eBusiness

eBusiness

2nd edition

PAUL BEYNON-DAVIES

Professor of Organizational Informatics,
Cardiff Business School, Cardiff University

palgrave
macmillan

First edition 2004
This edition 2013
Published by
PALGRAVE MACMILLAN

Palgrave Macmillan in the UK is an imprint of Macmillan Publishers Limited, registered in England, company number 785998, of Houndmills, Basingstoke, Hampshire RG21 6XS.

Palgrave Macmillan in the US is a division of St Martin's Press LLC, 175 Fifth Avenue, New York, NY 10010.

Palgrave Macmillan is the global academic imprint of the above companies and has companies and representatives throughout the world.

Palgrave® and Macmillan® are registered trademarks in the United States, the United Kingdom, Europe and other countries.

ISBN: 978–0–230–30456–7

This book is printed on paper suitable for recycling and made from fully managed and sustained forest sources. Logging, pulping and manufacturing processes are expected to conform to the environmental regulations of the country of origin.

A catalogue record for this book is available from the British Library.

Library of Congress Cataloging-in-Publication Data

Beynon-Davies, Paul.
    eBusiness / Paul Beynon-Davies. – 2nd ed.
      p. cm.
    Rev. ed. of: E-business. 2004.
    Includes bibliographical references and index.
    ISBN 978–0–230–30456–7
    1. Electronic commerce. 2. Business enterprises – Computer networks – Management. 3. Expert systems (Computer science) I. Title.
HF5548.32.B485 2013
658.8′72—dc23   2012036712

10 9 8 7 6 5 4 3 2 1
22 21 20 19 18 17 16 15 14 13

Printed in China

Contents

Illustrations

Figures

Tables

About the author

Paul Beynon-Davies is Professor of Organisational Informatics at Cardiff Business School, Cardiff University. He received his BSc in economics and social science and PhD in computing from University of Wales College, Cardiff. Before taking up an academic post he worked for several years in the informatics industry in the United Kingdom in both the public and private sectors. He still regularly acts as a consultant to public and private sector organisations and has been consistently rated one of the top information systems scholars worldwide.

He has published widely in the field of information systems and ICT and has written 12 books, including *Business Information Systems*, *Database Systems* and *Information Systems Development*. He has also published more than 70 academic papers, on such topics as the foundations of information systems, electronic business, electronic government, information systems planning, information systems development, database development and artificial intelligence.

Paul Beynon-Davies has engaged in a number of government-funded projects related to the impact of ICT in the economic, social and political spheres. He was involved in an evaluation of electronic government in Wales and was seconded part-time to the National Assembly for Wales (NAfW) as an evaluator of its Cymru-ar-Lein/Information Age strategy for Wales. From 2006 to 2008 he was director of the eCommerce Innovation Centre at Cardiff University, which also included the Broadband Observatory for Wales.

His research work has explored some of the foundations of informatics. This involves an attempt to build a more coherent and unified conception of Informatics as an inter-disciplinary area focused on the accomplishment of organisation through the entanglement of signs, patterns and systems. A summary of this work to date has been published by Palgrave Macmillan in the book *Significance: Exploring the Nature of Information, Systems and Technology.*

Preface to 2nd edition

Positioning

There are many texts on eBusiness or eCommerce. However, one of the reasons for writing the first edition of this book and now publishing a completely revised second edition was the belief that there continue to be a number of deficiencies with offerings in this area. The vast majority of texts on eBusiness are US in origin and naturally take the point of view of the North American continent. Many also tend to focus solely on the business issues and fail to correctly locate the technical issues within the business context. A large proportion of those texts that do focus on the interaction of ICT and organisations tend to be directed towards consultancy rather than providing academic balance. As such they have been more interested in 'selling' various aspects of the phenomenon of electronic business than in providing a systematic survey of the field, in the sense of identifying clear patterns and synergy with established practice. The available literature in the way of academic textbooks tends to be structured in terms of an accumulation of topics rather than a theory-driven form of presentation. Many textbooks also seem to multiply the number of concepts needed to understand and manage the phenomenon of eBusiness. Finally, there is a primary focus on the private sector in the existing literature, but the dynamics of eBusiness are not exclusive to the commercial enterprise. The application and exploitation of ICT for organisational change is equally relevant to the public sector and more recently to the voluntary sector organisation or social enterprise.

Our text continues to be clearly positioned in terms of these perceived limitations. It offers a worldwide perspective on eBusiness: many of the examples cited are taken from the UK and European experience of this phenomenon as well as from the US experience. From the start we position eBusiness as a socio-technical phenomenon which can be understood only through a balanced perspective: the appropriate application of technology within organisation. This book therefore provides a balanced and integrated account of business and technical issues.

We build an account of eBusiness from first principles, considering first the inter-relationship between activity, communication and representation and how this helps form organisation. This provides the proper context for explaining the modern application of ICT in business and understanding the value of ICT to organisation.

The approach taken in this book has been field-tested in a number of advisory and consultancy projects undertaken by the author and is constructed as a holistic account of the phenomenon. It provides a rounded focus on the application of eBusiness principles in the private, public and voluntary sectors. This means we cover the relevance of principles of eBusiness to all forms of organisation, including the modernisation of public sector services. We have also attempted to use the principle of Occam's razor in this text. In other words, we have attempted to use only sufficient concepts for the tasks of understanding and explaining the phenomenon of eBusiness. Three particular concepts we take to be foundational – those of sign, pattern and system. The idea of system drives the discussion of both theory and practice in the text. But we explain how the facets of a sign help stitch together patterns of activity, communication and representation in organisations. It is within such organisational patterns that eBusiness takes its rightful place. Finally, this text provides a systematic account of the field structured around a model of the eBusiness domain presented in the opening chapter and elaborated upon in various parts of the book. Clear linkage is also made to a number of my other texts published by Palgrave Macmillan – *Business Information Systems*, *Database Systems* and the more recent *Significance: Exploring the Nature of Information, Systems and Technology*.

Changes for the second edition

Most of the core content has transferred into the new edition from the first edition. However, a large number of improvements have been made in response to feedback from lecturers, students and the business and technology communities. The structure has been modified significantly to better organise the key discussion. Material has been combined into larger chapters which build to form a conception of eBusiness from first principles. Discussion of the growing body of literature exploring the theory behind eBusiness is expanded and better integrated into the flow of presentation. A number of new topics are included, such as mobile commerce, electronic government and cloud computing. Certain chapters have also been significantly updated with new material. Finally, the case material in the book has been extended, updated and better organised and a much greater range of pedagogical resources are included at the end of each chapter, such as a review test, exercises, projects, a critical reflection section and an exploration of case material presented at the end of the book.

Acknowledgements

My thanks to Ursula Gavin and Ceri Griffiths at Palgrave Macmillan for their encouragement to produce this second edition. My thanks also to a number of reviewers who provided many helpful suggestions in designing this new, revised edition.

Message to students

This book covers essential core material in the area of eBusiness. My aim in writing this book has been to create a coherent path through the subject which addresses some of the needs I have identified during more than three decades of experience in the area. Care has been taken to ensure that only material that is critical for the business student is included. Therefore, some material which you might find in other texts has been excluded to provide you with a more coherent and more relevant exploration of the subject.

Many textbooks on eBusiness consist of a collection of interesting but disconnected topics. In this manner, eBusiness is portrayed as something different from everyday business – sometimes radically different from conventional business. This book challenges that viewpoint. We consider eBusiness as modern business and assemble material to portray this topic as an integrated and seamless web of ICT application in organisations. This book therefore makes it easier for you to make sense of the subject as a whole. It also makes it easier for you to see how different elements of the subject inter-relate.

We provide balanced coverage of both theory and practice in this text. The aim is to use precise definitions of a number of foundation concepts to provide an understanding of the place of information, information systems and ICT within business. Such understanding then enables us to identify and explain a number of key lessons of use to professionals working in all forms of organisation.

So what you will get from reading this book is a *rounded* but *grounded* conception of this important area. The book will equip you with knowledge which will enable you to better perform as a business professional in the modern, complex organisational world.

Creativity involves, in the psychologist Edward De Bono's words, 'breaking out of established patterns in order to look at things in a different way'. Most of all this book is designed to get you to think differently: not only about organisations of all forms, but particularly about the place of technology within such organisations. After all, thinking differently is a necessary precondition for any successful innovation.

Message to lecturers

Audience

The material in this book is intended to impart a balanced, holistic introduction to the phenomenon of eBusiness. As such, it covers the key business and technical issues associated with electronic business and electronic commerce. The material is intended to act as a foundation for further investigation in eBusiness, information systems or information and communication technology. As a core text the likely audience will be undergraduates in business-related subjects, information systems (IS) or computing. As a reference text its audience is likely to be MSc or MA students taking an IS course or a substantial number of IS modules on an MBA or related programme. For all such students, this text will provide intellectual structure to the apparent but important chaos that is modern eBusiness.

Innovative approach

This book takes the innovative approach of building an account of eBusiness from first principles. To do this we use theory from a range of areas such as systemics and semiotics, and bring these ideas together to demonstrate how eBusiness is not just about the application of ICT within and between organisations: it is continuously created in the dynamic relationship between data, information, decision-making and activity in organisations. Indeed, we shall demonstrate how organisation is produced and re-produced from this interaction. This innovative approach we think serves to better place eBusiness in its proper context: it hopefully provides new life to demonstrating the centrality of eBusiness issues to modern business.

Ancillary material

A website has been produced to accompany the book and can be accessed at: www.palgrave.com/business/ebusiness2. Ancillary material includes a teaching guide and a number of PowerPoint presentations containing figures from the book. From this website instructors can also download an innovative ancillary database which provides one centralised repository for all additional material associated with the text. This database includes data about:

- Potential modules
- Potential lectures
- Revision questions
- Projects
- Exercises
- Exam questions
- Cases
- Web links
- Readings
- Book sections
- References to additional content from previous books by the author that is available on the website

All of these elements are cross-referenced to a list of several hundred topics. This means that a number of flexible but detailed reports can be produced to aid the use of the text in teaching.

About the book

Structure of the book

The book starts with an orienting chapter that provides an overview of the material presented in the content chapters of the work. The first three full content chapters – eBusiness organisation (Chapter 2), eBusiness systems (Chapter 3) and eBusiness value (Chapter 4) – cover essential background theory. They help the reader understand the importance of eBusiness and the way it is based upon some features found in all organisations. This leads us to consider three topics which help establish the context for eBusiness: the layers of infrastructure relevant to business systems (Chapter 5), the technical infrastructure for eBusiness (Chapter 6) and the eBusiness environment (Chapter 7). All this enables the reader to better understand the key application areas of modern eBusiness, which we discuss in two chapters (Chapters 8 and 9). Chapter 10 considers the essential activity infrastructure required to plan for, construct and maintain the eBusiness. We conclude the core content with an examination of some of the likely trends that will impact eBusiness over the coming years (Chapter 11).

Structure of the chapters

The large number of chapters in the first edition of the book have therefore been brought together in 11 major chapters. Each chapter is made up of a number of sections, and each section contains a description of a pertinent concept and an example or examples to illustrate its application in the domain. Across certain chapters we re-iterate coverage of key concepts. This has been shown to improve comprehension on the part of the reader.

In addition to the revised content, the pedagogical material in this new edition of *eBusiness* has been significantly extended. Each chapter opens with a set of features designed to orient readers and prepare them for what follows.

Learning outcomes set out what the student can expect to gain from the material that follows. Each learning outcome is linked to a core principle which can be applied to business so that students are able to see how each piece of knowledge is relevant. *Chapter outlines* give an overview of the content of the chapter. A brief *introduction* sets the scene.

At the end of each chapter, the main points are highlighted in a *chapter summary*. This is followed by an extensive section of activities consisting of a review test, a series of exercises and suggestions for student projects. The *review test* comprises a series of items designed to test understanding of the content of each chapter and ability to recall appropriate answers. Answers to questions can be obtained by re-reading the relevant chapter. *Exercises* are opportunities for the reader to take what has been learnt and extend knowledge or apply it to some other situation. They are deliberately open-ended and may be used in tutorials or other learning opportunities to structure more extensive learning about the topic under discussion. *Projects* are a larger piece of work in terms of both effort and duration than a student exercise. Typically they will involve the following: some form of independent investigation, including the activities of formulating a project proposal, producing a plan of work, conducting some form of data collection and analysis, and presenting of the results. Ideally, a student research project should display elements of independent/critical thinking. It should be noted that the suggestions are expressed merely in the form of some interesting research questions; they will demand much further work to develop into a working project proposal.

At the suggestion of previous adopters of this text we have also included a critical reflection section. This is meant to challenge the student and consists of a series of questions which should lead the reader to explore the area in greater depth and analyse it critically.

The case matrix

The first few chapters of the book contain integrated cases to help explain concepts. A range of other cases are collected together in a portfolio at the back of the book. The cases provide real-world examples of eBusiness issues relevant to the private and public sectors, as well as three cases specifically focusing on key industries impacted heavily by the continuing rise of eBusiness. The cases have been specially written by the author on the basis of published sources and are designed to integrate tightly with the concepts discussed within the chapters of the book (these relationships being specified in a detailed case matrix within the portfolio). The case studies are deliberately written as independent but rich resources of educational content and can be used both as sources of consolidation and for discussion across a range of chapters and topic areas. They are referred to throughout the book and each is supported by a list of issues for discussion and a 'key terms' section.

Glossary and bibliography

Two sources of material are provided as supplements to the main body of material. A glossary defines key terminology and enables quick access to individual topics in the main text. A complete bibliography highlights some key texts that may be used to pursue further study of key areas.

The eBusiness domain

Introduction

You the reader will be engaging with the topic area of this book, probably every waking hour of your life. You may be using your mobile phone to text or email friends, or to access your page on a social networking site. You might use your personal computer at home to order goods online, or pay your taxes to government as a banking transaction, or apply for a job using a company website. You might use your interactive digital television to download and watch a movie. You might use your netbook or tablet or eBook reader on the train to read the latest crime thriller or perhaps even a textbook.

It should be evident from this description that information and communication technology (ICT) is constantly present as it underpins so many aspects of our modern daily life. But you probably have not taken any serious time to ponder on the way in which such technologies actually work or how such technologies support the activities we pursue. Why should you? The very presence and contribution of ICT frequently comes to attention only when there is a breakdown in its appropriate use or a malfunction in the technology itself.

So when you find that you cannot access the *internet* because your *broadband* connection has failed, you are likely to feel frustrated. When your personal details have been accessed on your social networking profile by a potential employer, you might feel somewhat uncomfortable. When you are sent targeted emails by companies who have analysed your web surfing activities, you might feel somewhat aggrieved. When someone steals your online identity to pilfer funds from your bank account, you might feel very angry.

So it may be that, when things are running smoothly, ICT is effectively 'invisible' to all but ICT professionals. But in order for such smooth-running to be achieved, it is crucial that businesses are able to anticipate future needs, plan and implement the relevant developments and continuously seek to protect their customers. And to do this, they need employees and managers who are able to understand and reconcile the needs of the market and the organisation with the ever-evolving capability of ICT.

Electronic business or *eBusiness* is that area which involves the interaction of ICT, information systems and information with organisational activity. Not surprisingly, in such terms, eBusiness is modern business, because ICT, information systems and information are essential to the effective working of any modern organisation.

Information is so important to activity within the modern world that some have even referred to our current age as the information age. In this book we examine the very nature of information and use this to help the reader unravel the ways in which information underpins business activity of all forms. We shall demonstrate that information underlies the work of not only the high-ranking business executive but also the shop-floor worker.

Organisations have established *information systems* as systems for communication for many hundreds if not thousands of years. Such systems are used not only to control their current activities but also as the basis for changing and improving their ways of doing things. We describe how groups of inter-related information systems within businesses drive operations. We also describe the ways in which information systems are critically important for managing activities and relationships with customers, suppliers and partners.

Information and communication technology refers to any technology that is used in support of information systems. Much of the way modern businesses work is embedded or encoded in its ICT. Without *ICT systems* many organisations would cease to function. This book is a business book, not a technology book. However, we provide essential coverage of such technology to enable business professionals to better understand the ways in which ICT is being and can be used to increase the efficiency and effectiveness of both information systems and business practice.

Over a number of decades economic markets globally have been subject to two inter-dependent trends: the increasing centrality of information to effective activity and the increasing reliance on electronic networks for effective communication. Not surprisingly many contemporary markets are electronic markets or *eMarkets*: markets in which economic exchanges are conducted in whole or part through ICT. Modern trade or commerce is heavily reliant upon electronic commerce or *eCommerce*. This book provides you with a roadmap of the major ways in which such eCommerce impacts the world economy and world trade.

Hence, an understanding of eBusiness is critical to both current and aspiring business professionals. Any successful management of modern business must be based on a good understanding of eBusiness and how eBusiness fits with wider business and economic concerns. The management of eBusiness itself and the development of *eBusiness strategy* are thus critical to organisational success.

Our aim in this opening chapter is to take you on a high-level 'flight' over the terrain of contemporary eBusiness. We want to explore the major features in this terrain that we shall cover in greater detail within each chapter in the book. We do this to provide you with adequate bearings or sign posts which should help you better navigate through the material and better assimilate its key lessons. You should therefore not expect to understand the topics discussed here in one pass. Instead, you should feel free to follow links to further chapters at any time. However, once you have read through this chapter, you will find it particularly useful at some later point as a way of reviewing the material covered on the whole area of eBusiness.

Elements of the eBusiness domain

The mosaic represented in Figure 1.1 represents a tessellated structure. A tessellated structure or tessellation is a two-dimensional plane or surface which is completely covered by repeated application of one or more shapes. A honeycomb is an example of a natural tessellated structure in which one of the two regular polygons that tessellate – the hexagon (the other being the square) – is used to cover a surface. Hexagons are used within this figure to name and position the major elements of the eBusiness domain and also to illustrate the underlying structure for this book. In other words, each of the component elements contained in this mosaic is covered in more detail as a chapter of the book:

eBusiness organisation (Chapter 2). We start by covering essential core theory which helps us better understand the nature of eBusiness. This involves considering any organisation as performing business activity, communicating the nature of such activity and representing aspects of such activity in *records*. Hence, in this chapter we explore in some detail the nature of and inter-relationship between business records, business decision-making and business activity.

eBusiness systems (Chapter 3). We recognise the existence of organisation by the patterning of activity, communication and representation. This means that eBusiness is based on three types of systems: activity systems, information systems and data systems. In this chapter we distinguish between each type of system and demonstrate how they relate in building the eBusiness through layers of what we shall refer to as business infrastructure.

eBusiness value (Chapter 4). As a whole, organisations can be considered value-creating systems. The value created comes in three major forms: products, services and social capital. Products and services can also be tangible or intangible. The growth in intangible products and services is a major driver for eBusiness. ICT now not only supports value-creation within a wider value-network, but it also allows delivery of certain intangible products and services over this value-network.

eBusiness infrastructure (Chapters 5 and 6). So infrastructure plays an important role in both supporting eBusiness, as well as providing the platform for innovation. *Technical infrastructure* refers to the necessary arrangements of information and communication technologies that make eBusiness possible. We use a high-level model of such infrastructure to provide an overview of the key technical components necessary within any form of eBusiness.

eBusiness environment (Chapter 7). Any system operates within a wider environment. As a system the business organisation can be considered as interacting with four major facets of such environment: economic, social, political and physical. The economic environment provides the motive force for the existence of business organisations as well as constraining the ways in which such organisations act and interact. The social environment critically determines issues of access to eBusiness as well as concerns such as data protection and the management of personal identity. The political environment not only sets the legislative background for business activity but also acts as a key application area for the principles of eBusiness. Finally, the physical environment is a growing concern for business and sets the context for the movement in so-called green ICT.

Forms of eBusiness (Chapter 8). eBusiness has been undertaken for over 50 years in the sense that ICT has been applied to improving aspects of the internal operations of business organisations. Over the past couple of decades, the primary innovations in eBusiness have taken place within the area of commerce. Therefore, in Chapter 7 we examine four major forms of electronic commerce or eCommerce. Business to Business (B2B) eCommerce is one of the older and more established forms of ICT innovation in the area of trade and is distinguished from Partner to Partner or P2P eCommerce in terms of its emphasis on competition rather than collaboration. Business to Consumer (B2C) eCommerce has grown exponentially with the increasing penetration of the internet and the web into households. Consumer to Consumer (C2C) eCommerce is probably the most radical and recent form of ICT innovation in the area of commerce and is particularly related to growth in online social networking.

Further forms of eBusiness (Chapter 9). But the principles of eBusiness are not only relevant to the *internal value-chain* of businesses or to the major systems of activity that form their wider value-network. We also examine the use of eBusiness principles within the public sector in the form of eGovernment, as well as exploring the growth of commerce on the move: mobile eCommerce. This leads us to explore two significant aspects of B2C and B2B eCommerce: *eMarketing* and *eProcurement.*

Activity infrastructure for eBusiness (Chapter 10). eBusiness by its very nature is located at the interaction of technology with social systems. Hence, it is insufficient just to understand technology; you must also understand the importance of the social or activity infrastructure for eBusiness. Activity infrastructure refers to the necessary processes of strategy planning, management, implementation and evaluation that must occur within organisations if they are to be successful in eBusiness.

eBusiness futures (Chapter 11). As we have already mentioned, on one level, in terms of the use of ICT to improve internal business operation, eBusiness has a pedigree of over 50 years of experience. On another level, we have spent the past 20 years or so building infrastructure for effective eCommerce. More recently, only over the past five years or so, we have seen the explosion in the use of ICT to support online social networking. All this suggests that eBusiness is becoming embedded within the infrastructure of the world economy and is therefore here to stay. But how will this business phenomenon develop? In this final content chapter we examine some of the latest trends in the area that are likely to shape the nature of eBusiness over the coming decades.

eBusiness cases. Cases are used in two major ways in this book. First, most chapters utilise an embedded case to help illustrate the application of key concepts discussed. Second, a portfolio of specially written cases is deliberately placed at the end of the book. The case matrix provided in this section of the book provides a breakdown of the relevance of particular cases to particular topic areas discussed within content chapters.

So let us provide more detail on what we shall explore in this text...

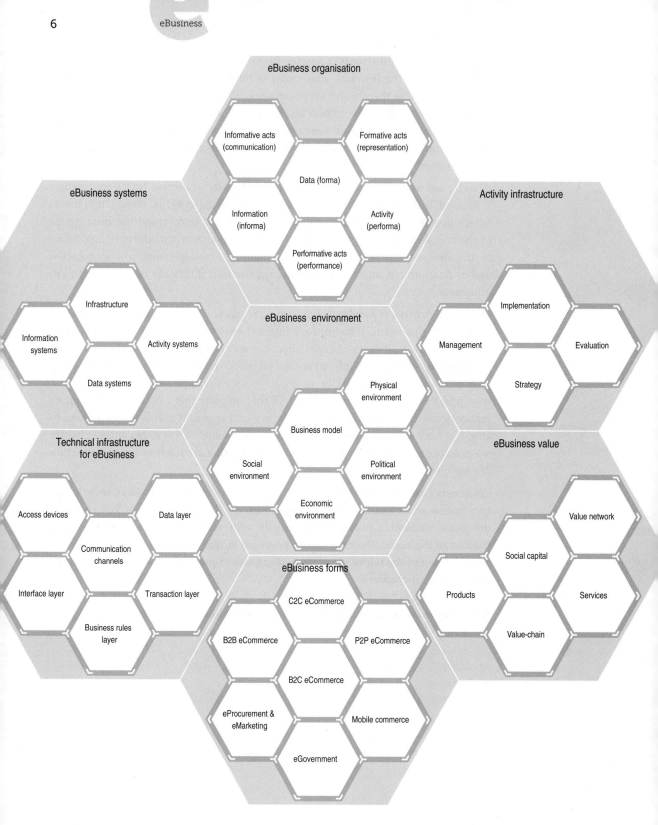

Figure 1.1 The eBusiness domain

eBusiness organisation

We use three inter-related ideas to develop a platform of theory on which eBusiness is built: signs, systems and patterns. First we explain how organisation emerges from the interaction of activity, decision-making, information and data. To help us do this we introduce a fictitious case, but which is based on real-world experience, which helps ground concepts from the eBusiness domain (Figure 1.2). We deliberately discuss this case as a history of one organisation's attempt to improve its ways of working through the application of ICT. This is the essence of eBusiness.

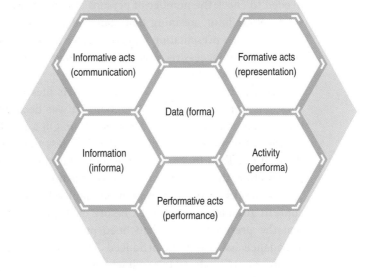

Figure 1.2 eBusiness organisation

USC case

Back in the 1980s a UK university decided to offer a series of short courses to industry. At the time it was particularly interested in offering courses in ICT of some three to four days' duration. For this purpose, it decided to set up a commercial arm – USC (University Short Courses) – to develop, market and administer such courses. Each short course offered by the company was created and maintained by one member of university staff, known as the course manager. However, depending on the popularity of the course, a course might be presented by a number of different lecturers in addition to the course manager.

USC presented such courses both at a specially prepared site on the university campus and at commercial and industrial sites throughout the UK. The former types of course were described within the company as scheduled presentations, while the latter were described as on-site presentations. Students on scheduled courses generally came from a number of different industrial organisations, while students attending on-site courses typically came from the same organisation. On-site courses gradually became a lucrative part of the business of USC as a number of companies began to use USC courses as part of their in-house training schedule for new employees.

A number of administrative activities were eventually established to manage the growing portfolio of courses and clientele. During the first couple of years of its establishment USC administrators created and maintained physical files containing paper records of courses, lecturers, presentations and attendance. The administration of financial transactions between organisations, individuals and USC was initially handled by the university's finance department, and hence no records were held by USC itself on financial matters.

During this period, bookings were taken over the telephone for courses. When a person telephoned to register for a particular presentation of a course, USC staff needed to check the number of persons already registered. Each presentation was set a course limit, meaning that staff had to ensure that the number of people registered for a presentation was not greater than the course limit. This meant that staff needed to access records about how many people had already booked for a particular presentation.

Periodically staff had to also access their files to check that particular presentations were viable to run. Eventually it was decided that four students was a break-even point for costing a presentation. On a regular basis USC staff needed to search for those presentations that had less than four students registered for them. If less than four persons were registered one month before the scheduled presentation, then the presentation was postponed and scheduled for a later date.

Two weeks before a presentation, staff telephoned each booked student to confirm attendance. One week before each presentation, staff needed to check that the presentation fee had been paid. Assuming a viable presentation, an attendance list was then produced. USC also needed to keep track of which lecturers were qualified to teach which courses. Using such records lecturers had to be assigned to scheduled courses at least six months ahead of a given course presentation.

After each course presentation, evaluation forms were handed out to attendees. On this basis data were gathered on the performance of lecturers and of courses. These data were used in decisions about revisions to the course portfolio, which took place at a special meeting held every six months.

Signs

Signs are critically important in all forms of activity, including business. Signs are important because they establish what it is to be human. Without signs we could not think, we could not communicate what we think and we could not ensure that we collaborate together successfully in our working activity.

Very broadly a sign is anything that is significant. In a sense, everything that humans have or do is significant to some degree. Sometimes not having or doing anything is regarded as significant. The world within which humans find themselves is therefore resonant with systems of signs. Signs are core elements serving to link issues of human collaborative activity, human communication and the representation of things in records.

Therefore, it is useful to view a sign as being composed of three aspects, which we call *forma*, *informa* and *performa*. Forma stands for the substance of a sign and concerns its physical representation as data. Informa relates to the meaning associated with a sign and concerns the interpretation of data as information. Performa relates to the use of the sign to facilitate coordinated activity or performance.

Activity

Humans rarely engage in totally individual activity. Instead, our individual activity is normally part of a complex web of collective activity. Whenever a group of people get together and attempt to engage in collective activity the issue of coordination arises. In other words, some way must be found of answering the question: 'how do I coordinate my activities with others in pursuit of common goals?'

For instance, in the case of USC the activities of lecturers and students needed to be coordinated. A particular lecturer needed to appear at a particular site at a particular time to deliver a particular course. Likewise, the employees of particular companies needed to know where to go and at what time and date to receive instruction in a particular course.

Information

To enable coordination of activities performed by particular business actors such as lecturers and students in pursuit of a collective goal, then communication is needed. In the case of USC, administrators needed to be able to communicate to lecturers when and what they were teaching and to students when and what instruction would be received. This could of course have been done through verbal communication: we could telephone lecturers to tell them what they are teaching and we could telephone students to tell them when to come on a particular course.

Data

However, as the number of students and lecturers increases as part of the business of USC, relying upon verbal communication and the individual memory of particular USC staff, lecturers and students is likely to prove difficult. Hence, most organisations keep records of the things of interest or significance to them. For this purpose USC started to construct and maintain structured records of data on things of interest to them: their lecturers, courses, students and presentations.

Hence, data are *symbols*. For example, if we were to inspect one of the attendance records used by USC at this time we would see the string of digits – 023563 – was used. As a collection this forms a symbol. However, the symbol by itself is meaningless beyond being a set of digits. Symbols are given meaning through the assignment of convention or context. Hence, this symbol amongst others of the same type was conventionally treated as a code by USC administrators to stand for given students: it was a student identifier. Information is thus data given meaning and used for communication in support of activity.

Decisions

Data and information are clearly critical to decision-making. A decision involves selecting an appropriate course of action in particular circumstances. Records are not only useful for making everyday operational decisions about actions such as whether to run a course presentation or not. The making of records also allows business actors to 'model' their understanding of business activities and on this basis to make strategic or longer-term decisions about future business activity. Hence, representing information about past attendance on particular courses as well as the evaluations obtained back from course presentations helped USC managers make decisions about which courses to perhaps drop from their portfolio and which courses to promote to potential clients in the future.

eBusiness systems

Along with signs, the other idea which we use to help build our explanation of eBusiness is that of a system. A systemic analysis of eBusiness corresponds to a holistic account of this phenomenon. We take eBusiness to be fundamentally concerned with the way in which various social and technical systems interact and form business organisation (Figure 1.3).

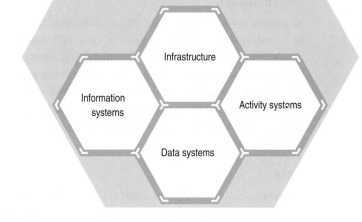

Figure 1.3 eBusiness systems

When somebody calls something a system they are normally referring to the patterning of something. In other words, they are identifying the interaction of a number of regular and recurring things. The systems concept, as we shall see, is particularly valuable because of the way in which it can be applied to patterns that exist in three inter-related areas: technology (data system), information (information system) and human activity (*activity system*).

Therefore, eBusiness is founded in the interaction of these three types of system: systems of activity, systems of information and systems of information and communication technology. Such systems amount to the patterning of performance, communication and representation respectively. Every activity system will rely on information for effective collaboration and coordination of activity. Information will be communicated by associated information systems which in turn will rely upon systems of representation. Data or ICT systems are an inherent part of most contemporary information systems because they manage the data resource on which much communication is based in the modern business world.

Activity systems

Organisations, particularly business organisations, consist of complex chains of activity systems. An activity system is a social system, and as such is often referred to as a 'soft' system. It comprises a logical collection of activities performed by some group of people, normally in fulfilment of some goal or goals. Another term now much used as a synonym for an activity system is organisational or business process.

We can understand an activity system as consisting of a recurring pattern of *performative acts*. For instance, one crucial activity system for USC is that series of activities required to run a particular course. The pattern of performative acts evident in this activity system looks something like this: create course, assign lecturers, schedule presentations, take bookings, deliver presentations, evaluate presentations. This pattern of activities is repeated continuously within the operation of USC as an organisation by different persons or business actors.

Information systems

An information system is a system of communication between people. As we have seen, information systems support activity systems in the sense that information is important for the coordination of human activity to meet established goals. We can understand an information system as consisting of a recurring pattern of communicative acts. Hence, to schedule a given presentation of a course USC administrators have to communicate with potential lecturers as to their availability. They then have to gain commitment from a chosen lecturer to present a given course on a nominated date in the future. This leads to communication with potential customers who may have declared their interest in taking a particular course of instruction.

Data systems

Because a number of USC staff need to coordinate their performative and communicative activity, records have to be created, updated and retrieved. Hence, one member of USC staff may take a telephone call from a potential customer asking to know when the next available presentation of a particular course will take place and who will present this course. They also wish to know whether any space is left on this course. To ease the burden on human memory the USC member of staff consults a record previously made for this purpose by some other administrator and communicates the result of this to the enquirer.

Data systems are therefore 'hard' systems because they are physical or technical systems. At a high-level a data system can be seen to consist of recurring patterns of formative acts operating upon data structures. In this sense, we use the term data system to stand for not only modern ICT systems but also traditional, so-called manual record-keeping systems. This allows us to correctly position the role of much modern ICT within the business. It also however allows us to demonstrate the value of modern ICT over older forms of information and communication technology such as filing cabinets, file folders and paper forms.

Control and management

The recurrent patterning of activity, communication and representation char-acteristic of organisations is evidence of control in organisations. Control is the process that implements regulation and adaptation in systems. Systems generally exhibit some form of control to maintain systems in some form of equilibrium but also to enable systems to adapt to changes in their environment. Control can be viewed in terms of a monitoring *subsystem* or process that regulates the behaviour of other sub-systems. This monitoring or *control subsystem* ensures defined levels of *performance* for an operational system by imposing a number of *control inputs* upon the system.

In such terms, management is clearly a control process within organisations. Management is an activity system that controls other activity systems. The primary activity of management is making decisions concerning organisational action. Effective management decision-making is reliant on good information. Effective management decision-making is reliant on the effective definition of performance and the construction of effective performance management systems for managerial activity. The recording of data about performance is thus critical to performance management.

Consider the case of USC in this light. USC needs to sell course attendance to customers to generate income. As part of their on-going activity USC needs to collect data on sales of courses to particular customer groups. Such sales can then be compared against targets (control inputs) set by the company for such sales activity. If current sales are below target then actions need to be taken to increase sales. This is the essence of organisational control as regulation. But evaluation data gathered from customers can also help USC adapt its educational services. For instance, it might find continuous requests in its evaluation data for particular topic areas of interest. It can use this data to change its course portfolio in response to changing customer demand.

Infrastructure

Organisation requires infrastructure. By infrastructure we mean the entire collection of systems necessary for an organisation to achieve its goals. From our discussion above it should be clear that there are at least three vertical layers of infrastructure crucial to eBusiness. Activity systems infrastructure constitutes the entire collection of activity taking place within activity systems necessary for supporting the creation and distribution of value. *Information systems infra-structure* consists of the entire set of inter-related information systems needed to support communication activity within the organisation. Data systems infrastruc-ture fundamentally consists of the necessary systems of record-keeping necessary to supply information for decision-making. As we shall see, within the modern organisation this consists of the hardware, software and communication technolo-gies available to the organisation necessary to maintain effective data systems.

Such layers are clearly organised in a *hierarchy*. The information systems infrastructure supports the activity infrastructure. In turn, the information systems infrastructure of some organisation will be supported by an *ICT infrastructure*. It is also possible to think of infrastructure in terms of a horizontal division between those systems concerned with external activities and those systems associated with internal activities. The former is frequently referred to as the front-end or front-office of the organisation. The latter is often called the back-end or back-office of the organisation.

eBusiness value

The primary goal of most organisations is to produce some form of value. Therefore, organisations are value-creating or value-producing systems. Organisations can be thought of as chains of inter-related activity systems associated with the production and dissemination of value. For commercial organisations such value will typically constitute goods. For public sector organisations value will typically consist of the services such organisations provide. Within the community, value will consist of social capital – networks of information, trust and reciprocity.

A good is some form of product produced by an organisation and distributed to the customer. A service is some form of activity performed by an organisation for a customer. Goods and services are the end-points of activity systems performed in business organisations. They are thus typically outputs delivered to the customer of the organisation.

It is possible to distinguish between two types of good: physical or tangible goods and non-physical or intangible goods. This distinction has a bearing, as we shall see, on the degree to which such forms of value can be delivered through aspects of electronic commerce. Tangible goods have a physical form and hence cannot be delivered to the customer electronically. Intangible goods may fundamentally be represented as data. They are hence sometimes called digital goods because they are amenable to digitisation and consequently may be delivered to the customer over data communication networks.

Similarly, services can be classified as either tangible or intangible. Certain services are tangible in nature and hence not amenable to electronic service delivery. Other services are intangible by nature and thus primarily constitute communication services. They are hence open to delivery through electronic channels.

The value produced by USC is primarily one of services. A course is an educational or training service delivered to particular customers. The value USC produces is therefore bound up with the perceived quality of the courses it delivers. A course traditionally is a tangible service in the sense that it demands actual persons to deliver material in a physical setting to a group of other persons that are co-present. The so-called correspondence course started to break down this form of instructional delivery and in its original form involved packaging all course material as an instructional paper package posted to the student and undertaken by the student at her own pace. Such forms of instruction or 'content' are clearly amenable to digitisation. Hence, with the rise of the internet and web (see Figure 1.4), USC started to produce a limited range of its courses for electronic delivery. As such, a proportion of their tangible services started to become intangible in nature.

Associated with the flow of any goods and services is a corresponding flow of transactions. A *transaction* is a data structure that records some coherent unit of activity, typically an event within some activity system or between activity systems. As we have seen, data and information are needed to support not only the internal activity of organisations but also exchanges between organisations and individuals. Transactions are hence critical to the recording of organisational activity – past, current and future. Transactions typically write data to the *data stores* of some data system. Such data, interpreted as information, are important to the measurement of organisational performance and critical to effective decision-making by business actors.

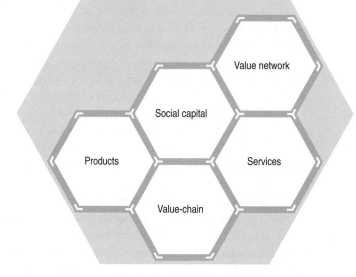

Figure 1.4 eBusiness value

Hence, organisations can be seen as consisting of a series of interdependent chains made up of related activity systems that deliver value. Organisations, as systems, also exist within a wider value-network consisting of chains of value between the organisation and external actors. Types of such external business actor include customers, suppliers and partners. This means that five value-chains are significant for most businesses:

1. the internal value chain consisting of a series of activity systems by which the organisation produces value;
2. the supply chain consisting of those activity systems by which an organisation obtains goods and services from other organisations;
3. the customer chain consisting of those activity systems by which an organisation delivers value to its customers;
4. the community chain consisting of those social networks surrounding the business that support value generation between individuals and groups;
5. the partner chain consisting of those activity systems that support coordinated or collaborative value creation by two or more organisations to the same set of customers.

Fundamentally, as we shall see, eBusiness and eCommerce focus around innovation within such organisational value-chains. The trend to use ICT to re-structure aspects of the internal value-chain of organisations has been on-going for a number of decades. In more recent years, ICT has been used to re-engineer aspects of the customer and supply chains important to a particular organisation. ICT is also being used to build bridges between an organisation and the larger community, as well as between the organisation and its partners in value creation.

Therefore, each organisation such as USC has a distinctive internal value-chain and external value-network. The internal value-chain of this company consists of activity systems such as course production, course delivery, marketing, course sales, on-site negotiation and course administration. The external value-network of this company involves its relationships and activities with its suppliers such as printers of publicity material and venue providers like hotels. It also includes its relationships and activities with its customers – students – and its partners – academic and administrative staff within the university.

Commerce

Commerce consists of the exchange of products and services between businesses, groups and individuals. Commerce or trade can hence be seen as one of the essential activities of any business. Commerce of whatever nature can be considered as an activity system of exchange between economic or business actors with the following generic phases or sub-systems: pre-sale activities occurring before a sale occurs; sale execution comprising activities involved with the actual sale of a product or service between *economic actors*; sale settlement involving those activities which complete the sale of product or service; and, after sale, consisting of those activities which take place after the buyer has received the product or service from the seller.

It is also possible to distinguish between three major patterns of commerce in terms of their frequency of occurrence. *Repeat commerce* is the pattern in which regular, repeat transactions occur between trading partners. Credit commerce is where irregular transactions occur between trading partners and the processes of settlement and execution are separated. Cash commerce occurs when irregular transactions of a one-off nature are conducted between economic actors. In cash commerce the processes of execution and settlement are typically combined.

USC clearly engages in commerce with a range of organisations. The pre-sale phase of its commerce activity primarily involves the enquiries it takes from potential clients and the bookings it makes with such clients for particular course presentations. Sale execution corresponds to the actual delivery of a course presentation to a particular client. Most customers of USC traditionally have their organisations pay USC some short period of time after taking a particular course – this form of sale settlement is characteristic of credit commerce. After delivery of material to customers, USC normally follows up with the particular organisations, checking quality issues and attempting to gain repeat business. This is a major part of USC's after-sales phase.

Technical infrastructure for eBusiness

The key message of eBusiness in recent years is that ICT is an enabler for organisational change focused around the re-design of the delivery of services and products to key *stakeholders* – customers, suppliers, partners and employees. Hence ICT is seen to offer the potential for more efficacious, efficient and effective delivery of value along supply, customer, partner, internal and community value-chains (Figure 1.5).

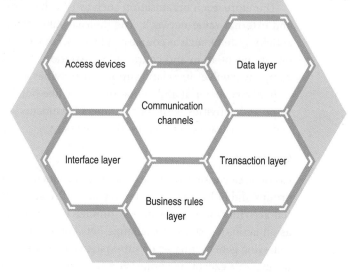

Figure 1.5 Technical infrastructure

As we argued above any organisation needs to represent in its records data about things or objects, as well as data about events or activities it regards as significant. The latter form of record, as we have seen, is frequently referred to as a transaction. Hence, in the case of USC, records were maintained about persons such as customers as well as events such as a booking by a particular customer for a particular course presentation. Transactions typically involve ways of recording the delivery of products and services and hence are the essential raw data for modelling and evaluating organisational performance. Reducing the costs associated with the administration of transactions is also a typical way of introducing cost savings with ICT.

ICT

Information and communication technology is any technology used to support data gathering, processing, distribution and use. ICT provides means of constructing aspects of information systems, but is distinct from information systems. Core elements of modern ICT include hardware, software, data management and communications technology, which are used to construct the ICT infrastructure of organisations.

It is important to recognise that information systems have existed in organisations prior to the invention of digital computing and communications technology, and hence ICT such as that described above is not a necessary condition for an information system. However, in the modern, complex organisational world most information systems rely on hardware, software, data and communication technology to a greater or lesser degree because of the gains possible with the use of such technology.

It is possible to describe the technical infrastructure required for eBusiness as consisting of three major and inter-connected aspects of ICT infrastructure: access devices, communication channels and ICT systems.

Access devices

Internal and external actors need to access organisational systems through access channels. Internal actors include managers and other employees, while external actors include customers, partners and suppliers. In terms of interaction with the customer, face-to-face contact and telephone conversation have traditionally been two of the most commonly used channels for accessing an organisation's value: its services or products. However, over the past decade, organisations both in the public and private sectors have implemented access channels that allow customers to interact with the organisation remotely using ICT.

A remote access channel typically is composed of some access device and associated communication channel. Typical remote access devices supported within the current environment for eBusiness are the internet-enabled personal computer (PC), interactive digital television (iDTV) and smart phones. There are a number of advantages to both the organisation and its external stakeholders in the provision and use of such access channels. For instance, an organisation may be able to reduce its costs of operation while providing for its customers access to its services and products 24 hours a day, 365 days a year.

Communication channels

Access devices are used to connect to organisational ICT systems through communication channels. Communication channels within the technological infrastructure for eBusiness rely on two critical technologies: the internet and the web.

The internet is a set of inter-connected computer networks distributed around the globe and can be considered on a number of levels. The base infrastructure of the internet is composed of *packet-switched networks* and a series of communication protocols. On this layer run a series of applications such as electronic mail (e-mail) and the World Wide Web – the web for short. The web is effectively a set of standards for the representation and distribution of *hypermedia* documents over the internet. A hypermedia document consists of a number of chunks of content such as text, graphics and images connected together with associative links called hyperlinks.

The web has become a key technology for constructing interfaces to the ICT systems of organisations. Hence, the company website has become a significant way of providing electronic delivery to business actors such as customers. The term website is generally used to refer to a logical collection of web documents or pages normally stored on a web server. Because of the increasing use of such technologies by customers, major investment has been undertaken by companies in increasing levels of interactivity on their websites. Most websites provided by medium-to-large companies are now fully transactional websites in which customers undertake a substantial proportion of their interaction with an organisation online.

ICT systems

An ICT system is a technical system. Such systems are frequently referred to as examples of 'hard' systems in the sense that they consist of physical components. An ICT system is an organised collection of hardware, software, data and communication technology designed to support aspects of some information system. An ICT system takes data as input, manipulates such data as a process and outputs manipulated data for interpretation within some information system. Hence, most ICT systems are effectively data manipulation or data processing systems.

It is useful to consider a modern ICT system as being made up of a number of subsystems or layers:

- *Interface layer.* This subsystem is responsible for managing interaction with the user. This subsystem is generally referred to as the user interface, sometimes the human–computer interface, and as we have mentioned, is now typically created using web technology.
- *Rules layer.* This subsystem manages the logic of the ICT system in terms of a defined set of business rules. These rules are typically handled by business rules engines.
- *Transaction layer.* This subsystem acts as the link between the data subsystem and the rules and interface subsystems. Querying, insertion and update activity is triggered at the interface, validated by the rules subsystem and packaged as units (transactions) that will initiate formative actions in the data subsystem.
- *Data layer.* This subsystem is responsible for managing the underlying data needed by the ICT system and stored within a set of inter-related data structures.

In the contemporary ICT infrastructure each of these parts of an ICT system may be distributed on different machines, perhaps at different sites. This means that each part or layer usually needs to be connected together in terms of some communications backbone.

Data management infrastructure

Data management is normally portrayed as one critical aspect of *back-end ICT infrastructure.* The back-end ICT infrastructure of the organisation will particularly manage the operational data of the organisation through *database systems.*

A key focus of many eBusiness strategies is to re-engineer service delivery around the customer. This requires the effective integration and inter-operability of back-end ICT infrastructure. Hence, for example, when a customer enters personal details such as their name and address into one ICT system this information should ideally be available to all other ICT systems that need such data within the organisation.

To enable fully transactional websites, the information presented to the user needs to be updated dynamically from back-end databases. Also, the information entered by customers needs to update company information systems effectively.

This demands integration and inter-operability of front-end and back-end systems within the ICT infrastructure.

USC case

As we have seen, in the early years of its administration USC used a paper-based records system. However, the company experienced a number of problems with this manual data system. For example, to ensure effective coordination of activity data needed to be communicated amongst a number of people such as venue operators, lecturers and a multitude of USC administrators. This meant that copies had to be made of documentation such as presentation schedules, consuming much-needed time and resource. A considerable amount of time was also spent in transferring data from manual records on to other documents such as course schedules. Administrators frequently made errors in entering the wrong data onto records or other forms of documentation. Further valuable time and effort was therefore expended in resolving such errors by administrative staff. Finally, it proved difficult to use the data stored in records for strategic as well as operational purposes. For example, it was difficult for managers to collate and analyse data to determine trends such as the popularity or otherwise of particular courses. To conduct such analyses meant a considerable investment of time and effort on the part of both administrative and managerial staff.

At the start of the 1990s, problems such as these persuaded USC to consider investing in the construction of an ICT system to handle basic administrative functions. Computing technology was also becoming much more affordable for the small- and medium-sized enterprise during this period.

Since ICT systems are essentially data processing systems, they rely on a core repository for the data used within the system. This repository is normally referred to as a database and is controlled by the *data management layer*. The design for the structure of the database at the heart of the ICT system is referred to as a data model. Essentially, this data model defines what data will be stored within the system and in what form. The USC data model consisted of a series of definitions for the data structures making up the database, as illustrated in Figure 1.6.

Courses	Course No	Course name	Course manager	Course duration		
Lecturers	Lecturer code	Lecturer name	Home address	Work address	Home tel no	Work tel no
Students	Student No	Student name	Student address	Student TelNo		
Presentations	Presentation No	Course No	Presentation date	Presentation site	Lecturer code	
Attendance	Student No	Presentation No	No Fee paid			
Qualifications	Lecturer code	Course No				

Figure 1.6 USC data model

Each data structure in this specification is made up of a number of data elements. Hence, the courses record consisted of an identifier for each course (courseNo), the name of the course appearing in the course portfolio (courseName), the identifier of the lecturer responsible for creating and maintaining the course materials (courseManager) and the number of days specified for the training (courseDuration).

These data structures are updated by a number of update functions which trigger transactions fired at the database. Transactions change the *state* of a database from one state to another. Hence, in the USC case sample update functions might be *Create a new course record* or *Create a new booking* or *Assign a new lecturer to a course presentation.*

A considerable amount of the way in which of an ICT system works is also taken up with so-called business rules. Such rules ensure that the data held in the data management layer of the ICT system remains an accurate reflection of the activity system it represents. Hence, in the case of USC, the data stored in the data structure *Attendance* should accurately represent the students that have either participated in a past presentation, are undergoing a current presentation or have booked for a future course presentation.

The interface layer is responsible for managing interaction with the user and traditionally has been generally made up of menus, data entry screens and data retrieval screens. Hence, in the case of the USC system a bookings screen allowed administrators to enter details of a new booking and a presentations screen allowed administrators to see instantly current numbers of bookings against the presentation schedule for a particular course.

eBusiness environment

We have argued above that an organisation can be considered as an activity system or more accurately as a series of interdependent activity systems. However, an organisation is not an isolated entity; it is what we shall refer to as an open system. By this we mean that it receives inputs from its environment and feeds outputs into its environment. The environment is hence a critical enabler of organisational activity; it also constrains what an organisation is able to do in terms of its activity.

Therefore, by environment we mean anything outside of the organisation. The environment of most organisations can be considered in terms of the interaction between four major environmental systems: an economic system, a political system, a social system and a physical system. The environment of some organisation constitutes a complex network of relationships and activities between the organisation and other actors in the social, political, economic and physical spheres (Figure 1.7).

An open systems model of the organisation emphasises that the relationship between environments and organisations is reciprocal. In other words, organisations are both affected by and affect their environments. The shape of and trends within each area of the environment will exert an impact on the eBusiness activities of some organisation. Likewise, the eBusiness activities of organisations are likely to impact the social, economic, political and physical environment.

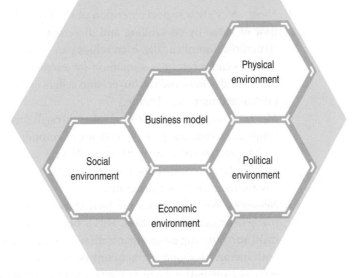

Figure 1.7 eBusiness environment

Economic environment

For commercial organisations the economic environment of the organisation is probably the most important. Business organisations exist and operate within some economic system. At the level of the nation-state we speak of such an economic system as being an economy. An economic system is the way in which a group of humans arrange their material provisioning and essentially involves the coordination of activities concerned with such provisioning.

Three major activity systems at the macro-level are important to economic systems: production, distribution and consumption. Production is that set of activities concerned with the creation of value: goods and services required for human existence. Distribution is the associated activity system involved in the collection, storage and movement of goods into the hands of consumers and providing services for such consumers. Consumption is clearly the activity system through which consumers receive and use goods and services.

Therefore, production and distribution are activities that deliver value while consumption is an activity that uses value. Hence, economies can be seen as a complex of value-networks that cause value to flow both within and between economic actors. This means that economic actors, such as suppliers, customers, partners and organisations themselves, interrelate and interact in complex networks of value production, distribution and consumption. A particular economic actor will take on different roles within a number of different value networks. Hence, an organisation may be both a supplier of some other organisation as well as being a customer of another within its value-network.

Economies have three basic mechanisms for controlling the flow of goods and services in such value-networks: hierarchies, markets and networks.

1. *Hierarchies* are a logical extension of the firm itself. Hierarchies coordinate the flow of value by controlling and directing it at a higher level in management structures. Simplistically, hierarchies can be seen as systems of cooperation. A managerial hierarchy is a medium for exchanges between a limited number of buyers and sellers and the buyers and sellers exchange goods and services within established patterns of trade.

2. *Markets* coordinate the flow of value through forces of supply and demand. Put simply, markets are typically systems of competition. A market is a medium for exchanges between many potential buyers and many potential sellers and, at least for larger companies, a series of markets forms the immediate competitive environment of the organisation.

3. *Networks.* We deliberately referred above to value networks rather than value-markets or value-hierarchies. This is because the immediate economic environment surrounding most organisations typically consists of some combination of both hierarchical and market control. In this sense, economic networks can be seen as a mediating form of control between hierarchies and markets in which forms of competition but also forms of cooperation exist between economic actors.

With the growth in ICT many contemporary markets and hierarchies have become eMarkets and eHierarchies. By an eMarket we mean one in which economic exchanges are conducted through ICT. In an eMarket, electronic transactions between employees, buyers and sellers enable the efficient and effective flow of goods and services through internal, supply, customer and community chains. In terms of eHierarchies, *inter-organisational information systems* and their associated ICT systems have been developed and maintained by consortia of partnering companies to provide infrastructure to control the flow of mutual value.

Consider the case of USC. In terms of its suppliers the company initially built a long-term relationship with a limited range of suppliers. This relationship was managed by one USC administrator to ensure the steady flow of supplies into the company, effectively constituting a managerial hierarchy. In contrast, for most aspects of its customer-chain USC entered the market and competed with other companies to supply technical training to customers. However, USC managed to build a relationship with a limited range of customer organisations to deliver major aspects of their internal training programme. These *contracts* in repeat business were originally managed by a couple of dedicated USC administrators, but eventually with the growth in electronic communications it became possible for one administrator to manage this business.

The social environment

The social environment of an organisation concerns the cultural life of some grouping such as a nation state. In terms of eBusiness the social environment particularly concerns ways in which people relate to organisational activity.

Although most organisations are producing strategies to encourage their external stakeholders such as customers to use remote modes of access to their services and products, a number of pre-conditions exist to the successful uptake of such modes of access. These pre-conditions represent the interaction of a range of factors in the social environment that affect take-up of electronic delivery and include *awareness, interest, access, skills* and *impact*. People must be aware of the benefits of using various remote access channels and interested in using them. They must also have access to remote access channels using convenient access devices and must have the skills necessary to use access devices such as the internet-enabled PC or the Smartphone effectively. This is frequently referred to as eLiteracy. Finally, people must actively use remote access devices on a regular basis in core areas of life such as work and leisure. Such use must approach a threshold that encourages the provision of more content and services delivered electronically.

There has been an inevitable trend for organisations to increase their use of remote access channels. However, it is still the case that there are differential rates of take-up of such channels both within nation-states and between nation-states. This is sometimes known as the *digital divide*. The digital divide fundamentally refers to the phenomenon of differential rates of awareness, interest, access, skills and use amongst different groups in society. For instance, there is continuing and substantial evidence to suggest that within nation states the older you are the more likely you are to be the least aware, the least interested, have the least access to ICT, the lowest levels of eLiteracy and use electronic services the least. Disparities in economic inequality between nation-states also account for lower levels of access to electronic delivery within the developing world.

USC provides a graded range of low-entry ICT skills courses based around the European Computer Driving Licence or ECDL scheme. This scheme, which provides graded training in eLiteracy, is provided not only to business organisations but also to the community through public-sector funded programmes by USC. Training in ECDL is meant to address directly many of the pre-conditions of electronic delivery discussed above.

However, other social factors affect take-up. For instance, as more and more business is conducted online there have been increasing cases of the misuse of data held about individuals such as in the area of personal identity theft. This has affected levels of trust placed in eCommerce but also raised expectations amongst customers about the degree of data protection and privacy that organisations should provide.

The political environment

The political environment clearly concerns issues of power. Political systems are made up of sets of activities and relationships concerned with power and its exercise. The political environment is particularly concerned with government and legal frameworks within nation-states and is a major constraining force on organisational behaviour. Hence, the practice of both individual governments and trans-national bodies such as the European Union continues to drive policy in the eBusiness and eCommerce areas.

The rate of development of the internet as a tool for conducting business has brought challenges to legal systems at a greater rate than previously experienced with the advent of other innovative forms of remote communication. For instance, conventionally law involves a centralised sovereign actor such as a nation-state exerting power within its territorial boundaries. This traditional concept of law is challenged by eCommerce since this phenomenon lacks geographical boundaries and there is no centralised authority controlling activity in this area on the global scale. This is a key area of concern for certain aspects of eBusiness such as the effectiveness of legislation for the enforcement of contracts and *intellectual property rights*.

The political environment of many countries has also been directly subject to the influence of ICT in areas such as electronic government (*eGovernment*) and electronic democracy (*eDemocracy*). ICT and information systems have been used to re-engineer aspects of governmental processes and the relationship between government and the citizen. For instance, government services such as tax collection and benefit payment are frequently conducted through ICT systems infrastructure. Aspects of democratic representation between government and citizen as well as certain democratic processes associated with the government have also been impacted by ICT.

Most companies in the UK and Europe more widely interact with some form of eGovernment. In the case of USC, for instance, the company regularly produces its accounts as an electronic document and transfers this document to central government administration electronically. It also completes its business tax return online and submits its payments electronically to the fiscal authority.

Physical environment

The problem of climate change and the consequent growth in sustainability concerns within business have clearly affected business practice. Businesses are now called upon by governments to take direct steps to reduce their 'carbon footprint'. One significant way in which organisations can do this is by considering their ICT infrastructure in 'green' terms. This might involve taking steps to reduce power consumption or the recycling of computer equipment. It might also involve looking for ways in which ICT can be used to reduce polluting activities such as air travel. Hence, companies might use remote conferencing and VoIP (Voice over Internet Protocol) technology to support business meetings between dispersed actors at low cost.

USC, as part of its organisational strategy, put a plan in place over the past five years to encourage green ICT. As part of this plan simple steps were taken to eliminate the standby operation of equipment such as personal computers and printers. Shared network printers were also introduced rather than the previous practice of giving each administrator their own printer. A policy of controlling upgrades of hardware and software across the organisation also increased the lifecycle of equipment and includes a path to the safe disposal of such equipment for recycling.

Business models

The concept of a *business model* has become popular in recent times as a way of thinking about business change, particularly the ways in which such change incorporates some form of technological innovation. The idea of a business model implicitly casts organisations as open systems that can change their activities to better respond to environmental changes. In other words, the key test of any business model is whether it enables the organisation to survive in its environment.

A business model is typically seen as specifying the structure and dynamics of a particular organisation in terms of features including major products and/ or services provided, key stakeholders involved, costs and benefits of particular modes of operation and key revenue flows. A business model in our terms can be described as the core logic for creating value that applies to a particular organisation. Business strategies specify how a particular business model can be applied to a particular market sector to improve competitive position. As such, the business model idea is useful in relating business strategy to business activities to information systems and to technology. This idea presupposes that a given business has a number of different options in terms of the particular business model it may choose to adopt. With the rise of eBusiness and eCommerce such options multiply.

Traditionally, the business model of USC has depended on the delivery of its courses at physical events – course presentations – to customers from various organisations. A smaller part of its revenue was derived from on-site physical presentations for partner organisations. More recently, USC has developed an online business model for a range of courses from its portfolio. Certain customers are able to take an entire course through electronic learning or eLearning. This enables the company to reach international as well as national customers with parts of its course portfolio.

Forms of eBusiness

It should be evident from the previous section that unlike other texts we see a seamless link between eBusiness and eCommerce. Some prefer to use the term eBusiness to refer to the use of ICT solely to improve internal operations while eCommerce involves the application of ICT in supporting trading relationships. We think this distinction is artificial and use the term eBusiness to encompass that of eCommerce. eBusiness is the use of ICT to support and improve all aspects of the business: internal and external.

The principles of eBusiness discussed in previous sections have been applied in different ways in both private sector organisations and their public sector counterparts. eBusiness involves all aspects of organisational transformation with ICT, including transformation of the internal value-chain. But eBusiness also includes eCommerce which focuses upon transformation of aspects of the external value-network associated with particular organisations. eCommerce involves the use of

ICT to enable and transform trading activities and relationships of the business with individuals, groups and other businesses.

Generally we may distinguish between four distinct forms of eCommerce corresponding to the application of ICT transformation to major aspects of the value network: the customer-chain (B2C eCommerce), the supply-chain (B2B eCommerce), the community chain (C2C eCommerce) and the partnership chain (P2P eCommerce). It is also possible to discuss micro-strategies associated with particular aspects of the customer-chain and the supply-chain respectively. In this light we consider the importance of eMarketing and eProcurement to modern business (Figure 1.8).

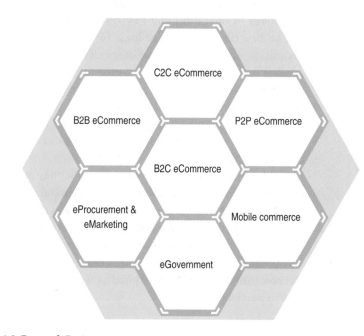

Figure 1.8 Forms of eBusiness

B2C eCommerce

Business-to-Consumer eCommerce is sometimes called sell-side eCommerce and concerns the enablement and transformation of the customer-chain with ICT. Customers or consumers will typically be individuals, sometimes other organisations. B2C Commerce typically follows a cash commerce model, which for low- and standard-priced goods normally follows the four stages of the generic model of commerce described earlier quite closely.

For medium- to high-priced items some form of credit commerce will operate. In other words, organisations will search for a product, negotiate a price, order a product, receive delivery of the product, be invoiced for the product, pay for the product and receive some form of after-sales service. Typically, B2C eCommerce will utilise a market model of economic exchange and hence B2C eCommerce generally works within an encompassing environment of electronic markets.

In the late 1990s USC took the strategic decision to open up B2C eCommerce as part of its operation. In the early stages it produced a very simple website which merely provided static details about the business of the company as well as providing contact details for customers. After a year of operation it then decided to perform a major upgrade of this website, including facilities for customers to dynamically view course presentation schedules and to book themselves onto a particular course presentation. Invoices to customers were sent out at some later date by the financial department of the university. The latest version of this website now includes a direct payment facility which expects a customer either to pay up-front or to supply details of payment online.

B2B eCommerce

Business-to-Business eCommerce is sometimes called buy-side eCommerce and involves supporting and transforming the supply chain with ICT. B2B commerce is clearly between organisational actors – public and/or private sector organisations. This form of eCommerce invariably concerns the use of ICT to enable forms of credit commerce between a company and its suppliers or other partners. For high-priced and customised goods traded between organisations some form of repeat commerce model operates. In other words, the same processes occur as for credit commerce but the processes cycle around indefinitely in a trusted relationship between *producer* and consumer. Hence, typically some form of managerial *eHierarchy* is employed to control the operation of such commercial relationships.

As the business of USC grew it proved increasingly difficult for USC administrators to manage an increasing range of venues spread across the UK and into Europe. A decision was therefore taken to engage a major hotel chain as the primary supplier for USC course presentations. To enable efficient management of such course presentations, USC was given access to a restricted part of the hotel chain's bookings system. This allowed USC administrators to quickly maintain a venue list against a yearly course presentation schedule.

C2C eCommerce

Consumer-to-Consumer eCommerce concerns the enablement of the community chain with ICT. C2C eCommerce occurs primarily between individuals and typically involves forms of cash commerce generally for low-cost services or goods. Consequently, it tends to follow a market model for economic exchange. However, other forms of value may be generated in the communities or social networks engaged in C2C eCommerce. Of particular interest is the degree of social capital that may be located in such social networks. *Social capital* is the productive value of people engaged in a dense network of social relations and consists of those features of social organisation – high levels of interpersonal trust, reciprocity, etc. – which act as a resource for individuals and facilitate collective action.

As part of its commitment to its developing customer-base USC decided to build a community of interest around its 'alumni' – students who had taken and been credited with one or more of its courses. Market research with such alumni showed a wish to keep in touch with fellow course participants but also a wish to use this network to learn more about new technologies and as a source of help in areas such as technical trouble-shooting. USC initially extended its website with an alumni area, allowing previous customers to post their contact details and areas of interest. Eventually, with the rise of social networking websites such as Facebook and LinkedIn, USC employed a dedicated person to facilitate electronic marketing to its customers and networking amongst its customers. It is believed that this provides significant added-value to its current customers.

P2P eCommerce

Partner-to-Partner (P2P) eCommerce concerns the enablement of the partnership chain with ICT. Business organisations now engage in networks of collaboration as well as networks of competition. This means offering a range of different products or services from a number of different businesses at the same time to the same customer through the same access channel. Hence, USC has taken a strategic decision to partner with a partnership network already established through its hotel supplier. Customers can hence book a course and at the same time book discounted accommodation at the venue through the USC website. For European destinations, flights and hire-car reservation can also be booked as part of the instructional package at a discounted price.

eMarketing and eProcurement

Two key aspects of B2C and B2B eCommerce respectively are important because of their contemporary significance as key process strategies for improving organisational performance: eMarketing and eProcurement. The internet and web offer innovative ways of engaging in pre-sale activity with the customer. One of the most significant of such innovations over the past decade has been the growth in the electronic marketing (eMarketing) of goods and services. As part of B2C eCommerce, eMarketing is an important way of impacting the efficiency and effectiveness of the customer chain. eMarketing not only involves the use of electronic channels for the delivery of promotional material: it also involves the conception and pricing of products and services. In the case of B2B eCommerce, engaging in electronic procurement is an important way to improve the efficiency and effectiveness of an organisation's supply chain. The pre-sale activity of search, negotiate and order in the supply chain is frequently referred to under the umbrella term of procurement. Sometimes the term procurement is used to refer to all the activities involved in the supply chain.

As mentioned, electronic marketing is now a significant part of the overall marketing strategy of USC. As an example of this, USC partners with a number of major technology suppliers and places banner and target advertisements for its courses on the websites of these suppliers. It also uses its growing customer records database to send out targeted emails, texts and tweets on new and upcoming courses. More recently it has attempted to build so-called viral marketing campaigns on social networking sites such as Facebook.

eGovernment

ICT and information systems are being used to re-engineer aspects of governmental processes and the relationship between government and the citizen. The interface between government and citizen in terms of services such as tax collection and benefit payment and the associated use of ICT systems to deliver these services via government agencies is typically referred to as electronic government. The term eDemocracy tends to be used to refer to the use of ICT in the service of democratic representation between government and citizen and the associated use of ICT within democratic processes in government. In many nations, a significant proportion of B2B eCommerce and eProcurement is actually enabled through eGovernment systems. This is because public sector organisations are significant purchasers of products and services from the private sector. Hence, for instance, USC regularly tenders for business on government eProcurement portals at the regional, national and European levels.

Mobile commerce

Mobile commerce or mCommerce can be seen to be a natural extension of the technological capabilities of the technical infrastructure associated with eBusiness. Modern communications infrastructure, particularly the increasing penetration of wireless infrastructure, makes it possible for workers to access organisational systems from a vast range of places and while on the move. Hence, course lecturers are able to access a central repository of material on courses and schedules provided by USC from almost anywhere in the UK or most parts of the world.

The same applies to customers who may access B2C websites not only from access devices such as laptops but also from smartphones. In the latter area, an increasing range of Smartphone applications or 'apps' form a significant part of the intangible products being offered.

Activity infrastructure for eBusiness

The activity infrastructure for eBusiness consists of those activity systems central to supporting the conduct of eBusiness. In addition to the conventional competencies in areas of activity such as finance, sales and production, the eBusiness must develop informatics competencies if it is to survive in the marketplace. These include competencies in eBusiness planning, management, implementation and evaluation. In systems terms, these processes can be envisaged in terms of a hierarchy of control. Planning controls management which in turn controls implementation. Evaluation feeds-back into planning, management and implementation. The major point is that effective eBusiness planning, management, development and evaluation is critical for the effective alignment of activity systems, information systems and ICT within business (Figure 1.9).

eBusiness planning

eBusiness planning is the process of deciding upon the optimal eBusiness infrastructure for some organisation and may involve the transformation from

Figure 1.9 Activity infrastructure for eBusiness

one eBusiness infrastructure into another. As described above, eBusiness infrastructure includes both activity systems infrastructure and informatics (information, information systems and ICT) infrastructure. The key output from eBusiness planning is eBusiness strategy. Part of the input to the planning process is performance monitoring – information fed back from the operational and management processes – which is critical to the on-going evaluation of strategy.

eBusiness strategy

eBusiness concerns itself with the juncture of ICT and organisation. Therefore, an eBusiness must concern itself with the development of both organisational strategy and informatics strategy. In a sense, eBusiness strategy is both organisational and informatics strategy. This is because there are at least three different viewpoints as to what eBusiness strategy constitutes. The appropriate viewpoint is defined by organisational context.

1. *eBusiness strategy is organisation/corporate strategy*. In this viewpoint there is little or no distinction between organisation strategy and eBusiness strategy. This definition is appropriate if the eBusiness is effectively the entire corporation as is the case in so-called *clicks-only* companies – companies that run their entire business through electronic channels.
2. *eBusiness strategy is business unit strategy*. In many companies the eBusiness strategy may be applicable only to a particular business unit. For example, some

companies run their eBusinesses as separate but parallel operations to their offline business.

3. *eBusiness strategy is a process strategy.* A key organisational process or activity system, or perhaps an integrated set of such processes, may be chosen for radical re-design through ICT innovation. For example, a company may decide that it wishes to concentrate on re-designing its supply chain or customer chain processes with ICT innovation. It is likely that this is the most common form of eBusiness strategy because many organisations are so-called *clicks-and-mortar* companies – traditional businesses which have established an online presence.

Being a traditional company that has grown into eBusiness, USC is best described as a clicks-and-mortar company. As a result its strategies, as we have already seen, have tended to be process strategies. ICT has been particularly used to improve aspects of its B2C, B2B and C2C operations.

eBusiness management

Two forms of management are important: *eBusiness management* and project management. eBusiness management is the process of putting eBusiness plans into action and monitoring performance against plans. eBusiness management will implement a portfolio of projects by defining and resourcing such projects. However, individual projects need to be managed as autonomous fields of activity and progress reported to general management processes – this is project management.

eBusiness development

eBusiness development is the process of implementing the plans documented in strategy and resourced from management. eBusiness systems are inherently *sociotechnical systems* consisting of data systems, information systems and the activity systems they support. Data and information systems will be constructed by a development organisation and nowadays frequently employ web-based standards and technologies. Detailed requirements are likely to be supplied by potential users of such systems to the development organisation. Clients such as managerial groups will typically supply key resources to the development organisation to enable such acts of 'engineering'.

USC, being a medium-sized company, has never had sufficient internal resource to undertake much eBusiness implementation itself. Its first, simple website was produced by an USC employee. However, it soon became evident that to build the sort of additional functionality they required demanded the use of external suppliers. Therefore, USC has contracted a dedicated ICT supplier to design, maintain and host its website for a number of years. However, the company recognises that this outsourced relationship has to be carefully managed over time and for this purpose has created a small group of in-house ICT people, who also have responsibility for monitoring its internal and external ICT infrastructure.

eBusiness evaluation

One critical sub-process within management is that of evaluation. Evaluation is the process of assessing the worth of something. At the highest level, evaluation is critical to the continuous assessment of strategy. At the lowest level, evaluation is critical to the assessment of ICT systems within their context of use and application, namely activity systems.

eBusiness strategy, project parameters and project plans are all control inputs in a hierarchy of control. Development progress, project reports and strategy evaluations are all forms of feedback. Planning, general management, project management and development are continuous processes. As in any activity system it is important that feedback loops work effectively for the activity infrastructure of eBusiness to be viable. Information systems are equally critical to such processes as conventional business processes such as sales and manufacturing.

eBusiness futures

Predicting the future is by its very nature prone to error, particularly in the area of technology and its impact. In 1949 for instance, ENIAC, an early computer, was equipped with 18,000 vacuum tubes and weighed 30 tons. It was predicted at the time that computers in the future may have only 1,000 vacuum tubes and perhaps weigh 2 tons. A few years later in 1977, the president of a large hardware manufacturer – Digital Equipment Corporation – predicted that no one would ever want to have a computer in their home.

So we will be circumspect in our predictions within this book and will base these on extrapolating from a number of trends evident in the current domain of eBusiness. We shall use these to provide a picture of some of the issues in the area of eBusiness that are likely to arise over the next ten years or so.

So what are the current trends? First, there is an increasing use of ICT infrastructure not only within organisations but also between organisations and external actors such as customers. In 1997, for instance, there were some 100 million users of the internet. This has progressively grown over the years: 200 million in 1998, 390 million in 2001, 640 million in 2003, 1 billion in 2005, 1.5 billion in 2008 and an estimated 1.9 billion in 2010. In 2010, 30 million adults in the UK accessed the internet every day and 17 million adults watched TV or listened to the radio over the internet. Seventy-three per cent of Europeans now engage in some form of online shopping and in 2009 £408 billion of eCommerce sales were taken in the UK alone.

It is therefore not unreasonable to expect the provision of broadband communication channels to assume its position as a utility alongside electricity, gas and water over the next 10 years. Ubiquitous communication infrastructure will become increasingly important for economic, social and political activity. ICTs will continue to converge around common standards leading to greater inter-operability between ICT systems and greater convergence amongst access devices, which will increase in functionality.

Growing ICT infrastructure will support a growing range of consumer applications, much of this based on the personalisation of content. A mixed economy in the development of content will stabilise over the coming decade with broadcasting and narrowcasting of content co-existing. The increasing penetration of high-bandwidth broadband into the home and into public places will foster an increase in remote and nomadic working. In the near future we can expect an increasing range of services and intangible goods in the private, public and voluntary sectors to be delivered electronically in an increasing number of areas of life.

The competitive advantage of businesses will thus be increasingly reliant on effective and efficient data communication infrastructure as business activity becomes increasingly designed around location-independence. As levels of remote interaction between individuals and organisations increase, situations in which the management of the personal identity become important multiply. We would therefore expect that the management of personal identity will assume increasing significance both in terms of internal organisational activity and particularly in cross-organisational infrastructure. As more and more activity moves online, securing data and systems will also become increasingly critical for organisations both in the public and private sectors.

Generally within business we would expect the continued embeddedness of information systems and ICT within organisational life. This will involve continued attempts to innovate within aspects of the value-chain distributed over internal communication networks. It will also increasingly involve attempts to integrate the wider value-network with the internal value-chain.

A tipping point in B2C eCommerce has already been reached. We can expect an increasing penetration of traditional B2C eCommerce such as online retail within the economy. We can also expect that B2B eCommerce will merge with P2P eCommerce over the longer term. Some have referred to the development of a digital business ecosystem in which both competition and cooperation activity is supported through ICT. The community chain is likely to assume greater levels of significance over the next decade and the social networking effect will become incorporated more clearly into forms of eBusiness.

In essence then, electronic business is definitely here to stay...

Introducing eBusiness cases

Case material is always important to keep theory grounded and needs to be sufficiently rich to be used in a variety of ways to illustrate key themes discussed. The cases collected together in a portfolio at the end of this book are deliberately chosen to reflect the global nature of eBusiness. While US-based companies still dominate eBusiness, we have also included cases from the UK and Europe more widely, to illustrate its impact within business activity in other parts of the world.

Wherever possible we have attempted to provide sufficient background and the history associated with a company's growth into eBusiness. This is to demonstrate that eBusiness is more a process than an end-state for organisations. As well as cases addressing a specific company we have also included cases exploring the way in which eBusiness has changed and is likely to continue to impact upon particular industries: music, movies, books. Detailed teaching notes for all the published cases are included for instructors on the book's website – www.palgrave.com/business/ebusiness2. Here you will also find links to additional teaching cases published by the *Journal of Information Technology*.

Summary

Electronic business or eBusiness is the utilisation of ICT, information systems and information to support all the activities of business. eBusiness is a superset of eCommerce which in turn is a superset of mobile eCommerce or mCommerce. eCommerce focuses on the use of ICT to enable the external activities and relationships of the business with individuals, groups and other businesses. mCommerce focuses on the use of various ICTs to enable work on the move.

In a sense, eBusiness builds upon the platform of naturally occurring phenomena found in all organisations. This platform is constituted at the intersection between signs, patterns and systems. Signs are critically important in all forms of activity, including business, and can be seen as being composed of forma, informa and performa. Forma stands for the substance of a sign and concerns its physical representation as data. Informa relates to the meaning associated with a sign and concerns the interpretation of data as information. Performa relates to the use of the sign to facilitate coordinated activity or performance. We shall argue that eBusiness is founded in the interaction of three types of system: systems of activity, systems of information and systems of ICT. Such systems amount to the patterning of performance, communication and representation.

In such terms, an organisation can be considered as an activity system or more accurately as a series of inter-related activity systems. An organisation is an open system. It receives inputs from its environment and produces outputs into its environment. The environment also constrains what an organisation is able to do in terms of its activity. The environment of most organisations can be considered in terms of the interaction between four major environmental systems: an economic system, a political system, a social system and a physical system.

The key message being promoted by eBusiness is that ICT is an enabler for organisational change focused around the re-design of the delivery of services and products to key business actors – customers, suppliers, partners, employees and managers. Economies are systems for coordinating the production and distribution of goods and services between business actors. Economic activity is organised in terms of markets, hierarchies and networks. Markets are systems of competition. They are mediums for the exchange of value between buyers and sellers. Hierarchies are systems of cooperation. Value exchange is conducted on the basis of established trading arrangements. Networks are a mediating form between markets and hierarchies. Electronic Business and eCommerce are features of eMarkets and eHierarchies. eMarkets and eHierarchies are environments in which economic exchanges are conducted using ICT. eMarkets are electronic environments for competition, while eHierarchies are electronic environments for collaboration.

The political environment is particularly concerned with government and legal frameworks within nation-states. The practice of government determines policy in the eBusiness and eCommerce areas. However, eBusiness is also a significant force within government itself. The political environment of Western countries has been much subject to the influence of ICT in the areas of electronic government and electronic democracy in recent times. In contrast, the social system concerns ways in which people relate to organisational activity. Social attitudes to issues such as data protection and privacy, as well as the trust in eCommerce systems, affects the practicality of eBusiness. A number of pre-conditions exist for the successful take-up of electronic service delivery, which include awareness, interest, access, skills, use and impact. The increasing use of ICT for private and public sector transactions is seen as potentially creating a 'digital divide' between those that successfully engage with these pre-conditions and those who do not.

The objective of re-designing organisational processes or activity systems with ICT to support electronic delivery of products and services typically involves remote access channels, delivery of intangible goods and services, constructing *front-end ICT systems* to manage customer interaction, ensuring effective back-end systems integration and front-end/back-end systems integration and ensuring the security of data and transactions.

Commerce of whatever nature can be considered as a process with the following phases: pre-sale, sale execution, sale settlement, after-sale. The precise form of the process of commerce will vary in terms of the nature of the economic actors involved, the frequency of commerce and the nature of the goods or services being exchanged. Electronic commerce is the use of ICT to enable the external activities and relationships of the business with individuals, groups and other businesses. Generally we may distinguish between four major forms of such eCommerce: B2C eCommerce, B2B eCommerce, C2C eCommerce and P2P eCommerce.

Two key sub-processes of B2C and B2B eCommerce are important because of their contemporary significance as key process strategies for improving organisational performance. Electronic marketing is the use of electronic channels for the delivery of promotional material. Electronic procurement is an important way to improve the efficiency and effectiveness of an organisation's supply chain.

The activity infrastructure for eBusiness consists of those activity systems central to supporting the conduct of eBusiness. In addition to the conventional competencies in areas of activity such as finance, management and production, the eBusiness must develop informatics competencies if it is to survive in the marketplace. These include competencies in eBusiness strategy planning, management, implementation and evaluation.

Critical reflection

Each chapter in this book contains a section such as this in which we would like you the reader to question and reflect upon the portrayal of eBusiness you will receive from this text. This is an opportunity to challenge conceptions and debate effectively with the nature of eBusiness in particular as well as the developing nature of business in general.

We began this chapter by stating that modern business is eBusiness. You might reflect on this statement in a number of ways. For instance, can you conceive of any successful businesses that do not use ICT? How critical is ICT to their success? If, for some reason their ICT failed, would they still be able to function and in what way? Is perhaps modern commerce too dependent on ICT infrastructure? Is there a downside as well as an upside to such dependence? Are organisations necessarily more effective with greater adoption of ICT? Has, for instance, the general standard of customer service from companies improved with electronic delivery? Are social networking sites truly social networks? Has communication between people actually improved with the widespread adoption of technologies such as Smartphones and email?

eBusiness organisation

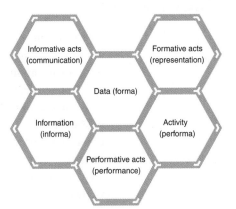

Learning outcomes	Principles
Explore the central role of signs in business activity, communication and representation.	Three distinct but inter-related forms of action are undertaken by actors and these three forms of action serve to accomplish what we mean by organisation. Actors engage in instrumental activity, make decisions and communicate about such activity and represent aspects of such activity in records. Signs inter-relate between and within these three different patterns of order.
Understand business activity as performative action.	Business can be seen to consist of performative patterns: recurring sequences of performative acts. Performative acts consist of the enactment of performa: the performance of coordinated and instrumental action within human groups.
Understand the relationship between business action, decision-making and information. Relate the nature of business communication as informative action.	Decision-making involves choosing between alternative courses of action. Such choice is informed by data. Coordinated action relies upon information generated in informative patterns: recurring sequences of informative acts. Informative acts constitute the enactment of informa: acts of decision-making and communication involving message-making and interpretation.
Distinguish between data and information. Explain how business communication is reliant upon formative action and explore how formative action consists of business representation.	Data are symbols. Information is interpreted data – data supplied with some meaning. Communication within business relies upon formative patterns: recurring sequences of formative action. Formative acts amount to the enactment of forma: acts of data representation and processing.

Chapter outline

Introduction

Electronic business is clearly an organisational phenomenon. Hence, to understand eBusiness we have to understand something of the nature of organisation. The term organisation can be treated either as a noun or as a verb. Hence, when people speak of an organisation they can view it as either a structure or a process: a static or a dynamic thing. As we shall see, these two views are in fact complementary. It is possible to see structure as emergent from action, indeed, from three inter-related types of action – performance, communication and representation. These three forms of action are linked together through the concept of a sign. As such, signs are closely entangled with all forms of organisation. They help us establish the key value that ICT provides to organisation within eBusiness.

In walking down a high street in downtown San Francisco I spotted a sign in a store window. The sign consisted of a large piece of paper with just three words written upon it in large type. It said, 'SIGNS MEAN BUSINESS'. In a sense, those three simple words, taken together, sum up what we are trying to achieve within this chapter. Signs are critically important in all forms of activity found within business. Signs are important because they establish what it is to be human. Without signs we could not think, we could not communicate what we think and we could not ensure that we collaborate together successfully in our working activity.

This chapter considers the nature of signs as units of significance and demonstrates how they are crucial building blocks in what we consider as organisation. It is no accident that the terms sign, significant and significance in English have the same root. Very broadly a sign is anything that is significant. But what does significant mean? To help answer this question, we make a three-fold distinction between the forma, informa and performa of a sign. This helps us relate notions of data, information, decision-making and activity in organisations and these fundamental things establish the platform upon which any eBusiness is founded.

To help ground our discussion we shall consider a different case in this chapter. In Chapter 1 we considered the case of a service organisation: an organisation delivering technical training. In this chapter we offer the contrast of a manufacturing organisation: an organisation producing steel products. Again, many of the details of the case are taken from a real organisation but we have changed its name and some of the details about its operation to protect confidentiality. Because we need to establish the nature of eBusiness from first principles we primarily consider the operation of this company prior to mass computerisation. Again, this historical portrayal enables us to demonstrate that technological innovation within organisation is a continuous process.

Organisation

Since eBusiness is an organisational phenomenon, to understand eBusiness and why it is important we first need to establish what organisation is (Morgan, 1986). In fact, there are two viewpoints on organisation. One views organisation as an institution or a structure. The other views it as a continuing process of human action.

In essence, the institutional perspective focuses on the unit of organisation and is interested in the features of organisations as wholes. The institutional perspective views organisations as entities which exist independently of the humans belonging to them. Human actions are directed or constrained by such larger social structures. Institutions have a life over and above the life of their members.

In contrast, the action perspective focuses on the process of organising rather than the unit of organisation. The critical interest here is in how humans generate structures of coordination and cooperation in work. For the action perspective social institutions such as business organisations are fundamentally constructed in action performed by human beings. This means that organisations do not exist independently of the humans which participate in their existence.

For much of its history the theory of organisation has tended to portray the institutional and action perspectives on organisations as mutually exclusive. In practice, of course each is a legitimate or valid position. We all act and interact with fellow human beings within organisations and appreciate the fluidity of organisational life. We all also experience the monolithic nature of organisations and the constraints placed upon our actions by these institutional structures.

We primarily take the action viewpoint on organisations within this book, partly because eBusiness fits naturally with a dynamic viewpoint on organisation. However, in this and the following two chapters we shall demonstrate that these two viewpoints on organisation are not incompatible. We shall demonstrate how the idea of organisation as structure or institution emerges from organisation as process or activity.

Let us first consider a very simple case of an organisation to help introduce this idea. Three fellow business students who are all keen cyclists look for some manageable weekend work to help with financing their studies. After expending some effort, they successfully manage to obtain a small contract to deliver leaflets to houses in specified areas of the major city in which they are resident. This contract demands that they will be given a different batch of leaflets each weekend and will be expected to deliver them to specified parts of the city. They will get paid on the basis of how many leaflets they deliver to houses in specified areas.

Initially, because the volume of leaflets they have to handle is small, they decide merely to divide up the leaflets equally and assign to each of them a major part of the city to cover. At the end of each weekend they verbally communicate to each other how many of the leaflets and to what areas have been delivered.

After a few weekends of working like this, the contracting company gets in touch with one of the students and demands to know how many of a particular type of leaflet has been delivered over the last week to a specified number of streets in the city. The student taking the call was unfortunately not the person delivering to this area and cannot get in touch with the actual person who did this until some days later. The contracting company is not particularly happy with this but says it will continue their contract. However, from now on they intend to contact them on a regular basis and expect the students to be able to provide definite answers to their questions promptly.

As a consequence, the leafleting group decides to *organise* themselves more appropriately. They decide that in order for anyone to be able to respond effectively to a phone call from the contractor they need to note on a regular basis which leaflets have been delivered to which streets in the city. This is initially done through a set of records made up of pieces of card for each batch of leaflets on which they note a list of nominated streets that need to be delivered to. At the end of each delivery day the organisational members tick the streets they have completed. This set of cards is then checked on the next working day to determine which streets to deliver to next.

In this simple example we have all of the component elements making up organisation and which we shall consider in some depth in this chapter. The group members or actors perform on a repeating basis a set of activities such as delivering leaflets to houses. Each group member needs to coordinate his or her activities with those of other actors: other group members. As a group they also need to coordinate their collective activity with that of the contracting organisation. For such coordination, communication is needed. Communication relies upon some mutually agreed system of signs between coordinating actors. Statements in spoken language are clearly acts of communication between two or more actors which rely on such a common sign-system. But statements in spoken language do not persist beyond the communication in which they take place. Hence, groups of actors that wish to coordinate their performance across time and possibly space have to create records. In other words, records ensure that multiple actors are informed of the actions of others some time after such actions have been completed and likely or not in a different place from which the actions took place. Such records are thus by their very nature used to do different things such as to assert that certain things are true in the current state of some organisation or to direct future actions of group members. In this sense, records are particularly important for making decisions about future courses of action.

Therefore, any organisation consists of a multitude of business actors. An actor is any entity that can act and we deliberately use the term actor here rather than person because we wish to emphasise that actors include humans, animals and machines. In the past, for instance, animals such as pit ponies were significant actors within industry. Nowadays, machines, such as vans, cranes and even ICT systems, as we shall see, are significant actors in the activity infrastructure of most organisations. From the leafleting example it should be apparent that three distinct but inter-related forms of action are undertaken by actors and that these three forms of action serve to accomplish what we mean by organisation. Actors perform instrumental activity, make decisions and communicate about such activity and represent aspects of such activity in records.

However, business actions do not normally occur in isolation. The actions of one business actor are normally entangled with or bound to the actions of other actors and as such form coherent patterns of action. A pattern consists of a set of elements that repeat in a predictable manner. Inherent in the idea of a pattern is the idea that it is reproduced across more than one situation. We will argue that what we mean by organisation consists of the patterning of performance, communication and representation by actors. Such patterning produces or accomplishes the order characteristic of human organisation and produces its institutional properties. Hence, in the leafleting example the business actors reproduce on a weekly basis the delivery of leaflets to designated areas. They also regularly communicate about such activity to each other and to facilitate communication between each other and their customer make records of their activities.

Such patterning of order is stitched together through the use of signs. Signs interrelate between and within these three different patterns of order which we will refer to as forma, informa and performa. Forma constitutes the substance or representation of signs, informa the content and communication of signs and performa the use of signs in coordinated action. Another way of viewing this is to say that the patterning of order characteristic of human organisation is enacted through three inter-related forms of action. *Formative acts* amount to the enactment of forma: acts of data representation and processing. *Informative acts* constitute the enactment of informa: acts of decision-making and communication involving message-making and interpretation. Finally, performative acts consist of the enactment of performa: the performance of coordinated and instrumental activity within human groups.

Signs: units of business significance

Medical practitioners are prime examples of professionals that use signs to create order. They first diagnose your illness on the basis of signs. In other words, they read your symptoms as a means of highlighting what may be wrong with you. They then use some esoteric term (usually with Latin roots) to stand for your illness. On the basis of this sign they will prescribe perhaps a range of treatment, probably including drugs, again with many weird and wonderful names, some proprietary, some generic.

Take also the example of advertising. Advertising is composed of signs that are used to attempt to influence the actions of consumers. What marketing people attempt to do is to manipulate our responses to products and services in subtle ways through signs. They attempt to affect not only our perceptions of products and services but also how we think about such things; this is in the hope that they can influence our consumption of such products and services.

But signs are not only critical to activity between producers and consumers; they are also critical for ensuring the effective operation of business organisations themselves. Signs, for instance, are critical to most aspects of management. Managers issue instructions or directives using signs. They also receive reports or assertions of what is happening in their business from other business actors. Signs are thus critical component elements of business communication and as such are crucial to the control of business operation.

Very broadly a sign is anything that is significant. In a sense, everything that humans have or do is significant to some degree. Sometimes not having or doing anything is regarded as significant. The world within which humans find themselves is therefore resonant with systems of signs. For the eminent theorist of signs, Charles Pierce (Pierce, 1931), signs relate people, objects and ideas: 'A sign is something which stands to somebody for something in some respect or capacity'. Signs therefore relate for some actor the symbol which stands for some *referent*: something that is referred to.

Consider Figure 2.1. Here we have the same symbol '434' interpreted in different ways by different business actors. For the business actor in the leafleting

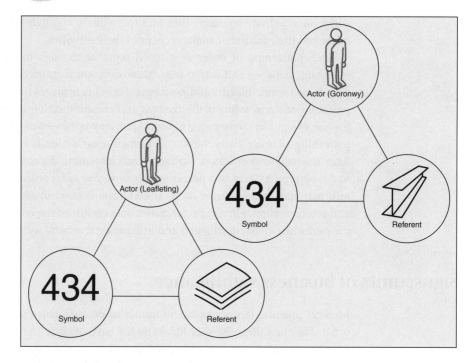

Figure 2.1 Symbols, referents and actors

case 434 stands for a number – perhaps the number of leaflets delivered in one day to a particular area of the city. For the business actor in the case of Goronwy galvanising, which we shall describe in the next section, 434 is not a number, it is part of a code; it stands for a particular type of steel girder of a certain length which is treated with a zinc coating by the company.

But signs don't exist in isolation. They normally form parts of an organised system of representation. The cognitive scientist Steven Pinker (2001) argues that our genetic makeup predisposes humans to be excellent manipulators of sign-systems. A sign-system is any organised collection of signs and relations between signs. Everyday spoken human language is probably the most readily identifiable example of a sign-system. However, the concept of a sign-system is much broader than spoken human language. Signs exist in most forms of human activity since signs are critical to processes of human communication and understanding. For example, within a face-to-face encounter, humans communicate through non-verbal as well as verbal sign-systems, colloquially referred to as 'body language'. Hence, humans communicate a great deal through facial expression and other forms of bodily movement. Such movements are also signs. The importance of such signs to human communication is evident in the recent explosion of business and personal development books purporting to reveal the 'secrets' of such body language.

Business signs

Signs mean business because signs are critical not only to business communication but also to business activity. A sign within business is anything that a business regards as significant: signs are critical things of interest to a business organisation. The American philosopher John Dewey suggested that a word is three things: a fence, a label and a vehicle. The same could be said more generally of the concept of sign. A sign is a 'fence' in the sense that it sets a conceptual boundary around something and is used to distinguish one thing from another. A sign is a 'label' in that it acts as a convenient reference standing for something else. Finally, a sign is a 'vehicle' in the sense that used with other signs as a sign-system it is a means for describing and debating with the world as well as acting upon it.

The arrow, embodied in the idea of the pointing hand, represents these properties of a sign. In other words, a sign 'points'. When a human forms her hand in this way she is using it to direct the gaze of some other actor to some particular thing. The act of pointing, which appears unique to our species and our nearest evolutionary cousins, the great apes, serves to highlight something from its surroundings. That thing is normally given a label, perhaps in some bit of business jargon. Finally, the labels for things are used to make a record of such things. These records are in turn crucial for the coordination of business activity.

Figure 2.2 illustrates the importance of business signs by using some standard words or terms found within communication by various forms of organisation. For instance, a manufacturing company such as the one we consider in this chapter would be interested in products, orders and sales. In contrast, a service company

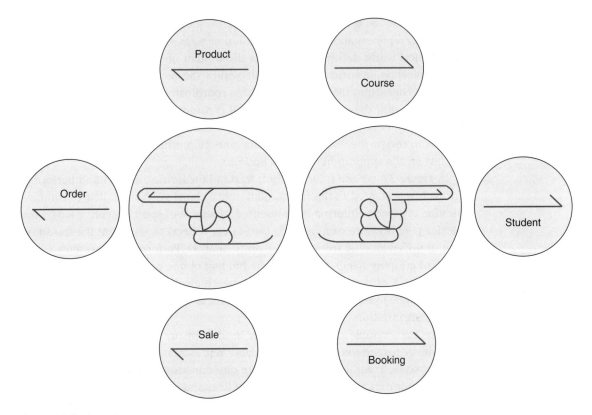

Figure 2.2 Business signs

such as USC, considered in the opening chapter, would be interested in courses, students and bookings, Finally, a public sector organisation such as a government agency would be interested in citizens, claims and benefit payments.

The term *universe of discourse* (UoD), domain of discourse or more recently ontology is used to describe the context within which a group of signs is used continually by a group of actors. Take for instance a university. Most universities need to record information to help in the activities of teaching and learning. Most universities need to record, amongst other things, what students and lecturers they have, what courses and modules they are running, which lecturers are teaching which modules, which students are taking which modules, which lecturer is assessing against which module and which students have been assessed in which modules as well as the grades they receive. All these things form part of the universe of discourse of a typical university. They are all things about which actors within the higher education institution wish to communicate or have discourse about. They are all things about which the university makes records. Finally, on the basis of what they know about such things, actors within the organisation in question take action: they teach students, mark assessments and award grades to students.

In essence then a sign consists of a significant pattern. Signs are key examples of such repeating patterns treated by two or more actors as significant. It is possible to unpack any sign as a pattern which has three distinct but inter-related facets which we denote as forma, informa and performa. These distinctions serve to link three worlds critical to all business organisation: they link the physical or technical world with the social world through the psychological world. Forma constitutes the substance, representation and manipulation of signs and falls within the physical or technical world. Informa constitutes the content of signs and their use within communication. As such, informa falls within the psychological world. Finally, performa constitutes the use of signs within coordinated, instrumental activity and thus falls within the social world. We shall consider each of these aspects of the sign in more detail in the following sections and shall then draw together these aspects to review the issue of business organisation, which provides the necessary context for the application of ICT in business.

In Figure 2.3 we use three symbols to stand for forma, informa and performa. Forma is represented as the representation of a signal symbol familiar to communication engineers. Informa is represented by a cycle of speech glyphs used by the Mexica people (more commonly known as the Aztecs) to represent the transmission of understanding from one person to another. Performa is represented by a series of grasping hands to indicate the binding of one person's actions to that of another. Each of these symbols – signal, speech glyph and hand – is indicated as part of a cycle to represent the patterning of these three facets of a sign within any form of organisation.

Take the example of a simple sign used in many modern organisations: a barcode. A barcode is a machine-readable representation of a code, typically a product code. Traditionally, barcodes are one-dimensional representations which serve to code data in terms of the widths of lines and spaces between lines.

Barcodes are commonplace in the modern world. Almost every food retail store, from the largest to the smallest, now sell products that contain barcodes. Patients

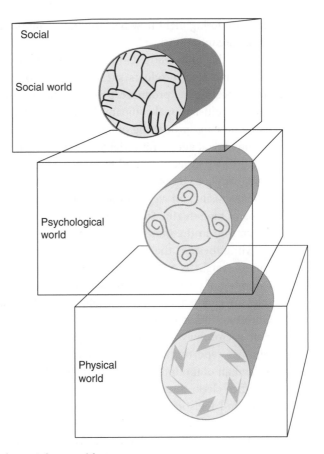

Figure 2.3 Performa, informa and forma

in hospitals are frequently tagged with plastic bracelets containing barcodes. Books and other forms of document are now given barcodes for ease of tracking. Airline luggage is frequently tracked across the world using barcodes.

The relationship or mapping between a barcode as forma and what it represents as informa is frequently and perhaps confusingly referred to as a symbology. The most common form of symbology is that of standard commodity coding. Most food retail outlets in the UK use a form of commodity coding known as the European Article Number. This allows such companies to engage in various aspects of performa: track goods from suppliers, control stock in warehouses, manage food displayed within supermarkets and associate products with sales to customers. So a simple business sign is critical to a vast amount of organisational communication, decision-making and action.

Business activity: performa

Let us utilise another more detailed case to unpack the distinctions between performa, informa and forma, made in the previous section. We shall also use this case to highlight how performance, communication and activity relate within actual organisations.

It is the mid-1980s. Goronwy Galvanising is a small company specialising in treating steel products such as lintels (beams), crash barriers and palisades (fence posts) etc., produced by other manufacturers. Goronwy is a subsidiary of a large multi-national company, Rito Metals, whose primary business includes the extraction and processing of base metals such as zinc as well as the production of various metal alloys. Rito Metals maintains ten galvanising plants on similar lines to Goronwy situated around Europe. Each plant is relatively autonomous in terms of managing its day-to-day business.

Galvanising, in very simplistic terms, involves dipping steel products into baths of molten zinc to provide a rustproof coating. Untreated steel products are referred to in the industry as being 'black'. Treated steel products are referred to as 'white'. Besides the obvious addition of a zinc coating, there is usually a slight gain in weight as a result of the galvanising process. Goronwy galvanises steel for a number of major steel manufacturers. However, as much as 80% of their current sales are conducted with Blackwalls steel, which places a regular set of orders with Goronwy. Other manufacturers order galvanised steel on an irregular basis. The staff at Goronwy consists of two layers of management: an overall plant manager who has reporting to him a production controller, an inbound logistics controller and an outbound logistics controller. The production controller is in charge of an office clerk, three shift foremen and 40 shop-floor workers. The inbound and outbound logistics controllers each have five operatives working for them. The plant remains open 24 hours a day, seven days a week. Therefore, most of the production workers, including the foremen, work shift-patterns.

As mentioned, unfinished, 'black' materials consist of steel-fabricated products of various forms. This raw material is delivered to Goronwy on large trailers in bundles referred to as batches. On arrival at the galvanising plant the black material is unpacked by an inbound logistics operative and checked for discrepancies such as material being unsuitable for galvanising. Such unsuitable material is referred to within the company as non-conforming black material and this is returned to the customer. If satisfactory, the products are referred to as conforming black material and this is transported to the galvanising plant where it is hung on racks and then dipped into large baths of zinc. The racks are removed from the baths after a few minutes of treatment and then left to dry. After an hour or so the white material is checked and unsatisfactory (non-conforming) white material is sent to be re-galvanised. Satisfactory (conforming) white material is then bundled back into batches, loaded onto trailers and eventually dispatched back to the customer.

Performa corresponds to the 'performance' of actors in various situations. We particularly focus on instrumental action in such terms. A performative act amounts to some transformation of the world undertaken by a particular actor at a particular time and in a particular place in an attempt to realise some particular goal.

In terms of our description of the case above we can identify a number of performative activities critical to Goronwy as an organisation. In essence performa relates to the fundamental question of 'what does an organisation such as Goronwy

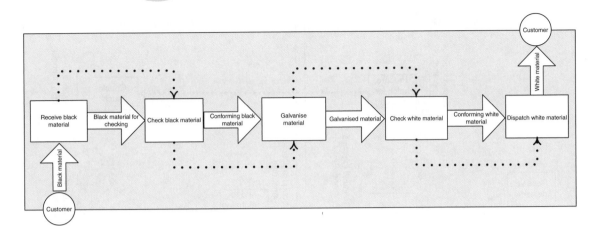

Figure 2.4 The primary performative pattern at Goronwy

do?' The response to such a question normally indicates the central performative activity of the organisation: in this case galvanisation. But galvanisation relies on one set of activities that handles raw material from the customer, and yet another set of activities that transports galvanised products back to the customer. Hence, it is possible to think of the activities of Goronwy related by precedence. In other words, to perform a particular activity another activity needs to be performed first and the performance of such activity will normally be a prerequisite for some other activity, and so on. Figure 2.4 illustrates such a set of activities relevant to Goronwy. The dotted arrows on the diagram represent the order in which activities are performed and the broad arrows indicate the *physical flow* of material that is transformed by such activities, represented as labelled rectangles on the diagram.

Performative acts normally correspond to the 'work' of people in collective interaction, typically using 'tools' to transform 'objects' in the world. Hence, performative acts typically occur in sequences where one performative act is reliant upon the completion of one or more other performative acts. A set of such coherent activities that repeats on a regular basis is what we refer to as a *performative pattern*.

Any business activity can be considered in more detail as a series of performative acts. In other words, we can take any performative activity and break it down into more detail. Hence, in Figure 2.5 we illustrate how we might provide more detail on the receive and check black material activities from the performative pattern outlined in Figure 2.5. This form of representation is particularly useful because it highlights the central role of particular business actors in particular performative activity. For instance, an inbound logistics operative unloads a batch, prepares it for checking and makes a decision about whether it is conforming or not.

Business information: informa

On Figure 2.5 performative acts are represented as boxes, while the diamond shape represents a decision point. As is evident from this diagram, decisions are choices

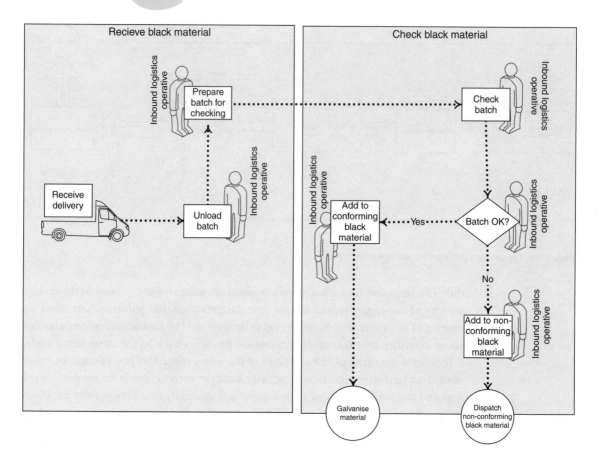

Figure 2.5 Performative acts

between alternative courses of performative action – in this case as to whether the batch is fit for galvanising or not. The choice made by particular business actors has to be communicated in some way to other business actors. This realm of decision-making and communication is the realm of informa. Hence, along with the patterning of performative activity in organisations there will be a patterning of communication and decision-making and we refer to such a form of order as informative acts and *informative patterns*.

Informative acts involve the transmission and receipt of messages. An informative act is some aspect of performance designed by one actor, the sender of some message, to influence the performance of some other actor, the receiver of some message. In any organisational activity business actors normally communicate in five major ways in support of coordination, and these ways amount to five major forms of informative act: five major ways in which actors seek to influence the actions of others and as a by-product of this to ensure coordination of their mutual activity.

Consider three examples of informative acts that appear regularly within business organisations: [*Please take the customer order*], [*Will you take the order?*], [*You will take the order*]. The content of these three messages is the same – [*that you will process the customer order*]. However, the intent of these three verbal statements is clearly different: the first is a request, the second a question and the third a prediction.

Hence, it is possible to formulate five key types of communicative or informative act in terms of differences in the intentions that the actor performing the communication has: assertives, directives, commissives, expressives and declaratives. We can thus use the notation I[c] to refer to a communicative act, where I stands for the intent of the communicative act and c its content. We shall provide a different symbol to designate the intent behind each of these five types and we shall place the content of some informative act between square brackets.

Assertives are communicative acts that explain how things are in a particular part of some universe of discourse, such as reports of business activity. Such acts commit the speaker to the truth of the expressed proposition. We express an assertive as ⊢[p]. For instance, within some business organisation a given business actor might make the statement ⊢[*Our orders have fallen by 10% this month*] or in the case of Goronwy an inbound logistics operative might make the statement to the plant manager, ⊢[*15% of all the black material we received over the last year was non-conforming*].

Directives are communicative acts that represent the senders' attempt to get the receiver of a message to perform or take an action, such as requests, questions, commands and advice. We express a directive as ?[p]. Hence, an actor might ask of another actor: ?[*Please ensure that our production target is met next quarter*] or in the case of Goronwy the plant manager might request of his production controller, ?[*Please ensure that all conforming black material is galvanised on its day of delivery*].

Commissives are communicative acts that commit a speaker to some future course of action such as promises, oaths and threats. They are communicative acts that represent a speaker's intention to perform an action sometime in the future. We represent a commissive as #[p]. Hence, a business actor might issue statements such as: #[*I promise to write a letter to company X*] or #[*I refuse to pay that invoice from company Y*]. In the case of Goronwy the manager might make the following commitment to its major customer Blackwalls: #[*We promise to turnaround all products within a three day period*].

Expressives are communicative acts that represent the speakers' psychological state, feelings or emotions towards some aspect of a domain, such as apologies, criticisms and congratulations. They express a speaker's attitudes and emotions towards some proposition. We represent an expressive as ![p]. Hence, some user of Facebook might indicate his feelings towards some content by implicitly communicating ![*I like content X*] or a managerial actor might state, ![*I am unhappy with Joe's overall performance this month*] or in the case of Goronwy the production controller might comment, ![*I am pleased with our production over the last quarter*].

Declaratives are communicative acts that aim to change some aspect of a domain through the communication itself. For instance, in the organisation of most Christian churches, declaring someone baptised or pronouncing someone husband and wife is sufficient to change the status of certain individuals. In most legal systems, sentencing a prisoner is sufficient to incur punishment for an individual. We express a declarative as ≡[p]. Within business settings declaratives are frequently used to represent that some state of performance has been achieved such as in the case of Goronwy, ≡[*That batch Z has been galvanised*] or ≡[*That batch Y has been dispatched back to customer X*].

Such informative acts form the component elements of informative patterns which parallel and support performative patterns in organisations. An informative pattern that occurs frequently in many organisations consists of the sequence: Assertive, Directive, Commissive, Declarative. This sequence forms a critical element of a so-called control loop which we shall discuss in some detail in Chapter 3. Figure 2.6 illustrates a typical pattern of this nature found in the Goronwy case which supports the performative pattern represented in Figure 2.5. Here, an assertion of a delivery triggers a directive to unload a trailer. This directive in turn triggers a commitment to unload and an eventual declaration that the trailer has been unloaded.

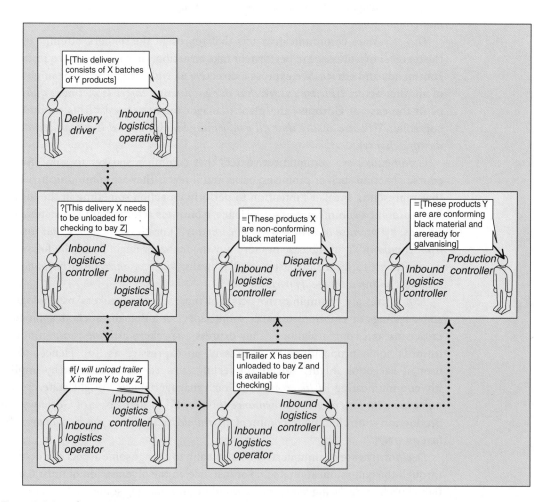

Figure 2.6 An informative pattern

Informa is not only about communication between two or more actors; it must also involve the way in which actors accomplish collective meaning through both internal and external communication. For example, when one inbound logistics operative speaks to another inbound logistics operative making the utterance – 'Trailer X has been unloaded to bay Z and is available for checking' – both actors must be using a common sign-system for such a statement to be understood. This sign-system clearly consists of a set of coherent sounds forming spoken words, each of which is taken to stand for something. In making this association between what we referred to earlier as symbol and referent, meaning is accomplished. Hence, when one actor speaks the word 'trailer' there is a mutual understanding of what this sound pattern refers to.

Informa is therefore a psychological accomplishment reliant on some collective agreement between actors about symbols and what they stand for. But this agreement about meaning is not inevitable or fixed. Most signs used within human activity and communication are arbitrary in nature. By this we mean that there is no inherent or universal association between symbol and referent. The stands for relation exists merely through establishment of some acceptance or expectation amongst a group of actors as to these relations – it is a convention.

This can be illustrated in relation to hand gestures, which are an important part of non-verbal sign-systems we referred to earlier. Six commonly used hand gestures are illustrated in Figure 2.7. What do each of the hand gestures mean to you? Many of these hand gestures in fact mean different things depending upon the culture of which you are a part. For instance, the upper left hand sign is generally taken to mean something like OK within a country such as the UK. Hence, a stock market trader on the trading floor of a major investment bank may just use this sign to indicate that she is happy with a particular share deal. However, if you use this sign in social situations within a country such as Tunisia it is likely to be interpreted as 'I'll kill you'!

Information provided through communicative acts using agreed signs is the basis of making decisions such as whether to buy traded company shares or what

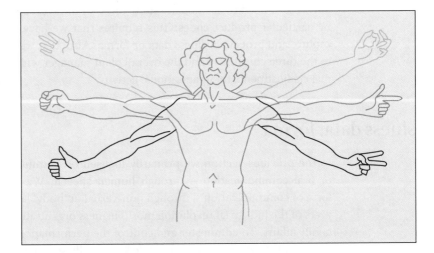

Figure 2.7 Hand gestures

material to galvanise. Action is then taken on the basis of decisions made: if the information is incorrect or inappropriate, then the wrong decisions will be made and the organisation will not perform effectively. Information – and more particularly, *quality* information, is therefore essential for the effective coordination of activity within organisations such as Goronwy, and to the way in which the overall purpose of this organisation is achieved.

Information therefore supports performative activity in the sense that it enables *decisions* to be made about appropriate actions in particular circumstances. Therefore, decisions and decision-making mediate between information and action and such decisions are particularly the responsibility of layers of management within organisations. In other words, the primary activity of management is making decisions concerning organisational action.

But effective management decision-making is possible only if a number of pre-conditions are in place. First, clear definitions of what performance means to some organisation need to be defined. This involves turning the agreed purpose or purposes of some organisation into a defined set of performance measures. Second, effective performance management systems for managerial activity need to be constructed. This means establishing clear ways of monitoring the performance of operational activity against performance measures. Third, to ensure this, data need to be collected from operational activity. This means establishing effective systems to capture and manipulate the data required for performance management. Fourth, such data must be communicated to management and appropriate decisions made on this basis.

Take the example of the activity at Goronwy Galvanising. One definition for the performance used by this organisation might be to achieve efficient through-put of materials through the galvanising process. This definition of performance can be measured in a number of different ways. For example, we might measure the amount of non-conforming black and white material identified over a particular period such as one month. To effectively manage performance in this area we therefore not only need to accurately record the amount of non-conforming material, but we also need to accumulate some totals of these exceptions perhaps organised by particular product codes. This requires that we have a set of activities which capture and process business data or forma. Also, that we communicate such data to the three controllers and the overall plant manager within Goronwy so they can make adjustments to organisational activity.

Business data: forma

In the previous section we primarily focused on communication through verbal or oral communication – through human speech. We also mentioned another form of communication – through non-verbal or 'body' language. During the early years of the industrial revolution most business organisations were relatively small, family affairs. To administer and control the performance of work in such organisations informal communications were generally sufficient. Verbal and non-verbal communication was used for immediate purposes and written letters were used for communications that had to travel some distance or were about events in the future.

By the 1840s in Great Britain large-scale administrative offices had developed to handle the increasing complexity and size of business operation. A new philosophy of management arose around the same time which emphasised the use of standard and formal communications ('forms') for numerous purposes such as the issuing of managerial orders, tracking of worker activity and the production of summary reports. We tend to forget that the use of the 'form', consisting of a set of defined and named areas for representing things, originally on paper, is as a convention a comparatively recent invention. This conventional pattern of forma appears to date back only a few hundred years.

Much communication in modern-day organisations still occurs through use of informal messages created using a verbal sign-system. However, formal communications represented in forms are now part of the essence of what we mean by organisation, even in the modern-day electronic business. But why do we represent things in such manner? The main reasons lie in the limitations of human cognition. Human memory, for instance, is sufficient to support cooperative and simple activities between individuals in small groups. As groups grow, activities, particularly those reliant on economic exchange, need to take place between strangers and generally are more complex in nature, reliant typically on some division of activities amongst a multitude of different actors.

At some point in human development signs started to be used to make persistent records of things. The key purpose of such records is to extend and compensate for the limitations of human memory. Records of economic transactions, for instance, institutionalise memory of past economic exchanges and the obligations placed upon individuals engaged in such exchange. Accurate record-keeping is also critical in establishing and sustaining trust between strangers engaging in economic exchange. Economic records account not only for the types and quantities of commodity exchanged, but they are also important for supporting social relationships such as ownership and debt.

Therefore business forms are clearly artefacts of communication used to represent things. Take three business forms that were used by Goronwy Galvanising in the 1980s, before mass computerisation by the company. The flow of such documents served to inform coordination of activity within this company and the storage of such forms in files acted as a record or collective memory of activity which had either occurred or should occur. This data infrastructure, as we shall see, was the eventual basis on which ICT systems began to be developed by the company.

As we have seen in our description of the activity at Goronwy, each trailer arriving from a customer might be loaded with a number of different types of steel product. Each batch of such products was therefore labelled with a unique order number. As a whole, each trailer was given its own delivery advice note detailing all associated batches on the trailer.

Since Goronwy mainly processed steel products for Blackwalls, the delivery advice note supplied with Blackwalls products was identified by a delivery advice number specific to this manufacturer. Each batch was identified on the delivery

Black Walls Products	Steel	Delivery Advice				
Advice No.: A3137	**Date:** 20/01/1988	**Customer Name:** Goronwy Galvanising		**Instructions:** Galvanise and Return		
Order No.	*Description*	*Product Code*	*Item Length*	*Delivery Qty*	*Weight*	
13/1193G	Lintels	UL150	1500	20	145	
44/2404G	Lintels	UL1500	15000	20	145	
70/2517P	Lintels	UL135	1350	20	130	
23/2474P	Lintels	UL120	1200	16	80	
Haulier: International	Received in Good Order:					

Figure 2.8 Sample delivery advice note

advice note by an order number generated by Blackwalls. Figure 2.8 illustrates a typical delivery advice note received from this company detailing all the black material on a particular trailer.

The delivery advice note in Figure 2.8 effectively acts as record of particular batches arriving on a given trailer. Data about a particular batch upon this form were referred to as an order-line. Each order-line effectively served to communicate an assertion from a customer such as Blackwalls to a particular business actor such as the inbound logistics controller at Goronwy about the type of product, its quantity and weight.

On arrival at the galvanising plant the black material was unpacked by an inbound logistics operative. It was then checked for discrepancies with the data supplied on the delivery advice note. Two major types of such discrepancy tended to occur on a regular basis:

- A *count discrepancy* occurred when the number of steel items actually found was less than or greater than the amount indicated on the delivery advice note.
- A *non-conforming black* discrepancy arose when some of the material was unsuitable for galvanising. For instance, a steel lintel might be bent or the material might be of the wrong product type.

Both types of discrepancy were written as annotations within the appropriate box on the delivery advice note by the inbound logistics operative.

When all the material had been checked, the delivery advice note was then passed on to the production controller. He and the office clerk transcribed details by hand, including any discrepancies, from the advice note to a job sheet. A separate job sheet was filled in for each order-line on the delivery advice note, such as the one illustrated in Figure 2.9.

The job sheet was next passed down to the shop floor of the factory where the shift foreman used it to record details of processing in the galvanising plant. Most jobs passed through the galvanising process smoothly. As mentioned, the steel items would be placed on racks, dipped in the zinc bath and left to cool. The site foreman would then check the condition of each completed job. If all items in a job

Job Sheet		Job No.: 2046			
Order No.	Description	Product Code	Item Length	Order Qty	Batch Weight
13/1193G	Lintels	L150	1500	20	145
Count Discrepancy	Non-Conforming Black	Non-Conforming White	Non-Conforming No Change		
Galvanised	Despatch No.	Despatch Date	Qty Returned	Weight Returned	
Y					

Figure 2.9 Sample job sheet

galvanised properly he would put a Y for yes in the galvanised box on the job sheet and pass it back to the production controller.

Occasionally, some of the items would not have galvanised properly. Such items would then be classed as non-conforming white and the number of such items placed in the appropriate box on the job sheet. Non-conforming white items would typically be re-galvanised at some later date.

When the shop-floor had treated a series of jobs the production controller would issue a dispatch advice note and send it to the outbound logistics section. Workers in this section would then stack the white material on trailers according to the data represented on this document, ready to be returned to the appropriate manufacturer. Each trailer for dispatch would have an associated dispatch advice note detailing the white material on the trailer.

Because of discrepancies, partial dispatches might be made from one job. This meant that the trailer of white material need not correspond to the trailer of original black material supplied to Goronwy. Hence, the data on delivery advices did not need to correspond precisely with the data on dispatch advices. The production controller would therefore need to record separate dispatches associated with one particular job on the correct job sheet. A typical dispatch advice note is represented in Figure 2.10 – note that the final order, 23/2474P, has not yet been delivered in full.

It is possible to step back from the specifics of a particular case such as Goronwy and consider forma as concerned with the operation of a number of types of formative act upon data structures. The forms discussed above are all examples of such data structures – all are structures for representing data. Such data structures consist of a set of data elements which in turn consist of a set of data items. For instance, as a data structure the job sheet consists of at least three data elements, each consisting of a number of data items. Hence, on this form there is a section

Goronwy Galvanising		Dispatch Advice						
Advice No.:	Date:	Customer No. and Name:						
101	22/01/2012	BL01 BlackWalls						
Order No.	Description	Product Code	Item Length	Order Qty	Batch Weight	Returned Qty	Batch Weight
13/1193G	Lintels	UL150	1500	20	150	20	150
44/2404G	Lintels	UL1500	15000	20	150	20	150
70/2517P	Lintels	UL135	1350	20	130	20	135
23/2474P	Lintels	UL120	1200	16	100	14	82
Driver:	Received by:						

Figure 2.10 Sample dispatch advice

which describes the original order with the data items OrderNo, Description, Product Code, Item Length, Order Qty, Batch Weight. There is also a section which is used to indicate any non-conforming material and a section which references eventual dispatches from the order.

Four sorts of action are taken by business actors at Goronwy in terms of data structures such as the delivery advice, the job sheet and the dispatch advice described above (Figure 2.11). The first is that we might create a new data structure, element or data item. Hence, the production controller might create a new job sheet. The second is that an element or a data item on an existing data structure might be updated. Hence, a production controller might place a 'Y' in the count discrepancy box of a particular job sheet. The third is that an existing data structure, element or item might be deleted. For example, after a period of a year or so job sheets would be destroyed within the paper filing system of Goronwy. Finally, data structures, data elements and data items will be read by business actors. Hence, various business actors within Goronwy will read the data on such forms, interpret what they mean and use this information to help determine further action.

Business organisation

In an operational sense, there are four inter-related questions that all organisations, particularly business organisations, must answer. 'What do we do?' 'What do we need to know to do things?' 'How do we communicate what we know?' 'How do we represent what we do, know and communicate?' These questions correspond to questions about performance or performa, communication or informa and representation or forma.

Any sign such as 23/2474P can be considered merely as forma, in this case as a set of characters. Such forma is useful only for communication when some business actor assigns some meaning to the forma, turning forma into informa.

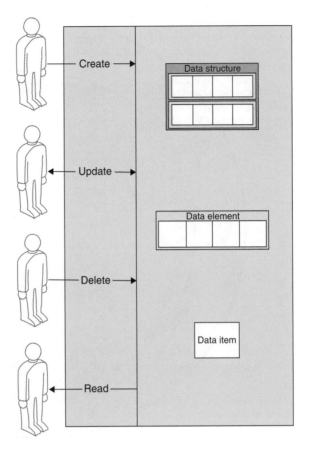

Figure 2.11 Formative acts

Hence, we know from inspecting or 'reading' the form displayed in Figure 2.10 that the symbol 23/2474P stands for a particular product type handled by Goronwy, namely, a steel lintel of 1200 cms in length and weighing 100 kg. But the purpose of identifying something in this manner is evident only when we consider the context in which the sign is used. This context is defined by the way in which the sign is used in coordinated activity. In this case it served to identify the appropriate product type of a particular batch and job as it travelled through the galvanising process.

In the way we have necessarily discussed the three patterns of organisation or order above, one would perhaps assume that the *direction* of influence between such patterns is linear: from forma, through informa to performa. In actuality, these three patterns form a cycle of influence: that performa enacts forma which enacts informa and in turn enacts performa. This is illustrated in Figure 2.12.

Creating forma is inherently an aspect of performa, but a limited aspect of performa. The creation of forma is typically directed at communication and such communication is typically directed at the coordination of performance. Take a contrasting example from the public sector. You are lying ill in a hospital bed. Your treatment or care depends upon the effective coordination of work of many

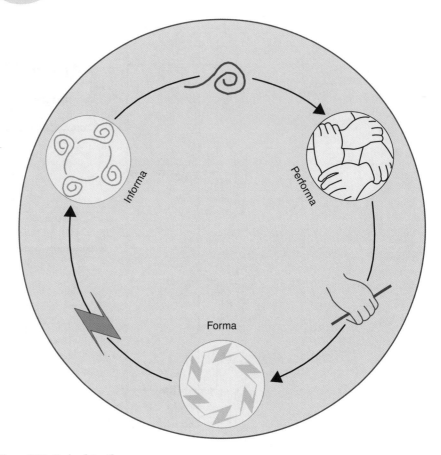

Figure 2.12 Cycle of significance

different care workers such as doctors, nurses, radiographers, pharmacists, porters, cleaners etc. Such coordination demands much communication amongst such actors. This communication will still involve much use of forma such as speech to make assertions about the state of the world or to issue directives as to what should be done by other actors. But such forma makes demands such as that the actors involved in such communication are co-present and also that they have sufficient capacity of memory to remember the content of the communication some time after it has occurred. Usually however, much forma is implemented as persistent records. After all, you would not want one nurse to give you a prescribed medicine (to be taken only once in any 24 hours) which another nurse gave you on an earlier shift only some eight hours earlier! This helps explain why care workers such as doctors and nurses spend over 40% of their time making records, such as diagnoses, prescriptions and care plans.

Therefore, when we speak of any human organisation we are actually referring to a complex system composed of at least three types of entangled patterns: patterns of performa, patterns of informa and patterns of forma. This can be illustrated within the case at Goronwy. Figure 2.13 represents what is called a storyboard of the major patterns evident in the case we have been considering. On the left of

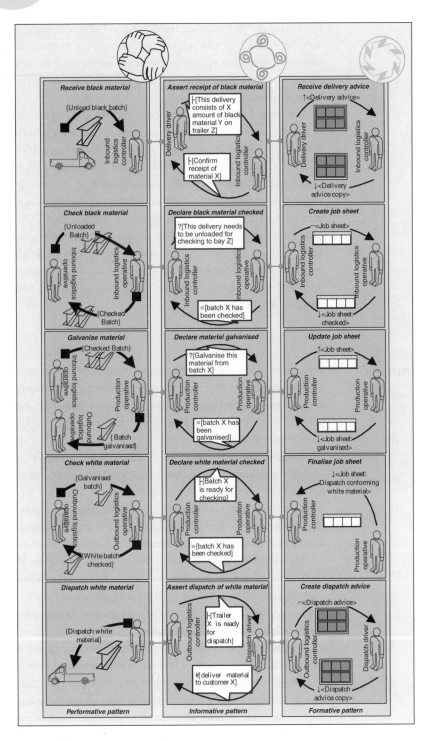

Figure 2.13 Performative, informative, formative organisation

the figure are represented the high-level elements of the performative pattern. In support of each of the related performative acts there is a corresponding pattern of informative acts. In turn, each informative act can be seen to be based in one or more formative acts, which in our example consisted primarily of the manipulation of paper forms.

We have spent such time considering the nature of organisation within this chapter to establish the actual context within which both business and as a consequence eBusiness takes place. As we shall see, it is traditional to see the impact of ICT on organisation as effectively providing a more efficient and effective platform of forma. In other words, according to this view, modern ICT provides value to organisations in enabling them to process data much more efficiently and effectively. But hopefully you should be convinced after reading this chapter that changing forma is likely to impact on both informa and performa, because these three realms of order or organisation are closely entangled. This helps explain the true transformative capacity or potential of such technology. It also helps us explain why ICT can potentially make things worse as well as better in organisations, if handled inappropriately.

Summary

Any organisation clearly consists of a multitude of business actors. Three distinct but inter-related forms of action are undertaken by such actors and these three forms of action serve to accomplish what we mean by organisation. Actors engage in instrumental activity, make decisions and communicate about such activity and represent aspects of such activity in records.

However, the business actions of actors do not normally occur in isolation. The actions of one business actor are normally entangled with or bound to the actions of other actors and as such form coherent patterns of action. What we mean by organisation consists of the patterning of performance, communication and representation by multiple actors. Such patterning produces or accomplishes the order characteristic of human organisation and produces its institutional properties.

Any patterning of order within organisation is stitched together through the use of signs. Signs interrelate between and within these three different patterns of order which we have referred to as forma, informa and performa. Forma constitutes the substance or representation of signs, informa the content and communication of signs and performa the use of signs in coordinated action.

The patterning of order characteristic of human organisation is enacted through three inter-related forms of action. Formative acts amount to the enactment of forma: acts of data representation and processing. Informative acts constitute the enactment of informa: acts of decision-making and communication involving message-making and interpretation. Finally, performative acts consist of the enactment of performa: the performance of coordinated and instrumental action within human groups.

Within the next chapter we consider how the patterning of order forms a number of critical and inter-related systems that are important to our understanding electronic business.

Review test

There are two major perspectives on organisational life	Select two
Institutional Perspective	
Bureaucratic Perspective	
Action Perspective	
Social Perspective	

Very broadly a _____ is anything that is significant.	Fill in the blank

A _____ is any organised collection of signs and relations between signs.	Fill in the blank

Any sign is a pattern with three distinct facets	Match the pattern with the appropriate definition
Performa	The content and communication of signs
Informa	The use of signs within coordinated action
Forma	The substance or representation of signs

An informative act is ...	Select the most appropriate answer
Some transformation of the world undertaken in fulfilment of some goal	
Some aspect of performance designed by one actor to influence the performance of some other actor	
Some operation which manipulates a data structure	

Business actors normally communicate in five major ways	Match the type of communicative act with the appropriate definition
Assertive	Communicative acts that attempt to get a receiver to perform some action
Directive	Communicative acts that commit the speaker to some future course of action
Commissive	Communicative acts that explain how things are in the world
Expressive	Communicative acts that aim to change the world through the communication
Declarative	Communicative acts that represent the senders psychological state

There are four types of formative action	Select all that apply
Delete	
Create	
Transform	
Update	
Read	

Exercises

- Find one other example of data known to you. Try to separate out issues of data (representation) from information (interpretation).
- Find some visual sign used within some business. Try to separate out what the sign is from what it represents. In other words, separate out the symbol from the referent.
- Identify some area of activity known to you. Determine the pattern of informative acts supporting it.
- Identify one activity system known to you and identify its key components.
- Consider some decision made in an organisation known to you. Work back from the decision to the information required to support it. What alternative forms of action are possible as results from the decision?
- Consider the Highway Code as a sign system. What activity does it support? How do such signs help determine activity?

Projects

- Various signs such as '-:)' have been invented within email systems to attempt to provide emotional content via this communication medium. Investigate the range and use of such symbols (emoticons) and analyse them as examples of business signs.
- Records have been maintained for many hundreds if not thousands of years in organisations of many different forms. Nowadays, the issue of records management is seen to be a significant problem for organisations. Investigate the term *records management*; determine why it is a significant problem and why it is increasingly important for organisations.
- The idea of speech acts and the theory of speech acts underlie the five types of business communication discussed in this chapter. Investigate some of this literature and critically assess the relevance of speech act theory to informatics work.

Critical reflection

Try reflecting on the nature of organisation in simple settings known to you. For instance, when you go into a coffee shop you probably participate in a performative pattern. You are a business actor – a consumer – and you interact with another business actor – a barista. Can you draw a storyboard (such as the ones drawn in this chapter) to describe this typical performance? What informative pattern normally accompanies such performance? Is there any formative pattern evident in support of the informative pattern?

Much has been published on business decision-making. How does such decision-making relate to the idea of organisation discussed in this chapter? How do we judge whether decisions are good or not? Does better communication improve decision-making? Is good record management important to decision-making?

Case exploration

Pretty much any of the organisations provided as cases at the end of the book can be considered in terms of the concepts discussed in this chapter. For instance, you might consider Tesco as an organisation consisting of activities, communications and representations. What activities does it undertake? What communication occurs within a Tesco supermarket store between business actors? What records do Tesco keep and for what purpose? What sort of decisions are continuously taking place and by whom? How important are good data to decisions within an organisation such as Tesco?

Further reading

As in all the chapters within this book we have deliberately omitted copious referencing of the strong underlying theory which supports the concepts discussed. This is to avoid disturbing the flow of the discussion. The ideas presented within this chapter are taken from a number of sources. The distinction between performa, informa and form is originally due to Jan Dietz (2006). The idea of informative acts is due to John Searle (1970) and the so-called language-action tradition in philosophy. Readers wishing to follow up on these literatures in more detail should first visit my book *Significance: Exploring the Nature of Information, Systems and Technology* (Beynon-Davies, 2011).

References

Beynon-Davies, P. (2011). *Significance: Exploring the Nature of Information, Systems and Technology*, Houndmills, Basingstoke, Palgrave Macmillan.

Dietz, J. L. G. (2006). *Enterprise Ontology: Theory and Methodology*, Berlin, Springer-Verlag.

Morgan, G. (1986). *Images of Organisation*, London, Sage.

Pierce, C. S. (1931). *Collected Papers*, Cambridge, MA, Harvard University Press.

Pinker, S. (2001). *The Language Gene*, Harmondsworth, Middx, Penguin.

Searle, B. J. R. (1970). *Speech Acts: An Essay in the Philosophy of Language*, Cambridge, Cambridge University Press.

3 eBusiness systems

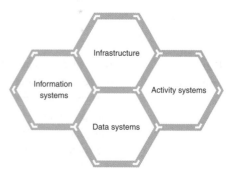

Learning outcomes	Principles
Understand the concept of system as consisting of patterns of organisation: applied across representation, communication and activity.	A system is an organised collection of things with emergent properties and with some definable purpose. The idea of a system and the associated concept of control have had a profound influence on the domain of eBusiness. Hence, the concept of system has been applied both to technology such as data systems ("hard" systems) and to human activity systems ("soft" systems). Information systems mediate between data systems and activity systems.
Consider the issue of control in the regulation and adaptation of business organisations.	Control is the mechanism that implements regulation and adaptation in systems. Systems generally exhibit some form of control that enables the system to maintain state within defined parameters and to adapt to changes in its environment.
Describe business organisation as emerging from the interaction between activity systems, information systems and data systems.	Data systems occur at the level of forma and are concerned with the form and representation of symbols in storage and signal transmission. Data systems are systems of symbols operated upon by recurring patterns of formative acts. Information systems deal with informa and are concerned with the meaning of symbols and their use within human action. Information systems are systems of communication and consist of recurring patterns of communicative or informative acts. Activity systems deal with performa: they are systems of performance and consist of recurring patterns of performative acts.
Explain the relationship between communication, decisions and control in organisations.	On the level of the individual, internal communication is critical to the control of individual activity. On the level of the social, activity by two or more actors, communication is critical to the performance of coordinated action. Decisions and decision-making therefore mediate between information and action. Decision-making is the activity of deciding upon appropriate action in particular situations. Decision-making is reliant upon information in the sense that information is seen as reducing uncertainty in decision-making.

Chapter outline

Introduction

The concept of *system* is central to thinking in numerous fields. For instance, in medicine it is seen as important to consider our bodies as being made up of various systems such as a digestive system and a central nervous system. In terms of astronomy we live on a planet that is part of the solar system. From the perspective of the social sciences we engage with people in groups that form social, political and economic systems. In mathematics we are educated in the use of number systems. Modern organisations are systems of activity that would collapse without effective information systems.

At first sight these varied systems appear to have little in common. However, on closer examination we see that all these examples represent what we might describe as a patterning or ordering of things. Systems theory, systems thinking or as we prefer to call it – *systemics* – is the attempt to study the generic features of such patterning.

The topic of the previous chapter – signs – take their shape within a number of different types of system and form patterns of significance in such terms. This chapter utilises concepts from systemics to help us understand the way in which such patterns of significance emerge within business organisation and how such patterns bridge between the social and the physical through the psychological. Within human organisation we are particularly interested in the way in which signs are used to express intentions, make decisions and generate action. This is clearly the realm of the social world or social action. However, we are also interested in the relationship between signs and the physical world – particularly in the ways in which signs are represented and manipulated using 'technology', notably so-called information and communication technology.

Therefore, we use the term system not only to encapsulate the notion of the organisation of signs. It is also used to denote the organisation of activity, communication and representation. It should be evident from the discussion in the previous chapter that signs are socio-physical or sometimes socio-technical phenomena. This means that signs interrelate between and within three different patterns of order, which we referred to in the previous chapter as forma, informa and performa. Forma, as we have seen, consists of the substance or representation of signs, informa the content or communication of signs and performa the use of signs in coordinated action. These different domains of patterning allow us to more clearly define three levels of system of interest to human organisation: activity systems, information systems and data systems.

Hence, we shall maintain that eBusiness is founded not only in the concept of a sign but also in the concept of a system and that these two concepts, along with the connecting idea of a pattern, are key 'tools of thought' for understanding and explaining the impact of ICT on private, public and voluntary sector organisations. Electronic business, as we shall see, involves interaction between activity systems, information systems and ICT systems. In this chapter we begin by describing the general nature of systems and then use this understanding to help form our notions of systems of activity, information and technology.

We again ground our discussion with examples from a central case. In previous chapters we considered two organisations working within the private sector: one in manufacturing, one in services. As a contrast, within this chapter, we consider a key organisation from the public sector, that of the emergency ambulance or response service.

Systems: patterns of organisation

The discipline devoted to the study of the general nature of systems is often referred to as systems thinking or systems theory. We prefer to refer to it as systemics because it has become popular in numerous aspects of life to refer to problems as systemic. But what actually underlies a systemic approach to things? A system very broadly is an organised set of interdependent elements that exists for some purpose, has some stability and can be usefully viewed as a whole. Five key principles are significant within this definition: that of holism, identity, organisation, purpose and emergence.

First, one of the fundamental principles of systemics is summed up in the ancient Greek philosopher Aristotle's dictum that *the whole is more than the sum of its parts.* This suggests that when we attempt to investigate and understand complex phenomena, such as how businesses work, we should attempt to do so holistically – in terms of the whole phenomena rather than parts of the phenomena. Second, a system has an *identity.* By this we mean it can be clearly distinguished from other phenomena. We can draw a boundary around what is inside the system and what is outside the system. We also can see a system as persisting through time. Third, systems display *organisation.* Systems are different from aggregates or collections of things because in a system we observe the continuous patterning of some phenomena. Fourth, to say a system displays organisation implies that a system is organised to do something: it has some explicit or implicit *purpose.* This means that systems are normally seen as organised to achieve some goals. Fifth and finally, a consequence of a system having identity, displaying organisation and achieving purpose is that systems accomplish *emergence.* A system is a complex entity that has properties that do not belong to any of its constituent parts, but emerge from the relationships or interaction of its constituent parts. This is really what is meant by *the whole is more than the sum of its parts.*

Consider a simple example. A road network can be viewed as a system. It is made up of component parts such as roads, road intersections and vehicles which travel along this network. The purpose of some road network is likely to be to convey people and goods between points within some geographical space. In a road network a bottleneck experienced at some road intersection is the result of the interactions of a large body of components or parts (vehicles) coming together in particular ways. A bottleneck is not a property of any one component of a system such as a vehicle; it is only a property of the system as a whole; it is an emergent effect of the operation of this system.

As we shall see, systemics has been applied to both 'hard' and 'soft' systems. Hard systems are not hard in the sense of being any more complex than *soft systems.* Instead, they are hard in the physical or technical sense. In such situations it is possible to use system concepts as a means of investigating complex situations and taking rational action with the objective of achieving what are seen to be defined, unquestioned and frequently unproblematic goals. For instance, large integrated manufacturing plants such as petro-chemical plants can be treated as hard systems in the sense that the design of such plants to achieve production goals is relatively unproblematic. Most technological systems, including, as we shall see, ICT systems, can be considered as hard systems in a similar manner.

In contrast, most human systems are soft systems because they are social in nature. They are collections of people undertaking activities to achieve some purpose. However, within human systems the boundaries or scope of the system may be fluid and the purpose of the system may be problematic and certainly open to interpretation from many different viewpoints. Hence, the purpose of a private, public or voluntary sector organisation may be open to different interpretations depending upon the viewpoints of particular actors that are not only members but also observers of the system. Hence, a university, for instance, might be considered a system for educating students, for conducting research, for engaging with industry or for contributing to the wider community.

The emergency ambulance service

Now let us consider in more detail one aspect of human organisation that will provide us with material to examine the relevance of the system concept to organisations in general and eBusiness in particular.

Within modern healthcare an effective system is required for responding to emergency health incidents. Most countries in the world rise to this challenge by establishing and maintaining specialist staff such as paramedics and specialist equipment such as ambulance vehicles to enable emergency response. Such service units are clearly called by different names across the globe. Ambulance services in the UK have the freedom and responsibility to establish their own forms of activity, communication and technology. This means that there is variation amongst activity systems, information systems and data systems within ambulance services in the UK. The description below is therefore based on a composite of the systems experienced amongst a number of such services. Let us describe the operation of this organisation in terms of the typical life-cycle of an emergency incident.

Getting specialist ambulance staff in their vehicles to an incident in the shortest period of time is a key goal or purpose for such an ambulance service. This demands effective coordination and control of activity amongst multiple actors to ensure that resources such as ambulances and paramedics are used most effectively and that patients receive appropriate emergency healthcare as promptly as possible.

The service is first aware of an incident when telephone operators take an emergency call and identify the caller's area code or closest mobile phone cell from the call. The call is then routed to the ambulance control call centre. A call-taker matches the number calling with an address using a computerised place map of the area covered by the service and then asks a set series of questions prompted by a set of rules embedded in the ICT system. On the basis of answers to the questions supplied, the system suggests appropriate action.

It used to be the case that the ambulance service in the UK worked using a first-come, first-served basis in terms of their response to emergency calls. However, most ambulance services now institute a process of 'triage' to enable prioritisation of response to incidents. This means that decisions are made as to the medical importance of incidents and on this basis further decisions are made about the dispatch of ambulance crews to such incidents.

A dispatcher will have been listening to the call since the location was identified. If the call is category A (life threatening) or category B (serious) then a paramedic dispatcher may have been asked for assistance. Some ambulance services employ paramedics within the control room who can be consulted in the case of any doubt as to the priority of the incident. The dispatcher assesses manually the nearest appropriate ambulance by using a number of computer screens: a screen indicating a plan designed to maximise the efficient use of resources (known as the system status management or SSM plan), a screen listing the status of all current resources and a screen which plots the current location of ambulance resources against a computerised map and a touch-screen telephone. The SSM plan is an attempt to dynamically deploy vehicles around the area covered by the ambulance service according to demand patterns established for day and time, geographical area and clinical urgency. As part of the functionality of the ICT system the SSM plan is capable of prompting control room staff to shift resources such as ambulances on a continual basis to stay within plan.

Using this technology and her knowledge of the local area the dispatcher assigns an ambulance to the emergency incident. This means that the dispatcher does not always send the nearest ambulance in terms of distance to an incident. For example, it would be inappropriate to dispatch a spatially near ambulance if the incident is called in during rush hour and the ambulance would need to travel in the direction of the major traffic flow. In this case, it is preferable to send a slightly more distant ambulance that can travel against the primary traffic flow. Not surprisingly, many ambulance services institute a policy of recruiting control room staff from their pool of operational ambulance crews because of the critical importance of such domain knowledge to effective dispatch.

During this process the call-taker will be giving pre-arrival advice to the caller prescribed both by the ICT system and their own training. While the call-taker continues with this interaction the dispatcher typically uses a radio message to alert the chosen ambulance crew that they are required to attend an incident. Details of the location of the incident (including a map grid reference) and the reported details of the patient's condition are also transmitted in this way. Some ambulance services also employ communication systems enabling control staff to transmit information as to incidents to ambulance crews.

Having received an incident alert from the control room, a member of ambulance crew presses a button on their communication set indicating the point at which they go mobile. Ambulances are fitted with global positioning system equipment that updates the dispatch system every 13 seconds with the location of ambulance crews. Crews are guided by satellite navigation to the incident location, supplemented by radio communication with the control room. When the crew arrive at the incident they press an *arrive* button on the communication set. They then administer any immediate treatment required at the scene and eventually move the patient into the ambulance. When ready to leave the scene of the incident, they press a *leave scene* button and when they arrive at the general hospital they press an *at hospital* button. Finally, they press a *clear* button when they are available to be allocated as a resource again.

Core system constructs

The emergency ambulance service described above can clearly be regarded as a system. This phenomenon has a clear identity in that we can draw a boundary around what forms activity in this area and what forms activity in the rest of the UK National Health Service. The activity which accomplishes emergency ambulance response is continuously reproduced in a patterned way and it is through such patterning that this organisation persists through time. The purpose of this organisation is to provide emergency healthcare at the point of incident. Such purpose is achieved or emerges from the complex coordination of the activities of a multitude of different actors: humans and machines.

The term *system* has a Greek origin; derived from *syn* meaning together and *histemi* meaning to set. In very broad terms, and from a static point of view, a system can be seen to consist of a collection of objects that are related or set together. But by setting together is also meant that a system is dynamic in the sense that the objects potentially influence each other.

Our very general definition of a system clearly encompasses a vast array of phenomena. For a certain interesting class of systems (open systems) on which we shall focus, a popular way is to specify certain types of objects and relations to be of interest. Systems of this type are generally portrayed in terms of an input-process-output entity existing within a given environment (Figure 3.1). In this view, systems can be seen as being composed of the following elements: one or more operational *processes* or mechanisms of transformation, one or more sets of *inputs* from and *outputs* to actors in the environment, one or more *control* processes.

Processes represent the dynamic elements of systems. A process is a mechanism of transformation. It consists of an inter-connected set of actions (behaviour) necessary to transform some input(s) into some output(s). It is possible to define two major types of process as relevant to any type of system: operational processes and control processes. Operational processes achieve the defined purpose or transformation of some system. Control processes, as we shall see, maintain the behaviour of operational processes in desired directions and hence maintain the overall identity of the system. The *inputs* to a system are the resources it gains from actors in its environment, some of which may be other systems. The *outputs* from a system are those things that it supplies back to actors in its environment.

For example, a manufacturing firm such as Goronwy Galvanising can be considered as a system that transforms raw materials (inputs) from its customers (actors) into finished products (outputs) for such customers. Similarly, a training company such as University Short Courses uses resources such as lecturers and venues (inputs) to deliver technical training (output) to its customers. Finally, the ambulance service can be considered as a process which uses ambulances and paramedics (inputs) to deliver emergency healthcare (output) for patients at the point of incident.

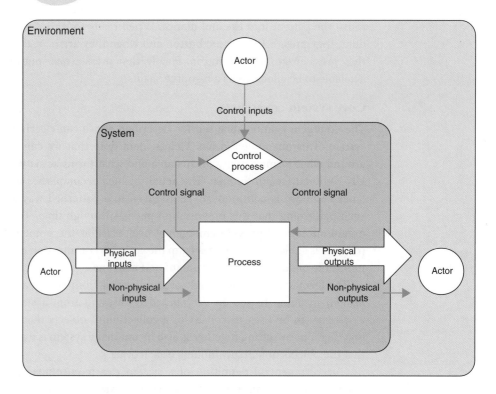

Figure 3.1 Core concepts of a system

These three institutions are best seen as complex systems. Two constructs are useful for specifying and managing the complexity inherent in many systems such as these: that of variety and the associated idea of a sub-system.

The complexity of any system can be defined in terms of the notion of state, which is defined by the values appropriate to the attributes of some system. At any point in time, a value can be assigned to each of these attributes. The set of all values assumed by the attributes of a system defines a system's state. Variety may be defined as the number of possible states of a system. For many systems, particularly those involving human activity, the variety of the system may be quite large in the sense that the number of possible states may not be precisely countable. Variety is therefore useful as a measure of the complexity of some system.

We can illustrate this idea using a simple example. Consider a collection of actors, each of which we represent as a node labelled A-F in the diagram illustrated in Figure 3.2. We assume that each actor within this system can theoretically communicate with each other actor in the group. We draw arrows between actors to represent such communication and draw such arrows in both directions between any two actors to indicate that, for instance, relation A → B is different from B → A. In other words, actor A can make an utterance to actor B and actor B can make an utterance to actor A; each is a separate speech or communicative act. In this sense, each relation or communication channel in this system is effectively a 'switch' that may be turned on or off, perhaps indicating the effect of one actor in

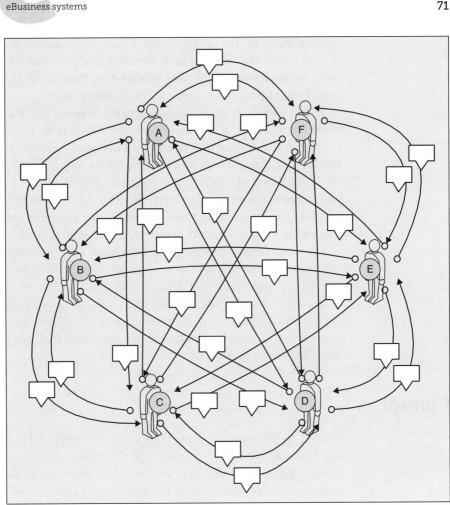

Figure 3.2 A simple dynamic system

the network on another through communication. Here we have a simple system in which a collection of things now interacts; it operates or behaves.

Hence, we could consider this as a simple model of a human communication network in which perhaps we wish to study the movement of communication around the network, perhaps the way in which some particular business communication, such as one of the types considered in the previous chapter, travels amongst group members. In this system, one state of the system is when one particular communicative act such as A → B takes place. Another state is when B → C as an act of communication takes place, and so on.

As we have seen, using the idea of a system's states, variety may be defined as the number of possible states of a system. Hence, since there are 2 possible communication relations between each of the 6 actors in the network, there are n(n-1) or 6 times 5 possible relations between actors, which is 30 possible relations. If we regard a state of the system as being a particular configuration of active and inactive communication relations then there are over 2^{30} (1,073,741,824) possible states for the entire system. This is a measure of the variety inherent in this comparatively simple system. Hence, for many actual social systems in which there are many more actors and relationships than in our example, the variety or complexity of such systems may be incomprehensibly large.

At first glance, we might conclude that this suggests that it is impossible to understand the workings of any reasonable complex system. But one way of handling the complexity of systems is to apply the notion of hierarchy to understanding and representing them. In this way, systems can be seen as being composed of various levels, each level of which can be conceptualised in terms of a system. Hence, the environment of a system may be viewed as a system in its own right and a process which is part of one system may be treated as a system in turn, and so on. In this way we can build a hierarchy of system, sub-system, sub-sub-system and so on.

For example, within emergency healthcare we can identify a number of subsystems of activity. These include maintaining resources such as ambulances and paramedics, deploying such resources to incidents, providing healthcare at incidents, transporting patients to hospitals and returning resources such as ambulances to the pool of such resources. Each of these subsystems can be seen to consist of a number of inter-related processes. Each process, in turn, can be considered a system in itself.

Control

Control is effectively the process by which the order within some system is built and sustained. We know, having read Chapter 2, that something is ordered or organised if we see evidence of patterning. In other words, we observe a common pattern across situations. Such patterns may be examples of representation as in the case of signals, communication as in the case of elements of a conversation or of behaviour or activity such as in routines found in organisations or various roles undertaken by individual actors.

Control is the process by which such patterning of order is created and maintained across situations. We recognise something as having a distinct identity – as being a system – through some patterning in the world. *Control* is the process by which a system ensures continuity through time. It is thus the means by which system identity is sustained and the system maintains its viability in terms of changes in its environment. Control is the means by which system behaviour is reproduced. In our terms, control produces the patterning evident in systems of action, communication and representation amongst groups of actors.

Hence, control can be conceived both as a process of regulation and a process of adaptation applicable to systems. The typical meanings associated with the term *control* are stability and conservation. This side of control is frequently referred to as *regulation* and is typically concerned with the internal operations of some system. In terms of regulation, control ensures that a system will recover some stability after a period of disturbance and maintain its viability over time. For instance, if we were to observe the work of a particular ambulance service in close detail for a number of weeks we would see clear evidence of such patterns. Different actors within such settings will reproduce modes of action, communication and record-keeping, time and again.

However, there are alternative meanings associated with the process of organising. This side of control is frequently referred to as *adaptation*. Adaptation is the evolutionary side of control and is concerned with the external relationships between the system and its environment. Systems generally exhibit some form of control that enables the system to adapt to changes in its environment, changing its behaviour to ensure a degree of 'fitness' between system and environment.

Hence, if we consider a manufacturing organisation such as Goronwy as a system then the internal operations of this organisation must be regulated to ensure that it performs effectively and efficiently. But such an organisation also has to adapt to its competitive environment; it must ensure that it produces things demanded by its customers at appropriate prices.

Control can be viewed in terms of a monitoring sub-system, or a hierarchy of such sub-systems, that 'steers' the behaviour of other operating sub-systems. Hence, this monitoring sub-system is frequently referred to as a control mechanism, sub-system or process.

In terms of systems 'designed' by human beings, such as organisations, control can be considered an imposed process. In the process of designing and constructing a system, necessary processes of control for regulation have to be established. This is because, any coherent element of a system must inherently have a control mechanism or process embedded within it. In other words, a system with operational or productive processes must have at least one controller for such processes. Applying the idea of systems hierarchy, we can refine the idea of a control process within some system as consisting of inputs, outputs and processes (Figure 3.3). For a control process to work effectively it must have three things: resources to deploy to regulate the behaviour of the system in a particular direction, control inputs which implement the 'purpose' of the system, control signals enabling the process to monitor and instruct operational processes.

The control process ensures defined levels of performance for the system through use of a number of control inputs. This sets the key decision strategy for the controller. Such a decision strategy then works in interaction with three other key elements of a control process: sensors, comparators and effectors. *Sensors* are processes that monitor changes in the environment of some system or in the system itself (sensed signals) and send further signals to comparators. *Comparators* compare signals from sensors against some decision strategy and on this basis make some decision to send signals to effectors. Sometimes referred to as actuators or activators, *effectors* cause changes to a systems' state. In other words, they introduce changes to system variables by sending signals to particular parts of a system.

Consider the process of triage described above, which is critical to the control of the dispatch of ambulances to incidents. Triage can be considered a decision strategy which takes as input an assessment of the condition of the patient at the incident. This is sensed by the call-taker using responses obtained from the call-maker to a series of questions determined by the ICT system. The overall triage category determined for the patient will then determine a priority setting for the

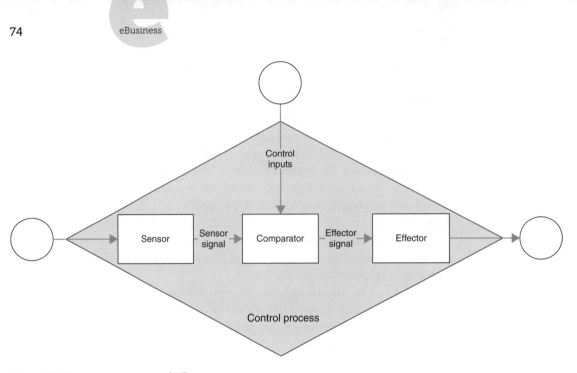

Figure 3.3 Comparators, sensors and effectors

dispatch of ambulance crews. This is likely to be achieved through triggering rules such as:

- if the condition of the patient is considered life threatening (category A) then set dispatch priority as immediate;
- if the condition of the patient is assessed as serious (category B) then set dispatch priority as urgent and issue immediate paramedic advice over the line;
- if the condition of the patient is non-life-threatening then set dispatch priority as non-critical and place in queue to be dispatched after category A and B cases, or to be directed to a source of medical advice.

The dispatch priority then acts as a stimulus to the dispatcher who makes changes to the state of the ambulance fleet under her control.

Control and performance

From this discussion it should be evident that the process of control and the concept of information are inherently inter-linked. This is because in order for a control process to work effectively it must continually monitor the state of the system it is attempting to control. Such monitoring occurs through sensing signals from its operating process. The control process must also contain a model of the system it is attempting to control. Critical to this model will be defined measures of performance. Signals transmitted from the monitoring process are compared against this model and interpreted in this manner. On the basis of such interpretation, decisions are made as to appropriate action and further signals are transmitted back to the operational system to maintain the system's performance within defined parameters.

Thus there is an inherent association between control, performance and measurement. In order to control the performance of a system a control process must 'measure' features of its operational system and compare such measurements against its goals. In such terms, all forms of measurement can be considered in terms of what we referred to in the previous chapter as a sign-system. Points on a temperature scale, for instance, can be taken to stand for ambient energy within some physical space. Particular points on this scale are likely to be calibrated to certain natural signs. Hence, in the centigrade scale zero degrees C stands for the freezing point of water while 100 degrees C stands for the boiling point of water.

Alternatively, consider performance and its measurement in the case of the ambulance service. A review of ambulance service performance in the mid-1990s within the UK concluded that more clinically relevant performance measures were needed for the service. It suggested that the focus of such measurement should be on the potential for saving lives with shorter response times to patients suffering with life-threatening conditions. Over the last decade demand for emergency ambulance services in the UK has increased by over 50% whilst funding has increased by only 17.5%. The review recommended a long-term performance target of 90% of life threatening calls responded to within eight minutes. Subsequently, an interim target of 75% of life-threatening calls to be responded to within eight minutes was introduced.

A control process makes decisions about appropriate action by comparing signals from the operating system against its decision strategy. Such performance levels will be defined by higher-level systems and consist of control inputs. Such control inputs in the case of the ambulance service would amount to response targets, such as those described above. In terms of a manufacturing plant such as Goronwy Galvanising, a defined level of performance might be productivity level per manufacturing unit. In terms of a training organisation such as USC performance might be judged in terms of the number of attendees successfully completing particular courses.

In systems terms the issue of performance can therefore be judged in terms of the central transformation of the system. Three main types of performance measures can be distinguished around this transformation principle: efficacy, efficiency and effectiveness: *Efficacy* is a measure of the extent to which a system achieves its intended transformation and is fundamentally a check on the output produced by some system. *Efficiency* is a measure of the extent to which the system achieves its intended transformation with the minimum use of resources. Fundamentally, measures of efficiency involve a check on the resources (inputs) used to achieve some output. Finally, *effectiveness* is a measure of the extent to which the system contributes to the purposes of a higher-level system of which it may be a sub-system. Effectiveness amounts to a check on the contribution being made by the system to the purpose of some super-system of which it is a part. Therefore, the 'e' in eBusiness does not only mean electronic; it should mean efficacious, efficient and effective business.

Consider performance in the ambulance service case from these three view points. The efficacy of a particular ambulance service can be measured in terms of average response times to incidents. The efficiency of the unit can be measured in terms of some ratio of resource such as ambulances and paramedic staff against number of incidents responded to within a defined period. The effectiveness of the service can be measured in terms of its contribution to overall healthcare within the population such as by recording the survival rates of life-threatening patients treated.

Control and communication

The management guru and systems theorist Peter Senge (1990) believes that one of the most important and valuable characteristics of systemic thinking is its ability to handle cycles of cause and effect. This is inherently what is meant by *feedback*. Control is normally exercised within a system through some form of feedback. Outputs from the process of an operational system are fed back to the control process. The control process then adjusts the control signals to the operating process on the basis of its interpretation of the data it receives (Figure 3.4).

Control is typically exercised through a *negative feedback* loop. Sometimes known as a balancing loop or damping feedback it involves the control process monitoring the outputs from the operational process through its sensors. The comparators in the monitoring system detect variations from defined levels of performance provided by control inputs. If the outputs vary from established levels then the monitoring subsystem initiates some actions that *reduce* or decrease the variation through its effectors.

For example, a company maintaining cash flow can be conceived of as a system with negative feedback in which the cash balance continually influences company

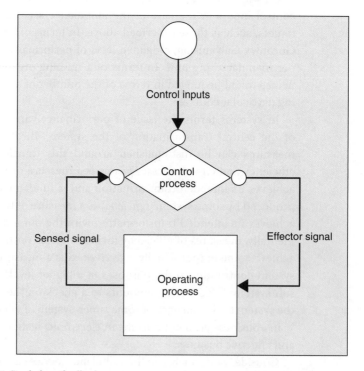

Figure 3.4 Single-loop feedback

decisions on expenditure and borrowing. Within ambulance control, the deployment of ambulances needs to be continuously adjusted to reflect the location and frequency of emergency incidents.

Negative feedback can be exercised either within a single- or double-loop. *Single-loop feedback* is primarily concerned with regulation. In this type of feedback a single control process monitors variations in the state of an operational process, compares this state against some planned levels of performance and takes corrective action to bring performance in line with plan. In single-loop feedback the plans for performance (the control inputs) remain relatively unchanged (Figure 3.5). Sensors only monitor the behaviour of internal processes and effectors only act upon such internal processes.

Double-loop feedback is primarily concerned with adaptation. In this type of feedback the control process must not only monitor variations in the state of an internal process, but it must also monitor changes in its environment. Hence, there are two control loops involved and the feedback from the higher-level controller will cause adjustments to the decision strategies of lower-level controllers.

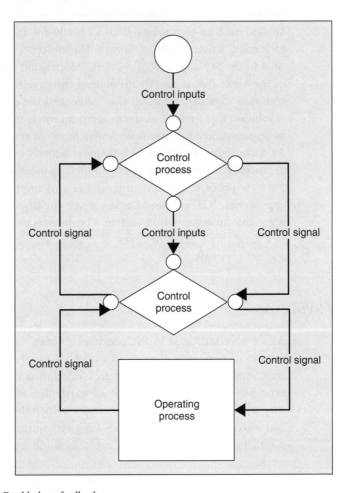

Figure 3.5 Double-loop feedback

Double-loop feedback is consequently a higher-level form of control in that it is essential to ensure that a system adapts effectively to changes in its environment. Double-loop feedback is that form in which the monitoring of lower-level single-feedback control systems as well as monitoring of the environment triggers examination and perhaps revision of the principles on which the control process is established.

Consider feedback in the domain of healthcare. The environment of healthcare consists of the human population and its illnesses. Since the National Health Service in the UK is divided up on a regional basis, particular healthcare units have to adjust their delivery of healthcare to changes within their population. Hence, one particular regional population may, for a number of reasons, experience a higher rate of cardiac arrests or strokes than other comparable populations. An ambulance service delivering emergency response to such a population will need to ensure that its equipment, the training of its staff and most importantly its healthcare practices are appropriate to changing need. This is clearly an example of double-loop feedback.

The idea of a system and the associated concept of control has had a profound influence on the domain of eBusiness. Hence, the concept of system has been applied both to technology such as hardware and software ('hard' systems) and to human activity ('soft' systems). The concepts of system and control contributed to the development of modern information and communication technology in the sense that it heavily influenced the design of devices such as the modern computer. Systems thinking also influenced the creation of the communications revolution that underpins the modern internet. We shall argue that the treatment of organisations as systems underlies much of contemporary eBusiness thinking. As a consequence much of eBusiness activity is based in the assumption that organisations can be designed by modelling them in system terms and implementing new processes within organisations to improve performance. Within such approaches, ICT is seen as a key agent for organisational change. But we shall argue that an organisation such as a business is not just one system: it is a complex of a least three different types of system: activity systems, information systems and data systems.

Activity systems

As we have indicated in the previous chapter, activity systems occur within the domain of performa: the ways in which actors transform things in the world in an attempt to realise particular goals. Performa is enacted through performative acts. But the performative acts of particular actors do not occur in isolation. Any performative activity is normally undertaken in response to other actors and activities. Therefore, performative acts normally correspond to the 'work' of people in collective interaction, typically using 'tools' to transform 'objects' in the world.

Consider the ambulance service in such terms. Performative action in this situation includes call-takers taking incident calls, health-care professionals driving to the scene of some incident in ambulances and paramedics administering emergency health-care at incidents. In terms of any such performative act we can decompose it into its constituent elements such as in the case of an emergency response worker driving an ambulance to an emergency incident. In this case the key actor is the emergency response worker and the key transformation is the navigation of a vehicle from some point A to the location of the incident at point B. This act therefore takes place at particular locations and at a particular time and is performed to achieve the goal of getting skilled personnel to the point at which they can deliver emergency healthcare.

But the performative acts of any one particular actor are normally stimulated by the acts of other actors and support performative acts of yet further organisational actors. Hence, the stimulus for the dispatch of some ambulance is normally the reporting of a particular incident and the dispatch itself will put in train provision of further health-care by paramedics and other health-care professionals.

A pattern is a regular set of differences which is reproduced across more than one situation. At the level of performative activity, actors within a population recreate patterns or reproduce performative acts from one situation to the next. This is important to the ordering of mutual action. Performative acts therefore tend to occur in conventional patterns that repeat across situations, which we shall refer to as a performative pattern. This means that a performative pattern is an abstraction of the regularity of performance. We refer to a coherent collection of such performative patterns as an activity system (Figure 3.6).

Within organisations many activity systems are explicitly designed. If activity systems are designed there must be someone doing the designing: defining the boundary of such a system as well as the patterning of activities within the system. Following conventional practice we shall say that such design should take place by those actors who have some 'stake' in the system. Hence, we refer to them as stakeholders in the activity system. This is to highlight the fact that stakeholders may be different from the actors in an activity system. A stakeholder is an actor that has some interest in the performance of some system, but who may not necessarily be part of the system itself.

Activity systems are normally designed and re-designed continuously within organisations in an attempt to improve performance. Activity systems are therefore always problem situations for organisations: they are situations in organisational life that are regarded by at least one person as being problematical. Facing up to most problem situations are what we might call 'would-be-improvers' of it, people looking for a solution to the problem situation; these are the stakeholders for the activity system in question.

Therefore, the decision as to what is contained within an activity system and what forms part of the environment of some activity system is dependent on the viewpoint of the stakeholder in such a system. Stakeholders normally exist as groups of actors to which a particular activity system is relevant. Different stakeholders may hold different viewpoints as to the boundaries of systems and the key elements of systems. There may also be conflict over perceptions as to the intended purpose of some system. Such differences are likely to reflect the differing viewpoints of different stakeholders.

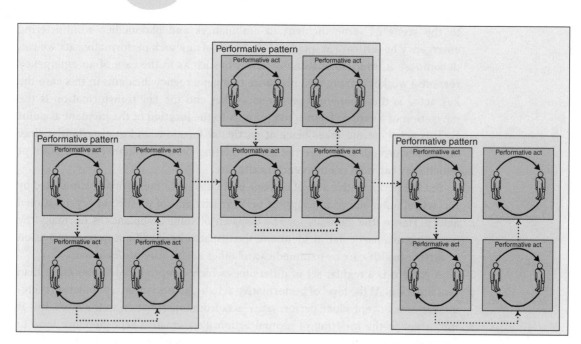

Figure 3.6 Activity system

Consider the ambulance service as an activity system. From the point of view of the 'customer' – the patient – this form of organisation might be described as a system designed to offer quality emergency healthcare at the point of incident. Alternatively, from the viewpoint of the manager it might be seen as a system to achieve optimal utilisation of a limited healthcare resource in fulfilment of targets. Hence, organisational purpose is a dynamic not a static issue. The purpose of some activity system is continually negotiated, understood and disseminated throughout the organisation by its stakeholders.

Consider the purpose of the ambulance service. In talking to certain stakeholders we might get a definition of the purpose of this activity system as something like: *providing rapid response to incidents and providing appropriate emergency healthcare at the point of incident.* We can turn this purpose into the central process or transformation of this activity system. In Figure 3.7 we abbreviate this to *providing emergency healthcare.*

Clearly, this central performative activity relies on other activities that input into the central transformation and those which output from the central transformation. Following the practice we established in the previous chapter, activity boxes are joined in Figure 3.7 with dotted arrows to indicate dependencies or precedence of activities. Hence, to provide emergency healthcare in response to incidents we first need to maintain resources such as ambulances and paramedics and to deploy such resources at ambulance stations and hospitals such that they are likely to be close to the point of incident. These are input activities. Once emergency healthcare has been delivered at an incident the patient is likely to need to be transported to the nearest general hospital, and following this, the ambulance needs to return quickly to its base of operation. These are output activities.

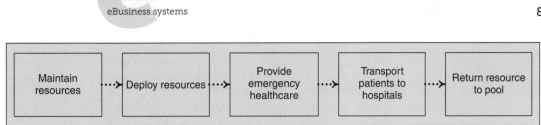

Figure 3.7 Emergency ambulance service as an activity system

For each of the processes added in turn to the activity system, the modeller might consider their inputs and outputs. However, for our purposes, this high-level model of the activity system is sufficient to indicate the regular patterning of performative activity within this system.

We next need to consider the issue of control. By this we need to answer the question of how does one evaluate whether the key purpose of our activity system is being achieved? Also, how do we implement this purpose in terms of the three Es of performance discussed in an earlier section: efficacy, efficiency and effectiveness? This involves specifying four additional types of activity familiar to the idea of a control process we discussed earlier. First, we need to consider planning activities which supply criteria for assessing performance in terms of the resources to be used and how they will be measured. This effectively means specifying control inputs. Second, we need to specify control processes that need to be in place to assess performance against criteria set. Such processes implement decision-making strategies necessary to assess the performance of some operational process and as such represent comparators. Third, we need to consider monitoring processes which collect measurements of activities against performance criteria set. Such processes are necessary to supply data about performance to control processes and effectively amount to sensors. Finally, we need to consider change processes necessary to enact regulation of operational activities, which amount to effectors.

These processes need to be joined together with appropriate dependencies. Hence, in terms of our example (Figure 3.8), each of these main operational activities may need to be controlled. For instance, to deliver rapid emergency healthcare at incidents we first need to define what we mean by rapid, perhaps by implementing targets such as response times to incidents (control inputs). We then need to identify the geographical location of incidents (sensors) and dispatch ambulances to incidents (effectors). We may then monitor the degree to which target response times are being met over some prescribed period.

However, there is a danger in this approach to modelling activity systems. We should not forget that the diagrams in Figures 3.7 and 3.8 represent models at a very high-level of abstraction. The model is not the reality. We need to always keep in mind that an activity such as *dispatch ambulances* actually comprises a complex, entangled network of performative acts which is reliant in turn on networks of informative and formative acts: all such acts being undertaken by business actors. It is to such informative and formative acts we turn next.

On Figure 3.8 the control loop actually represents at a high-level a great deal of performative, informative and formative activity. For instance, to determine actual response times to incidents we have to continually make records of dispatch

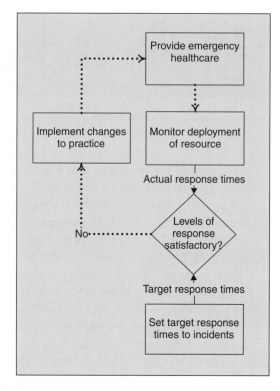

Figure 3.8 Example of ambulance service control

times and arrival times of particular ambulances over some period of time. Such response times then have to be communicated to somebody who makes a decision as to whether the response level is satisfactory and if not what changes to practice to initiate to address the problem.

Information systems

When the activities of two or more actors are directed towards a common goal then issues of coordination come into play. If multiple actors pursue a common goal they have to organise their joint actions. This extra layer of organisation is coordination. When the actions of two or more individuals are coupled we speak of coordinated action. Coordination is normally achieved through the imposition of convention, either through specifying some procedure to be followed in relation to a particular situation and/or in terms of conventions of communication and representation. Communication therefore facilitates coordinated action, which in turn is facilitated by representation. Another way of expressing this is that activity systems are reliant upon information systems which in turn are reliant upon data systems.

As discussed in Chapter 2, information systems are fundamentally specialised forms of communication system. As we have seen, a communicative or informative act is some aspect of performance designed by one actor, A, to influence the performance of some other actor, B. We would argue that an information system consists of recurring patterns of communicative action: acts of communication in which actors create and send messages in an appropriate context with certain intentions. The communication of such intentions is important for the coordination of performative action. Hence, communicative acts normally inter-relate in a network of precedence. By this we mean that one informative act normally precedes another in some regular and repeating sequence to form a coherent pattern (Figure 3.9).

Consider the representation of the information system relevant to the ambulance service from our description in an earlier section and illustrated in Figure 3.10. This consists of a pattern of inter-connected communicative acts that are reproduced by actors continuously. Callers continuously are making calls to the ambulance service asserting that particular incidents have taken place at particular locations and involving particular persons. The call taker within the ambulance service is likely to consult an experienced paramedic to determine the priority of the incident. This will determine instructions given to the caller and instructions given to the resource allocator. The resource allocator in turn will issue instructions to an ambulance driver who will respond with a commitment to attend a particular incident. This commitment will be communicated back to the caller. The ambulance driver will also assert the start of the journey to the incident and the treatment administered at the incident. Finally, the paramedic team will also assert when they leave an incident and when they arrive at the hospital.

Effectively this cycle of assertive, declaratives, directives and commissives implements patterns of information underlying what many have referred to as a sense and respond strategy within organisations and which is similar to the control loop described in the section above. Organisations implement feedback and control their operations through communicative action. In other words, the control loops we have described in previous sections consist typically of patterns of both informative and formative acts.

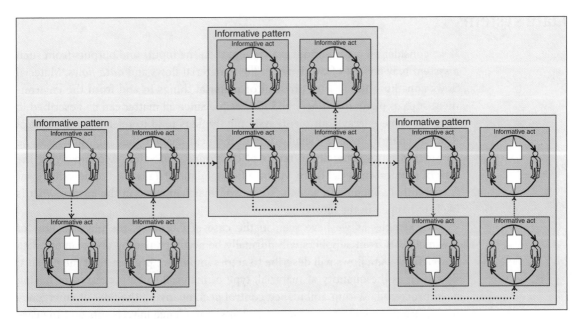

Figure 3.9 Information systems as a collection of informative patterns

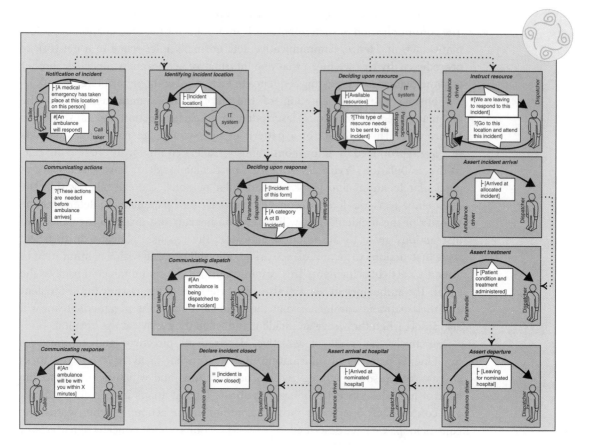

Figure 3.10 Ambulance service information system

Data systems

If we consider an organisation as a system, then the inputs and outputs from such a system may consist of two types of flow: material flows and *data flows*. Material flows constitute the flow of physical or material things to and from the environment such as plant, machinery and foodstuffs. Since all matter can be described in terms of some energy equivalent, systemic thinkers tend to refer to such physical flows as energy flows. We shall argue in the next chapter that such flows can be considered more generally in terms of the concept of value. Accompanying the flow of physical material there will be a flow of data. Data is used to describe what is currently happening in some system, what has happened in the past or what is likely to happen in the future.

For example, as we have seen in the case of Goronwy, the physical flow of raw materials from suppliers will normally be accompanied by one or more data flows. These data flows will describe to actors important properties of the physical flow such as the quantity of material, type of material to be processed or having been processed. Within ambulance control accompanying the flow of emergency healthcare there will be records of incidents, ambulance movements and the care delivered to patients.

A coherent set of patterns of data flow comprises a data system (Figure 3.11). Data systems work at the level of forma. Forma is concerned with patterns of data representation and use. A data system consists of physical patterns (symbols) which can be combined into structures and manipulated to produce new structures. A data system therefore consists of both data representation and data processing.

Data representation involves the use of data structures, data elements and data items. Data processing involves sets of formative acts which operate upon data structures, elements and items, which collectively we refer to as data representors. In general then, a formative act consists of the operation of one or more operators on one or more representors. 'Create' or 'write' actions involve creating new data structures or representing new data elements within data structures. 'Update' actions involve changing the value of data items in the sense that the symbols appropriate to the data item are changed. 'Delete' actions involve removing entire data structures or data elements from within data structures. Retrieval or 'read' actions involve accessing data from data items, data elements and data structures.

We can represent a create formative act using the symbol $\llcorner$ – the opposite of the mathematical symbol for 'not' – $\neg$ –, which is used to represent a delete formative act. Hence, $\llcorner$<d> represents the bringing into existence of the named data representor d enclosed in angled brackets, while $\neg$<d> represents the removal from existence of a named data representor. Likewise, we represent an update formative act as ($\downarrow$<d>) and a retrieval or read formative act as ($\uparrow$<d>).

Consider the data system of relevance to the ambulance service example. In Figure 3.12, we have illustrated the typical sequence of formative actions necessary to support the information and activity system described in previous sections. Various actors use the ICT system to create, update and read various records. First, an incident record is created. This record is then updated with location and resource details and read by a dispatcher. During the response to the incident both

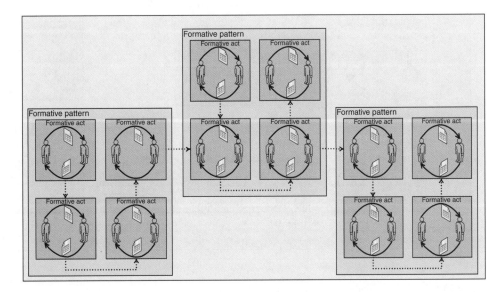

Figure 3.11 Data systems as collections of formative patterns

a resource record and the incident record is updated to reflect the changing situation on the ground.

The idea of a data system is therefore much larger than that of modern ICT. Indeed, it allows us to plot a clear historical path from embodied forma such as human speech through persistent forma such as paper-based forms to forma which is processed automatically by machines. Many modern ICT systems can be considered in terms of some collection of business rules which implements some form of decision strategy, such as the one discussed earlier in relation to triage. The key input into this decision strategy is data read from certain data structures. The key output from this decision strategy is a series or writes, updates or deletes to data structures. In abstract terms this describes the operation of two fundamental technologies embedded in modern ICT systems: databases and business rules.

The mathematician and computer scientist Ted Codd had the key insight of mapping aspects of set theory – particularly the idea of tuples – onto a data structure that had been around for many thousands of years. The most common data model that has been employed for representation of persistent forma as we have seen has been referred to as a file-based data model and this data model uses the inter-related constructs of fields, records and files. Codd proposed mapping the data structure of a file onto that of a mathematical relation, being a set of tuples. This data structure fundamentally underlies the data systems used within most modern digital computing systems exploited for business purposes.

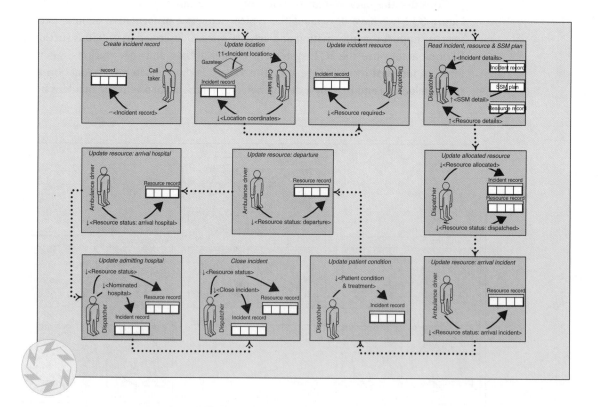

Figure 3.12 Emergency ambulance service as a data system

Codd's relational data model underlies most modern databases which are referred to as relational databases. Within this data model, there is one data structure: the relation. Each relation is made up of a number of data elements called tuples and each tuple is made of a number of data items known as attributes. Most ICT practitioners tend to use the terms *table*, row and column as synonyms for relations, tuples and attributes. Hence, within the ambulance service case there is likely to be an incidents table. All the rows within this table are made up of the columns *incident no.* (a unique identifier for the incident), *incident description*, *patient no.* (a unique identifier for each patient treated), *an incident category* (A, B or C) and an *incident status*. We consider relational databases in more detail in Chapters 5 and 6.

Decisions and control

Information emerges from the process of communication: both internal communication and external communication. Internal communication is what is frequently labelled as thought. Thinking is the process by which a given actor uses signs to reflect upon the world and to build plans for action in relation to the world. External communication is the use of signs to negotiate a collective meaning and purpose between two or more actors.

On the level of the individual, internal communication is therefore critical to the control of individual activity. On the level of the social, activity by two or more actors, communication is critical to the performance of coordinated action. But internal and external communication are not separate processes; they are necessarily entangled. Much of the reflection that an individual engages in is directed at the accomplishment of social action.

Information is therefore not stuff that is transmitted around the nervous system of an individual actor. Neither is it stuff that is transmitted between actors. Information is in-formation. In-formation is a critical and continuing accomplishment that drives human action. Information particularly supports both individual and social activity in the sense that it enables decisions to be made about appropriate actions in particular circumstances. Decisions and *decision-making* therefore mediates between information and action. Decision-making is the activity of deciding upon appropriate action in particular situations. Decision-making is reliant upon information in the sense that information is seen as reducing uncertainty in decision-making.

Consider the simple case of an individual actor undertaking a sequence of activities (Figure 3.13). In the first scenario there is no uncertainty about the course of activity: the actor performs activity A, then activity B, then activity C. No decisions need to be made about what activity to perform next because each activity is certain. In the second scenario we introduce the simplest form of uncertainty. The actor has performed activity A but there are now two alternative courses of activity open to him: B or C. He now needs to decide or choose what activity to perform next. The key question is how should such a decision be made? The normal answer to such a question is in terms of information. Information

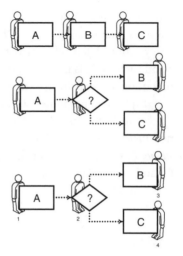

Figure 3.13 Decision-making in action

enables the actor to reduce the uncertainty in the situation by directing choice of future action.

Suppose activity A involves checking a batch of steel products delivered to Goronwy Galvanising by a particular actor. The key decision to be made by this actor is whether this batch of black products is fit to be galvanised (activity B) or should be returned to the manufacturer (activity C). This decision is clearly based upon information this actor gleans about the condition of steel products in the batch. The actor communicates with himself about the state of the batch and on this basis decides what to do next. If they are all conforming he chooses action B (sending them on to be galvanised): if some are non-conforming then he separates these products from the batch and returns this non-conforming material to the manufacturer (activity C).

Let us add a small further level of complexity. Rather than one actor performing activities A, B and C and making a decision about such activity, these activities and the act of decision-making are parcelled up in a division of labour: actor 1 performs activity A, actor 3 performs activity B and actor 4 performs activity C. The decision between activities B and C are taken by yet another actor: actor 2. This is clearly an example of social or coordinated action. The various actors in this performative pattern have to coordinate their joint activity through external communication.

Critical forms of external communication within business relate together in informative patterns. The informative pattern which underlies the performative pattern described above might look like that in Figure 3.14. Here, the actors in the group communicate through assertives, directives and commissives and through such instrumental communication ensure the coordination of their activity.

Such communicative acts can be unpacked in turn in terms of forma. For instance, it is perfectly possible for all these communicative acts to be formed as utterances: as speech acts. In practice, it is likely that acts of communication will be formed as paper-based representation – as data items on paper forms. More recently Goronwy has encoded such acts of communication in the records of an

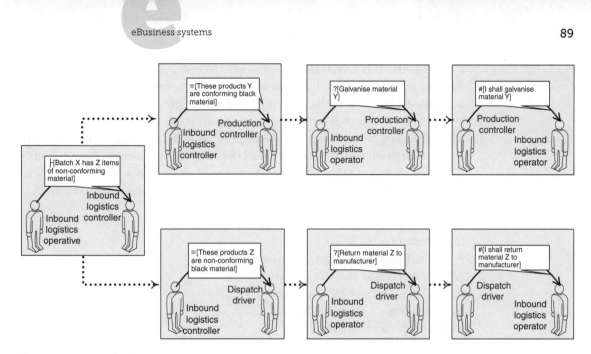

Figure 3.14 A typical informative pattern at Goronwy

ICT system, perhaps as the rows of some table within a relational database. As such, the database acts as a form of collective memory for the organisation, from which decisions can be made.

Therefore, much modern-day decision-making within organisations is not performed any longer by humans. It is enacted by machines: by ICT systems. Consider a simple case in which you are one business actor (a consumer) who wants to hire a car from another business actor (an organisational actor). Traditionally, you as a consumer would turn up in person at some outlet of the care hire company and you would engage in a dialogue with some car hire operative to get what you want.

This dialogue might follow a typical pattern such as:

- *Consumer*: I would like to hire a car please.
- *Car hire operative*: Certainly sir. And what type of car are you looking to hire?
- *Consumer*: A compact please.
- *Car hire operative*: A compact, certainly sir. For what period would you like to hire this car sir?
- *Consumer*: For a period of four days please.
- *Car hire operative*: And when would you like the hire period to start sir?
- *Consumer*: Next Monday please.
- *Car hire operative*: That would be in five days time. And could I ask sir whether you are one of our loyalty members?
- *Consumer*: Yes, I am.
- *Car hire operative*: Excellent sir. In which case I can offer you a 10% discount on our normal car hire prices. ...

Whilst engaging in this communicative pattern the operative will be entering details of the car hire transaction into an ICT system using a screen on his desktop computer. This screen actually prompts the operative to ask the questions he does. In this sense, the ICT system is gathering data from which it can make an automated decision as to the amount of discounting, if any, to apply to the car hire purchase. Such data include the car rental group required, the period of the rental, whether or not the customer is a member of the rental club run by the company and how far in advance the car has been booked. So in this scenario there are actually three communicative actors not two: one of these actors is a machine. This machine is making an automated decision based upon business rules, such as:

RULE***********************
IF Customer rents Car
AND Car Rental Group ISA Compact
AND Rental Period ISA Day Rental
AND Customer ISA Club Customer
AND Booking > 3 Days in Advance
THEN Customer Discount = 10%
RULE***********************
IF Customer rents Car
AND Car Rental Group ISA Compact
AND Rental Period ISA Day Rental
AND Customer ISA Club Customer
AND Booking ≠ 3 Days in Advance
THEN Customer Discount = 5%

Summary

In this chapter we have argued that eBusiness is founded in systems thinking or systemics. A system is an organised collection of things with emergent properties and with some purpose that can be defined. Critical ideas from systemics of relevance to all systems are sub-systems, input-process-output, environment and control. Control is the mechanism that implements regulation and adaptation in systems. Systems generally exhibit some form of control that enables the system to maintain state within defined parameters and to adapt to changes in its environment. Control processes are built of sensors, comparators and effectors working in feedback loops and are normally exercised in terms of defined measures of performance – efficacy, efficiency and effectiveness measures.

The idea of a system and the associated concept of control have had a profound influence on the domain of eBusiness. Hence, the concept of system has been applied both to technology such as data systems (hard systems) and to activity systems (soft systems). Information systems mediate between data systems and activity systems.

Data systems occur at the level of forma and are concerned with the form and representation of symbols in storage and signal transmission. Data systems are systems of symbol operated upon by recurring patterns of formative acts, which are built from two sets of primitives: representors and operators. Representors are primitives of data representation or organisation: operators are primitives of data manipulation or processing. In terms of data representation, a data model can be described at a high level of abstraction in terms of a hierarchy of data items, data elements and data structures. A data item is the lowest-level of data organisation. A data element is a logical collection of data items and a data structure is a logical collection of data elements. In terms of data processing we distinguished between four core types or classes of formative act from which all forms of such processing can theoretically be built: create, read, update and delete.

Information systems deal with informa and are concerned with the meaning of symbols and their use within human action. Information systems are systems of communication and consist of recurring patterns of communicative or informative acts. We limit our account of communicative acts to those which support performative acts. For this purpose it is possible to identify five key types of communicative act: assertives, directives, commissives, expressives and declaratives. Such informative acts relate together in patterns that compose an information system. The key output of an information system is in-formation: the construction and communication of meaning both by actors themselves and between actors.

Activity systems deal with performa: they are systems of performance and consist of recurring patterns of performative acts. Performative acts are acts of production, distribution and consumption. They therefore relate people to objects and involve people collectively creating, moving or using such objects. Performative acts are the atomic units for performative patterns: a performative pattern being a regular and repetitive sequence of performative acts. Performative patterns inter-relate within activity systems. The key output from activity systems is instrumental action, that as we shall see in the next chapter, produces value: goods, services and social capital.

Review test

A _____ is an organised collection of things with emergent properties and some defined purpose.	Fill in the blank

Systemics considers phenomena by dissecting a problem into its smallest parts, attempting to understand the workings of parts and building up a conception of the whole from this understanding.	True or False?
True	
False	

A bicycle considered as a set of bicycle parts would be regarded as a system.	True or False?
True	
False	

The key elements of any system are inputs, outputs and what else	Select the most appropriate answer
Process	
Agent	
Sub-system	

Systems generally can be seen as being composed of _____. Hierarchy seems to be an inherent property of most systems.	Fill in the blank

Variety refers to how flexible a system is	True or False?
True	
False	

Control enables a system to … .	Select all that apply
Sensors	
Processes	
Comparators	
Effectors	

An activity system consists of a collection of informative patterns.	True or False?
True	
False	

A _____ consists of a collection of performative acts.	True or False?
True	
False	

A _____ consists of a collection of formative acts operating upon data structures.	Fill in the blank

Exercises

- Consider the purposes of a private sector and public sector organisation as a system. What are the purposes of such organisations? How do such purposes differ?
- In what way is it appropriate to identify the inputs, processes and outputs of the educational system? What physical and non-physical flows are relevant to the educational system?
- What contributes to the high variety of most human systems such as businesses?
- What constitutes control in a human system such as a business? In what way is a business strategy a set of control inputs?
- What sort of difficulties might be experienced in specifying efficacy, efficiency and effectiveness measures of performance for the business?
- In some business organisation or business process what constitute likely sensors, comparators and effectors?
- What sorts of feedback are experienced in economic systems such as markets?
- Consider an educational organisation such as a school or university as a system. Try to identify some possible sub-systems. Try to represent in high-level terms a university or school as an activity system. Identify appropriate measures for the efficiency and effectiveness of university teaching as an activity system.
- Negative feedback is frequently used to maintain the homeostasis of some system. Investigate the term homeostasis in greater detail.

Projects

- Attempt to apply some aspect of systems thinking to a non-trivial problem in business or commerce. For instance, consider the problem organisations such as Tesco has in managing its supplies and suppliers. Attempt to model this supply chain as a system and analyse the usefulness of applying a systems approach to this area.
- The systems approach has been criticised by a range of authors in the areas of organisation theory and organisation behaviour. Investigate this literature and use it to critically determine the degree to which it is appropriate to use a systems model for describing and understanding organisations.
- The whole is greater than the sum of its parts or the system is greater than the sum of its subsystems. What do you think is meant by this in terms of the three levels of business systems (activity systems, information systems and ICT systems) examined in this book? Provide some examples of the way in which these principles reflect organisational life.
- Attempt a small project in activity, information or data re-design within an organisation known to you. For instance, consider the admissions process at a university. How can this process be improved and how important is ICT to the re-design of your chosen process?
- A number of different graphical notations exist for specifying activity models. Investigate two distinct notations for specifying either activity models or organisational processes. Develop some criteria of comparison (such as number of constructs, ease of drawing etc.) and analyse each approach in terms of your set criteria.
- Models are useful as a means of joint understanding not only within a particular organisation but also between organisations. Some have proposed the development of high-level or generic process models that may be applicable across organisations within the same industrial sector. Suggest some of the benefits but also the problems of this proposal. Determine to what degree it is possible for organisations to re-use existing generic process models to help in business analysis and design.

Critical reflection

In what way is a higher education institution such as a university a system? Who are the key actors in a university? What would you say constitutes the key activity systems of a higher education system? How true is it to say that different persons will have different ideas about what constitutes an activity system and what it is made up of? Consider a university in this light. On what information systems does such activity rely? What data systems do you feel are important to decision-making in a university setting?

Case exploration

Again, many of the organisations provided as cases at the end of the book can be considered in terms of the concepts discussed in this chapter. For instance, you might consider the primary activity system of an organisation such as IKEA. How would you define the key purpose of this activity system? What input activities are important for fulfilling this purpose? What output activities arise from this central transformation? How are each set of activities controlled? For instance, how does IKEA ensure it has a sufficient number of products in store to meet customer demand? What information systems are essential for managing control such as this? Try to think of one example of a record that IKEA might use to help it perform its business.

Further reading

Most of this chapter is founded in the well-established literature on systems theory or systemics. Readers should first visit chapter 2 of my book *Significance* for more detail on such literature (Beynon-Davies, 2011). Michael Jackson (2003) provides a good introduction to the application of systems theory to organisations as does the work of Peter Senge (1990). The work of Peter Checkland (1999) is a specific example of the application of concepts from systemics to understanding and designing organisations.

There are many books on organisational theory and organisational behaviour. Bratton *et al* (2010) provide a recent and comprehensive review of the field. This chapter has provided an overview of systems theory as applied to organisations, particularly designed to act as foundation to our consideration of informatics. Checkland (1987) provides the definitive account of soft systems work upon which the approach to activity systems described in this chapter is based. The idea of an information system is built upon John Searle's idea of speech acts (2010) and the theory behind data systems is founded in work on data modelling (Tsitchizris and Lochovsky, 1982; Beynon-Davies, 2004).

References

Beynon-Davies, P. (2004). *Database Systems*, 3rd edn. Houndmills, Basingstoke, Palgrave Macmillan.

Beynon-Davies, P. (2011). *Significance: Exploring the Nature of Information, Systems and Technology*, Houndmills, Basingstoke, Palgrave Macmillan.

Bratton, J., P. Sawchuk and C. Forshaw. (2010). *Work and Organisational Behaviour*, 2nd edn. Houndmills, Basingstoke, Palgrave Macmillan.

Checkland, P. (1987). *Systems Thinking, Systems Practice*, Chichester, John Wiley.

Checkland, P. (1999). *Soft Systems Methodology: A Thirty Year Retrospective*, Chichester, John Wiley.

Jackson, M. C. (2003). *Systems Thinking: Creative Holism for Managers*, Chichester, John Wiley.

Searle, J. R. (2010). *Making the Social World: The Structure of Human Civilization*, Oxford, Oxford University Press.

Senge, P. M. (1990). *The Fifth Discipline: The Art and Practice of the Learning* Organisation, New York, Doubleday.

Tsitchizris, D. C. and F. H. Lochovsky. (1982). *Data Models*, Englewood-Cliffs, Prentice-Hall.

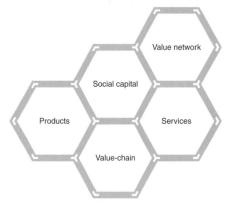

4 eBusiness Value

Learning outcomes	Principles
Describe organisations as value-creating systems positioned within a wider value network.	Organisations are value-creating systems that interact with a wider value-network. The primary environment of any commercial organisation is the economy. Economies are systems or networks of exchange for value. Economies consist of systems not only of value production but also of value distribution and value consumption. An organisation's value is hence determined by its position within a wider value network.
Understand the many different forms of value and distinguish between tangible and intangible value.	Two types of value are normally associated with an organisation: services and/or products. Value also emerges from wider social networks: in the form of social capital. Goods and services can be distinguished in a number of ways. Tangible goods and services have a physical form. Intangible goods and services have a non-physical form and hence are amenable to representation as data.
Understand forms of control within the value-network.	Exchange between business actors is typically controlled either in terms of markets or hierarchies. Markets are systems of competition. In contrast, managerial hierarchies are systems of cooperation. In practice, the value-networks of organisations are forms of economic control in which both cooperation and competition are evident.
Describe key parts of the wider value network.	The activity systems of the typical business are collectively referred to as the internal value-chain. Two other chains of value are normally seen as critical to the value-network of most organisations: the supply chain and the customer chain. These three value-chains overlap with another frequently ignored chain of value of increasing significance to organisations: the community chain.
Understand the concept of a business model and its relationship to the wider value network.	The concept of the internal value-chain and the wider value-network provide ways of considering the potential of changes to business systems. Hence, the design of business models and the value-network of organisations are inherently inter-twined.

Chapter outline

Introduction

The concept of value is a common thread which ties together a range of topics considered in this book. The Oxford English dictionary defines value as the importance or usefulness of something. One aim of this book is to consider the value of ICT to organisations: since this underpins the essence of eBusiness. ICT is important and useful to organisations in many different ways. However, an understanding of such value is possible only by considering the layered contexts within which ICT is used and applied.

The management guru Michael Porter (1985) uses the term value to describe, at a high-level, the key output of the business organisation. This enables him to focus on the processes or activity systems which produce such value: collectively referred to as the internal value-chain. In such terms, organisations are considered as value-creating systems.

But economies are systems not only of value production but also of value distribution and value consumption. An organisation's value is hence determined by its position within a wider value network. Typically, the value associated with an organisation equates with the services and/or products provided by the organisation. However, value also emerges from dispersed forms of 'organisation' evident in wider social networks. Such forms of value relate to social capital; the resources for mutual support available in forms of community. Social capital is the key value that members gain from participation in such social networks.

As considered in previous chapters, electronic business can be considered fundamentally a matter of organisational analysis and design, underpinned with ICT innovation. Our emphasis on analysis and design focuses on the options an organisation has to do things differently, not only in terms of its internal value-chain but also in terms of positioning itself within the wider value network. There is hence key value in the concept of what we shall refer to as a business model in that it relates issues of strategy, activities and technology.

Information and communication technology in particular has affected the value-proposition of not only particular organisations, but also whole industries. It has increased the range of business models open to organisations within such industries, and this is particularly true of the so-called content industries. Thus, we ground our consideration of the changing concept of value within this chapter in an industry of global reach: that of the movie industry.

Value and value-creating systems

In a sense, this chapter is about *axiology*: the study of what people value or find to be of worth. In a purely materialist sense we could equate value with the satisfaction of human needs such as the need for food, water and shelter. For the psychologist Abraham Maslow (1954) these constitute basic human needs which must be satisfied before other human needs such as the need for safety, love and belonging, esteem and self-actualisation are achievable. In this manner, a hierarchy of needs is specified that translate into forms of value. Some of this value is material in nature such as food while other forms of value are non-material in nature such as a sense of esteem or personal status.

The upshot of this is that value is a complex issue and one which is particularly associated with the different activity, communication and representation systems within which people engage. Hence, people have valued different things at different times and in different places. In this sense the concept of value is a significant concept in that value is arbitrary: it depends on what is considered of worth by some community of people.

In his famous book *Argonauts of the Western Pacific* (1922) the eminent anthropologist Bronislaw Malinowski described a curious case of axiology. This involved the Kula exchange, sometimes known as the Kula ring: a system of goods exchange conducted amongst 18 island communities, including the Trobriand Islands, in the South Pacific. Participants in this exchange system travel hundreds of miles by canoe in order to exchange Kula, which consists of two types of good: disc necklaces formed from a red seashell and armbands formed from a white seashell. Kula goods have no value as useful objects, but are traded purely for the purposes of raising social status. The act of giving a necklace or armband is used as a sign of the greatness of the giver. This exchange network is known as a ring because Kula necklaces are traded to the north in a clockwise direction and kula armbands are traded to the south in an anti-clockwise direction. In this way, kula valuables never remain in the hands of recipients for long. Instead, they must be passed on to other partners in the kula exchange system within a certain amount of time and thus constantly are circling around the exchange network. However, even temporary possession of kula by a participant brings prestige and status for the temporary owner.

A similar system was conducted on the Pacific Northwest Coast of North America in terms of what was known as potlatch. Potlatch is a festival ceremony which was practiced by indigenous peoples of this area, the word coming from the Chinook meaning 'to give away' or 'a gift'. At potlatch gatherings, a family or hereditary leader hosted a feast for guests. The main purpose of the potlatch was the re-distribution of wealth. Within it, hierarchical relations within and between clans, villages and nations, were observed and reinforced through the distribution or sometimes destruction of wealth. The status of any given family was raised not by who had the most resources, but by who distributed the most resources.

Figure 4.1 represents the 'Kula ring' as a network, or more precisely as an exchange network. In very abstract terms, a network is a set of nodes connected by links of some form. In communication networks, which we shall consider in Chapter 6, the nodes are usually types of computing device and the links are data communication lines. In social networks, the nodes are people and the links or relations are various forms of social interaction and/or social bonds. The actual type of link, relationship or more formally relation represented in Figure 4.1 is that of an exchange relation. Within an exchange network, people exchange things they regard to be of worth: they exchange value.

Even within systems or networks of gift exchange such as the Kula or Potlatch, the *value* exchanged traditionally comes in two forms: goods and services. It is no surprise that in English the word *good* is used to refer not only to something of worth

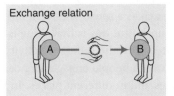

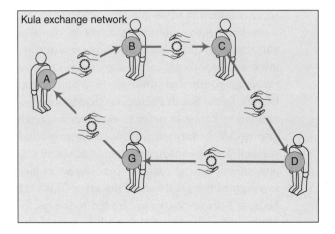

Figure 4.1 An exchange network

but also to denote a type of value. A good is normally some physical thing which is valued and exchanged between one actor and another such as food or a kula neck-lace. In contrast, a service is usually some valued activity which is performed for one actor by another actor such as tilling a field, providing a potlatch festival or operating upon a malignant tumour. Later in the chapter we shall argue for consid-eration of a third type of value which we refer to as social capital. Social capital is a non-material form of value which is also 'exchanged' between actors and bears a close relationship with the status derived from potlatch and kula described above.

As we have indicated in previous chapters, business actors can consist of organisations as well as human groups, individuals and even 'machines'. In the modern world a *good* is normally considered to be some form of product produced by an organisation and distributed to customers of that organisation. Similarly, a *service* is typically some form of activity performed by an organisation for its customers. As such, goods and services can be considered the end-points of business processes or activity systems performed within business organisations (Chapter 2). They are outputs from such value-creating systems delivered to the customer of the organisation.

For instance, in a manufacturing organisation key aspects of value will be associated with properties of the products manufactured. Hence, an automobile manufacturer will be judged in terms of criteria such as the price of its manufac-tured cars and their reliability and safety. In the public sector, an organisation's value will typically be associated with properties of the services it delivers. Hence, a university may be judged in terms of the quality of the education it provides or the research it conducts.

However, it is important not to confuse the notion of money with that of value. Within the modern capitalist world, money is frequently seen as comprising the sole source of value. This is incorrect: money is instead a conventional proxy for value. Treated literally money can be considered a sign (Chapter 3) which serves to stand for or refer to value in other forms. Money in most of its manifestations has no intrinsic use value in and of itself. It merely serves as a measure of exchange value. Hence, within modern exchange networks if some individual sells you some good such as a book you impart a certain amount of money in exchange for this book. That person can then use such money to engage in another relationship of exchange: they can perhaps exchange the amount of money received for some foodstuffs. This is why it becomes possible to represent money as data: as records in data systems supporting networks of exchange.

Having said this, the management guru Michael Porter (1985) uses the term *value* in its strictly economic or monetary sense. This means that for him non-monetary expressions of value have to eventually be expressed in monetary terms: '...value is the amount buyers are willing to pay for what a firm provides them. Value is measured by total revenue, a reflection of the prices a firm's product commands and the units it can sell. A firm is profitable if the value it commands exceeds the costs involved in creating the product.'

We alluded to the materiality of value earlier. This helps us distinguish between two types of good: physical or tangible goods and non-physical or intangible goods. This distinction has a particular bearing, as we shall see, on the degree to which such forms of value can be delivered over data communication networks and hence will be important in considering the degree to which electronic commerce is both feasible and desirable for some company or for some industry (Chapter 7).

Tangible goods have a physical form and hence must be distributed over physical channels to the consumer. *Intangible goods* may be fundamentally represented as data. They are hence amenable to digitisation and as such may become digital goods. Such goods clearly may be delivered to the customer electronically over communication networks.

Examples of tangible goods are mechanical goods such as automobiles, electrical goods such as DVD players and perishable goods such as foodstuffs. Examples of intangible goods are text (as in books, magazines and academic papers), images such as in prints or photographs, audio (such as music) and video (as in movies). Many such recent forms of intangible good, as we shall see, are frequently denoted with the label *content*.

Similarly services can be classed as either tangible or intangible. The inspection of goods, the ordering of such goods and the delivery of goods are data-based services that support the sale of tangible and intangible products. However, certain services are tangible in nature and hence not amenable to electronic service delivery. Other services are intangible by nature and thus primarily constitute communication services. They are hence open to delivery through electronic

Table 4.1 Types of goods and services

	Goods	Services
Tangible	Automobiles Foodstuffs	Health care Waste disposal
Intangible	Music Movies	Legal advice Monetary transfers

channels. *Tangible services* include health treatments such as operations and beauty treatments such as hairdressing. *Intangible services* include legal advice, news reports and monetary transfers. Table 4.1 illustrates these distinctions.

Goods and services are, of course, not mutually exclusive; indeed in many businesses the sale of a particular tangible good will normally be associated with a range of services, some tangible, some intangible. When purchasing a tangible good such as an automobile, for instance, the customer may be able to inspect images of the product, order the product and pay for the product using forms of electronic delivery. The customer may also, of course, inspect, order and pay for intangible goods such as music electronically. After purchase it is likely that the car will need regular servicing and inspection – tangible services.

The movie industry

The movie industry is a particularly good example of an industry that has continuously been affected by the changing nature of value and the impact of technological change on its value-proposition. A movie or motion picture was originally a story conveyed with moving images and the first true movies emerged during the 1880s with the invention of the motion picture camera and projector. In the 1920s new technology enabled a soundtrack to be added to and synchronised with the moving image. In the mid-1930s the first colour movies were produced. Originally invented in the 1990s, digital cinematography started to be used seriously in the 2000s. Over the past couple of years major movies have been shot entirely in digital format. This opens up a number of new access channels to movies. Not surprisingly, over the next decade, the movie industry is likely to undergo fundamental change because of the way in which ICT transforms fundamental business models within the sector.

Hence, movies are modern examples of digital content. The term content, as we shall see, used to be restricted to web-based documents. Nowadays, the term is used to refer to all forms of good that can be represented in digital form as data. Many forms of good that now can be delivered as digital content such as books, music and movies have for most of their history been tangible in nature. Hence, you can still buy a physical book or music on CD or a movie on DVD. However, there has been a gradual movement of the so-called content industries to produce such goods in a form that can distributed and consumed over data communication networks. This enables a number of different business models for such industries which exploit the potential of digital access channels and associated devices.

Social networks and social capital

According to the poet John Donne, 'no man is an island entire of itself'. Similarly, organisations are not isolated entities. Organisations exist within a wider community of actors. Such communities generate a distinct form of value, which is not so easily measured in monetary terms. This form of intangible value is known as social capital. For instance, managers spend a considerable amount of time 'networking'. This is because a manager's social network is a particularly valuable resource for the individual. For instance, studies of personal careers shows that the higher one moves up the managerial hierarchy the more important are social networks to promotional prospects.

People have argued over the term 'community' and its key features for centuries. It is fruitful to consider the issue of community from the point of view of social networks. Consider Figure 4.2. In a similar manner to the exchange network illustrated earlier, in this figure we have represented individuals as circles and links as double-arrowed lines. Suppose each line in this network is taken to represent a relationship of friendship. Hence, in network 1 the line between individual A and individual B indicates that A is a friend of B, and vice versa. This is because, unlike an exchange relation, that is asymmetric, a friendship relation is symmetric. When you exchange something with somebody else you pass on value from yourself to that someone. When you are a friend of someone however, that someone is also your friend.

In examining the three friendship networks in Figure 4.2 the individuals considered remain the same but a transformation occurs through networks 1 to 3. More people are connected together through friendship in network 3 than

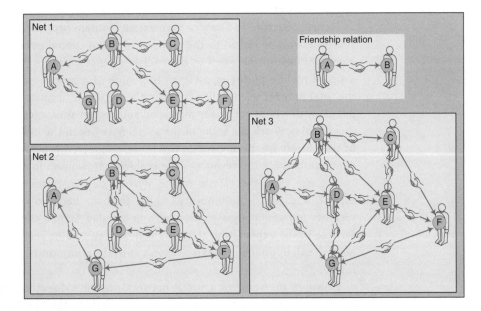

Figure 4.2 Social networks

in network 1. Suppose we also overlay relationships of trust, collaboration and cooperation on these networks. In a community we would expect the connectivity – a measure of the inter-connectedness of the nodes in a network – in all four types of social network to be high. Hence, network 3 is closer to most definitions of a community than network 1 in Figure 4.3.

In recent literature, authors have argued that communities generate value just like organisations and hence it becomes possible to consider a chain of value that a community generates. However, the value of a community lies not in its physical or financial capital but in its social capital. The American sociologist Robert Putnam (2000) defines social capital as being 'features of social organisation such as networks, norms and trust that facilitate coordination and cooperation for mutual benefit.'

Capital is traditionally defined as the financial assets available to some company. It is hence a key resource for production. In contrast, social capital is the productive value of people engaged in a dense network of social relations. Social capital consists of those features of social organisation such as networks of secondary associations, high levels of interpersonal trust and reciprocity which act as resources for individuals and facilitate collective action. Therefore, it is argued, a community rich in social capital is more likely to possess effective civic institutions and more likely to be effective at maintaining law and order.

This is similar in conception to so-called Metcalfe's law in relation to the value of a communication network. Metcalfe's law (proposed by the communication engineer Robert Metcalfe) states that the value of a communication network for a particular user of such a network is proportional to the square of the number of users of the system (n^2). In Chapter 2 we used this notion to define the variety of a system as a network. The concept of variety in this sense and the density or inter-connectedness of a social network is related as a maximum to the number of unique connections in the network ($n*(n-1)/2$).

Hence, Metcalfe and to a certain extent Putnam propose that the variety of a social network is linked to the amount of social capital generated. The value of a communication network to the user is a function of its variety. For example, a single mobile phone is useless. The value of a mobile phone increases with the total number of mobile phones in the network, because the total number of people with whom each user may send and receive messages increases. Likewise in a social network the value of the social network to the individual is a function of the variety of the network. The more connected a person is to others in a community the more resources she is able to draw upon in collective action.

A scene from the classic movie *Witness* demonstrates the power of social capital. The Amish community, which forms a backdrop to the story, come together to build a large wooden barn in one day. People contribute their labour for free in the expectation that this will be returned or reciprocated when they need to call upon the collective resources of the community at some point in the future.

However, the value of a social network does not directly correspond with its density or connectedness. Of equal importance is the 'quality' of links in the network. A common theme in the literature on social capital and community is that changes towards the mass *globalisation* and urbanisation of society have led to a decline in community and hence a consequent decline in social capital. This supposes that not only are social networks in the modern age less dense or more widely dispersed, the links in such networks are in some sense less binding.

For example, trust between human beings is normally developed over time as individuals (actors) gain confidence in the reliability of the performance of other actors through inter-action. Social capital rests on the transitivity of trust as a human relationship – A trusts C because B trusts C and A trusts B (Figure 4.3). This allows large social networks to exhibit trust without their necessarily being close contact between particular individuals.

The sociologist Mark Granovetter (1973) distinguishes between two forms of link (relation) in a social network – strong links and weak links. Strong links exist between people who are regularly in contact and who share much in common. Hence, strong links typically exist between close friends, work colleagues or family members. Weak links exist between people in irregular contact such as between acquaintances, business contacts and distant friends. Strong links are particularly important in support networks, typically in the early and later stages of life. Weak links deliver new social and economic opportunities.

More recently it has been proposed that technology, particularly ICT, can be important to maintaining social networks of both strong and weak links. In the *information society* a large proportion of interaction between individuals is conducted remotely using forms of ICT. It is therefore proposed that this remote

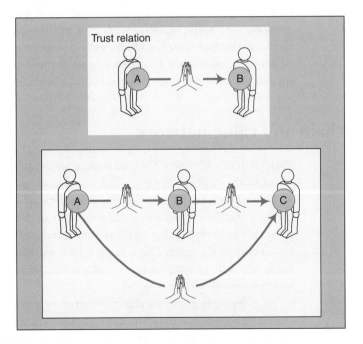

Figure 4.3 Transitivity of trust

interaction may become more and more critical to the maintenance of strong links in social networks. Because of the location-independence of remote communication, the size and scope of weak links within social networks may also grow.

So why are businesses interested in social networks? The main reason is that the social capital embedded in social networks and its emergent effects such as increased trust amongst the members of such networks may become increasingly important to company activity, particularly sales. This is because there is an inherent association between networks of friendship and networks of trust. Generally speaking, you are more likely to trust your friends than acquaintances. For instance, you are more likely to trust a recommendation received for a particular product or service from a friend than a stranger. Businesses have known for some time of the part social networks play in the positive reporting of goods and services and the relationship this has to growth in sales. Many organisations have therefore attempted to foster what we shall refer to as adjunct communities – online social networks associated with particular business activity. Organisations have also attempted to exploit the connections in such social networks to conduct so-called viral marketing. This is based upon the idea that word-of-mouth recommendations can travel through a social network in much the same way as viruses travel through epidemics.

The movie industry

The digital nature of movie content opens up its potential for marketing using social networks. For instance, movie companies now release snippets of movie content on so-called social networking sites such as YouTube as a means of stimulating interest and in the hope that recommendations to view such content will travel along the links in trusted social networks. Some movie producers have even experimented with the use of such sites to allow possible consumers to engage in the design of the eventual content, such as in gaining feedback on the attractiveness of particular plot-lines. It is therefore no surprise to find big players in the movie industry investing in these new *marketing channels*.

Value-chain and value network

Porter offers a template for considering an organisation's key activity systems in terms of the concept of value. This is a generic model of an organisation known as the value-chain. In this view organisations are seen as social institutions that produce and deliver value to customers through defined activities. The activities or processes in Porter's value-chain are modelled on the ideal manufacturing organisation such as Goronwy Galvanising, which we considered in Chapter 2. However, these key activity systems can be adapted to service organisations such as USC, which we considered in Chapter 1.

An organisation's value chain is therefore a series of interdependent activity systems that in combination deliver products and/or services to a customer. According to Michael Porter, such activities are of two types: primary and secondary activities. Primary activities constitute the core competencies of the

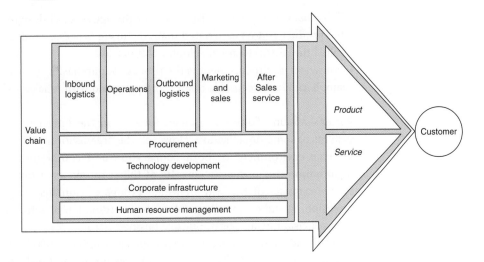

Figure 4.4 The value chain

organisation. Secondary activities are important to the successful operation of primary activities. This is illustrated in Figure 4.4.

According to Porter, *primary activities* in the value chain consist of the following:

- *Inbound logistics*. This process involves the receiving and storage of raw material needed by a company to produce its products. It also involves the associated activity of distributing relevant raw material to manufacturing premises.
- *Operations*. This would traditionally be called production or manufacturing. It involves transforming inputs (raw materials) into finished products.
- *Outbound logistics*. This involves the storage of finished products in warehouses and the distribution of finished products to the customer.
- *Marketing and sales*. Marketing is the process of planning and executing the conception, pricing, promotion and distribution of ideas, goods and services to create exchanges that satisfy individual and organisational goals. Sales as a function is the associated activity involved in the management of purchasing activities.
- *After-sales service*. These are services that maintain or enhance product value by attempting to promote a continuing relationship with the customer of the company. After-sales may involve such activities as the installation, testing, maintenance and repair of products.

Secondary activities consist of the following:

- *Infrastructure activities*. These are support activities for the entire value-chain such as general management, finance, accounting, legal services and quality management.
- *Human resource management*. This involves the recruiting, hiring, training and development of employees of a company.

- *Technology development*. This involves the activities of designing and improving the product and its associated manufacturing process. Traditionally, it would be called the research and development function.
- *Procurement*. Procurement is the process of purchasing goods and services from suppliers at an acceptable quality and price and with reliable delivery.

Porter's notion of the value chain focuses on the internal processes or activity systems of some organisation. However, the organisation as a system exists within a wider environment of both cooperation and competition. For the business organisation this primarily consists of the economic environment. An economic system consists of the way in which groups of humans arrange their material provisioning and essentially involves the coordination of activities concerned with such provisioning amongst multiple business actors.

As already mentioned, three major forms of activity are relevant to all economic systems: production, distribution and consumption. *Production* is that set of activities concerned with the creation of goods and services for human existence. *Distribution* is the associated process of collecting, storing and moving goods into the hands of consumers and providing services for consumers. *Consumption* is the process by which consumers receive and use goods and services.

Consider the movie industry in this manner. The movement of movies onto digital formats has affected the production, distribution and consumption of movies. For example, in terms of distribution, traditional channels involve the use of cinemas and broadcast television channels to provide controlled access to movie content. The movement of movies onto digital format opened up new avenues for distribution of this content, particularly distribution via DVD. It is a short step from the DVD to offering access to such content via electronic delivery channels over the internet. There is every reason to expect that consumers will want increasing access to movie content online just as they access music, newspapers, television and radio.

Production, distribution and consumption are activities that deliver value. Hence, economies can be seen as consisting of a multitude of chains of value both within and between economic actors. This means that economic actors inter-relate and interact in complex networks of value production, distribution and consumption. A particular economic actor will take on roles within a number of different chains of value within such networks. For instance, organisations may be both buyers of goods and services and sellers of goods and services. Organisations may both compete with other organisations in the sale of particular goods and services as well as cooperating in the delivery of goods and services to particular customers.

Therefore two other chains of value flow are critical to the competitive environment and assume some significance for most commercial organisations: the supply chain and the customer chain. They are both chains of value flow in the sense that both customers and suppliers will typically be other organisations, who in turn will have relationships and engage in activities with further organisations. Hence, an economic system will be composed of a complex network of such chains and we refer to this as the wider value network.

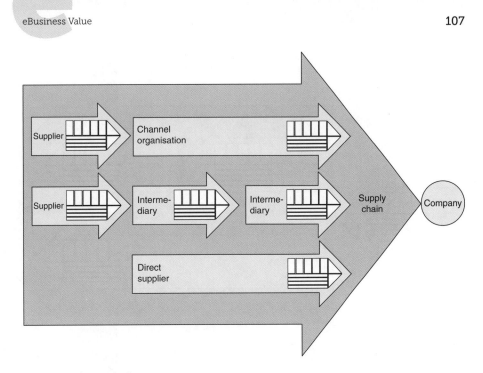

Figure 4.5 The supply chain

The *supply chain* for a typical business is illustrated in Figure 4.5. The broad arrows on the diagram indicate the flow of goods and services between organisations. On the diagram we distinguish between direct suppliers one step removed in the supply chain and indirect suppliers more than two steps removed in the supply chain. Indirect suppliers are sometimes referred to as channel organisations or *intermediaries*. Typical intermediaries include warehousing companies, independent wholesalers, retailers and distributors.

The *customer chain* is the demand chain of the business. Figure 4.6 illustrates the customer chain of a typical organisation. Within such chains we may distinguish between local customers in the immediate marketplace of some organisation and export customers in some form of global market place. For both forms of customers, but particularly in the global market place, forms of channel organisation or *intermediary* (such as distributors and retailers) may mediate between an organisation and its customers.

Clearly the shape of the value-network, including the supply and customer chains, will vary depending upon the type of industry an organisation is in. In Figure 4.7 we illustrate three value chains from different industrial sectors. In automobile manufacturing components are produced both by subsidiaries of the major car manufacturers and external component suppliers. Such components are used to assemble cars which are passed on to the dealer network which sells cars to consumers. In food retail foodstuffs are supplied to supermarkets from warehouses and foodstuff suppliers and are sold on to the consumer. Within insurance there is little in the way of a supply chain. Insurance products are sold on to consumers via agents and brokers.

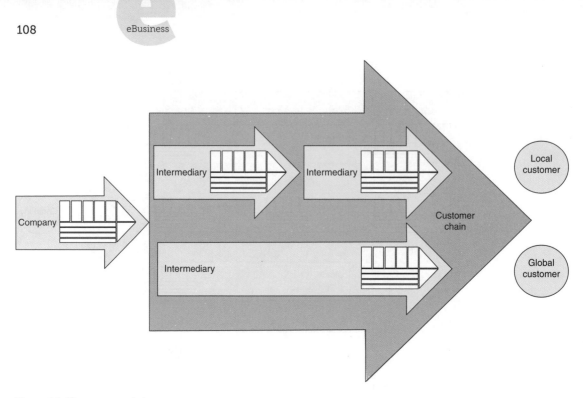

Figure 4.6 The customer chain

The supply chain and customer chain define the immediate external environment for organisations and helps define commerce or trade. However, one might argue that such chains overlap with two other frequently ignored chains of value of increasing significance to most organisations: the community chain and the partnership chain.

The *community chain*, as we have argued earlier, is founded on social networks of individuals. The value of the community chain lies in its ability to generate social capital: the productive value of people engaged in a dense network of social relations. One indicator of high social capital is a high level of inter-personal trust in a social network. This is an increasingly important pre-requisite for many forms of business and commerce.

Many modern companies also conduct trade or commerce in networks of partnerships. This is because participation in such partnership networks reduces costs and risks of operation for business. For instance, an airline might partner with both a car hire company and a hotel chain. Each member of the partnership network agrees to promote the goods and services of the other organisations in the network and may also share customer data to facilitate this. The key advantage of participation for the organisation in the partnership network is the ability to provide end-to-end value to the customer. This in turn is likely to improve both customer acquisition and customer retention for the companies involved in the partnership.

Intermediation, disintermediation and re-intermediation

Aspects of the external value chains of organisations have been critically affected by the creation of electronic markets. As we have seen, the traditional retail value

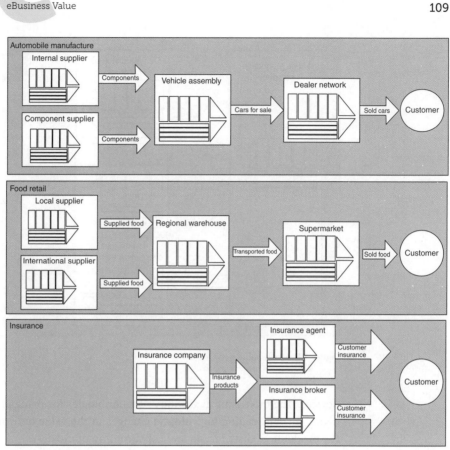

Figure 4.7 The value networks

network is one of wholesalers, distributors and retailers. However, by using the internet and applications built using the World Wide Web, producers can now sell directly to their customers. This process is known as *dis-intermediation* in the sense that intermediaries are removed in the customer chain. But the internet and web suffers from being a large and complex medium for supporting a market. Potential customers for particular products and services frequently find it difficult to locate the precise company meeting their needs. Hence, in recent times a new breed of intermediaries – electronic intermediaries have emerged. Such organisations re-impose middlemen between the producers of products and services and the consumers of such products and services. They supply a service to the consumer in locating companies fulfilling their needs and they supply a service to the producer in identifying potential customers. This process is known as *re-intermediation*.

The movie value-network

Changes are taking place in many content industries such as in the movie industry, all founded on the process of *digital convergence*. Digital convergence is the process, occurring on the global scale, of certain media converging around representation in a restricted range of digital formats. This allows inter-operability of a number of technologies, particularly what we shall refer to in the next chapter as access

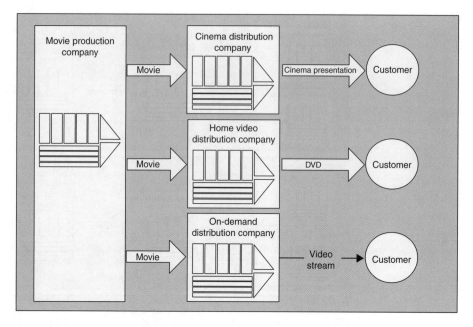

Figure 4.8 Movie value networks

devices. The increasing availability of technologies for managing movie content in digital form is leading to profound changes in the value network for this industry: the production, distribution and consumption of movies.

The value network for the current movie industry is illustrated in Figure 4.8. A movie production company creates a movie, sometimes under the umbrella of a film studio or as an independent. This movie then has to be taken up and distributed by a number of different types of distributor. Traditionally, the movie would be played for a set period in selected cinemas, perhaps owned by major cinema chains. A short time after this the movie will be released on DVD for distribution by video rental companies. More recently, the movie will be offered for digital download or for watching via some video-streaming service.

The conventional method of making a movie involves a sequence of three processes: pre-production, shooting and post-production. Pre-production involves performative activities such as establishing production schedules, establishing budgets, obtaining permits, hiring staff and purchasing equipment. Shooting involves the actual capture of pictures onto storage media using capture technology on and off set. Post-production involves the editing of movie content, including adding effects, music and other audio.

For movie companies, the whole process of production is normally a costly exercise because production staff and particularly actors are expensive. Studio space and the traditional equipment used to shoot and edit movies are also expensive. Filming certain scenes, such as action and stunt scenes, can prove particularly costly. With digital format, in terms of production, the cost of producing movies potentially decreases. For instance, the equipment required to produce high-quality movie content in terms of capture and editing has decreased substantially. The use of computer-generated imagery (CGI) has particularly reduced the costs of producing action and stunt scenes. This means that potentially barriers to entry are lowered to production in the movie industry, meaning that new producers can potentially enter the industry.

Distribution involves traditionally 'printing' the movie onto some storage medium, as well as shipping and marketing the movie. These processes in the past cost distribution companies many millions of US dollars. For this reason, the release of movie content is normally tightly controlled in a windowing sequence of cinemas first, then DVD for rental and release to pay-per-view television channels, then DVD for purchase and finally release to broadcast television.

The introduction of digital projection equipment into cinemas has been undertaken not only to improve the quality of the projection itself but also to reduce distribution costs. Digital content can be transmitted electronically to cinemas around the world for a fraction of physical distribution costs. Potential supply-chain savings of billions of US dollars have been estimated in digital content submission to cinemas. The cost of storage of film content is also much reduced. For such reasons, the movie companies themselves have made heavy investment in digital projection equipment in cinemas. However, this has meant that the movie producers wish to recoup their investment from the conventional delivery channels of cinema release before any new access channels are considered. Successful films clearly allow the film industry to recoup such investment quickly. However, the film industry points to a vast number of other films making a considerable loss.

We mentioned above that the movement of movies onto digital format also opens up new avenues for distribution and consumption of this content such as video download and video streaming. As digital content, movies are normally considered as a form of data known as video. The term video is used to refer to a number of commonly used storage formats for moving pictures. As data, video can be delivered in one of two ways. The consumer can request the whole of the video file which is delivered over some communication network to an access device such as a personal computer. The film is then stored on the access device and can be played at some later date. Alternatively, the video may be delivered as a continuous stream of data to the access device over the communication network. The video is not stored on the access device and is played at the point of access.

A number of websites now offer access to movie content, either as video downloads or as video streams. However, film producers and distributors have been slow to adopt these new business models because of both the risk it takes in film production and because until quite recently there was little incentive to move from a lucrative DVD market. Many now believe that DVD sales may have reached their peak and that the movie industry will need to investigate new ways of making revenue.

There are a number of key advantages to the online distribution of movie content. One key advantage is that movie producers and distributors can release their whole back-catalogue of content for the consumer to access. They can also distribute such content through a variety of what we shall refer to as access channels: direct-to-home movies on demand, via conventional satellite/cable into the home, via P2P sharing or IP television. Promoters of online distribution also point to the potential that digital movie content has in providing an added-value service to the consumer such as increased interactivity and personalisation of such content. Some have argued that once people are able to easily buy or rent films on demand over data communication networks, the chances are they will pay for and watch more movie content.

Others have raised difficulties posed to the distribution of movie content over the internet, particularly the increasing potential for digital piracy. Until recently, online piracy has been seen to cost the movie industry less than physical copying of DVDs. However, the gap is seen to be diminishing and some see this trend undermining key revenue models for movie producers. It is even seen by some as possibly contributing to the demise of the movie industry as we know it.

Transactions and transaction costs

Associated with the flow of any goods and services between business actors, in relations of exchange, is a corresponding flow of transactional data. As we have already seen, a transaction is fundamentally a set of formative acts (Chapter 2) operating upon one or more data structures which serves to record some coherent unit of activity, typically an event within some activity system or between activity systems.

Data are needed to support not only the internal communicative and performative activity of organisations but also the exchanges between organisations and individuals. Transactions are hence critical to the recording of organisational activity – past, current and future. Transactions typically write data to the data structures of some data system and such data are used within information systems for the measurement of organisational performance.

For instance, a customer sales order is a crucial transaction for most commercial organisations. A customer sales order effectively amounts to the representation of what we called a directive communicative act in Chapter 2. It amounts to an instruction from the customer to the organisation which details the good or service desired for a nominated price. In practice, this sales transaction will trigger a create formative act which writes a new record to a sales order file. This record acts as a memory of who made the order, when the order was made, for what goods or services and in what quantities. Such records are critical for triggering other performative activities such as the picking of goods from warehouses and the distribution of goods to customers. It is also likely to be important to measuring the sales performance of the company. Hence, each exchange event between business actors generates a transaction. As well as records which record the order and transfer of goods and services, one of the most prominent types of transaction type is that of payments.

One of the key questions that has concerned economics for many decades is why the economy is populated by a number of business firms, instead of consisting exclusively of a multitude of independent, self-employed people who contract with one another in complex networks of exchange, which is what classical economics would predict as the natural state of affairs based upon models of supply and demand. Transaction costs, or what we shall more accurately refer to as coordination costs, are critical to providing answers to this so-called question of the nature of the firm. Coordination costs also, as we shall see, helps explain the increasing importance of ICT to commerce and the ways in which such technology can and is being used to transform economic systems.

The economist Ronald Coase, way back in the 1930s, used the idea of *transaction costs* or coordination costs to develop a theory as to when certain economic tasks would be performed by firms and when they would be performed by the market. A transaction or coordination cost is a cost incurred in making an economic exchange. For example, when buying or selling a financial security a commission is normally paid to a broker; the commission is a coordination cost of undertaking a deal on the stock market. Or consider purchasing a textbook. The 'costs' in such a purchase not only include the price of the book itself but also the energy and effort expended in finding the most appropriate textbook for the most appropriate price from the most convenient bookselling outfit.

Hence, Coase noted that there are a number of coordination costs to using any exchange network for the trading of goods and services. Firms attempt to balance production costs against coordination costs. Production costs include the processes necessary to create and distribute goods and services. Coordination costs or transaction costs include the costs of information and data processing (communication and representation) necessary to coordinate the work of people and machines.

This idea he used to suggest that firms will arise when they can arrange to produce all that they need internally and thus reduce their coordination costs. This theory has also been used to attempt to explain why firms engage in relationships with other firms and what form such relationships take. This is fundamentally an issue of how the organisation controls its activities: does it perform them in-house or does it farm them out to other organisations in the wider value-network?

For example, the movie industry can be considered to consist of a complex assemblage of business actors including film production companies, suppliers of cinematography equipment, specialist pre-production and post-production personnel, film directors, actors and other film personnel. This list does not include a vast range of potential movie distributors. During the 1940s and 1950s the Hollywood movie industry was dominated by a number of large studios. These studios pulled as many of the activities of the movie industry in-house. This enabled them to better control their activities both in terms of the costs of production and the coordination of the numerous peoples and activities involved. However, the modern movie industry, partly in response to technological change, consists of a much more diverse network of actors. A number of Hollywood studios still exist but large centres of film-making also exist in India, Hong Kong and Nigeria. The value-network in the movie industry is now much more diverse and distributed globally.

Control in the value network

The upshot of conceiving of organisations as value-creating systems raises the critical question of what activities the organisation itself needs to perform in-house and what activities it can outsource to other organisations. If the organisation decides to outsource activities it also needs to decide how it will manage or govern the interaction with other organisations. These questions can hence be seen to revolve around the issue of how to control parts of the value network.

This means that it is possible to see the 'design' of the value network of a particular organisation as a response to the issue of control which we considered in Chapter 2. As we have argued in previous sections, a wider economy can be considered as a system or network of exchange. Within such networks of exchange, ways have to be found of controlling the flow of value (goods and services) amongst a multitude of business actors. It is useful to define two polar types of such control which are referred to in the literature as managerial hierarchies and markets. These forms are actually two poles of a dimension which help define a range of intermediate forms of control evident in actual value networks. These types of economic control process are important for understanding why various parts of the value network, such as supply chains, develop as they do. They also help us understand how both existing forms of eBusiness are formed in particular ways as well as the value of emerging forms of eBusiness (Chapter 7).

Hierarchies

Hierarchies, or more accurately managerial hierarchies, are a logical extension of the firm itself. Hierarchies coordinate the flow of value by controlling and directing it at a higher level in management structures. In hierarchies, order is designed and consciously organised to achieve outcomes. This is the traditional form of control exercised within and between public sector organisations. In government this typically constitutes bureaucratic control since behaviour is very much governed by rules and procedures. In hierarchies, the mechanisms of operation involve bureaucratic monitoring and interventions and as such hierarchies demonstrate overt, planned, purposeful governance.

Simplistically, hierarchies can be seen as typically systems of cooperation. A managerial hierarchy is a medium for exchanges between a limited number of buyers and sellers and the buyers and sellers exchange goods and services within established patterns of trade. Hence, hierarchies form the cooperative environment of organisations and, typically because of the established nature of relationships between economic actors, they rely on smaller volumes of communication and associated data flow than is the case in terms of markets (see next section).

Most companies have established trading relationships with a limited number of suppliers and as such these relationships are traditionally managed in terms of managerial hierarchies. Hence, an automobile manufacturer is likely to build established trading relationships with a limited range of component suppliers. It is also likely to distribute its products through a specialised network of dealerships. Hence, both the supply chain and the customer chain within traditional automobile manufacture will be organised as a series of hierarchies. Within the movie industry a production company will normally interact with a limited range of suppliers such as equipment suppliers and agents of actors.

Markets

Markets coordinate the flow of value through forces of supply and demand and external transactions between actors in some exchange relationship (Figure 4.10).

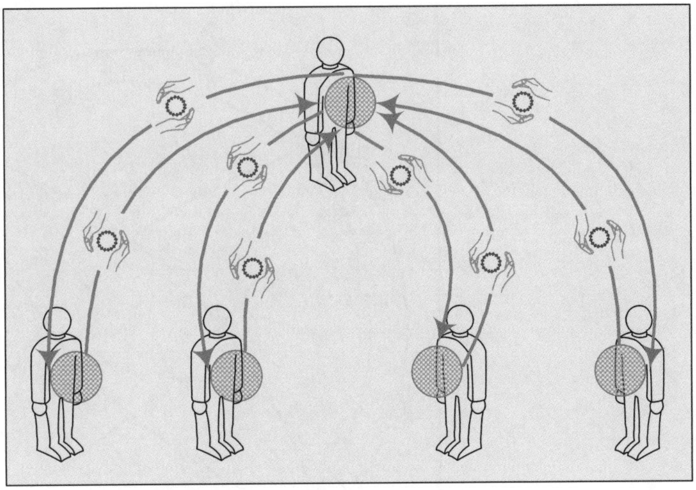

Figure 4.9 A managerial hierarchy

In markets, order is not pre-defined: it develops or emerges from spontaneously generated outcomes. This is the form of control seen as typical in the private sector since in markets behaviour arises from private competitive decisions. Within markets operations are governed by price, competition and self-interest. Hence, markets do not display any overt form of governance. Instead, governance is implicit and emergent rather than planned.

Put simply, markets are typically systems of competition. A market is a medium for exchanges between many potential buyers and many potential sellers and, at least for larger companies, a series of markets forms the immediate competitive environment of the organisation. However, because of its many-to-many nature a market is heavily reliant on large volumes of data and communication flow. Participation in markets traditionally generates what we referred to above as a large amount of 'transaction costs' for a company.

One of the crucial markets for financial companies is the stock market. The stock market is a market for the exchange of shares and other forms of securities. Companies trade shares through financial intermediaries to a vast range of financial consumers many of which will be other companies. The price of a particular company share is determined by the forces of supply and demand. In other words, the more demand for a particular security, the higher its price. The movie industry also partakes in a number of markets. For instance, it sells its movies to cinema chains, distributors of DVDs and more recently to online video on-demand operations.

Value networks

We have deliberately used the term network in this chapter in terms such as social network, the value network and exchange network because such networks can be seen as a model of control that accommodates both market structures and managerial hierarchies. The value-network of a particular company, for instance, is likely to involve both cooperation with other business actors and competition with such actors.

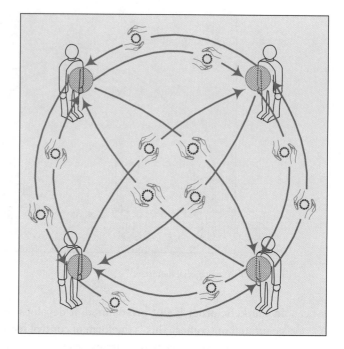

Figure 4.10 A market

As we have seen, many modern companies conduct trade or commerce in networks of partnerships. This is because participation in such partnership networks reduces costs and risks of operation for business. For instance, an airline might partner with both a car hire company and a hotel chain. Each member of the partnership network agrees to promote the goods and services of the other organisations in the network and may also share customer data in the process.

Production costs and coordination costs

We can bring together the idea of control and transaction costs to help us understand how value networks develop as they do for a particular company and what influence technology plays in this process. Malone *et al* (1987), for instance, argue that markets and hierarchies can be distinguished in terms of the balance of production costs to coordination (transaction) costs.

As we have seen, production costs include the processes necessary to create and distribute goods and services. Coordination costs or transaction costs include the costs of communication necessary to coordinate the work of people and machines. As we have argued above, markets are generally characterised by low production costs and high coordination costs. In contrast, hierarchies typically have high production costs and low coordination costs.

Malone *et al.* argued in the 1980s that the increase of ICT use would stimulate a trend towards electronic markets and electronic hierarchies. They also argued for the dominance of market forms because ICT would decrease the costs of coordination and would enable companies to greater personalised goods and services, thus enabling them to better handle issues of product complexity and asset specificity.

More recently, Don Tapscott and Anthony Williams (2006) have proposed that the internet and the web is critically changing the logic of the firm. The presence of such technological infrastructure is forcing a decline not only in transaction costs but also in the costs of 'production' as well. They attribute the latter to the growth in collaborative production facilitated by technologies built upon the global communication infrastructure. So-called open-source software production is a case in point. Open source software is produced by a large network of collaborating software developers. They infer from this that network forms of governance and control in economic systems will begin to overtake traditional pure hierarchy and market forms over the first quarter of the 21st century.

Business models

The concept of a business model has become popular in recent times as a way of thinking about business change, particularly as such change incorporates some form of technological innovation. We would argue that the business model concept implicitly uses a model of the organisation based in the idea of an open, value-creating system. This means that the patterns of organisation that produce particular forms of value are not fixed. Open systems can be designed and it is in this light that the concept of business model is frequently discussed.

Therefore, we would argue that there are clear similarities between the concept of a business model and that of a value-creating system (VCS). To refresh, according to this view, organisations are conceived of as chains of activity systems associated with the production and dissemination of value which in their entirety can be portrayed as value-creating systems. Such value-creating systems have to manage not only their internal operations but also their relationships with other business actors within the wider value-network.

As such, a business model can be considered the organisation's core logic for creating value. The business model idea, as we shall see, is useful in relating business strategy to activity systems to information systems to ICT systems. The pre-supposition of design implies that a given business has a number of different options in terms of the particular business model it may choose to adopt. With the rise of eBusiness and eCommerce such options multiply. Traditionally, business strategies specify how a particular business model can be applied to a particular industrial sector to improve competitive position. More recently such strategies must specify relationships with customers, partners and suppliers.

Osterwalder and Pigneur (2010) argue that any business model is built from nine basic building blocks: value propositions, customer segments, channels, customer relationships, revenue streams, key resources, key activities, key partnerships and cost structure. These building blocks form a canvas for specifying or designing a particular business model. We adapt these building blocks in terms of the theory we have established in this and preceding chapters.

First, a business model establishes the value proposition of the organisation. In other words, what does an organisation create, produce or provide? Second, value is created for particular customer segments. In other words, for whom are we creating value? Third, value is distributed to customer segments through access channels. This includes not only the physical delivery of a product or service but also the associated communication with the customer such as allowing customers to purchase specific products and services as well as providing after-sales support to the customer. Fourth, to be successful a business model must propose ways of building and sustaining customer relationships. This implies that it must suggest ways of managing what we shall call processes of customer acquisition, customer retention and customer extension. Fifth, a particular business model specifies the structure of activity, information and data systems appropriate for a particular business in terms of its environment. A key part of the argument used for adaptive systems is that the model of the business must fit environmental circumstances. The so-called model for the business must be founded in its key value-chains and be viable in this environment. Its activities must also be sustainable long-term. Sixth, a business model should specify not only the value delivered to customers within the wider value-network but also the value it gains from suppliers and partners. To create value for its customers an organisation needs resources from suppliers. It also needs to establish relationships with partnering organisations. Seventh, and finally, a business model should specify the major streams of revenue and how the costs of producing value for customers are outweighed sufficiently by such revenue to make the business both viable and sustainable.

The movie industry

Let us consider the movie industry in this light. This case demonstrates the way in which ICT is starting to re-structure a major industry. The changes taking place in the movie industry are illustrative of the fact that any technology has opportunities as well as threats for industries. In particular, technology adoption is likely to change business models because of the ways in which it affects the wider value network.

As we have seen above, the traditional value network in the movie industry consists of major film producers, major global distributors and mass consumers. The control of the content (value) along such a network has typically been heavily controlled in a sequence of release to cinema chains, then onto DVD to the rental network and finally for DVD sale to the general public.

For over 20 years the conventional business model for renting movies has been through a physical video and more lately DVD rental outlet. These are effectively intermediaries in the distribution of movie content to customers. However, over the past couple of years there has been a significant decline in the amount of exchange activity conducted with such physical rental outlets, partly due to the rise of online DVD rental, as exemplified by Netflix and LoveFilm. These companies have built new business models for the distribution of DVDs and are progressively establishing yet another business model for the distribution of such content via on-demand video streaming.

LoveFilm, for instance, is a British subsidiary of Amazon.com. It provides a number of services through its website including online DVD rental, DVD direct sales and more recently video streaming of movies over the internet. It provides an online delivery structure for an array of services in a series of partnerships with other companies. In 2011 it claimed to offer over 67,000 movie titles for 1.5 million customers and handled over 4 million rentals per month to customers located in five countries. In terms of online DVD rental LoveFilm charges a flat monthly rate to its customers. Depending on the amount paid, customers have delivered to their homes through the post a number of DVDs which they can keep for as long as they wish. DVDs are returned in pre-paid envelopes to the company. Members of a certain level are able to stream a selected range of movies to their home PCs or to their interactive digital televisions free of charge. Other movies can be streamed on a pay-per-view basis. Netflix is an American company operating a similar business model within the USA and Canada. This company, which was established in 1997, offers over 100,000 titles on DVD to a subscriber base of over 10 million subscribers.

Summary

We have considered organisations as value-creating systems that interact with a wider value-network. In such terms, organisations have the option to design their internal activity systems and their relationships and activities with the wider value-network to optimise their performance.

The primary environment of any commercial organisation is the economy. Economies are systems or networks of exchange for value. Economies consist of systems not only of value production but also of value distribution and value consumption. An organisation's value is hence determined by its position within a wider value network.

Typically, the value associated with an organisation equates with the services and/or products provided by the organisation. However, value also emerges from dispersed forms of 'organisation' evident in wider social networks. Such forms of value relate to social capital; the resources available for mutual support in forms of community. Social capital is the key value that members gain from participation in such social networks.

Goods and services can be distinguished in a number of ways. We have been particularly interested in the 'materiality' of such goods and services. Tangible goods and services have a physical form. Intangible goods and services have a non-physical form and hence are amenable to representation as data.

Associated with the flow of both tangible and intangible goods and services is a corresponding flow of transactions. A transaction is a data structure that records some coherent unit of activity, typically an event within some activity system or between activity systems.

Exchange between business actors is typically controlled either in terms of markets or hierarchies. Markets are systems of competition. They are complex systems of one-time exchange between buyers and sellers. In contrast, managerial hierarchies are systems of cooperation. Exchange within hierarchies is conducted on the basis of established trading arrangements. In practice, the value-networks of organisations organise as both markets and hierarchies. Value-networks are forms of economic control in which both cooperation and competition are evident.

Porter proposed a template for the activity systems of the typical business which he refers to as the internal value-chain and which consists of a defined set of primary and secondary activities engaged in by the typical businesses. However, two other chains of value are normally seen as critical to the value-network of most organisations: the supply chain and the customer chain. We have argued that these three value-chains overlap with another frequently ignored chain of value of increasing significance to organisations. This we have referred to as the community chain and proposed that it is founded on social networks of individuals. The value of the community chain lies in its ability to generate social capital – one indicator of which is a high level of inter-personal trust – an essential pre-requisite for many forms of business and commerce.

The concept of the internal value-chain and the wider value-network provide the business analyst with ways of considering the potential of changes to business systems in terms of not only competitive performance but also in improvements in managing networks of cooperative relationships both with other organisations and to the global network of individuals from which such businesses draw their customers. Hence, the design of business models and the value-network of organisations are inherently inter-twined.

Review test

Economic actors include ...	Select all that apply
Customers	
Suppliers	
Regulators	
Partners	
Controllers	

A _____ is some form of product produced by an organisation. A _____ is some form of activity performed by an organisation.	Fill in the blanks

Intangible goods are those that do not have a physical existence and are fundamentally information-based	True or False?
True	
False	

Inbound logistics is a primary activity in Porter's value-chain	True or False?
True	
False	

Human resource management is a primary activity in Porter's value-chain	True or False?
True	
False	

Match the type of value chain to the appropriate definition		Match the elements
Customer chain	A series of interdependent activities that produces a product or service for a customer/consumer	
Supply chain	A series of interdependent activities by which an organisation sources products or services from other individuals, groups or organisations	
Internal value-chain	A series of interdependent activities by which an organisation sells its products or services to customers	

_____ capital is the productive value of people engaged in a dense network of social relations.	Fill in the blank

A _____ cost is a cost incurred in making an economic exchange	Fill in the blank

How does the value-chain differ from the value-network?	Write two sentences

Define disintermediation	Write two sentences

Exercises

- Try to model a public sector organisation such as a university in terms of the internal value-chain.
- eMedicine is a developing area of medical practice and involves the remote treatment of patients using ICT. Experiments have even been undertaken in performing surgical operations using robotic devices controlled across communication networks. How would you class this form of service – tangible or intangible?
- Identify the elements of the supply chain, customer chain and internal value-chain of an organisation known to you.
- Consider a company which produces trucks for haulage contractors. Determine whether this business sector would be arranged as a market or a hierarchy.
- Provide one other example of a market and describe what is exchanged. Provide one other example of a managerial hierarchy and determine what established trading relationships exist in this hierarchy. Describe the actors, relationships, information and transactions in some segment of a market or hierarchy known to you.
- Unpack the example of LoveFilm in terms of the building blocks of a business model.

Projects

- Select one industrial sector such as retail or finance. Investigate and detail the changes caused within the sector over the past 20 years through the application of ICT. What effect has this had on competitiveness within the sector and on the shape of the sector generally?

- Investigate ways of measuring social capital in a community. For instance, develop some ways in which you might map the social network underlying some virtual community. What sort of bonds or links exists in this network? Are they strong or weak links and what level of mutual support is provided to members of the social network through such links?
- Investigate the relationship between transaction costs and consumer behaviour. For instance, what sort of transaction costs are involved in changing between particular utility (gas, electricity, water, broadband) suppliers on the part of the consumer? Has the web reduced such so-called switching costs?
- Investigate the degree to which music constitutes an information commodity (intangible good) and the consequences this has for the music industry. Try to treat the problem as one demanding some form of value-network analysis.
- Try to take a traditional business and specify its business model in terms of the concepts from this and preceding chapters. Consider whether in the information age there are alternative business models for such an organisation. Specify one of these business models.

Critical reflection

Consider an industry known to you such as perhaps banking, insurance or the publishing industry. Consider how these industries have changed over the past 20 years. Attempt to use the concepts of the value-chain, value-network and business model to help describe what has been happening to such industries. Is it possible to consider the effect of ICT upon such industrial change purely in relation to coordination costs as compared to 'production' costs?

How relevant is the idea of a value-chain for understanding the dynamics of public or voluntary sector organisations? What would constitute the supply and demand chains of a higher education institution such as a university? Would you say there is any disintermediation in the higher education sector?

Case exploration

Consider another content industry comparable to the movie industry discussed in this chapter and try to analyse its value-network. For instance, consider Apple (see case) and its use of the iTunes site and access devices such as the iPod and more recently the iPad to distribute music. In what way is digital music value? What type of value does it constitute? How is such value produced, distributed and consumed? Who are the major actors in the value network and how do they communicate? Try to consider why the Apple business model is particularly successful in terms of this form of content.

Two other content industries worth exploring in relation to the effect that ICT is having upon business models are that of book publishing and the music industry. Read the eBooks or the music industry case at the end of the book and try to identify similarities or differences with the way in which technology is affecting the movie industry.

Further reading

The theory of social networks has been around for some time – particularly in the work of Granovetter and others. The book by Christakis and Fowler (2010) has recently popularised the issue. Porter's original conceptions of the value-chain and his model of the competitive environment of the organisation are re-considered for the internet age (Porter, 2001). Sawney and Parikh (2001) consider the issue of value and ways in which value changes in a connected world. Paolini (1999) introduces the idea of the organisation as a value-creating system. Coase's (1937) work on transaction costs forms the basis for Malone *et al.*'s (1987) treatment of electronic markets and hierarchies and the more recent popular discussion of this in Tapscott and Williams' consideration of new collaborative forms of working supported through ICT (2006). Osterwalder and Pigneur (2010) provide a highly graphic account of the generation business models, with many examples from eBusiness.

References

Christakis, N. and J. Fowler. (2010). *Connected: The Amazing Power of Social Networks and How They Shape Our Lives*, New York, Harper Press.

Coase, R. H. (1937). The Nature of the Firm. *Economica* 4(16): 386–405.

Granovetter, M. (1973). The Strength of Weak Ties. *American Journal of Sociology* 78(6): 1360–1380.

Malinowski, B. (1922). *Argonauts of the Western Pacific: An Account of Native Enterprise and Adventure in the Archipelagoes of Western New Guinea*, London, Routledge Kegan Paul.

Malone, T. W., J. Yates and R.I. Benjamin. (1987). Electronic Markets and Electronic Hierarchies. *CACM - Communications of The ACM* 30(6): 484–497.

Maslow, A. (1954). *Motivation and Personality*, Cambridge, MA, Harper and Row.

Osterwalder, A. and Y. Pigneur. (2010). *Business Model Generation*, Hoboken, NJ, John Wiley.

Paolini, C. (1999). *The Value Net: a Tool for Competitive Strategy*, Chichester, John Wiley.

Porter, M. E. (1985). *Competitive Advantage: Creating and Sustaining Superior Performance*, New York, Free Press.

Porter, M. E. (2001). Strategy and the Internet. *Harvard Business Review* 79(3): 63–78.

Putnam, R. D. (2000). *Bowling Alone: the Collapse and Revival of American Community*, New York, Simon and Schuster.

Sawhney, M. and D. Parikh. (2001). Where Value Lies in a Networked World. *Harvard Business Review* 79(1): 79–86.

Tapscott, D. and A. D. Williams. (2006). *Wikinomics: How Mass Collaboration Changes Everything*, London, Atlantic Books.

5 eBusiness infrastructure

Activity Systems · Data Systems · Information Systems · Front-end · Back-end

Learning outcomes	Principles
Relate the importance of infrastructure to organisation.	By infrastructure we mean the ways in which performative, informative and formative action is conventionally conducted within organisations. Infrastructure is both enabling and constraining. Existing infrastructure is the platform upon which innovation can be built. But infrastructure also constrains the range of possibility available to organisational change.
Describe the four levels of infrastructure and how they inter-relate.	Organisational infrastructure consists of four layers corresponding to the distinction between activity, communication and representation. The activity infrastructure of any organisation relies on a corresponding information, information systems and ICT infrastructure.
Explain the workings of the major elements of information systems infrastructure.	In terms of information systems infrastructure, it is possible to distinguish between those information systems that directly interface with organisational stakeholders of various forms (front-end information systems) and those which form the core information-handling systems of the organisation (back-end information systems).
Relate the importance of information infrastructure.	The information systems infrastructure of some organisation is reliant on an integrated information infrastructure. High-level information models are therefore important to recognising and managing the inter-dependencies between information systems within organisations.
Explain the idea of data infrastructure.	Information and information systems infrastructure relies upon a corresponding data systems infrastructure. Such data systems consist of sequences of formative acts acting upon data structures.

Introduction

Organised activity of whatever form requires infrastructure. *Infrastructure* consists of systems of social organisation and technology that support human activity. For example, a road infrastructure is both a supporting social and technical (socio-technical) infrastructure for travel: the associated activity system. A road infrastructure enables traffic to get from point A to point B using motorways, carriageways and major or minor roads. This is the technological infrastructure of the road network which supports the activity system of transport or travel using vehicles such as automobiles.

In terms of business we shall argue that there are four layers of infrastructure: activity systems infrastructure, *information infrastructure*, information systems infrastructure and ICT Infrastructure (Figure 5.1). Each of these layers is critically dependent on the layer below it. As we have seen, organisations can be viewed as complex collections of activity systems and the wider environment within which they interact as a value network. Information is essential to the effective coordination of value-creating activity in organisations and is supplied by information systems. Modern information systems rely on ICT to a greater or lesser extent and data systems infrastructure is a crucial part of ICT infrastructure.

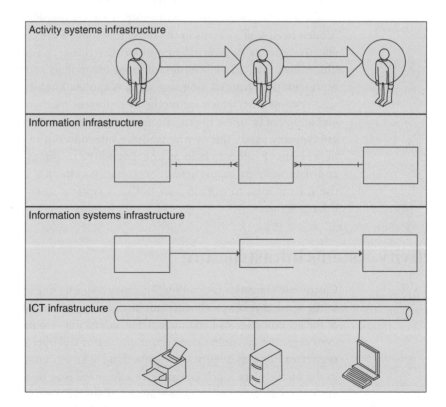

Figure 5.1 Levels of infrastructure

Business analysis and business modelling

Business analysis is that activity devoted to the analysis of business systems. To engage in business analysis we make models of business systems and such modelling is undertaken for three major reasons. First, a model is a simplification: it abstracts the things of interest from some situation and thereby manages the complexity inherent in the situation. Second, a model is a representation: we use some agreed signs to represent things of interest in the situation considered to be problematic. Third, a model is a medium for communication between multiple actors: we can use models to communicate and agree common understanding about some situation. On the basis of this common understanding we can take action.

Take the idea of a tube, metro or subway map as an example of a model. A map of a metro system is a particularly good, everyday example of the practical use of models in everyday situations. What is significant for the user of the London Underground, Paris Metro or New York Subway is the topology of this transport system; in other words, how stations within the underground railway system are connected. Such a map is hence a model of the actual underground railway network in the sense that it highlights or abstracts key features of the network for its users, typically by representing them as a sign-system: a series of circles (for stations) and coloured line segments (for tube lines). Such maps communicate to potential users of the tube or subway its role as an aid to mutual and coordinated performance by a multitude of human actors, to travel across some city-space.

There is hence a clear relationship between models and signs (Chapter 2). Models need sign-systems in the sense that models are created through signs and effectively act as an external communicative resource amongst a group of actors. This means that, all such representations are models and all models are forms of representation. Natural language such as spoken English is clearly the richest of sign-systems with which we model or represent our 'world'. Clearly, for analysis and design of business organisation, more restricted and formalised sign systems are typically used. This is why we have introduced a range of visual constructs in previous chapters to help us understand the workings of activity, information and data systems in particular organisations. In this chapter we continue to use such models to explain how business systems inter-relate to build business infrastructure.

Activity systems infrastructure

Clearly each business is different. This may be partly due to different environments in the sense that obviously different business organisations are in different sectors of the economy – retail, manufacturing, education – to name but a few. However, even organisations in the same economic sector will operate differently. Part of the reason for this may be to achieve something of an advantage over their *competitors* in the marketplace. Such competitive advantage may be achieved in a number of ways: through differentiation in human activity, efficiency of human activity and/or effectiveness in activity.

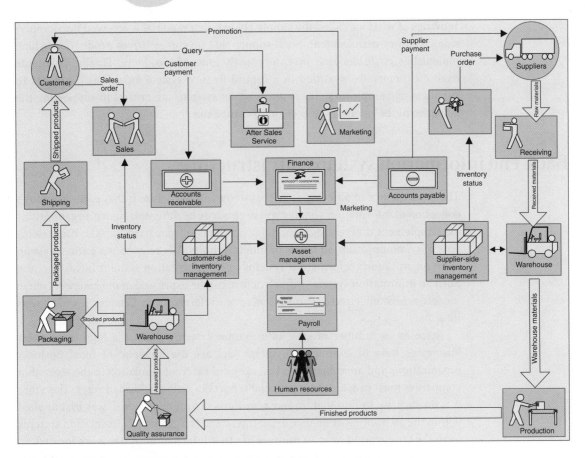

Figure 5.2 Activity systems infrastructure of a typical manufacturing organisation

Figure 5.2 provides a schematic of an *activity systems infrastructure* for a typical manufacturing company, which can be seen to be an elaboration of the idea of the value-chain discussed in the previous chapter. Such an activity systems infrastructure can be expressed in terms of activity system models, which effectively serve to represent what we called performa in Chapter 2. In the typical business organisation, infrastructure consists of a number of activity sub-systems such as sales, after-sales, marketing, purchasing, receiving, warehousing, production, human resources, packing and shipping. Such activity sub-systems relate together in flows of physical items (broad arrows) as well as data (narrow arrows).

The flow of data in support of activity defines the information systems infrastructure of relevance to the business. On the one side, sales orders from customers act as the major input into the organisation. Sales orders trigger packaging and shipment of goods from customer-side inventory back to the customer. This part of information systems infrastructure therefore supports activities within what we referred to in the previous chapter as the customer chain. Marketing and after-sales service also engage in an attempt to build a long-term relationship with the customer. On the other side, purchase orders from the company trigger the shipment of raw materials by suppliers. Hence, these information systems support the activities of what we called the supply chain. Such material is received into supply-side inventory management. Such supply-side inventory drives production which replenishes customer-side inventory with finished products. Finally, payments from customers are recorded in a central finance system as well as payments to suppliers and employees. These information systems are critical to supporting the activities of the internal value-chain of companies.

Back-end information systems infrastructure

The consequence of differing activity systems infrastructure is that each company's collection of information systems will necessarily be different. Hence, organisations may implement different operational procedures or may parcel up the basic elements of communication in terms of different units. We refer to the entire makeup of an organisation's information systems as its information systems infrastructure. Such an information systems infrastructure can be expressed in *information system models*, which effectively represent what we referred to in Chapter 2 as business informa.

There are a number of core information systems that, at a high level, most businesses have in common. Financial data are the lifeblood of most business organisations and are subject to a vast range of external regulation in the sense that companies must prepare their financial reports in well-established ways. Therefore it is no surprise to find that, in most business organisations, ICT was first applied within the accounting or finance department and that financial information systems form the core around which a number of other information systems are located.

Core information systems constitute the so-called *back-end* (sometimes referred to as the back-office) systems of some company. They are critical to the performance of core activity systems within business such as sales and production. Around this core a number of *front-end* information systems will exist. Such systems face the major stakeholders of the business: managers, employees, customers and suppliers. Hence, we refer to such information systems in terms of four groups: *management information systems, employee-facing information systems, customer-facing information systems* and *supplier-facing information systems*.

Most companies of whatever size will need an information system for recording orders for products/services from customers, orders made to suppliers for products/services and the amounts paid or due to employees. Many businesses that sell products are therefore founded around a number of such key information systems. Sales-order processing is an information system that records details of sales orders from customers. Inventory management is the information system that maintains an inventory of raw material from suppliers and finished goods stored in warehouses ready to be shipped to customers. Purchase order processing is that information system that records details of purchase orders to suppliers. Finance is that system that records amounts owed and paid by customers, amounts owed to and paid to suppliers, and amounts paid to and owed to employees. Finally, payroll is the information system that records details of wages and payments made to employees.

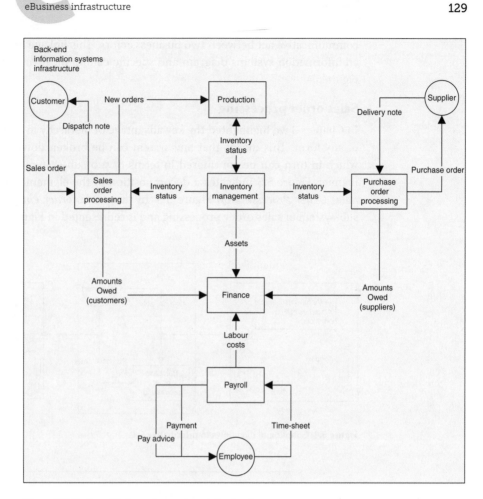

Figure 5.3 Back-end information systems infrastructure

Businesses which sell services will operate differently in the sense of having different activity systems. Hence, although they will have core information systems in similar areas these will operate differently from that described in this chapter. Figure 5.3 illustrates some of the flows of data (represented by labelled arrows) between these major back-end information systems.

It must be remembered that an activity system diagram is an abstraction of a number of performative patterns evident in some organisational situation. Likewise, an information system diagram such as the one in Figure 5.3 is an abstraction of a number of informative or communicative patterns supporting performative patterns. Hence, the arrow labelled delivery note in Figure 5.4, which flows between the actor *supplier* and the process *purchase order processing* can be seen to effectively represent an abstraction of an assertion that a particular order has been delivered between some business actor in the supplier organisation (such as a supplier clerk) and a business actor in the manufacturing organisation (such as a purchasing clerk). Likewise, the arrow labelled *purchase order* that flows between the same process and the supplier can be seen to represent a directive communicative act between two business actors. This linkage between elements of an information systems diagram and specific communicative acts is illustrated in Figure 5.4.

Sales order processing

In Chapter 3 we highlighted the key advantage of hierarchy in considering systems of any form. This means that any system can be broken down into sub-systems, which in turn can be considered in terms of sub-sub-systems, and so on. In this manner, Figure 5.5 indicates a decomposition of the elements of the process box *Sales Order Processing* on Figure 5.3. In turn, *sales order entry* can be seen as a sub-system of sales order processing and is represented in Figure 5.6.

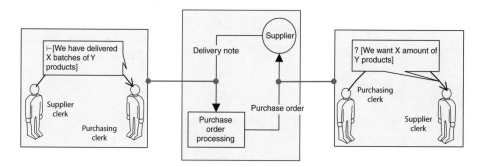

Figure 5.4 Coupling of data flows to informative acts

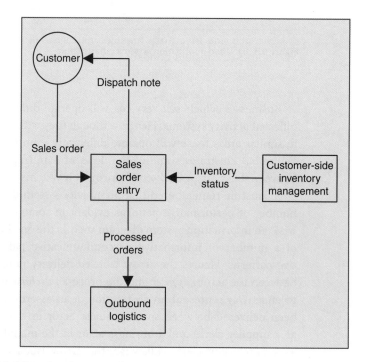

Figure 5.5 Sales order processing information system

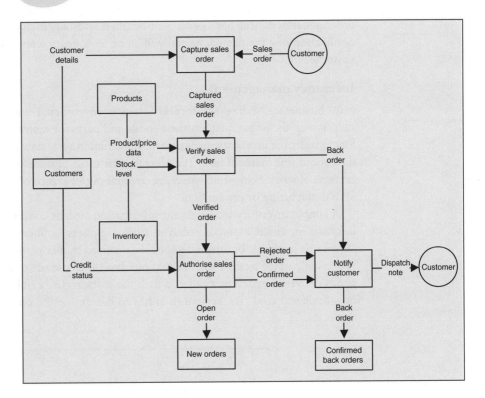

Figure 5.6 Sales order entry information system

Sales order processing is an information system that communicates with a customer-side inventory management system. This is necessary to check the availability of finished goods for the customer. It will also pass processed orders to an outbound logistics system which dispatches goods to customers matching original sales orders. The customer is notified of the form and timing of intended delivery.

A suggested decomposition of the order entry subsystem is given in Figure 5.6. Note, we have provided data stores on this diagram – repositories for data – represented by labelled, open boxes. This is to indicate the important reliance of actual information systems on records of the things of interest to some organisation, such as a company's products or customers. Such repositories, as we shall see, act as a crucial link between the information systems infrastructure and the data systems infrastructure.

Order entry is a key process that interfaces to the organisation's customers. Order entry captures the key information needed to process a customer order. Traditionally, orders might be expected to arrive through the post or over the telephone line. More recently orders may be sent electronically and come over the internet as XML documents.

Normally the order entry system would make an enquiry of the stock control system to check that suitable quantities of the desired item are available. If an order item cannot be filled then a substitute item might be suggested or a back order generated. This back order will be filled later when stock is replenished. A notification of a confirmed, partially filled or back order would be supplied to the customer.

Inventory management

Most businesses have several forms of stock or inventory. These include raw materials, materials for packing, finished goods and parts for maintenance of products. Stock control or inventory management information systems are designed to record data about this material flow. The objective for most businesses is to minimise the amount of stock held whilst ensuring optimal performance of other systems such as manufacturing or production.

A simple inventory management information system concerned with handling information about material received from suppliers is illustrated in Figure 5.7. When raw materials or finished goods are received by an organisation then a check is normally made against the original purchase order made to the supplier. If the goods delivered match that ordered then the stock record can be updated with the quantities supplied. The system then has to determine the optimal place to store

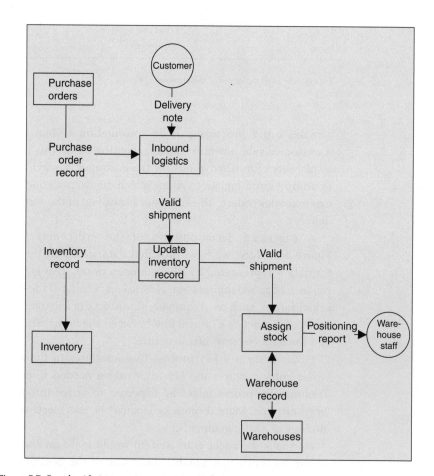

Figure 5.7 Supply-side inventory management information system

the stock in the company's warehouses. Once this is determined then a positioning report is generated for use by warehousing staff and the warehousing record updated.

Minimal stock levels are a crucial element of a modern business philosophy known as just in time (JIT) manufacturing. Providing facilities for storing stock of raw materials needed for manufacture is a critical cost to the business. The more stock held, the greater the costs incurred. JIT aims to store only enough stock to meet the short-term needs of production. Warehouses are replenished with raw materials *just in time* to ensure efficient production.

Purchase order processing

Figure 5.8 represents elements of a standard purchase order processing information system. Purchases may be generated in two ways. The inventory management

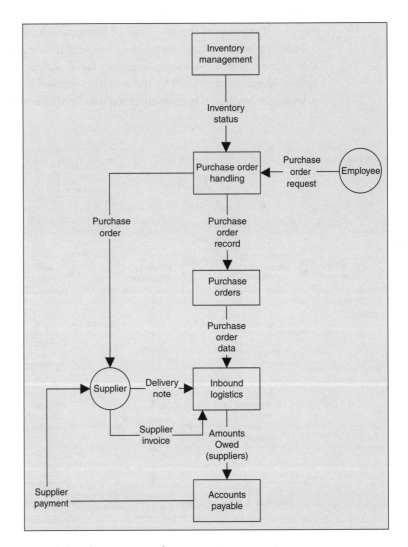

Figure 5.8 Purchase order processing information system

system itself may generate an automatic purchase order if the level of a stock item falls below a certain level. Most medium to large organisations will have a purchasing or procurement unit. Staff in this unit will be generating purchase orders on the basis of requests it receives from the inventory management system or from requests from staff for those items not included within the general remit of inventory management. Purchase orders will be produced by purchase order handling and then sent to relevant suppliers.

This information will then be used to update an inbound logistics information system that will check information it has on purchase orders against invoices it receives from suppliers. If the goods received from suppliers match purchase order information then financial information about the amounts owed to suppliers is passed on to a major sub-system within a financial information system: accounts payable.

Finance

Figure 5.9 represents the workings of a standard financial information system or accounting information system. Most financial information systems are divided up into three major sub-systems: accounts receivable, accounts payable and general ledger. The data store used by the accounts receivable system is generally called a sales ledger because it records financial details of all amounts owed by customers to

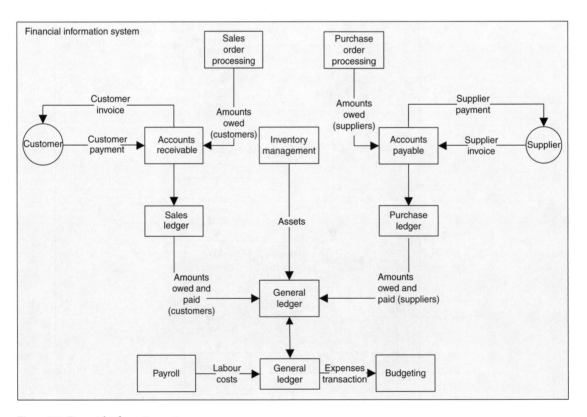

Figure 5.9 Financial information system

the organisation. The data store used by the accounts payable system is sometimes called the purchase ledger because it stores details of all monies owed to suppliers by the organisation. A third accounting system called a general ledger system is used to record details of all the financial transactions relevant to an organisation: income, expenditure and assets. It hence receives data from accounts payable, accounts receivable and inventory management systems.

The accounts receivable system is essential for managing the cash flow of the company. When goods are shipped to customers a record of the amount owed by customers is passed on to the accounts receivable system. This leads to the customer's account being updated. When customers send payments to the company the credit balance of the customer is reduced by the appropriate amount. The information about customer credit and amounts paid are regularly used to update the general ledger system.

The accounts payable system is also essential for managing the cash flow of the company. When goods are ordered from suppliers a record of the amount owed to suppliers is passed on to the accounts payable system. This leads to the supplier's account being updated. When the organisation makes payments to its suppliers the credit balance owed to suppliers is reduced by the appropriate amount. The information about credit owed to suppliers and amounts paid are regularly used to update the general ledger system.

The third key input into a general ledger system is a payroll system. The payroll system will regularly update the general ledger with the costs incurred in paying staff. There will also be an input into the general ledger from the inventory management system detailing the current financial position of assets held by the company.

Payroll

Figure 5.10 represents elements of a standard *payroll information system*.

Payroll produces two primary outputs: some payment to the employee, and a record (payslip or pay advice) of the details of payments made. The key input into a payroll system is some information of the work undertaken during a given time period such as a week or month. These details may be collected on time-sheets sent on from operational departments or may be automatically generated from a production scheduling and control system. The payroll system will need to access information stored on each employee such as pay rates, tax details etc. to produce given pay advices. Periodically, the payroll system will update the general ledger system with the financial costs of labour.

Front-end information systems infrastructure

In the previous section we described the typical back-end information systems infrastructure of the business. On this foundation a large number of other information systems are normally built. Such systems are front-end in the sense that they directly interface to the major stakeholders of the business: managers, employees, suppliers and customers.

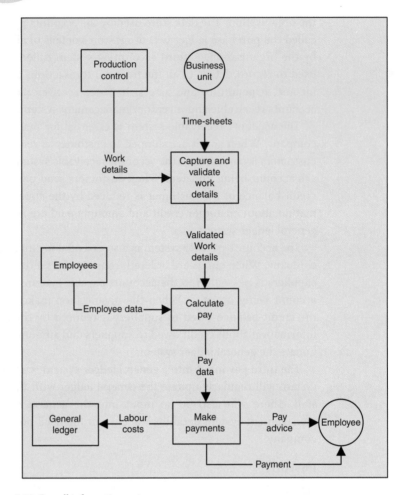

Figure 5.10   Payroll information system

Various information systems may feed off the information provided by core information systems in the back-end infrastructure and summarise such information for effective management and planning. In effect this is a vertical extension to the back-end information systems infrastructure. These are the *management-facing information systems* of the business.

Extensions may also be made horizontally out from the core information systems of the business. Connections may be made from the core information systems infrastructure to other information systems that interface to a company's customers, suppliers or employees. Such are the customer-facing, supplier-facing and employee-facing information systems of the business. Figure 5.11 illustrates some of the relationships between back-end and front-end information systems in the typical business.

For example, in a university setting, a key back-end information system would be a student information system that would handle information concerned with students, courses and modules. A number of key front-end information systems

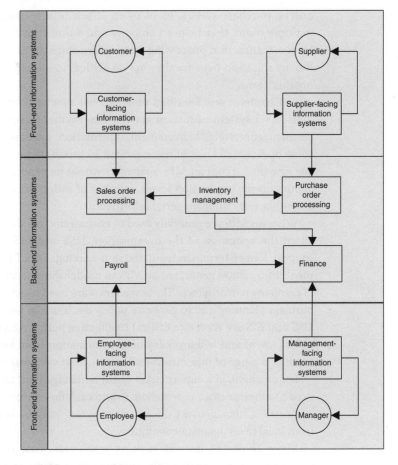

Figure 5.11 Front- and back-end information systems infrastructure

would run off this back-end information system. For instance, academics may use a system to report on students enrolled on a particular module, administrators may use a front-end information system to manage student fees and managers may use a front-end information system to plan for future student intake into the university over a number of years.

Management-facing information systems

In terms of the control processes of organisations we may distinguish between three major types of information system: *transaction processing systems* (TPS), management information systems (MIS) and decision support systems (DSS)/ *executive information systems* (EIS).

Transaction processing systems are the operational information systems of the organisation. In a business organisation examples include order entry, accounts payable and inventory management information systems, as described above. Such information systems process the detailed information generated in the day-to-day operations of the business. This detailed information is, as discussed earlier, normally referred to as transactions and include customer orders, purchase orders, invoices etc. Such information is essential to supporting operations that help a company add value to its products and/or services. Hence, transaction processing systems are sometimes referred to as life-blood of the organisation because they are so critical to effective everyday activity within organisations.

In Chapter 3 we described management as a key control process for organisations. As a system of human activity management needs information systems to perform effectively. Management information systems are used particularly by some operational layer of management to monitor the state of the organisation at any one time. From an MIS, managers would be expected to retrieve information about current production levels, number of orders achieved, current labour costs and other relevant managerial information.

Whereas MIS are generally used to enable effective short-term, tactical decisions about the operation of the organisation, DSS and EIS are generally expected to support longer-term, strategic decision-making. DSS/EIS will utilise the management information generated by MIS to model short-term and long-term scenarios of company performance. These scenarios are used to ask 'what-if' questions within business planning and to generate policy decisions in the area of business strategy. DSS and EIS are therefore critical to effective performance at the strategic level of management and will probably need information from key environmental sensors (such as a range of other front-end information systems) to function effectively.

For example, in a supermarket chain a management information system will be used to monitor stock in warehouses and cash flow through the company. In a local authority, a management information system may be used to monitor revenues from local taxes against expenditure.

Major things of interest such as employees, customers, orders, finance and inventory are important to the information systems infrastructure of our model organisation and data shared about such things are likely to form the key inputs into a management information system for some organisation. Using such a system, operational managers can continually monitor the state of the organisation. This is indicated in Figure 5.12 as one large management information system. In practice it may form a number of integrated MIS perhaps for particular business areas. One of the key outputs from the MIS will be summary reports on major trends affecting the company such as labour costs, current levels of assets and current levels of spending. This reporting may be written to a planning data store for use by an executive information system. The EIS is likely to be used to formulate high-level strategic decisions affecting the company.

Customer-facing systems

Customer-facing information systems support demand-chain activities and typically interface between back-end information systems such as sales order processing, inventory management and the customer. Traditional customer-facing information systems include sales, marketing, outbound logistics and after-sales systems. Recently, there has been increased emphasis on integrating such systems together to form a customer relationship management or customer chain management information system.

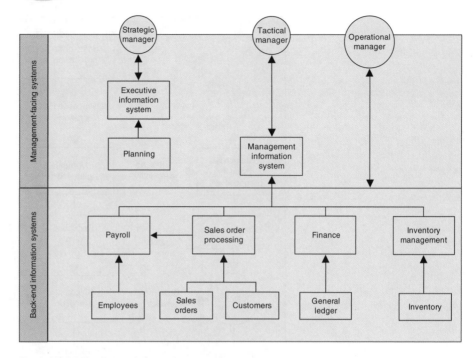

Figure 5.12 Management information systems

Sales. In some companies, particularly those associated with high-value products such as automobile sales or industrial equipment, customers would not normally fill out orders themselves. They are more than likely to interface with some sales-force in relation to making orders. Hence a sales information system is a common component of the information systems infrastructure of such organisations. This system will record the activities of the sales-force in terms of what sales have been made, to whom, by whom and when. This information will frequently be used to calculate commission owed to sales people on products sold.

Marketing. Marketing is the organisational process devoted to promoting the products and/or services of some organisation. Good marketing is reliant on good customer information. Marketing is likely to utilise the information held about its existing customers to prepare and manage advertising campaigns for company products and services. A marketing information system is also likely to store details of various promotions, which customers have been contacted and the results of contacts made.

Outbound logistics. The distribution of goods to customers is sometimes referred to as outbound logistics. Orders processed by a sales orders processing information system will typically be passed to an outbound logistics or distribution system. This is a particularly important information system for medium to large companies with lots of customers, minimal stock and many points of distribution. Delivering products to customers efficiently and effectively is critical to customer retention. Hence, aspects of this logistics system will be concerned with optimising the use of delivery channels to customers. Such channels may involve management of intermediaries such as parcel post distributors.

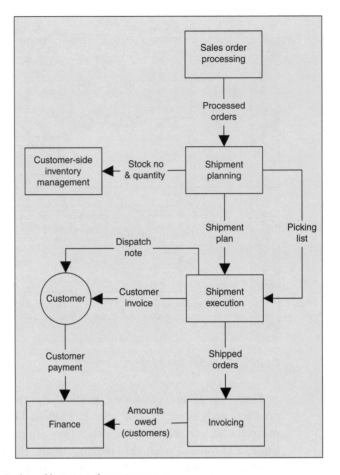

Figure 5.13 Outbound logistics information system

A diagram of an information system for outbound logistics is included in Figure 5.13. Shipment planning determines which orders will be filled and from which location they will be shipped. The system produces two outputs: a shipment plan which indicates how and when each order is to be filled and a picking list which is used by warehouse staff to select the desired goods from the warehouse. Shipment execution supports the work of the shipping function and is used to coordinate the flow of goods from the business to customers. The system will produce a shipping note that is attached to each despatch of goods. It also passes on details of the shipment to invoicing. Invoicing systems take the information supplied on shipping and produces invoices to customers using information stored about customers, orders, products and prices. Invoices may be sent at time of shipment or some time thereafter.

After-sales. An after-sales information system will be involved in tracking customer support and product-maintenance activities following a sale, probably on a continuous basis for a number of years. The complexity of this system will probably vary with the type of product or service sold by the company. For low-value goods such as books or CDs after-sales may merely track customer complaints and product replacements. For high-value goods such as automobiles after-sales is likely to involve the recording of maintenance or service schedules. For example, the lift manufacturer OTIS uses an after-sales system which pro-actively schedules maintenance of lifts by their engineers.

Customer Relationship Management. Each of the four systems of sales, marketing, outbound logistics and after-sales interacts with the customer in different ways and record different information associated with each interaction. Customer Relationship Management (CRM) has become a popular philosophy in the recent management literature. Winning new customers and keeping existing customers happy is seen to be critical to organisational success. But effective CRM demands a unified view of the customer. This is provided by a CRM information system.

A CRM system would ideally track all customer interactions with a company from initial enquiries through making orders to the whole range of after-sales services that might be offered to and consumed by the customer. Typically then, CRM systems integrate the range of front-end and back-end information systems that have a direct bearing on the customer. Some of the relationships between the key customer-facing information systems are illustrated in Figure 5.14.

Many online sites maintain forms of CRM system. Such systems log all interactions between an established customer and the site. The information they gather in this manner may be used for a variety of purposes such as pro-active marketing through email and the web.

Supplier-facing systems

Supplier-facing information systems support supply chain activities. Traditional supplier-facing systems include inbound logistics and procurement and typically interface with back-end information systems such as purchase order processing,

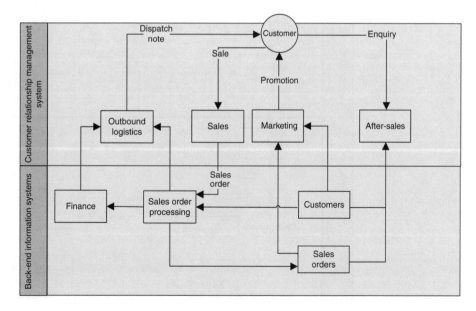

Figure 5.14 Customer-relationship management system

finance and inventory management. Not surprisingly, given the symmetric nature of buy-side and sell-side activities there has been increased emphasis on integrating supplier-facing information systems together to form an integrated supply chain management or *supplier relationship management system.*

Inbound logistics. Inbound logistics is that process devoted to managing the material resources entering an organisation from its suppliers and partners. In the retail sector for instance large food retailers are likely to have fleets of vehicles involved in the delivery of goods to stores. These vehicles may have to make up to 100 deliveries in any given working week. Clearly, effective and efficient systems are needed to plan and schedule routes for the vehicles to deliver foodstuffs to stores using the lowest mileage possible.

Procurement. Procurement is that process devoted to the purchasing of goods and services from suppliers at acceptable levels of cost and quality. It can be considered as the sister process of sales. A procurement system will be concerned with managing this process of procuring goods, services and raw materials needed by the company to operate effectively. It is likely to interact with both the purchase ordering information system and the inventory management information system.

Supplier relationship management. This is the sister system to the *customer relationship management system.* It keeps track of all supplier interactions with the company and integrates the information used by supplier-facing information systems such as procurement and inbound logistics. Some of the relationships between the key supplier-facing information systems are illustrated in Figure 5.15.

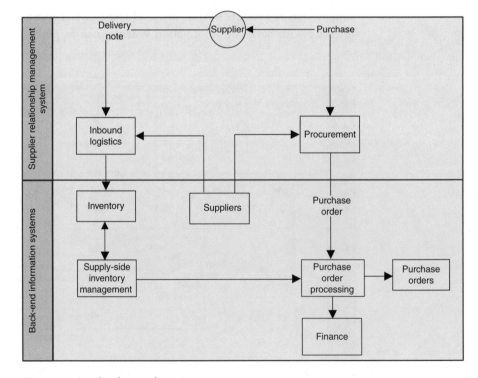

Figure 5.15 Supplier-facing information systems

Electronic procurement is the trend which involves using ICT to integrate many supply-chain processes. Procurement information systems and supplier relationship management information systems in general are important parts of electronic procurement.

Employee-facing systems

Employee-facing information systems support the internal value chain within organisations. Typical employee-facing information systems include human resource management and production control systems and they are likely to interact with key back-end information systems such as payroll.

Human resource management. A company is likely to need to build systems to record, process and maintain large amounts of information about its employees. Payroll information is only one facet of this information. Companies will also want to maintain detailed histories of the employment of their employees, such as job movements and appraisals.

Production system. This system will be involved in scheduling future production, monitoring current production and interfacing with the inventory management information system in terms of requisitioning raw material for production and replenishing supplies of finished goods. Some of the relationships between the key employee-facing information systems are illustrated in Figure 5.16.

For example, human resource management systems and production or manufacturing systems are likely to integrate around activity information. Hence detailed work patterns of employees may be integrated with production scheduling.

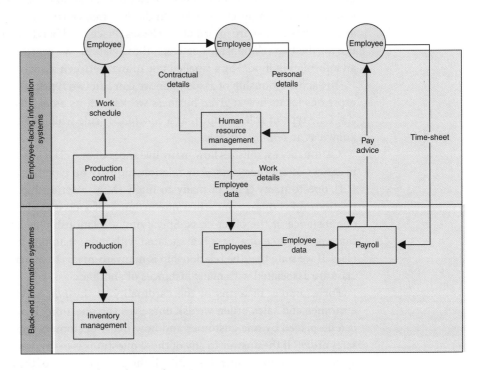

Figure 5.16 Employee-facing information systems

Information infrastructure

As well as expressing the flow of communication or information between activities we also need to express the relationship between the things of interest to some organisation: the things about which communication takes place. As should be evident from the information system models presented in previous sections, most business organisations need to know and communicate about its customers, products, suppliers, stock and sales, amongst many other things. To document such things of interest and the relationships between these things we need an information model. An information model indicates the structure of information required by activities and processed within some information system for the purposes of business communication. We may, in this manner, talk of an information infrastructure as a series of inter-related information models.

An information model is built using two major constructs: classes and relationships. A *class* may be defined as some 'thing' which an organisation recognises as important and communicates about on a regular basis. The data stores on an information systems model provide evidence of such 'things'. In the information system models presented in the previous sections, some of the classes which are clearly identifiable include delivery notes, dispatch notes, suppliers, customers, employees, purchase orders and sales orders. We represent such information classes by a labelled rectangle on an information model.

A *relationship* is some association between information classes. Typically these are binary relationships: associations between two classes. For instance, in analysing our business we might express the fact that a customer places a sales order or a supplier handles a purchase order. In these phrases customer, supplier, sales order and purchase order are information classes. Places and handles are labels we might use for the two relationships between these classes. We represent relationships on an information model by a labelled line drawn between associated classes.

To each relationship of association we can add two types of business rule, which expresses for us how a given business works with its associated information classes. One type of rule is known as a *cardinality* rule while the other type of rule is known as an *optionality* rule.

Cardinality establishes how many instances of one class are related to how many instances of another class. Any relationship may be typed as either a one-to-one (1:1), one-to-many (1:M) or many-to-many (M:N) relationship. If we state that the relationship is one-to-one, then one instance of a class is always associated with one instance of the other class. Specifying a relationship as one-to-many means that one instance of a class is associated with more than one instance of the other class. If we state that the relationship is many-to-many, then many instances of one class are associated with many instances of another class.

For example, in terms of the cardinality of the *places* relationship between customer and sales order, we ask ourselves the question: 'how many sales orders can be placed by one customer and how many customers appear on a particular sales order? If the answer to any of these questions is many, we place a 'crows-foot' symbol next to the respective entity. If the answer to any of these questions is one, we leave the crows-foot off the relationship for the respective entity. Hence, in the case of *customer places sales order*, customer is likely to have a cardinality of one and sales order a cardinality of many. In defining this we are actually making two assertions about the business situation we are modelling: that a customer may place many sales orders but that a particular sales order is placed by at most one customer.

Optionality establishes whether all instances of a class must participate in a relationship or not. Hence, each class participating in a relationship is either mandatory or optional in that relationship. A O (zero) is used to indicate that a class is optional in a relationship and a vertical line is used to indicate that a class is mandatory. Hence, in the case of *customer places sales order* the optionality is mandatory both for customer and sales order in the places relationship. This means that we make two further assertions about the business situation: that a customer must place at least one sales order to constitute being a customer of the company and that a sales order must always be associated with an existing customer.

In such manner, we can start to build a representation of some of the meaning of these business signs as well as indicating some of the structure of activities supported by these signs. We can then stretch such representation across key information systems to construct an information infrastructure for the organisation. Figure 5.17 illustrates part of the information infrastructure for our typical business that relates directly to some of the back-end and front-end information systems discussed in previous sections.

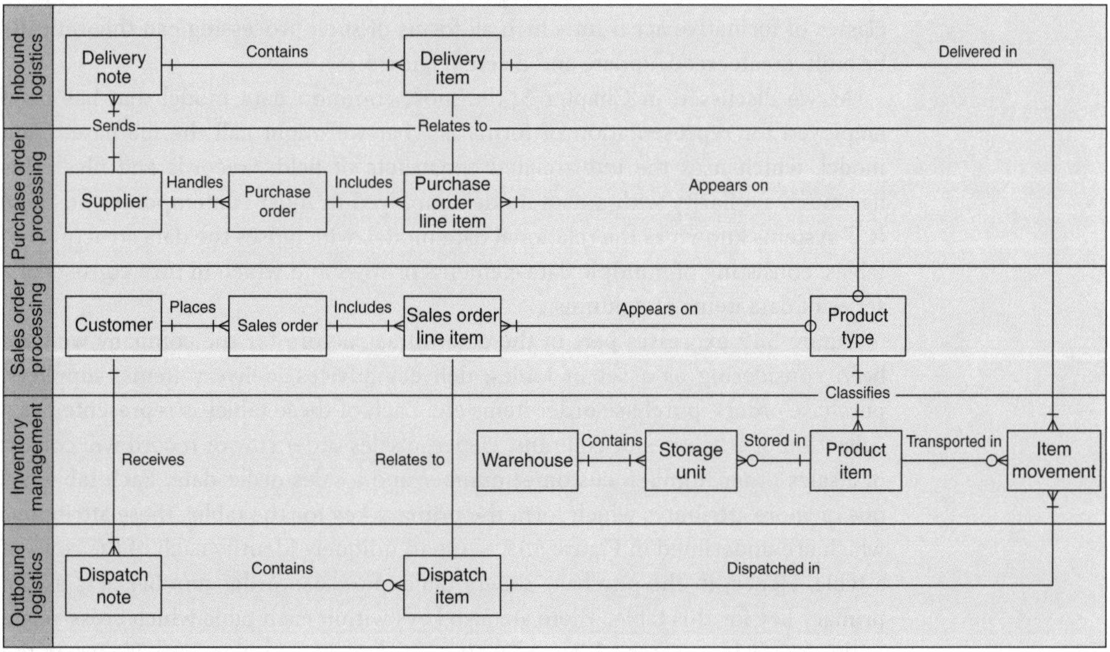

Figure 5.17 Information infrastructure

For example, it is evident from this diagram that a delivery note is a crucial class used by the inbound logistics system. Each delivery note is made up of a delivery item. The delivery items will be stored in warehouses and hence the movements of such items will need to be recorded within the inventory management information system.

Data systems infrastructure

As mentioned previously, associated with the flow of any goods and services within production, distribution and consumption along the value-chain and the wider value-network is a corresponding flow of transactions. In terms of informa a transaction can be considered a communication between business actors. As we have seen, in terms of forma, a *transaction* is a data structure that records some coherent unit of activity, typically an event within some activity system or between activity systems. Information is needed to support not only the internal activity of organisations but also the exchanges between organisations and individuals. Transactions are hence critical to the recording or representation of both internal and external organisational activity.

To represent the forma of such internal and external communications such as this we need a data model. Any data model can be seen to consist of two sets of inter-related primitives which we refer to as representors and operators. Representors are primitives of data representation or organisation: operators are primitives of data manipulation or processing. In terms of data representation, a data model can be described at a high level of abstraction in terms of a hierarchy of data items, data elements and data structures: a data item being the lowest-level of data organisation. In terms of data processing it is useful to define a number of core types or classes of formative act from which all forms of such processing can theoretically be built: create, read, update and delete (Figure 5.18).

As we discussed in Chapter 3, the most common data model that has been employed for representation of forma is what we might call the file-based data model, which uses the inter-related constructs of fields, records and files. This has much similarity with a data model employed in most contemporary business ICT systems known as the relational data model, which uses the data structures of tables, consisting of multiple data elements or rows and which in turn consists of a series of data items or columns.

Figure 5.19 expresses part of the data infrastructure for the company we have been considering as a set of tables: delivery advices, delivery items, suppliers, purchase orders, purchase order items etc. Each of these tables is represented as a collection of attributes or columns. Hence, a sales order row or record will consist of a sales order number, customer number and a sales order date. Each table has one or more attributes which form the primary key for the table. These attributes, which are underlined in Figure 5.19, serve to uniquely identify each of the rows of a table. Hence, in the purchase orders table, purchase order number acts as the primary key for this table. There are also keys within each table which cross-relate to the data held in other tables and which are known as foreign keys. Hence, in the purchase orders table the supplier number attribute serves to relate to a supplier

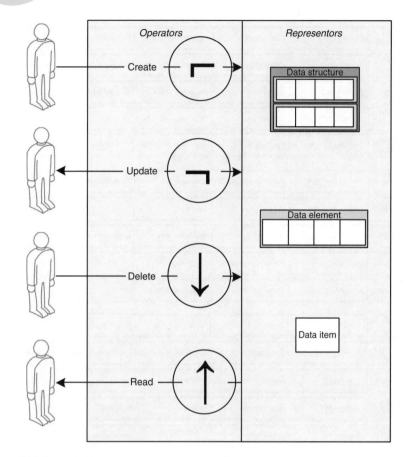

Figure 5.18 Formative acts

record or row held in the suppliers table, identified by the primary key supplier number.

Four main types of operation are performed upon data structures such as this. We referred to these operations in Chapter 3 as consisting of four types of formative act: create, delete, update and read. We also suggested using the symbol ⌐ for a create formative act, while ¬ represents a delete formative act. Likewise, we represent an update formative act as ↓ and a read formative act as ↑.

Hence, in terms of the rows within tables, new records or rows are created or inserted into such tables. Once records exist they may be updated or deleted from such tables. Existing records or rows may also be retrieved and read. Suppose, for instance, we wish to represent the data from a particular delivery advice issued by a supplier within the data structures indicated in Figure 5.20. We would undertake the following formative acts upon such data structures:

⌐ <Delivery note (123456, 12/12/2012, 654321, 'Deliver to bay 4')>
⌐ <Delivery items (123456, 01, AAB321, 20, 200, P234561)>
⌐ <Delivery items (123456, 02, ABC221, 40, 600, P234562)>
⌐ <Delivery items (123456, 03, BBB111, 60, 100, P234563)>

Delivery notes	Delivery no.	Delivery date	Supplier No.	Instructions		
Delivery items	Delivery no.	Delivery item No.	Supplier product code	Delivery quantity	Delivery item price	Purchase item No
Suppliers	Supplier no.	Supplier name	Supplier address	Supplier Tel. No.	Supplier email	
Purchase orders	Purchase order No.	Supplier No.	Purchase order date			
Purchase order items	Purchase order No.	Purchase item No.	Supplier product code	Purchase item quantity	Purchase item price	
Product types	Product type code	Product description	Product length	Product weight		
Product items	Product item code	Product type code	Item qty			
Item movement	Product item code	Movement type	Movement date	Movement time	Delivery No.	Dispatch No
Warehouses	Warehouse code	Warehouse location	No. Storage units			
Storage unit	Storage unit code	Warehouse code	Product item code			
Sales orders	Sales order No.	Customer No.	Sales order date			
Sales order items	Sales order No.	Sales item No.	Customer product code	Sales item quantity	Sales item price	Sales item No.
Customers	Customer No	Customer name	Customer address	Customer Tel.No.	Customer email	
Dispatch notes	Dispatch No.	Dispatch date	Customer No.	Instructions		
Dispatch items	Dispatch No.	Sales order No.	Customer product code	Dispatch quantity		

Figure 5.19 Data infrastructure

Summary

By infrastructure we mean the ways in which performative, informative and formative action is conventionally conducted within organisations. Infrastructure is both enabling and constraining. Existing infrastructure is the platform upon which innovation can be built. But infrastructure also constrains the range of possibility available to organisational change. Organisational infrastructure consists of four layers corresponding to the distinction between activity, communication and representation made in previous chapters.

The activity infrastructure of any organisation relies on a corresponding information, information systems and ICT infrastructure. Collectively this is referred to as the *informatics infrastructure*. In terms of information systems infrastructure, it is possible to distinguish between those information systems that directly interface with organisational stakeholders of various forms (front-end information systems) and those which form the core information-handling systems of the organisation (back-end information systems).

Organisations in the private sector rely typically on a core set of back-end information systems. Around such core systems a range of front-end information systems are normally constructed. It is important to represent the workings of this information systems infra-structure as an aid to better management. For this purpose, information systems models are critical.

The information systems infrastructure of some organisation is reliant on an integrated information infrastructure. High-level information models are therefore important to recognising and managing the interdependencies between information systems within organisations. Finally, information and information systems infrastructure rely upon a corresponding data systems infrastructure. Such data systems consist of sequences of formative acts acting upon data structures.

Review test

Information Systems are distinct from	Fill in the blank

Information Systems rarely stand still. They evolve to support _____ systems.	Fill in the blank

Information Systems are the same as Activity Systems	True or False?
True	
False	

Place the layers of informatics infrastructure in the order in which it supports activity infrastructure	Indicate the order using 1 to 3
ICT infrastructure	
Information Systems Infrastructure	
Information Infrastructure	

Core business information systems include ...	Select all that apply
Customer relationship management	
Sales Order Processing	
Finance	
Inbound logistics	
Purchase Order Processing	
Payroll	

Sales Order Processing is that information system which records details of purchase orders to suppliers. It is likely to support major elements of the procurement process.	True or False?
True	
False	

Customer-facing information systems include ...	Select all that apply
Sales	
Supplier relationship Management	
Outbound logistics	
Procurement	
Marketing	
Customer relationship management	

Supplier-facing information systems include ...	Select all that are relevant.
Sales	
Procurement	
Sales order processing	
Procurement	
Inventory management	
Supplier relationship management	

Employee-facing information systems include ...	Select all that are relevant.
Sales	
Human Resource Management	
Sales Order Processing	
Production Management	
Marketing	
Customer relationship management	

Exercises

- Determine why back-end systems are sometimes referred to as back-office systems.
- In a company known to you determine what constitute its core information systems.
- Identify a management information system in an organisation known to you and try to model its operation.
- Take a public sector organisation such as a local authority. Try to identify the key front-end information systems relevant to this organisation.
- Try to identify the types of activity data that might be generated from a production system. In what way might it update a human resources management system? What other information systems are likely to feed off a production system?

Projects

- Consider some historical information system and build a case description of its use. Some possible cases include Herman Hollerith's invention and use of his tabulating machine for running the US national census, the management of railway ticketing in the 19th century, the operation of Lloyd's insurance. Distinguish between the activity system, information system and the ICT used in each historical case.

- Construct a high-level map of some organisation's information systems, perhaps using the modelling notation for information systems discussed in the chapter. Include both computerised (ICT systems) as well as non-computerised information systems, by using document symbols to represent the paper flow in manual information systems. Consider the scope for extending ICT systems within the organisation.
- Consider the diverse ways in which data is captured in some organisation such as a retail chain. Determine the ways in which such data is validated and verified. Consider the extent to which the data collected by the organisation is of requisite quality. You might use such criteria as the degree to which it is accurate and useful.
- Investigate the degree of integration between information systems in some organisation. Recommend ways in which the systems can be better integrated in the future. Use information systems models for this purpose.
- Investigate the relevance of the distinction between management information systems and transaction processing systems in some organisation. In other words, is it possible to identify systems specifically used by management from those used by other workers in the organisation? Identify clearly the current users of such systems. Try to determine whether such systems are delivering the information required by such users.
- Draw a detailed map of the information systems used within some business organisation known to you, using a hierarchical series of information systems models. Determine the extent to which they diverge from the systems described in this chapter. To what extent do they map onto the systems described in this chapter?
- Attempt to develop a case study of the way in which ICT systems have been built over the past 20 years within some company. On the lines of the Goronwy Galvanising case in Chapter 1, try to determine how such systems were planned for and designed. Does it have explicit or implicit informatics infrastructure? Do people within the organisation describe such infrastructure as enabling or constraining?
- Extend the information infrastructure model detailed in this chapter to include information of relevance to all the back-end and front-end information systems discussed in the chapter.

Critical reflection

Infrastructure is both enabling and constraining. For instance, data systems infrastructure enables the coordination of organisational activities. But consider how current data systems infrastructure might constrain the development of new ways of doing things.

If core information systems tend to have common features across organisations, what potential is there for gaining competitive advantage through information systems? In what sense are these core information systems critical for regulating the business organisation? What role do management information systems play in the regulation of organisations? How important is it that the information systems in this back-end infrastructure transfer data between systems easily? What potential business problems might arise from poor data transfer between systems? What part do front-end information systems play in organisational performance?

In what ways may customer-facing information systems contribute to improvements in customer service? In what ways may supplier-facing information systems contribute to better management of the supply chain? Human resources are now frequently expressed in terms of human capital. How may effective employee-facing information systems contribute to better management of human capital?

***Case
exploration***

Amazon (see case) sees itself as a technology company first. But try to consider the information systems and activity systems which rely upon the ICT infrastructure of this company. What would customer information systems look like for Amazon? How heavily do you think it relies upon its supplier information systems? What sort of information classes might exist within its information model? In other words, what does it need to know about to perform its business effectively.

***Further
reading***

The concept of an information system is considered from a soft systems perspective in Holwell and Checkland (1998). I elaborate in more detail upon this idea in my book *Business Information Systems* (Beynon-Davies, 2009, new edition forthcoming). Front-end and back-end information systems in business are also covered in this text. Hay (1996) provides coverage of a range of 'patterns' or generic information models making up the information infrastructure of a typical company, on which the discussion of information infrastructure in this chapter is based.

References

Beynon-Davies, P. (2009). *Business Information Systems*, Houndmills, Basingstoke, Palgrave Macmillan.
Hay, D. C. (1996). *Data Model Patterns: Conventions of Thought*, New York, Dorset House.
Holwell, S. and P. Checkland. (1998). *Information, Systems and Information Systems*, Chichester, UK, John Wiley.

6 Technical infrastructure for eBusiness

Learning outcomes	Principles
Describe communication as a process and relate the way in which access devices and communication channels connect to front-end ICT systems.	An organisation's services or products may be accessed in a number of different ways. Each way we might describe as a channel of access. The access channel is used to carry messages between stakeholders such as customers, suppliers, partners and employees and the organisation's ICT systems. Any access channel consists of an access device and associated communication channel.
Identify some of the critical components of the internet and explain some of the technologies underlying the web and their relevance for business.	Modern communication infrastructure relies on two critical technologies: the internet and the web. The internet consists of a set of technologies which facilitate the inter-connection between data communication networks globally. The web is an application which runs on the internet and consists of standards for the transmission of hypermedia documents.
Understand the layers of an ICT system and how such layers are distributed around communication networks.	An ICT system can be seen to consist of four interacting layers: interface, business rules, transactions and data management. These four layers may be distributed on different machines around some communication network.
Distinguish between transactional data stored within databases and such data transmitted as electronic documents.	To enable the effective flow of transactions between organisations certain standards have to be defined for the format and the transmission of electronic messages. Historically, a standard for transactional flow has been based in something known as Electronic Data Interchange (EDI). More recently, standards have been defined using a web-based technology known as Extensible Markup Language (XML).

Chapter outline

Introduction

In the previous chapter we emphasised the central place of communication, mediating between activity and representation within human organisation. But this begs the question of what is communication? In other words, what do we mean when we say that one business actor A communicates with another business actor B? As we shall see, an understanding of the fundamentals of communication helps explain some of the value that modern digital computing and communications technology offers to the contemporary organisation.

The standard way of discussing communication is in terms of a classic model due to Claude Shannon, which focuses solely upon the medium of communication. In this chapter we discuss some of the limitations of this model and introduce an augmented model of communication closely coupled to the idea of business signs introduced in Chapter 2. Within this augmented model, human communication is seen as a process involving interaction of a number of elements: actors, intentions, messages, signals and communication channels.

One of the most familiar forms of human communication is face-to-face communication, and this is still a primary form of communication within business organisation. However, much modern communication is mediated communication: communication between humans mediated through the use of communication devices such as mobile phones and personal computers. Much organisational communication is also not between humans but between humans and 'machines', particularly between humans using ICT systems through some form of interface. When communication devices are used in this manner we refer to them as access devices. Electronic business, as we shall see, relies upon the use of various access devices within particular access channels not only to facilitate interaction between internal and external stakeholders of the organisation, but also to facilitate the delivery of goods, services and data to such stakeholders.

Communication

Way back in the 1950s two eminent US electronics engineers, Claude Shannon and Warren Weaver, developed a formal model of communication as a process (Shannon and Weaver, 1949). In this model, and not surprisingly given the background of the researchers, communication was treated as an 'engineering' problem. As Shannon himself stated, 'the fundamental problem of communication is that of reproducing at one point, either exactly or approximately, a message selected at another point'. In this model (Figure 6.1), a source is said to generate a message. This message is then encoded and transmitted as a signal along some communication channel. The signal may be subject to noise in the environment, meaning that the received signal at the destination may not be identical to that transmitted from the source. Hence, the process of decoding a signal may involve correcting errors introduced by noise to reproduce the original message.

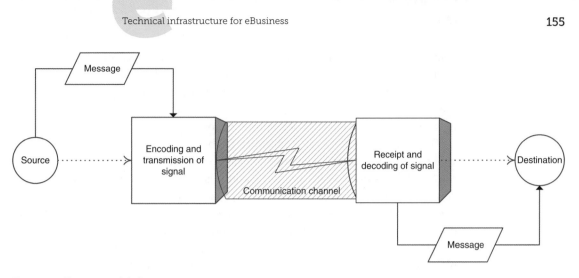

Figure 6.1 Shannon model of communication

Any form of energy propagation can be used for communication through signals: a signal being a physical pattern which travels along some communication channel. For instance, human speech travels as a signal consisting of a physical pattern of sound waves travelling through the communication channel of air. But the very idea of such a pattern implies that a signal is modulated. *Modulation* is the process by which variation or variety (Chapter 3) is introduced into a signal. If we are unable to modulate the pattern of a signal then no significance can be communicated between sender and receiver along a communication channel. Once we can vary the signal then it becomes possible to code certain messages using such variations in the signal. Coding is therefore the translation of a signal from one medium into the same pattern expressed differently in some other communication medium.

For example, assume we are listening to a live orchestral performance on the radio. For the musicians, the music being performed is represented as symbols on paper. The orchestra translates these into the physical gestures of playing instruments. Instruments being played excite a series of pressure waves in the air. These waves induce vibrations in a microphone and this device delivers a coded electrical signal to a transmitter. This causes an oscillating current to move back and forth in a transmitting tower. The current is accompanied by electro-magnetic radiation in the form of radio waves. Radio waves are received by our radio set. This device transforms the radio signal into a series of pressure waves produced from its speaker. The pressure waves impact upon our ear drum. Our brain/mind transforms this auditory sensation into the perception of something significant: music.

The Shannon and Weaver model has been instrumental in supplying theory for a number of technological advances, particularly the invention of effective data communications, which we consider in a later section. However, the model has been criticised on a number of grounds as an accurate representation of human communication, primarily because it is designed to address only what we have referred to in previous chapters as the forma of signs. In other words, this model considers communication solely as a problem of physical energy transmission. It therefore excludes consideration of the well-formedness of messages, the meaning of messages and the purpose of communication.

There are a number of additional problems, associated with the way in which communication is controlled between two or more business actors. First, the model assumes that communication is inherently linear, whereas most communication in business is normally transactional in nature. Human verbal communication, for instance, typically occurs in the form of dialogue, discourse or 'conversation'. Within such discourse business actors adjust their messages in response to a history of previous messages conducted within a particular dialogue. Second, the model tends to focus upon a limited subset of communication practice – dyadic communication – communication between two actors. In contrast, human communication within business organisation frequently occurs within and between groups of communicants. Finally, the model under-emphasises the role of records and record-keeping within human communication. We shall argue that, when human communication occurs between more than two people and particularly when messages have to be transmitted across time and space, the persistent record is an essential feature of much human communication. This last factor, in particular, is critical for understanding the importance of technical infrastructure to business.

Hence, to serve as a satisfactory baseline model of communication a number of elements have to be added to the Shannon and Weaver model, as illustrated in Figure 6.2. Within this augmented model communication is seen as a process involving the interaction of actors, intentions, messages, signals and communication channels. Business actors are the senders of communication or the receivers of communication. The intentions of a sender will be encoded in a message using

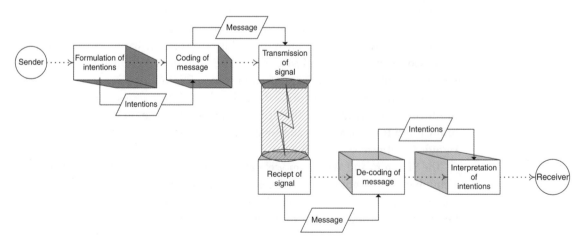

Figure 6.2 Augmented model of communication

elements from a particular sign-system. The message, consisting of a series of symbols, will be transmitted by the sender in terms of signals along some communication channel. One or more of the other parties will be a receiver, which have the ability to decode signals to reveal symbols and interpret the meaning of the message.

Consider a simple example of a business communication in such terms. Business actor A speaks the words 'our orders have fallen by 10% this month' to business actor B while at some meeting. In terms of intentions, this message, as we know from Chapter 2, represents an assertion: a report about the state of some 'world', in this case, the performance of some business. The assertion is made using signs from a particular sign-system – in this case a series of spoken English words. As spoken words these signs are encoded as phonemes (elementary pieces of sound which combine to form words), meaning that they travel along a communication channel based on sound transmission. The sounds impinge on the auditory or hearing apparatus of actor B. This actor is able to decode these sounds as symbols and is able to understand them as words of English and on this basis to infer the intention of actor A. On the basis of receiving this message he might decide to take appropriate action, such as calling a further meeting with sales staff.

Communication signals and channels

A signal is a key example of what we referred to in Chapter 2 as business forma: a coherent pattern of differences in matter or energy modulated along some communication channel. Theoretically, any form of matter, whether it be solid, gas or liquid, can be used as forma. Likewise any form of chemical or physical energy can be used to provide a signal for communication. For instance, as we have seen, human speech travels as a signal consisting of a pattern of sound waves (acoustic energy through air), while hand gestures and facial expressions rely upon the reflectance and transmission of light (optical, reflected, physical energy). In contrast, honeybees communicate through the transmission of particular odours (gases diffusing through air) and through vibrating honeycomb within the hive (manipulation of a solid).

Generally speaking, signals come in two major forms: digital and analogue. A digital signal has a small number of possible values, two for a binary digital signal. An analogue signal has values drawn from a continuous range. The value of the signal varies over this range. Hence, both light and sound can be considered as a waveform emanating from some source. Sound, for instance, can be considered as a pressure wave which travels through a solid, liquid or gas and can be represented as a sinusoidal wave as in Figure 6.3. The figure also illustrates how such a signal can be digitised, in this case by sampling the frequencies of sound at specific time intervals.

Since a symbol is any aspect of the world that can be modulated and used in communication, the degree of modulation possible determines the variety or complexity of a sign-system. To refresh, the variety of a system refers to the number of states the system may take (Chapter 3). In a sign-system the variety of this

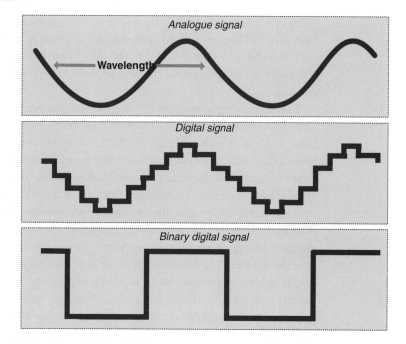

Figure 6.3 Analogue and digital signals

system is related to the degree with which signals composed from the sign-system can be modulated. Using Shannon's communication theory this can be used to describe the amount of significance that can be conveyed by the sign-system in communication. The essence of discrimination or difference is being able to 'draw' a boundary around something. In doing so an actor distinguishes that which is inside the boundary and hence part of the thing from that which is outside the boundary and not part of the thing. This is in essence a binary distinction and explains why the most basic unit of discrimination and hence the most basic way of coding data or forma is in terms of binary digits, otherwise known as bits.

Not surprisingly then, Shannon's theory of communication is a theory of forma measured in terms of binary decisions or bits. A statistical measure of the variety in a signal provides an indication of the level of significance being conveyed by a signal. Logarithms to the base 2 are used as a measure of the amount of significance in a message. To calculate this first translate the message into a binary code, then count the binary digits in the message string. This gives you a measure of the significant content of the message. It is therefore no surprise to find that most forms of communication technology nowadays use a form of binary coding (conceived as 0s or 1s similar to the dots and dashes of Morse code) and hence are binary communication channels.

Take an example. During the time of the Napoleanic Wars a communication system was set up by the Royal Navy consisting of a series of flags hoisted on the rigging of warships. The use of a particular sequence of flags was used to code a particular message such as the famous message *'England expects...'* at the battle of Trafalgar. Suppose a sailor wanted to signal a number between 0 and 127 by means of flags. Using a single flag for each number he would need 128 flags to achieve this. If he decides to use a decimal system to code the numbers being transmitted he needs 21 flags – ten for the units, ten for the tens and 1 for the hundreds. Using a binary system he requires just 14 flags – seven ones and seven zeros. 14 bits is therefore a measure of the significance of such messages.

The capacity of some communication channel refers to the amount of data or forma that can be transmitted along the channel in some given period of time. The *bandwidth* of a channel refers to the minimum and maximum frequencies allowed along a channel, which in a digital communication channel corresponds to bit rate: the number of binary digits (bits) that can be transferred per second between sender and receiver. For instance, the bit rate or bandwidth of human speech is around 50 bits per second, while the typical bandwidth available when connecting a personal computer to the internet from a UK home is of the order of 2 million (Mega) bits per second.

But communication is not only about the transmission of data as signals; it is also about the persistent storage of such data in records. This is fundamentally the difference between persistent and non-persistent forma. When human communication occurs between more than two people and particularly when messages have to be transmitted across time and space, the persistent record is an essential feature of much human communication.

In persistent forma symbols have to be represented in some way for storage and manipulation. From the discussion above it is evident why most data can be ultimately coded in terms of binary digital (bit) representation. However, within modern digital computing, the measure of the quantity of data stored is typically expressed in terms of the number of bytes rather than bits. A *byte* consists of 8 bits – the word being a contraction of 'by eight'. The capacity of some particular form of storage can then be described in terms of kilo-bytes (Kbytes: 1 thousand bytes – 10^3), mega-bytes (Mbytes: 1 million bytes – 10^6), giga-bytes (Gbytes: 1 billion bytes – 10^9) or tera-bytes (Tbytes: 1 trillion bytes – 10^{12}).

Persistent forma are an inherent feature of and a key problem for the modern world. New measures of the volume of data are becoming required as ICT becomes more and more embedded in modern-day life. For instance, Google's whole data storage was estimated as being 5 petabytes (10^{15} bytes) in 2004. It was also estimated that print, magnetic and optical storage media produced about 5 exa-bytes (10^{18} bytes) of data in 2002. Ninety-two per cent of this data were stored on magnetic media, mostly in hard disks. 5 exa-bytes is equivalent to the size of data contained in 37,000 new libraries the size of the Library of Congress book collection. More recently, it has been estimated that 1,200 exa-bytes of digital data was generated in 2010.

Mediated communication

The examples from the previous section implicitly assume that the actors involved in some communication are two humans and that such communication occurs in a face-to-face manner, typically using human speech as a channel of communication. We know, of course, that over the past hundred years or so many forms of technology have been used to enable *remote* communication within and between organisations. Such remote communication is sometimes called *tele-communication* because it is performed by actors at a distance: the actors are not present together in some location. To enable such tele-communication various forms of communication device must be used, each such device forming a node in a communication network.

Consider the communication necessary for a consumer to access the products and services provided by some organisation. An organisation's services or products may be accessed in a number of different ways. Each way we might describe as an *access channel*. Traditionally, such services or products would be accessed through face-to-face communication or postal channels. Nowadays, much communication between the individual and organisations is now mediated communication such as in the case of telephone communication. In such mediated communication the technology used, such as a telephone, we would refer to as an access device. More recently technology is not only used to mediate communication; it becomes an independent actor in organisational communication. Hence, when an individual orders some product using a company website they are not typically communicating with a fellow human directly: they are communicating with an ICT system.

ICT systems generally utilise a subset of telecommunications known as data communications. Data communication refers to the electronic collection, processing and distribution of data over tele-communication networks. The basic model of communication described in the previous section can be modified for data communication in the following terms. A *sender unit* formulates a message and transmits it as a signal to a *telecommunication device,* which is a piece of hardware that performs a number of functions on the signal, and then transmits the signal along a *communication channel* to another *telecommunication device* which reverses the process performed by the sending telecommunications device and passes the signal on to a *receiving unit* which decodes the signal as a message.

It is convenient to combine the idea of a sender unit and telecommunication device into the concept of an *access device.* The tele-communication device and receiving unit at the organisation end of the communication we shall refer to as the interface layer of some ICT system (Figure 6.4). This phenomenon, involving different mediated channels for the remote and interactive electronic

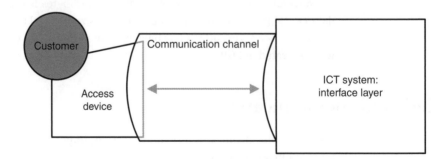

Figure 6.4 Electronic delivery

access to products and services, is frequently referred to as *electronic delivery*. Certain products and services such as digitised music or travel insurance will be accessible directly via remote access channels. For other more physical products organisations are likely to provide data and ordering services but distribute the products to customers through conventional physical channels such as the postal service.

Access devices

Therefore, in the modern electronic business various remote access channels can be used. Generally, there is inter-dependence between certain access devices and communication channels. Access channels are conduits for the delivery of certain goods and services and the recording of transactions. But access channels are not mutually exclusive. Certain intangible access devices and channels can be used in correspondence with traditional face-to-face access and certain organisations may wish to keep open traditional access channels such as a high-street outlet for reasons of coverage of the customer-base and overall effectiveness. However, in terms of a cost reduction strategy, many organisations are likely to wish to reduce the number of traditional access channels and increase the number of remote access channels. For instance, the cost of a typical high-street banking transaction such as a credit or debit to a bank-account over the counter in a high-street bank costs a few pence or cents for each bank to undertake. The cost of an online credit or debit to a bank-account costs a fraction of a penny or cent.

Electronic business and electronic commerce relies on individuals, groups and organisations being able to access electronic networks and systems through various access devices. Four main types of stakeholder or business actor are of interest to the typical business: customers, suppliers, partners and employees. Each type of stakeholder will have a variety of access devices and communication channels open to it. Each stakeholder type will also normally interact with a different interface to the ICT infrastructure of some organisation.

In this section we consider the options that exist for stakeholder devices which include: telephones, television, *personal computers*, *multi-media kiosks* and *mobile devices* (Figure 6.5).

Telephony

Telephony includes conventional audio telephones, modern video telephones and the now fading technologies of fax/telex for data transmission. Telephones have been used for a number of years as a form of retail access device. In more recent times a number of trends have enabled growth in the use of such devices for the ordering of products and services. Of these the most significant are the development of touch-tone services, intelligent networks and the growth of call centres. Telephony can be effectively combined with other access devices such as interactive television to provide a more complete electronic retail experience. Of recent interest is the increasing availability of voice communication over the internet through so-called Voice over Internet Protocol.

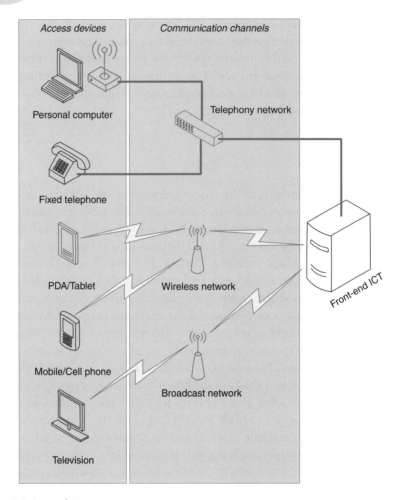

Figure 6.5 Access devices

Television

In many parts of Europe television has converted from an analogue to a digital terrestrial channel. Television is already used as a form of electronic retail channel through terrestrial broadcasting in the sense that commercial advertising is piped into the home using this medium. With the emergence of satellite and more lately digital broadcasting a number of pay-per-view channels have emerged. Retailing already occurs via the medium of pay-per-view television through specialist shopping channels.

Because service providers in the area of pay-per-view need a mechanism for extracting payments from their customers the broadcasting signal is usually encrypted. This means that service providers normally have to provide some form of decryption equipment or set-top box for each customer. Such a device can easily be converted to provide a backward channel to the service provider through conventional telephony services (using modems) to enable interaction.

More recently digital televisions have been enabled with wireless devices that allow connection to the internet directly though a home wireless network via conventional telephony.

Conventional television of both the terrestrial and satellite variety suffers from lack of personalisation and interactivity. This has changed with the possibilities offered by digital television. In a sense, the only thing that changes with the advent of digital television is the way in which the television signal is encoded. However, with digital television it becomes possible to deliver not only traditional television channels but also web content. This further opens up the possibility of interactive digital television (iDTV) in which hand-held devices or other input devices allow the customer to navigate through web material and also to input data such as orders and payments.

iDTV offers similar electronic retail capability to the internet-enabled PC (see below). However, it perhaps offers a lower level of actual content reflecting the lower bandwidth of this access mechanism and inherent difficulties experienced with using current handsets for controlling access. The high start-up costs for companies also mean that there tend to be fewer service-providers than that available in the area of Internet Service Provision.

Personal computers

Personal computers are currently the preferred mode of access to the internet. The vast majority of domestic users and small businesses connect to the internet via standard analogue or digital telephone lines. Since such lines were originally designed to handle analogue speech transmission a device known as a modem is typically needed to connect to analogue telephony channels. This converts the digital data transmitted by a computer into a series of analogue tones of various pitch and amplitude that can be transmitted over the analogue telephone network.

Hence, telephone lines to date have been the key technology supporting access to electronic organisations from personal computers in the home. Currently however a key constraint is the bandwidth that can be delivered into the home using a conventional modem. However, broadband technologies have impacted upon this market through technologies such as ADSL.

A key problem with this access channel is the variable penetration of this technology into the home from various regions within countries and between different social classes. Generally speaking, for instance, penetration varies between 20%–66% of households in the UK compared to 100% penetration of television.

A significant degree of standardisation of the home personal computer has been achieved over the past decade. This has encouraged a degree of domestication in its use. However, a key problem still remains. The average home user has to upgrade their hardware and software on a frequent basis, thus increasing the general cost of ownership above that involved in the maintenance of other access technologies such as television.

Multi-media kiosks/public internet access points

Personal computers are designed for use from the home or office. Multi-media kiosks (sometimes referred to as Public Internet Access Points – PIAPs) are specialist access points to services provided on the internet. Generally such kiosks are specifically designed for certain forms of access and normally placed in public places. Hence a kiosk situated in a shopping mall is likely to permit access to a range of shopping services while that sited in a hotel lobby is likely to offer access to tourist information. As the penetration of mobile access and electronic commerce increases it is likely that the need for PIAPs will decrease over time.

Mobile devices

Mobile devices include mobile phones, palm tops (sometimes referred to as personal digital assistants – PDAs) lap-top computers and the latest tablet devices. Here, the mobile computer appears either in its general-purpose or 'fat' form (the lap-top) or in more dedicated or 'thin' devices such as personal digital assistants or wireless application protocol (WAP)-enabled mobile phones. The main difference between mobile access and that available through the conventional fixed PC is that the access channel is likely to be the cellular phone network. WAP servers have enabled access to the internet from mobile devices such as mobile phones and tablet devices.

The idea of a tablet computer has been around for a number of years, and in its early forms overlapped somewhat with the idea of a personal digital assistant or PDA. In April 2010 Apple released the first iPad and sold 3 million of these devices in 80 days. In contrast to earlier tablet devices the iPad uses a touch screen display and a virtual onscreen keyboard for input. Tablets such as the iPad can use both WiFi and cellular phone networks to access the internet.

The mobility characteristic of devices such as smart mobile phones and tablet computers has encouraged a whole new range of ICT applications. For instance, mobile access devices of various forms are central to supporting the work of many utility companies such as gas and electricity suppliers. Workers in many gas supply companies, for instance, now use mobile devices to access corporate systems. Generally, such devices are used to enter data such as meter readings and to update customer billing services online, while in the field.

RFID tags

Radio-frequency identification (RFID) is an automatic identification method, relying on storing and remotely retrieving data using devices called RFID tags. An RFID tag is an object that can be attached to or incorporated into a product, animal or person for the purpose of identification. Data from the RFID tag is transmitted using radio waves. Some varieties of tag can thus be read over a distance of several metres.

Most RFID tags contain at least two parts. One is an integrated circuit for storing and processing data, modulating and demodulating a signal, and other specialised functions. The second is an antenna for receiving and transmitting the signal. A technology called chip-less RFID allows for identification of tags without an integrated circuit. This enables tags to be printed directly onto things such as clothing at a lower cost than traditional tags.

RFID tags are penetrating more and more parts of the business. For instance, such tags are now typically used within the supply chain to improve the efficiency of inventory tracking and management.

Multi-channel access centres

One should not assume that traditional organisations whether in the private or the public sector can entirely switch over to one or more remote access channels, since this may prove a risky strategy in the sense of excluding particular types of customers. Therefore, it is more than likely that such organisations will wish to maintain traditional access channels such as face-to-face contact and telephone access, alongside some of the access channels discussed above. Even those companies that began as entirely internet-based businesses have established a physical presence in an attempt to differentiate the quality of their service. Many organisations are also attempting to integrate various access channels within *multi-channel access centres*. Here, the organisation establishes a common entry point for all customer interaction of whatever form.

Communication networks

Access devices and channels are generally organised into arrangements called data communication networks: a set of devices joined by some communication technology enabling the transfer of data between such devices. Such data communication networks tend to be distinguished in terms of their coverage. A local area network (LAN) is a type of data communication network in which various nodes are situated relatively close together usually in one building or buildings in close proximity. The most common use of LANs is to link a group of personal computers together sharing devices such as printers usually through dedicated cables of communication line or through wireless communication. In contrast, a wide area network (WAN) is a type of data communication network in which nodes are geographically remote. WANs may consist of a mix of dedicated and non-dedicated communication lines as well as microwave and satellite communications. In terms of WANs, a number of alternatives are used for connecting the home or office personal computer to an organisation's front-end ICT.

Telephone network

The telephone networks in most countries are organised as wide-area telecommunication networks. Conceptually the topology of this network is that of a tapered star. There are a relatively small number of main exchanges connected by long-distance trunk cables. Main exchanges are connected to a much larger number of local exchanges. These local exchanges connect directly to customers in the home or the office.

Because the connections between main exchanges and local exchanges are much fewer in number than the cables that connect local exchanges to customers the cables are designed for high performance data transmission. These cables are typically of optical fibre and can handle transmission of many Mb/sec. Such cabling can also be much more easily upgraded than the cabling between customers and the local exchange.

The performance of the telephone network as a medium for data transmission is therefore heavily reliant on the performance of the so-called *local loop*: the physical characteristics of the communication medium between local exchange and customer premises. Within many countries such as the UK this part of the communication infrastructure typically consists of copper cabling. At the time of writing, companies have started to replace such cabling with optical fibre for selected premises within major cities in the UK.

Digital transmission

Telephone companies are clearly interested in increasing the speed of data transmission (the bandwidth) over the telephony local loop. Digital services have been developed that allow the simultaneous transmission of multiple voice circuits into business premises. This allows the business to treat their local telephone network as subsumed under the integrated services digital network (ISDN). The data rates available can be as large as the business requires.

However, ISDN has now been almost subsumed by the technology of the digital subscriber loop or digital subscriber line (DSL). DSL or xDSL is a family of technologies that provides digital data transmission over the wires of a local telephone network. DSL was originally developed as a means of providing video-on-demand services over the conventional copper telephony infrastructure within the local loop. It is now used as an effective means of providing fast, very high quality, access to the internet. Some of the main advantages of DSL are lower cost than ISDN and permanent connection to the internet.

However, DSL technology relies on short transmission distances between a local exchange and a domestic customer or business (typically 10 Km). Typically, the download speed of consumer DSL services range from 512 Kbit/sec to 80 Mbit/sec, depending on DSL technology used, line conditions and service level implemented. Upload speed normally is lower than download speed for Asymmetric Digital Subscriber Line (ADSL) and equal to download speed for Symmetric Digital Subscriber Line (SDSL).

Cellular networks

Radio networks are dominated currently by the use of cellular mobile phones. Such phones were originally devices capable of transmitting only voice traffic as analogue signals. However, the development of digital standards has enabled the development of integrated voice/data communications.

So-called third generation (3G) technologies enable cellular network operators to offer users a wider range of more advanced services while achieving greater network capacity through improved spectral efficiency. Services include wide-area wireless voice telephony and broadband wireless data, all in a mobile environment. Typically, they provide services at 5–10 Mb/sec. Certain countries have already upgraded their cellular networks with fourth generation (4G) infrastructure. 4G cellular networks can provide bandwidth of many hundreds of mega-bits per second.

WiFi and WiMax

3G and 4G networks are wide-area cellular telephone networks which evolved to incorporate high-speed internet access and video telephony. In contrast, so-called

WiFi networks based on the IEEE 802.11 standard are short-range, high-bandwidth networks primarily developed for data. Typical bandwidth for WiFi varies between 10 and 54 MB/Sec.

A Wi-Fi enabled device such as a PC, mobile phone or tablet can connect to the internet when within the range of a wireless network connected to the internet. The coverage of one or more interconnected access points, referred to as *hotspots* can comprise an area as small as a single room or as large as many square miles covered by overlapping access points. Hence, Wi-Fi is typically used to make access publicly available at Wi-Fi hotspots provided either free of charge or to subscribers by various providers. Organisations and businesses such as airports, hotels and restaurants often provide free hotspots to attract or assist clients.

WiMAX, the Worldwide Interoperability for Microwave Access, is a telecommunications technology based on the IEEE 802.16 standard aimed at providing wireless data over long distances in a variety of ways, from point-to-point links to full mobile cellular type access. The bandwidth and reach of WiMAX makes it suitable for a range of potential applications including connecting Wi-Fi hotspots with each other and to other parts of the internet and providing a wireless alternative to cable and DSL for broadband access within the last few kilometres. It has also been proposed as a technology for providing mobile connectivity. The actual bandwidth achievable through this technology depends on a range of factors but typically offers 2MB/sec rates over a few kilometres of distance between transmitters and receivers.

The internet and web

When people speak of communication technology, as we have done so above, they generally speak of the internet in the same breath. The internet – short for inter-network – began as a Wide Area Network in the United States funded by its Department of Defense to link scientists and researchers around the world. It was initially designed primarily as a medium to exchange research data but now it has become an essential part of the communication infrastructure of modern organisations both in the public and the private sector. Some have even claimed it to be fundamental basis of a global information society.

Currently the internet is a set of inter-connected computer networks distributed around the globe and can be considered on a number of levels. The base infrastructure of the internet is composed of packet-switched networks and a series of communication protocols. On this layer run a series of applications such as electronic mail (email) and more recently the World Wide Web, or the web for short.

Packet-switched networks

The early computer networks were modelled on the local and long-distance telephone networks that dated back to the early 1950s. Computer networks during the period tended to be composed of leased telephone lines. In these traditional telephone networks a connection between a caller and the receiver was established through telephone switching equipment (both mechanical and computerised) selecting specific electrical circuits to form a single path. Once the connection was established data travelled along the path. This is known as a *circuit-switching network.*

The process of circuit-switching works well for voice communication but proves expensive for data communication because of the need to establish a point-to-point connection for each pair of senders/receivers. Most modern computer networks therefore use a form of network technology known as *packet-switching.* In such a network the data in a message or file is broken up into chunks known as packets. Each packet is electronically labelled with codes that indicate the sender (origin) and receiver (destination) of the packet. Data travels along the network from computer to computer until they reach their destination. Each computer in the network determines the best route forward for the packets it receives and must transmit. Computers that make these decisions are known as routers. The destination computer re-assembles the packets into the original message.

There are a number of advantages to packet-switching networks for data communication. Long streams of data can be broken up into small, manageable chunks. This means that the packets can be distributed efficiently to balance the traffic across a wide-range of possible transmission paths in a data communication network.

TCP/IP

One of the key objectives of most computer networks is to achieve high-levels of connectivity: the ability of computer systems to communicate with each other and share data. To achieve such connectivity, standards must be defined to enable communication between sender and receiver. Such standards are encoded in communication software.

One approach to developing higher connectivity amongst systems is by using the idea of Open Systems. Open systems are built on public domain operating systems, user interfaces, application standards and networking standards. One of the oldest examples of an open systems model for data communication is the *Transmission Control Protocol/Internet Protocol* (TCP/IP). This was developed by the US department of Defense in 1972. TCP/IP is the communications software model underlying the internet. The advantage of this approach is that two different computer systems using TCP/IP are able to communicate with each other even though they may be based on different hardware and software platforms.

IP addresses

An *IP address* is the fundamental way of identifying uniquely a computer system on the internet. An IP address is constructed as a series of up to four numbers, each delimited by a period. It is hence called a dotted quad. In a 32-bit IP address each of the four numbers can range from 0 to 255. Generally the first of the four numbers identifies a computer network. The remaining numbers usually identify a node on this network. For example, 126.203.97.54 may be an IP address for a computer on the local area network at my university.

Universal Resource Locators

Internet users generally find IP addresses difficult to remember. Hence more memorable identifiers have been introduced which map to IP addresses. Computers attached to the internet and the HTML (see below) documents resident on such computers are identified by *Universal Resource Locators* (URL). URLs can thus be used to provide a unique address for each document on the web. The syntax of a URL consists of at least two and as many as four parts. A simple two-part URL consists of the protocol used for the connection (such as HTTP) and the address at which a resource may be located on the host. In the URL below the protocol – HTTP – is placed before the symbols ':// '. The address after these symbols identifies a specific web page on the host computer, in this case the home page of Cardiff University.

HTTP://www.cardiff.ac.uk

Domain names

The 'cardiff' in the URL in the previous example is short for 'Cardiff University', the 'ac' for academic and the 'uk' for United Kingdom. This constitutes a so-called *domain name*, an agreed string of characters that may be used to provide some greater meaning to a URL. In practice, a domain name identifies and locates a host computer or service on the internet. It often relates to the name of a business, organisation or service and must be registered in a similar way to a company name.

The World Wide Web

The internet is an inter-network on which a number of applications currently run. Examples of such applications include WWW, email, newsgroups and *chat*. The World-Wide-Web or the web for short dominates any discussion concerning the communication infrastructure for modern business. Frequently people confuse the internet with the web. The internet is the backbone communication infrastructure as described above. The web is effectively an application that runs on the internet and forms a set of core standards for most contemporary front-end ICT systems. Figure 6.6 illustrates the primary components of the web: hypertext/hypermedia, HTTP, HTML web browsers, websites and web portals.

The web is effectively a *client-server* (see below) application running over the internet. Web clients run pieces of software known as a browser. This enables

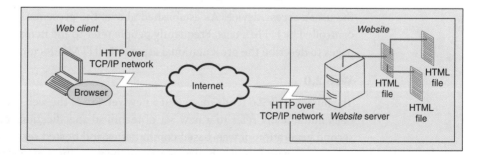

Figure 6.6 Components of the web

connection to web servers using two communication protocols – HTTP and TCP/ IP. Web servers deliver hypermedia documents in HTML format over the internet to web clients. HTTP is a protocol that defines how information can be transmitted between web clients and web servers typically over a TCP/IP network.

The web can be thought of as a collection of hypermedia documents residing on thousands of servers or websites situated on computers around the world. Electronic documents of any form are made up of two types of data. First, data that represent content such as text, graphics etc. and second, data which describe to ICT applications how the content is to be processed. Typical processing involves formatting the document on such media as the printed page and the PC screen. Process information is normally represented by a set of embedded tags that indicate how the content is to be presented. This process of tagging text with extra information is known as marking-up and the set of tags for doing this a mark-up language. In the 1960s work began on developing a generalised mark-up language for describing the formatting of electronic documents. This work became established in a standard known as the *Standard Generalised Mark-up Language* or SGML.

SGML in fact constitutes a meta-language: a language for defining other languages. Hence, SGML can be used to define a large set of mark-up languages. The inventor of the web, Tim Berners-Lee, used SGML to define a specific language for hypertext documents known as *hypertext mark-up language* (HTML). HTML is a standard for marking up or tagging documents that can be published on the web, and can be made up of text, graphics, images, audio-clips and video-clips. Documents also include links to other documents either stored on the local HTML server or on remote HTML servers. HTML has undergone a number of revisions since it was first introduced in 1991. A major part of the work of the World-Wide-Web consortium (W3C) has been to produce standard versions of HTML with increased functionality.

To access the web one needs a web browser. These are essentially programmes that let the user read web documents, view any in-built images or activate other media and hotspots. After the invention of the concept of the web the idea became established quickly in the scientific community. The term *website* is generally used to refer to a logical collection of HTML documents normally stored on a web server. We can distinguish between the content and presentation of a *web-page*. The content consists of the text and other media bundled in terms of HTML documents. The presentation concerns the way the content is displayed on the user's access device. As established above, the presentation of a document is controlled by HTML tags. Frequently people refer to the items on a website as web pages to describe the presentational aspect of a HTML document.

Web 2.0

The phrase *Web 2.0* tends to suggest a new version of the web. However, the phrase does not actually refer to a new set of technical specifications but to a perceived second generation of web-based communities and hosted services which facilitate collaboration and sharing between users of the web. The main technologies referred to under this banner are RSS feeds, social bookmarking, weblogs, folksonomies and wikis. *RSS* stands for 'Really Simple Syndication' and consists of a family of web feed formats used to publish frequently updated content such as blog entries, news headlines or pod-casts to subscribers. *Social bookmarking* refers to a technology which enables users to store lists of internet resources that they find useful. These lists are then made accessible to the public by users of a specific network or website. Other users with similar interests can view links by topic, category, tags or even randomly. A weblog or *blog* for short is a website where entries are written in chronological order and commonly displayed in reverse chronological order. Blogs typically provide commentary or news on a particular subject such as food, politics or local news. Some blogs operate as personal online diaries. A typical blog combines text, images and links to other blogs, web pages and other media related to its topic. The ability for readers to leave comments in an interactive format is an important part of many blogs. A *wiki* is a shared web page or site that can be updated using easy-to-use tools through a browser. Since such pages/sites can be directly edited by anyone with access to it, the main use of wikis is in collaborative content production. *Folksonomies* are sets of tags developed and used collaboratively by a community of users to classify and retrieve web content such as web pages, photographs and web links. Folksonomic tagging is intended to make a body of information increasingly easy to search, discover and navigate over time.

ICT systems

The internet and the web typically serve to connect the access devices used by various business actors with the ICT systems of organisations. It is useful to consider any such ICT system as being made up of a number of subsystems or functional layers (Figure 6.7):

- *Interface subsystem.* This subsystem is responsible for managing interaction with the user and is generally referred to as the user interface, sometimes the human–computer interface.
- *Rules subsystem.* This subsystem manages the logic associated with some application in terms of a defined set of update functions and business rules.
- *Transaction subsystem.* This subsystem acts as the link between the data subsystem and the rules and interface subsystems. Querying, insertion and update activity is triggered at the interface, validated by the rules subsystem and packaged as units (transactions) that will initiate actions (responses or changes) in the data subsystem.
- *Data subsystem.* This subsystem is responsible for managing the underlying data needed by the ICT system.

Take the example of an ICT system for storing details of research publications in a university. One part of the interface will be a data entry form to enter details of a journal publication. One of the rules or constraints used to validate data may be that the date entered for the publication must be less than or equal to today's date. A key transaction will involve insertion of new publication data into the system.

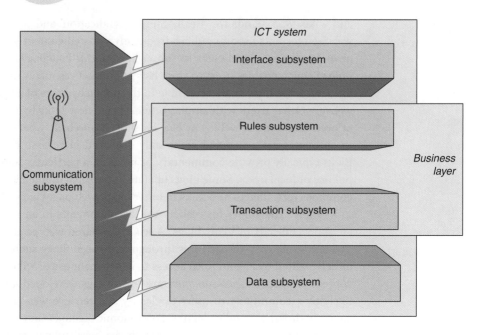

Figure 6.7 Layers of an ICT system

Part of the data management layer will have data structures for the storage of publication data.

In the contemporary ICT infrastructure each of these parts of an application may be distributed on different machines, perhaps at different sites. This means that each part usually needs to be stitched together in terms of some communication backbone. For consistency, we refer to this facility here as the *communication subsystem*.

The typical ICT infrastructure of the modern organisation will therefore tend to be built as a three-tier or N-tier client-server architecture with either thin or fat clients. Thin clients will run just the interface. Fat clients will run the interface and rules subsystems, sometimes also transaction management. In a *three-tier architecture* the functionality of the ICT system will be positioned in three layers consisting of a client or interface layer, a business or application layer and a data layer.

There are a number of advantages to constructing ICT systems in terms of a series of separate but interdependent layers. First, it makes for easier management of the maintenance of these systems. Hence, changes can be made to presentational issues separate from business rules and changes to business rules can be made separately from data. Second, N-tier architectures make for easier management and administration of ICT systems. For instance, thin clients, or so the argument goes, are likely to be considerably less expensive than a PC. Also, the network administrator will only need to buy and maintain one copy of each software application on the server. Hence, an N-tier architecture in principle can reduce the costs of operating an ICT infrastructure and contribute to reducing the total cost-of-ownership problem. Third, separation of critical aspects of functionality permits easier integration of systems. Hence, it becomes possible to share data structures and business rules across a range of separate systems.

Interface layer

Most contemporary ICT systems within organisations have been designed to be accessed through various access devices running a web browser. The *user interface* is therefore typically accessed through such a web browser and access channels may be over a local area network or over a wide area network. This is the client or interface layer.

User interface

In previous chapters we made the case for considering machines such as ICT systems as significant actors within modern organisations. As significant actors such ICT systems have to be communicated with. Such communication is normally defined in terms of some interface. Each ICT system has an interface or actually a series of interfaces. Collectively they are referred to as the user interface or sometimes the human–computer interface. Such a user interface defines how human actors can interact with and control the ICT system. It also includes the ways in which the ICT system communicates with humans.

In this sense, the user interface can be seen as a collection of dialogues: each dialogue being made up of a series of messages between the human user and the ICT system. Business actors use the interface to input data into the system and to receive data output from the system. Decisions are made on the basis of information interpreted from the data supplied and action is taken within the encompassing activity system. This is illustrated in Figure 6.8.

For example, a customer phones through an order for a certain quantity of an organisation's products to an order clerk working within a call centre. The order clerk inputs details of the order into the order-processing ICT system through an order-entry screen. In the act of doing this the ICT system may be able to automatically output details of an existing customer such that on the basis of previous orders the clerk may be able to make the decision to offer a discount on the purchase to the customer. At a later point in time the customer rings the call centre again to check progress against her order. This time a different order clerk accesses the ICT system and confirms the order by examining the results of a database query. This also enables him to confirm dispatch of the product to the customer.

Intranets and extranets

The data entry and retrieval screen described in the previous example is more than likely to consist of a web page extracted from a series of web servers. Such web servers are likely to provide electronic services to the major stakeholders of the organisation: customers, suppliers, managers and employees. Consider an ICT system run by a particular high-street bank which operates online banking for its customers. The client end comprises the web browser run on the customer's PC or some other access device. The client requests access to a web server run by the

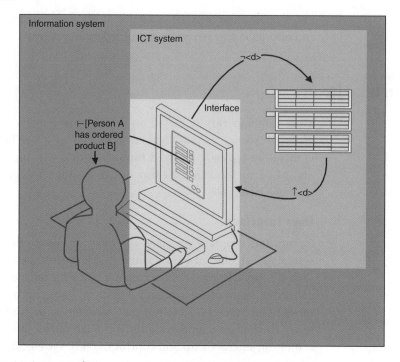

Figure 6.8 A user interface

bank and interacts with a number of data entry screens with associated dialogue particularly concerned with authenticating the customer. The web server will interact with a series of large banking databases storing data about customers and accounts. The mediating business or application layer is likely to consist of business rules such as *a customer should not be able to go overdrawn to a degree greater than his or her overdraft limit.* It will also contain update functions with embedded transaction types such *as check an entered customer identifier against a recorded identifier for the customer in the customer database* and *update the account balance of a customer by crediting or debiting a given account.*

Internet and web technologies are therefore being used to produce standard interfaces to ICT systems in organisations. Interfaces and communication channels will vary with the type of stakeholder and access devices used. Customers are likely to access services through some internet-enabled device to a general website on the *Internet*. Internal stakeholders such as employees and managers are likely to access ICT systems through some form of corporate *intranet*. An intranet is a corporate LAN or WAN that uses internet technology and is secured behind *firewalls*. The Intranet links various clients, servers, databases and applications together. While using the same technology as the internet, an Intranet is run as a private network. Only authorised users from within the organisation are allowed to use it.

In contrast, external stakeholders such as suppliers and partners are likely to access ICT systems through some form of *extranet* (Figure 6.9). Whereas an intranet is accessible only to the members of an organisation, an extranet provides

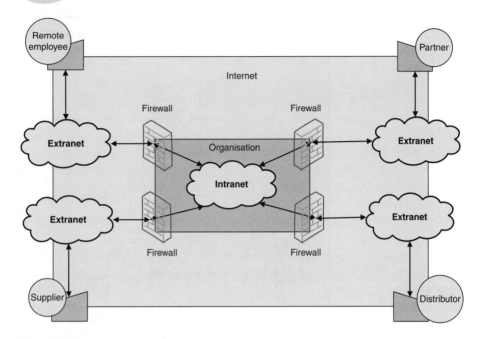

Figure 6.9 Intranet, extranet and internet

a certain level of access to an organisation's web-based information to outsiders. An extranet is an extended Intranet. It uses internet technology to connect together a series of intranets and in the process secures communications over the extranet. This it does by creating 'tunnels' of secured data flows. The organisation will also utilise firewalls to ensure that outside access is secure.

Websites and web content

Websites are now regarded as the most important mechanism for presenting content. The term *content* was originally used for what was known as hyper-text: networked text implemented through HTML. The term then expanded to include a growing range of media incorporated on websites (images, graphics, audio, video); hypertext became hypermedia. However, the term 'content' really came into its own with the rise of so-called content management and content management systems, introduced because of problems experienced in maintaining websites. Content as a term is also now used in terms of websites that display dynamic content, refreshed at query time from back-end databases. The term over the past few years has been used to include traditional media, as the channels of delivery for this media become subsumed by the internet, everything from magazines, television programmes, music and movies.

Typically, a commercial website will be organised hierarchically. The user enters at the site's *Home Page*. In terms of a commercial site, this usually establishes the range of products and services available from a particular company. From the home page the user may select a particular product or service by clicking on a hotspot or hyper-link, causing navigation typically to another page on the website. From here

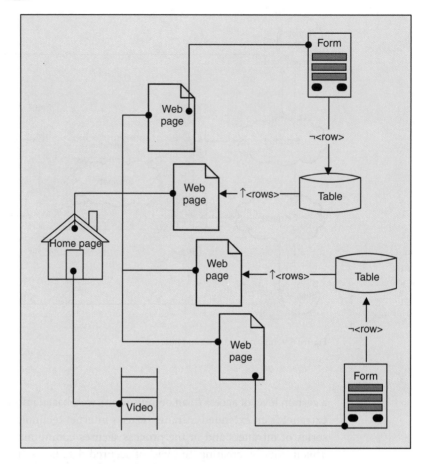

Figure 6.10 Structure of a typical website

the user may be able to access further detail or perhaps order from the website using a form consisting probably of a series of sub-forms (Figure 6.10).

Major investment is currently being undertaken by organisations to increase levels of interactivity on their websites. Therefore, a typical assessment of the functionality of websites is made in terms of three major forms of content. Assessments of the 'quality' of such websites are frequently conducted in these terms. *Publish* content is one-way content. It allows the user to retrieve general information placed on the website or web-page. In contrast, *interactive* content is two-way content. It allows users both to retrieve information as well as to communicate with internal organisational stakeholders and/or systems. *Transact* content is also two-way but allows users to transfer data to the organisation or receive personalised data from the organisation, such as making bookings or payments. Suppose a company sells toy soldiers. A *publish* site will provide simple details of the company and perhaps indicate how an order should be made. A *query* site would allow the user to search an online catalogue of toy soldiers for sale. A *transaction* website would allow the user to place an order online, perhaps even to pay for the order online.

Websites that primarily offer only information content typically use static web pages. A static web page is produced as a standalone HTML document. Any changes made to the page demands posting a new version of the page to the website. In contrast, a dynamic web page consists of both HTML code and calls to some *back-end ICT systems* such as database systems. A certain amount of the content may be retrieved from such back-end systems and displayed to the user. Hence, two tables from the back-end database are shown in Figure 6.10 being queried by web pages, while the two forms are shown creating rows within the tables of this database.

Business layer

The *business tier* of a typical business ICT application consists of three inter-related elements: update functions, business rules and transactions.

Transactions

On one level, as we have seen in a previous chapter, a transaction represents the recording of some event such as an economic exchange between two or more business actors. On another level a transaction represents a collection of formative acts which change a data structure or a set of data structures from one state to another.

As we have seen, a data system effectively records aspects of acts of communication which in turn serve to support coordinated activity in some activity system. Hence, one key use of data systems is to assert or declare that things become true in the wider information and activity system or alternatively to deny facts that cease to be true about these business systems. Hence, in a university activity system we might enrol the student *Peter Jones* in the module *business information systems*. A registry assistant communicates this as an assertion by using the student ICT system to write a new enrolment record to the enrolments table. This is an example of a transaction which changes the state of the enrolments table in the database.

A transaction therefore consists of one or more formative acts that operate upon data structures. Transactions consisting of create formative acts normally build new data elements within the data structures of some database, while retrieval or read transactions access data contained within the data structures of some database. In contrast, update transactions cause changes to values held within particular data items of particular data elements and data structures in a database, while delete transactions erase particular data elements within the data structures of some database.

Hence, in a banking ICT system a *create* transaction might be used to enter a new credit or debit record against a particular bank account. In contrast, a *read* transaction might be used to assemble a statement for a particular bank account for a particular period. An *update* transaction might be used to change the contact details of a particular customer. Finally, a *delete* transaction might be used to remove a particular standing order or direct debit placed by a customer.

Business rules

A considerable amount of the functionality of an ICT system is taken up with so-called *business rules*. Such rules reside both within the rules management subsystem of an ICT system as well as the data management subsystem. They ensure that the data held in the data management layer of the ICT system remain an accurate reflection of their universe of discourse (the business or activity system they represent). In other words, the data held in some ICT system should display integrity; they should accurately reflect the state of their activity system. For example, in terms of the universe of discourse relevant to a typical university an ICT system established for student records should provide accurate responses to questions such as *how many students are currently enrolled on a particular module?* In terms of an online banking application, customers should be able to accurately obtain the current balances for their bank accounts.

Data integrity is ensured through integrity constraints. An integrity constraint is a business rule which establishes how a database is to remain an accurate reflection of its universe of discourse. Integrity constraints may be divided into two major types: static integrity constraints and transition integrity constraints.

A static constraint is used to check that a transaction will not change a database into an invalid state. A static constraint is hence a restriction defined on states of the database. For example, a static constraint relevant to a university domain might be *students can only take currently offered modules*. This static constraint would prevent us from entering data, *John Davies takes Strategic Management*, into our current database. This would be because *Strategic Management* is not a currently offered module in our database.

In contrast, a transition constraint is a rule that relates given states of a database. A transition is a state transformation and can therefore be denoted by a pair of states. A transition constraint is a restriction defined on a transition. An example of a transition constraint might be *the number of modules taken by a student must not drop to zero during a semester*. Hence, if we wished to remove a fact relating John Davies to a particular module from our database we should first check that this would not cause an invalid transition. Within a banking application an example of a transition constraint would be *a customer should not be able to go overdrawn to a degree greater than his or her overdraft limit*. Hence, before debiting a bank account the application would need to check that there are sufficient funds in the bank account to handle the debit transaction.

Update functions

Update functions represent individual elements of functionality associated with a particular business application. As such they encapsulate both business rules and transaction types. Update functions are triggered by events usually activated from the interface or client management layer or sometimes from other update functions. The end-result of the activation of a particular update function is that transactions are fired at the data management layer of the ICT system.

An update function will usually have a series of conditions associated with it. Such conditions typically represent integrity constraints. There will also be a series of actions associated with the update function. These will specify what should happen if the conditions are true and typically constitute transactions types.

For instance, we might specify an update function appropriate for a university application as follows:

ON Transfer Student X from module 1 to module 2

IF
  student X takes module 1 AND
  student X does not take module 2 AND
  module 2 is offered

THEN
  update student X takes module 2

Here, X, module 1 and module 2 are place holders for values. Hence, we might initiate a transaction using this update function by assigning the value *John Davies* to X, *Business Information Systems* to module 1 and *eBusiness* to module 2. This would record that student *John Davies* has transferred from the module *Business Information Systems* to the module *eBusiness* and would occur only if there are data which indicates that *John Davies* currently takes *Business Information Systems*, that he does not currently take *eBusiness* and that *eBusiness* is a currently offered module.

Traditionally, update functions and business rules within the business layer would have been coded using a programming language as part of the wider application system. Such a business layer is now frequently constructed using a business rules engine which allows the developer to enter and maintain update functions and associated rules separately from interface and data management layers.

Data management layer

As discussed above, front-end ICT is likely to work in the modern business using internet and web technologies. Hence, the effective integration of front-office and back-office systems is critical to organisational effectiveness. For instance, to enable fully transactional websites, the information presented needs to be updated dynamically from back-end databases. Also, the information entered by customers needs to update company database systems effectively. For this reason we focus on a discussion of the technology of data management within this section, some of the ideas of which have already been introduced in Chapter 5.

Traditionally data management in ICT systems has been part of the file system managed by the operating system. During the 1970s a class of software started being used for the higher-level management of data: the database management system (DBMS). DBMS are software systems for managing databases and constitute the fundamental technology in the data management layer of most contemporary ICT systems. A database system is therefore composed of a database and a DBMS and both database and DBMS must conform to a given data model (Chapter 3). In this section we define these three terms in greater detail.

A *database* is an organised repository for data having a number of critical properties. A database can be viewed as a model of its activity system. The data stored in a database is usually an attempt to represent the properties of some objects in this activity system. A database is normally accessible by more than one person perhaps at the same time. One major responsibility of database usage is to ensure that the data are integrated. This implies that a database should be a collection of data that has no unnecessarily duplicated or redundant data. Another responsibility arising as a consequence of shared data is that a database should display integrity. In other words, that the database accurately reflects the universe of discourse that it is attempting to model. Besides integrity constraints discussed above, one of the major ways of ensuring the integrity of a database is by restricting access: in other words, securing the database. The main way this is done in contemporary database systems is by defining in some detail a set of authorised users of the whole, or more usually parts of the database.

Consider a database held by an insurance company. The data structures in the database emulate information classes of interest to the activities of this company. Hence, the database maintains records about insurance policies, policy-holders and insurance claims. These data are typically accessed by a number of different users in the organisation for the purposes of opening new insurance policies for customers and handling claims against particular insurance policies. These data must be consistent and accurate, meaning that if a policy-holder has a record in the database then this record should accurately reflect properties of this particular customer. One way of ensuring that data have integrity is by restricting access to data to particular types of users. Hence, only those employees working in the claims department should be able to create and update a claim record.

A *database management system* (DBMS) is an organised set of facilities for accessing and maintaining one or more databases. A DBMS is a shell which surrounds a database and through which all interactions with the database take place. The interactions catered for by most existing DBMS fall into four main groups. First, structural maintenance consists of adding new data structures to the database, removing data structures from the database and modifying the format of existing data structures. Second, transaction processing typically involves inserting new data into existing data structures, updating data in existing data structures and deleting data from existing data structures. Third, information retrieval involves extracting data from existing data structures and presenting this data for use both by end-users and application systems. Fourth, database administration consists of creating and monitoring users of the database, restricting access to data structures in the database and monitoring the performance of databases.

In Chapter 5 we used the term *data model* to refer to a model of the data required for some domain. The term is also used to denote the architecture for a particular database and DBMS in that it describes the general structure of how data are organised, stored and accessed within some database application. A data model in these terms is generally held to be made up of three components: data definition, data manipulation and data integrity.

Data definition describes the way in which data can be represented in terms of the data structures, data elements and data items relevant to the data model. Data manipulation comprises a set of data operators for the insertion of data, the removal of data, the retrieval of data and the amendment of data in data structures. Data integrity consists of a set of integrity constraints or rules that must form part of the database. Integrity is enforced in a database through the application of these integrity constraints. One of the most popular forms of data model used in contemporary data management is the relational data model, which we introduced in Chapter 5. Here, we consider what data definition, data manipulation and data integrity means within this particular data model.

Data definition consists of one and only data structure in a relational database: the table. Each table is made up of a number of data elements called rows and each row is made of a number of data items known as columns. Hence, we might represent data relating to the dispatch advice notes of Goronwy Galvanising as described in Chapter 2. The table named *Dispatch notes* in Figure 6.11 consists of four data items (Dispatch No., Dispatch date, Customer code and Instructions) and 3 data elements corresponding to 3 rows in the table, one for each dispatch note.

Data integrity in the relational data model corresponds to three types of integrity rule: entity integrity, referential integrity and domain integrity.

Entity integrity establishes that each row in a table is identified by values in one or more columns of the table, called the table's primary key. The values of a primary key must be unique and not null. In other words, we must have a value for each element of the primary key and each value must be unique in terms of other values of the primary key. For instance, in the *Dispatch notes* table the *Dispatch No.* data item is the only item having both these properties. It is therefore the most suitable candidate for a primary key for this table.

Dispatch notes	Dispatch No	Dispatch date	Customer code	Instructions
	101	22/01/2012	BLW	
	102	25/02/2012	TCO	
	103	10/03/2012	BLW	

Dispatch items	Dispatch No	Sales order No	Customer product code	Dispatch quantity
	101	13/1193G	UL150	20
	101	44/2404G	UL1500	20
	101	70/2517P	UL135	20
	101	23/2474P	UL120	14

Figure 6.11 A simple relational database

Referential integrity establishes that values in columns may also act as links to data contained in other tables. Such columns are called foreign keys. A value for a foreign key must either be the value of some primary key elsewhere in the database or be null. The primary key of the Dispatch items table is actually composed of two data items: *Dispatch No.* and *Sales Order No.* Both these data items individually are in fact foreign keys to two other tables in the database. Dispatch No. acts as a foreign key back to the primary key of the Dispatch notes table. Sales Order No. acts as a foreign key back to a Sales orders table. The values of these two foreign keys can never be null because we always must know which dispatch note and sales order a particular dispatch item relates to.

Data manipulation involves functions for entering new rows into tables, deleting rows from tables and editing data held within the rows of a table. These correspond to the four types of formative acts described in earlier chapters.

Communicating documents

In previous sections we have focussed upon the storage of transactional data in databases. But transactional data in the form of electronic messages have to be transmitted between the ICT systems of organisations. For this to work effectively three conditions must be satisfied. First, the electronic message comprising the transaction must have a defined format. Second, the receiver and sender of the message must agree the format of the message. Third, the message must be able to be sent and read by electronic devices. Historically, a standard for transactional flow has been based in something known as Electronic Data Interchange (EDI). More recently, standards have been defined using a web-based technology known as Extensible Markup Language (XML).

One of the main advantages of HTML is its simplicity. This enables it to be used effectively by a wide user community. However, this simplicity is also one of its disadvantages. Sophisticated users want to define their own tags particularly for functionality involved with the exchange of data. The World Wide Web Consortium thus developed *eXtensible Markup Language* or XML in 1998 to meet these needs. The term *extensible* means that new markup tags can be created by users for the exchange of data.

Like HTML, XML is another restricted descendant of SGML. Whereas HTML is used to define how the data in a document are to be displayed, XML can be used to define the syntax and some of the *semantics* of a document. Thus, XML can be used to specify standard templates for business documents such as invoices, shipping notes and fund transfers. XML is seen as a major way in which EDI may be replaced for electronic document transmission between organisations.

An XML document consists of a set of elements and attributes. Elements or tags are the most common form of markup. The first element in an XML document must be a root element. The document must have only one root element but this element may contain a number of other elements.

Suppose your company is a coffee wholesaler. You might wish to create XML documents for the exchange of shipping information to your customers. An appropriate root element might therefore be the tag <PRODUCTDETAILSLIST>.

An element begins with a start-tag and ends with an end-tag. The start tag in our document for the root element would be <ProductDetailsList>. The corresponding end-tag would be </ProductDetailsList>. Note that tags are case-sensitive in XML. Hence <PRODUCTDETAILSLIST> is a different tag from <ProductDetailsList>. Elements can be empty, in which case they can be abbreviated to <EmptyElement/>. Elements must also be properly nested as sub-elements within a superior element. Hence, the following XML element might be used to define a particular coffee product.

```
<ProductDetails ID='1234'>
<ItemName>Kenya Special</ItemName>
<CountryOfOrigin>Kenya Special</CountryOfOrigin>
<WholeSaleCost>20.00</WholeSaleCost>
<Stock>4000</Stock>
</ProductDetails>
```

Here we have a ProductDetails element with a number of sub-elements. Definitions for these sub-elements such as ItemName, CountryOfOrigin, WholeSaleCost and Stock are properly nested within ProductDetails.

In traditional database terms this would constitute a row in a products table. This row is made up of a number of columns including an identifier for the product, the name of the item, the country of origin of the product, the cost of the product and the number of product items in stock. Attributes are Name-Value pairs that contain descriptive information about an element. The attribute is placed inside the start-tag for the element and consists of an attribute name, an equality ('=') sign and the value for the attribute placed within quotes. In our coffee producer example the tag <ProductDetails ID='1234'> contains the attribute ID and the value '1234'. Within XML the ordering of elements is significant. However, the ordering of attributes is not significant. Hence, the two orders for the product information below would be regarded as different elements:

```
<ProductDetails ID='1234'>
<ItemName>Kenya Special</ItemName>
<CountryOfOrigin>Kenya Special</CountryOfOrigin>
<WholeSaleCost>20.00</WholeSaleCost>
<Stock>4000</Stock>
</ProductDetails>
<ProductDetails ID='1234'>
<ItemName>Kenya Special</ItemName>
<WholeSaleCost>20.00</WholeSaleCost>
<Stock>4000</Stock>
<CountryOfOrigin>Kenya Special</CountryOfOrigin>
</ProductDetails>
```

Traditionally, the structure or syntax of an XML document has been defined in terms of a document type definition or DTD. More recently, the trend has been to use XML Schema to define the structure of an XML document. It lists the names of all elements, which elements can appear in combination and what attributes are available for each type of element. It can also be used to specify certain rules on data elements such as whether an element is a piece of text or a number, and whether an element has a default value or not.

The cloud

In the 1960s the computer scientist John McCarthy made the prediction that 'computation may someday be organised as a public utility'. This is the aim of the cloud or cloud computing in which computing power is delivered to the user in much the same way as electricity or water is delivered as a utility over the internet. The user of a cloud application does not require knowledge of the location or configuration of the application to use it: she merely connects to it over the internet. Therefore, the term derives from the common representation of the internet on diagrams, such as the ones used in this book, as a cloud. But cloud computing is not one technology but a series of technologies including client-server computing, software as a service, data centres and virtualisation.

As we have discussed in an earlier section, ICT systems as applications are typically divided up into layers such as interface, rules, transaction and data. Each of these layers may be distributed on different machines, perhaps at different sites connected together through communication across some network. The most extreme version of this technical architecture is when a client machine runs little more than the user interface, probably through a browser. Most other parts of application are run on remote data servers. Clients communicate with such servers through open software standards such as the internet protocol and application programming interfaces.

Web standards are starting to support inter-operable systems across computer networks, particularly through the idea of a *Service Oriented Architecture* (SOA) and the related idea of a *web service*. SOA represents a computing architecture in which ICT system functionality is decomposed into small, distinct units known as services, which can be distributed over a network and can be combined together and reused to create business applications. Such services communicate with each other by passing data from one service to another, or by coordinating an activity between one or more services.

In this architecture, computing resources are typically owned and operated by a third-party provider located in one or more *data centres*. A data centre is a purpose-built facility which runs multiple computing servers, usually with associated infrastructure such as telecommunications, backup power supply and security. However, consumers of the resources provided by the data centre are not concerned with the underlying infrastructure as services such as web applications or data storage are available on demand to the consumer.

Hence, the architecture associated with cloud computing assumes a massive network of 'cloud servers' interconnected as if in a grid. The servers run applications in parallel and sometimes use a technique known as *data virtualisation* to maximise computing power per server. This involves making multiple physical resources such as storage devices or servers appear as a single virtual resource to the user.

One of the most publicised cloud applications is Salesforce.com's customer relationship management system. This ICT system is broken down into several broad applications such as Sales Cloud and Service Cloud so that business actors such as sales persons can access them through an internet-enabled mobile device or a connected computer. The Sales Cloud enables access to customer profiles and account histories, and allows sales persons to control data associated with the sales process such as contact data and marketing campaigns. The Service Cloud enables companies to track customer transactions coming in from a number of access channels, and automatically route these for handling by appropriate persons.

Some of the claimed benefits of cloud computing include device and location independence, improved scalability, improved reliability and reduced cost. Cloud applications can be accessed from various different access devices from any internet-enabled location. The dynamic provisioning of computing resources means that a user's needs for computing power can scale upwards without significant new investment. The application itself in terms of software and data can be separated from physical resources such as hardware. Hence, if more computing power is required to handle peak loads additional cloud servers can be applied to the task on an as-needed basis. Well-designed cloud applications can ensure business continuity and reliability of ICT use. Finally, it is claimed that the pricing structure of cloud computing, typically offered as a subscriber or metred service, offers a more cost-effective means of operating ICT infrastructure than in-house computing.

However, there are a number of concerns expressed in relation to cloud computing. Cloud computing is a form of informatics outsourcing and just like any form of outsourcing has to be closely controlled by the client company to ensure that the service provided meets changing need. Particular attention needs to be paid to the security of business data held on remote data servers and that records of personal data held on such servers such as customer data meet data protection standards.

Summary

An organisation's services or products may be accessed in a number of different ways. Each way we might describe as a channel of access. The access channel is used to carry messages between stakeholders such as customers, suppliers, partners and employees and the organisation's ICT systems. Any access channel consists of an access device and associated communication channel. The access device is used to formulate, transmit, receive and display messages. Stakeholder access devices come in many forms including telephones, interactive digital television, personal computers and mobile devices. Major ways of connecting access devices to front-end ICT systems include telephone networks, digital transmission and radio networks.

The most prevalent current example of the application of communication technology is the internet. The internet – short for inter-network – began as a Wide Area Network in the United States funded by its Department of Defence to link scientists and researchers around the world. The technical infrastructure of the internet consists of a number of components that include packet-switched Networks, TCP/IP, HTTP, IP addresses, universal resource locators (URLs) and domain names. Packet-switching networks employ protocols in which data in a message or file are broken up into chunks known as packets and distributed around the network using TCP/IP: an open systems model for data communication that employs a number of layers. Computers attached to the internet and the HTML documents resident on such computers are identified by URLs. A domain name provides more meaning to a URL and identifies and locates a host computer or service on the internet. Internet protocol addresses are mapped to domain names by domain name servers.

The World-Wide-Web or web for short is an application that runs on the internet. The primary elements of the web include the concept of Hypertext/Hypermedia, its implementation in HTML and the use of web browsers. Hypertext is an electronic or online version of network text. A hypertext document is made up of a number of textual chunks connected together with associative links called hyperlinks. Hypermedia is a superset of hypertext. HTTP is a protocol that defines how hypermedia documents can be transmitted between nodes in a communication network. HTML is a standard for marking up or tagging documents that can be published on the web, and can be made up of text, graphics, images, audio-clips and video-clips. To access the web one needs a browser. These are essentially programs that let the user read web documents, view any in-built images or activate other media and hotspots. The nodes of the web generally consist of websites and web portals. The term website is generally used to refer to a logical collection of HTML documents normally stored on a web server.

Various front-end ICT systems will interface with a multitude of internal and external stakeholders of the business and will typically involve some form of website accessible via the internet or on an Intranet or Extranet. An Intranet involves using internet technology within the context of a single organisation. An extranet is an extended Intranet. It uses internet technology to connect together a series of intranets, in the process securing communications over the extranet.

The business tier of a typical business ICT application consists of three inter-related elements: update functions, business rules and transactions. Update functions are elements of functionality associated with a particular business application and as such they consist of both business rules and transaction types. Such update functions are triggered by events which are typically initiated at the interface and activate a set of business rules. Once such business rules complete operation, transactions are fired at the data management layer of the ICT system.

Back-end ICT systems include the core systems in the business and tend to be located around databases storing important corporate data. Contemporary data management involves databases, DBMS and data warehouses. The integration of back-end ICT infrastructure is now frequently achieved through the implementation of ERP systems.

To enable the effective flow of transactions between organisations certain standards have to be defined for the format and the transmission of electronic messages. Historically, a standard for transactional flow has been based on something known as Electronic Data Interchange (EDI). More recently, standards have been defined using a web-based technology known as Extensible Markup Language (XML). XML can be used to define standard ways of specifying data structures for the transmission of documents as electronic messages between organisations.

Cloud computing is the idea of delivering computing power to the user in much the same way as electricity or water is delivered as a utility over the internet. The user of a cloud application does not require knowledge of the location or configuration of the application to use it: she merely connects to it over the internet. Cloud computing is not one technology but a series of technologies including client-server computing, software as a service, data centres and virtualisation.

Review test

The four primary components of the technical infrastructure supporting eBusiness are ...	Select all that apply
Access devices	
Communication channels	
Front-end ICT systems	
Messages	
Back-end ICT systems	

An access channel consists of an access device and what else ...	Select the most appropriate term
Communication channel	
Tele-communications device	
Receiver	
Message	
Cable	

An _____ is used to formulate, transmit, receive and display messages	Fill in the blank

Remote access devices include....	Select all that apply
Personal computer	
Satellite communications	
Mobile phone	
Multi-media kiosk	
Interactive digital television	

Communication channels include….	Select all that apply
Conventional telephone network	
ADSL	
Cellular network	
Satellite communications	
Modems	

The Web is different from the Internet.	True or False?
True	
False	

What is meant by packet-switching in the context of the Internet?	Write two sentences

An ____ address is the fundamental way of identifying uniquely a computer system on the Internet.	Fill in the blank

Internet Protocol addresses are mapped to domain names by _____ servers.	Fill in the blank

A Web browser is….	Choose the most appropriate description
A piece of security software	
A piece of software used for accessing hypermedia documents stored on the Web	
A form of search engine	

HTML stands for….	Choose the most appropriate description
Hypertext Markup Language	
Hypermedia Translation Language	
Hot-spot Tracking Language	

What is a universal resource locator and why is it important to the Web?	Write two sentences

XML stands for … .	Choose the most appropriate description
Extra manipulation language	
Extensible markup language	
Extensible manipulation language	

An ICT system can be considered to have five major layers or subsystems...	Place in order with that closest to the user first
Rules Subsystem	
Interface Subsystem	
Data Management Subsystem	
Transaction Subsystem	
Communications Subsystem	

Match the type of system to the most appropriate stakeholder type	
Internet	Customer
Intranet	Supplier
Extranet	Employee

DBMS stands for...	Select the most appropriate description
Data Biometric Migration System	
Database Management System	
Database Mission System	

A database is the same as a DBMS?	True or False?
True	
False	

Exercises

- In terms of traditional access modes such as face-to-face communication what represents the access device and channel?
- In terms of some remote access mechanism investigate the key costs for the stakeholder of maintaining such an access mechanism.
- Does a company known to you use any mobile devices to access systems? What types of system are accessed through such devices?
- Investigate some of the other common tags used in a HTML document.
- Investigate how academic material such as a textbook may be presented via the web.
- In terms of some access channel known to you, investigate the precise media used for data transmission.
- Determine whether an application known to you uses a three-tier client-server architecture.
- Try to find an organisation that maintains both an internet and Intranet website and determine how these two sites differ.
- Determine whether an organisation known to you uses an extranet. Attempt to determine the functionality of the Extranet.
- If you use a computer on some network try to determine the IP address of the computer.

- Determine the entire range of top-level domain names currently available for use.
- Identify core database systems in an organisation known to you?
- Find an example of the use of XML in some key industrial sector.
- Find an example of a cloud application. Determine its pricing model.

Projects

- HTTP is a stateless protocol. Determine more precisely what 'stateless' means in this context. Also determine some of the problems of this stateless nature in terms of building ICT systems on the foundation of such a protocol.
- Bandwidth is defined in this chapter as a key property of a communication channel. Concerns have been raised over the level of bandwidth required not only in the workplace but also in the home over the next decade. Investigate the limitations of bandwidth in supporting the informatics infrastructure in the near future.
- In terms of some remote access channel investigate the key costs for the organisation of maintaining such an access channel. For instance, what access devices are supported? How much does the communication channel cost to run and maintain?
- Every device on the internet has to have its own IP addresses. Not surprisingly, with exponential growth in the internet and devices connected to it, concerns have been expressed over the adequacy of the current addressing scheme to cope. Investigate this issue and proposed solutions to it.
- The internet and the web have created what may be referred to as a global marketplace. Define precisely what globalisation means in relation to communication technology. What consequences does communication technology play in globalisation? Would globalisation happen without communication technology?
- Technology does not stand still. Investigate likely changes to the technology of the internet over the next decade. What are the likely trends and what effect will such trends have on global business?
- Investigate the likely effect of Web 2.0 on business organisations. For instance, business organisations are grappling with both the potential and the pitfalls associated with so-called social networking sites. Some businesses are using such sites and software as means of enhancing collaboration amongst organisational members. Other businesses see social networking as a large security risk.
- Investigate the use of blogs for business purposes. Do web logs offer a distinctive new channel of communication for a business with its customers? How are blogs managed within the overall communication strategy of a company? Are blogs considered part of the content management process or are they managed separately?
- Gather data on a limited range of ICT systems within some organisation. Analyse their functionality in terms of the layered model discussed in this chapter. How easy is it to assign aspects of their functionality to a three-tiered model? Is an N-tiered model more appropriate?
- Most modern ICT systems projects utilise database technology. Investigate why this is the case and to what purposes such database systems are put. What DBMS

are used in association with corporate database and what facilities do such systems provide?

- Investigate the take-up of cloud computing amongst organisations in a particular industrial sector.

Critical reflection

Do you think we would have the internet today without defence spending? In what respect do you feel the internet is creating a global information society? One of the most important factors for business is the reach of the internet into their potential customer population. Is it likely that we will ever achieve 100% penetration of the internet into people's homes? What do you feel is the most important application of an intranet within business? In what ways may extranets be used to more tightly integrate the activities of partner organisations?

Can the performance of some organisation be determined by the degree to which its information systems infrastructure is enabled with ICT? How significant do you think HTML is to business communication and why? How important is it for a company to have a well-designed website and why? Databases have been seen to be perhaps the central technology for modern business. Why do you think this might be the case? To what extent do you think common *data formats* influence trading relationships between companies?

Case exploration

Take one of the dot com companies like Facebook discussed in the case section at the back of the book. Use the model of an ICT system discussed in this chapter to think through some of the technical infrastructure issues considered in this chapter. Consider the issue of how well-designed is the interface. How easy is it for users of Facebook to do things using its interface? When you do something with this interface, such as to add a new friend, what do you think happens in the business layer? What update functions do you think get triggered, what business rules might be applied and what transactions are fired at the data management layer? How do you think data about friends are stored by Facebook? What sort of tables might exist in this database and what columns might exist in a particular table?

Further reading

Chapter 3 of my book *Significance* (Beynon-Davies, 2011) covers the process of communication in more detail. More detail on the technical infrastructure underlying eBusiness is provided in Beynon-Davies, 2009. Tim Berners-Lee has described the genesis of the World-Wide-Web in his book (1999). Schneiderman and Plaisant (2009) cover the interface layer in their book on interface design. Graham covers the business layer in terms of service-oriented architecture (2006). Beynon-Davies (2004) covers the data management layer.

References

Berners-Lee, T. (1999). *Weaving the Web: The Past, Present and Future of the World Wide Web by Its Inventor*, London, Orion Business Publishing.

Beynon-Davies, P. (2004). *Database Systems*, 3rd edn. Houndmills, Basingstoke, Palgrave Macmillan.

Beynon-Davies, P. (2009). *Business Information Systems*, Houndmills, Basingstoke, Palgrave Macmillan (new edition forthcoming).

Beynon-Davies, P. (2011). *Significance: Exploring the Nature of Information, Systems and Technology*, Houndmills, Basingstoke, Palgrave Macmillan.

Graham, I. (2006). *Business Rules Management and Service Oriented Architecture: A Pattern Language*, London, John Wiley.

Schneiderman, B., C. Plaisant, M. Cohen and S. Jacobs. (2009). *Designing the User Interface: Strategies for Effective Human-Computer Interaction*, New York, Pearson.

Shannon, C. E. (1949). *The Mathematical Theory of Communication*, Urbana, University of Illinois Press.

7 ❬ eBusiness environment

Physical environment

Business model

Social environment

Political environment

Economic environment

Learning outcomes	Principles
Understand the relationship between the organisation as a system and the environment of the organisation.	The organisation as a value-creating system interacts with actors within the wider environment. It is useful to consider four major aspects of this environment: economic, social, political and physical.
Describe the nature of the economic environment of the organisation.	The primary environment of a commercial organisation is the economy. Economies are systems for coordinating the production and distribution of goods/products and services. Commerce is the term normally used for that process which deals with the exchange of goods and services from producer to final consumer.
Describe the nature of the social environment of the organisation.	There is clear evidence that modern Western societies are now information societies. The definition of the information society relies on a critical mass of the populace using what we have called electronic delivery as their preferred method of accessing the services and products of public and private sector organisations. A number of pre-conditions exist to the successful uptake of electronic delivery: awareness, interest, access, skills, use and impact.
Understand the political environment of the organisation.	Traditional conceptions of law are being challenged by electronic commerce, such as the use and enforcement of contracts and intellectual property rights.
Describe the nature of the physical environment of the organisation.	Any activity has an impact upon the physical environment. An increasing focus has been given to the proper management of ICT to mitigate effects upon the physical environment and to reduce an organisation's carbon footprint.

Chapter outline

Introduction
Economic environment
Social environment
Political environment
Physical environment
Summary
Review test

Exercises
Projects
Critical reflection
Case exploration
Further reading
References

Introduction

In previous chapters we portrayed an organisation as a value-creating system positioned within a wider environment. By *environment* we normally mean anything outside the organisation with which the organisation interacts. This way of considering organisation and environment is familiar in a technique from business analysis known variously as PEST or PESTLE analysis. A PESTLE analysis is a high-level way of investigating in strategic terms the environment of some organisation. This approach considers the environment as a series of necessary systems that must be considered when contemplating any form of organisational change. These include the political system (P), the economic system (E), the social system (S), the technological system (T), the legal system (L) and the environmental system (E).

We collapse this commonplace approach into a four-fold analysis of the organisational environment in this chapter. From our point of view, the environment of most organisations can be considered in terms of four major inter-dependent systems: an economic system, social system, political system and physical system. In this sense, the external environment can be seen to be made up of a network of activities and relationships in each of these systems between the organisation and other actors. In a sense, the previous chapter has already provided elements of a technology analysis for business, at least as far as ICT is concerned. We also choose to combine the consideration of political and legal issues together in a single section.

An economic system consists of the way in which groups of humans arrange their material provisioning and essentially involves the coordination of activities concerned with such provisioning. An organisation's *economic environment* is defined by activities and relationships between economic actors or agencies and the organisation. The economic environment is particularly concerned with the performance of national and international commerce and trade and is influenced by such factors as levels of taxation, inflation rates and economic growth. Information systems are critical to organisational performance within economic markets. Recently, growth has been experienced in specialised markets focused around the use of electronic networks. Not surprisingly, electronic business and electronic commerce have become significant strategies by which modern organisations improve their performance.

The *social environment* of an organisation concerns its position in the cultural life of some grouping such as the nation state. The social system can be seen to be made up of a series of social networks consisting of activities and relationships that serve to bind various social groupings together. In this chapter we are particularly interested in the ways in which people relate to organisational activity through communities of consumption.

The *political environment* or system concerns issues of power. Political systems consist of sets of activities and relationships concerned with power and its exercise. The political environment is particularly concerned with government and legal frameworks within nation-states and is a major constraining force on organisational behaviour. The political environment of Western countries has been much subject to the influence of ICT in the areas of electronic government and electronic democracy in recent times.

The *physical environment* constitutes the eco-sphere surrounding organisational activity. In recent years growing concerns have been raised as to organisational impact on the physical environment such as the negative effect CO_2 emissions are having on the atmosphere and the way this process contributes to global warming. As a consequence, business organisations are increasingly expected to take action to reduce their 'ecological footprint'. The construction and use of information and ICT systems have a part to play in this process. For instance, ICT makes it increasingly possible for many workers to work from home, reducing the need for commuting to work and consequently reducing their consumption of fossil fuels.

Economic environment

An organisation exists within some wider economic system. At the level of the nation-state we speak of such an economic system as being an economy. An economic system is the way in which groups of humans arrange their material provisioning and essentially involves the coordination of activities concerned with such provisioning.

In Chapter 4 we argued that an economy is a system for the production, distribution and consumption of value. These can be considered three major activity systems relevant to economic systems. *Production* is that set of activities concerned with the creation of goods and services for human existence. *Distribution* is the associated process of collecting, storing and moving goods into the hands of consumers and providing services for consumers. *Consumption* is the process by which consumers receive and use goods and services.

An economic system is thus a system for the exchange of value between diverse economic actors. Commerce is the term normally used for that process which deals with the exchange of goods and services from producer to final consumer. Commerce of whatever nature can be considered as a system or process with the following generic phases of activity: pre-sale, sale execution, sale settlement and after-sale. *Pre-sale* involves activities occurring before a sale occurs. *Sale execution* consists of the activities involved in the actual sale of a product or service between economic actors. *Sale settlement* involves those activities that complete the sale of product or service and *After-sale* involves those activities that take place after the buyer has received the product or service.

Consider the process of buying a book from a bookseller. Pre-sale activity might include the marketing of particular books though inclusion in various online and off-line catalogues. Sale execution clearly involves the purchase of the book by a customer. The customer may be an organisation, in which case, it is likely that sale settlement will occur through a process in which the bookseller invoices the organisation and the purchaser makes payment at some later date. After-sale service may include site visits by sales personnel to particular educational institutions and perhaps initiatives such as discounting particular book lines.

The precise form of this generic process of commerce will vary depending on the economic actors involved, the nature of the goods or services being exchanged and the frequency of commerce between the economic actors.

Generally speaking we may distinguish between organisational actors and individual actors. In terms of organisational actors we may further distinguish between private sector or commercial organisations, public sector organisations and other not-for-profit organisations such as voluntary organisations.

The most important feature of a product or service is typically its price. In such terms we may distinguish between low price items, low- to medium-priced items, medium- to high-priced items and high-price items. As considered in Chapter 4, another important distinction of relevance to eBusiness is whether the goods are tangible or intangible: tangible goods being those that have a physical existence, intangible goods those that can fundamentally be represented as data.

So commerce may involve different types of goods and services. There are also three major patterns of the frequency of commerce. *Repeat commerce* is the pattern in which regular, repeat transactions occur between trading partners. *Credit commerce* is where irregular transactions occur between trading partners and the processes of settlement and execution are separated. *Cash commerce* occurs when irregular transactions of a one-off nature are conducted between economic actors. In cash commerce the processes of execution and settlement are typically combined.

Cash commerce for low- and standard-priced goods typically follows the four stages of the generic commerce model quite closely. For medium- to high-priced items some form of credit commerce will operate. In other words, organisations will search for a product, negotiate a price, order a product, receive delivery of the product, be invoiced for the product, pay for the product and receive some form of after-sales service. For high-priced and customised goods traded between organisations some form of repeat commerce model operates. The same processes occur as for credit commerce but the processes cycle around indefinitely in a trusted relationship between producer and consumer. These three forms of commerce are illustrated in Figure 7.1.

Most purchases of small items over the internet occur in cash commerce mode. For example, the purchase of foodstuffs from an online supermarket chain by members of the general public commonly occurs as a form of cash commerce. In contrast, companies in established relationships tend to work with either a credit or repeat commerce model. Hence, a major supermarket chain will normally place a repeat order with a processed food supplier and will pay this supplier on a regular basis after invoicing on the part of the supplier.

Electronic delivery

The economic value of ICT lies in its ability to support communication and activity both internally within the business and externally with other business actors. As such, ICT is particularly promoted within both the public and private sector as a means of improving the performance of the delivery of services and goods to internal and external actors. The activity of re-designing activity systems and corresponding information systems to meet the challenges of electronic delivery

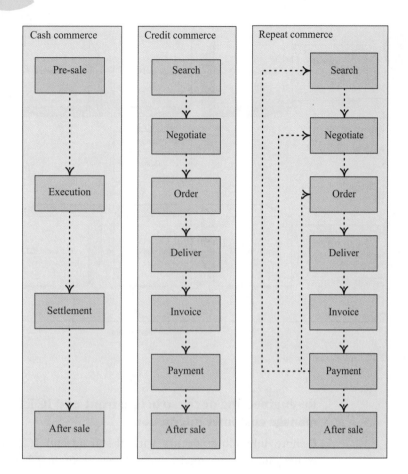

Figure 7.1 Forms of commerce

relies on the creation of effective ICT infrastructure (Chapter 6). Figure 7.2 illustrates elements from this infrastructure which we discuss in terms of business impact below.

Investigating and implementing various access channels for different stakeholders

As discussed in the previous chapter, ICT infrastructure supports remote communication between the internal and external actors of the business and the ICT systems of the organisation. Such interaction occurs through access channels. In terms of interaction with the customer, for instance, face-to-face contact and telephone conversation are two of the most commonly used channels for accessing services and products. However, most large- to medium-scale companies have implemented access channels that allow customers to interact with the organisation using devices such as the internet-enabled personal computer (PC), interactive digital television (iDTV) or the internet-enabled mobile phone. This enables organisations to provide access to company services and products 24 hours a day, 365 days a year. Such remote and mediated access is now a critical part of what eBusiness and eCommerce means for business organisations.

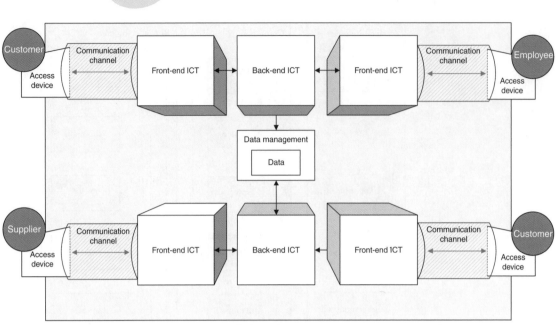

Figure 7.2 ICT infrastructure

Re-engineering or constructing front-end ICT to manage customer interaction

Remote interaction occurs with the front-end ICT of the organisation via communication channels. As we have seen in Chapter 6, the technological infrastructure for modern front-end ICT relies on two critical technologies: the internet and the web. The internet is a set of inter-connected computer networks distributed around the globe and as a concept can be considered on a number of levels. The base infrastructure of the internet is composed of packet-switched networks and a series of communication protocols. On this layer run a series of applications such as electronic mail (email) and more recently the World-Wide-Web – the web for short. The web is effectively a set of standards for the representation and distribution of hypermedia documents over the internet. It has also become a key technology for constructing the front-end ICT of organisations through websites. Because of the increasing use of technologies such as the internet and the web, major investment continues to be undertaken by companies to increase levels of interactivity on their websites. Many companies now provide fully transactional websites in which customers can undertake a substantial proportion of their interaction with a company online.

Providing effective delivery of intangible goods and services

As we have seen in Chapter 4, certain goods and services are information-based or intangible in nature. Examples include music, software, movies and books. As such they are prime candidates for electronic delivery. A large proportion of such intangible goods and services are now typically described as content and made available for access over the internet and the web. Other goods and services are tangible in nature. Examples include foodstuffs, electronic goods, automobiles and medical surgery. Such goods and services are clearly not amenable to electronic delivery. However, the management of the ordering, sale and delivery of such goods and services still relies upon information-based activity to record transactions.

Re-engineering or constructing back-end ICT

Not surprisingly, a key focus within the eBusiness agenda over the past decade or so has involved re-engineering service delivery around the customer. Hence, when a customer enters personal details such as their name and address into one system this information should ideally be available to all other systems that need such data. Such customer-focused strategy demands integration and inter-operability of ICT systems. Typically such integration is reliant on effective data management and data sharing.

Consider the case of a customer of some insurance company in this light. This customer holds three distinct insurance policies with the same company: life insurance, house insurance and car insurance. In the past the insurance company would have run three separate ICT systems for each type of insurance, meaning that the same customer would appear across all three systems. This meant that it was quite difficult to identify those critical customers that conducted multiple lines of business with the company. It also made it difficult to develop strategies such as discounting arrangements to help retain such customers. Not surprisingly, this insurance company decided to invest in re-designing its back-end ICT infrastructure around the customer rather than the insurance policy. This has made it much easier to identify and to retain critical customers.

Ensuring front-end/back-end ICT integration

But integration is not just about establishing linkages between back-end systems; it also concerns establishing linkages between front-end and back-end ICT. For instance, and as we have seen in Chapter 6, to enable fully transactional websites, the data presented need to be updated dynamically from back-end databases. Also, the data entered by customers need to update company information systems effectively.

Social environment

In recent times it has become popular to speak of the information society, thus identifying the important impact of information, information systems and ICT upon modern social systems. In this chapter we use a model of the pre-conditions for the electronic delivery of services and products to structure our discussion of a number of issues present in the social environment that critically affect both current and future eBusiness activity. Three factors are particularly considered as important to consider as key constraints on business activity: the emergence of a digital divide, concerns over the privacy of data and the trust placed in eCommerce transactions.

Pre-conditions for electronic delivery of services and products

The increasing penetration of electronic delivery into business strategies provides some evidence that modern Western societies are information societies. However, at its heart, the idea of an information society relies on a critical mass of the populace using electronic delivery as a preferred method of accessing the services and products of public and private sector organisations.

Although organisations are producing strategies to encourage their external stakeholders such as customers to use remote modes of access to their services and products, a number of pre-conditions exist for the successful uptake of such access channels. These pre-conditions represent the interaction of a range of social factors likely to affect take-up of remote access devices and channels and the use of such channels to interact with forms of electronic delivery.

Business actors or stakeholders must be aware of the benefits of using various remote access channels (awareness). Such benefits must also be seen to outweigh the costs of using electronic delivery in people's minds. However, awareness in and of itself is no guarantee of effective take-up. Actors must also be interested in using various remote access channels for specific purposes (interest). For people to change their conventional way of interacting with organisations over to new access channels there is a substantial and immediate set of transaction costs which include the costs of finding relevant information, the costs of learning new ways of conducting such interaction and the costs of correcting mistakes. These are all typically referred to as switching costs, because they refer to the costs incurred by individuals in switching from one mode of access to another. Evidence suggests that small, up-front transaction costs of this nature frequently discourage people from making a commitment to electronic delivery. To outweigh such transaction costs, interest from customers is likely to depend on substantial and perceived added value offered by using electronic access over traditional modes of access.

Assuming a suitable level of both awareness and interest, stakeholders must further have access to remote access devices from the home or some other convenient location. Measures of such access are frequently expressed in terms of forms of connectivity to the internet. Access can be determined by a whole number of factors, particularly income, since the money available to an individual or household will determine whether or not a computer and internet access (as well as its associated costs) are affordable. There is no such thing as 'free' access to the internet. All those who enjoy 'free' access do so because the university, organisation or other institution in which they work pay the costs. For those who cannot enjoy this luxury, internet access can include the costs of the hardware and software, payments to the Internet Service Provider (ISP), as well as telephone bills for those using internet access through fixed telephony. The cost of upgrading equipment and replacing obsolete software compounds the financial burden imposed on individuals with internet access.

But even if a person has access they must also have the skills necessary to use access devices such as the internet-enabled PC effectively. This is frequently cast as the problem of eLiteracy – the low-level skills required to use ICT. Such low-level skills include being able to use a keyboard and a computer mouse, to conduct basic

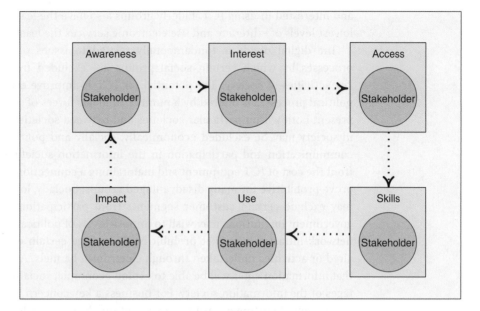

Figure 7.3 Preconditions of electronic service delivery

operations with operating systems such as Microsoft Windows, to use productivity packages such as office software, and to use internet and web tools such as browsers. Clearly there are a substantial number of transaction costs for the individual associated with learning such a range of new skills.

If a person is aware, interested, has access and is skilled enough he or she must commit to using remote access channels on a regular basis in core areas of life. In other words, people accept technological innovations if such innovations become 'domesticated' into personal, everyday routines, in a similar way that other technological devices such as telephones, televisions, fridges, washing machines and micro-wave ovens are domestic appliances.

Finally, use of various access channels must approach a threshold that encourages the provision of more content and services delivered electronically. The hope for many organisations is that a virtuous cycle is established in which better content and services, perhaps directed at particular social, economic or political groups will encourage greater awareness of, interest in and use of remote access channels as the preferred method of interaction with organisations.

Digital divide

Given the nature of technological innovation and the way such innovations diffuse throughout society it is perhaps no surprise to find differential rates of awareness, interest, access, skills and use of ICT amongst different groups in society. However, as more and more areas of everyday activity rely upon use of remote access channels and electronic delivery there is concern that a digital divide continues to disadvantage many groups. For instance, there is substantial evidence to suggest that the older you are the less likely you are to be aware and interested in using ICT. Elderly groups also have the least access to ICT, the lowest levels of e-literacy and use electronic services the least.

The digital divide is fundamentally related to issues of social exclusion – processes by which certain social groups are excluded from participation in key activities of society. The potential for ICT to improve economic, social and political processes is limited by a number of major forces of such social exclusion present both within particular societies and between societies. Particular sectors in society may be excluded economically, socially and politically from effective communication and participation in the information society. On the economic front the cost of ICT equipment and maintaining a connection to the internet may prove prohibitive for many disadvantaged groups. Socially, low levels of eLiteracy may exclude certain customer segments from participation. Finally, politically, government institutions may wish to impose levels of political/state control of the network infrastructure that prohibit or discourage certain opinions from being aired or activities undertaken through electronic channels. A key concern here is that information elites will be able to exploit economic, social and political advantages of the information society. For business a key concern is that major sectors of a potential customer-base will miss-out on electronic delivery of services and products.

Data privacy

As we have seen in Chapter 6, *transactional data* are data that record events taking place between individuals, groups and organisations. Transactional data are essential to the effective running of most organisations and markets. However, the increase in transactional data has potentially insidious consequences. Transactional data can be used to record the daily lives of almost every person in a nation state. These data can be combined with more traditional kinds of data such as people's age and place of birth to permit organisations to make decisions about the planning of their work. Therefore, some key privacy concerns associated with eBusiness include the collection and storage of personal data by companies, the disclosure of such data to third parties and the use of such data by companies or other agencies to impact upon a person's private space.

For instance, *cookies* are data files placed on an access device by a web browser. Such cookies are typically used to identify the user of the access device to the website visited and the date of the last visit to a site. This is particularly useful to companies because they can identify particular customers, monitor their surfing behaviour and tailor interaction with their own particular site in terms of data collected about the customer. However, many regard the use of cookies for the collection of data in this manner as an invasion of privacy. This is mainly because cookies are passed surreptitiously between web server and user. Another example is spamming – the sending of unsolicited emails to large numbers of people whose data are held on address lists of various forms. Sometimes these lists of personal data are sold between organisations.

Such concerns have brought to the fore the issue of ensuring the privacy of data held about an individual. In the UK the Data Protection Act of 1984, laid down a number of principles that enforce good practice in the management of personal data by organisations. In 2000 the UK government implemented new legislation to bring the act in line with the data protection directive of the European Union.

Data protection in the European Union is based upon five main principles: first, that personal data should be collected for a specific and declared purpose; second, that the collection and processing of personal data should be adequate, relevant and not excessive in relation to declared purpose; third, that organisations should maintain accurate and current data on persons and that inaccurate or incomplete data should be erased or rectified; fourth, that personal data should be preserved in a form which permits identification of individuals for a period no longer than that required for the purposes for which the data is stored; fifth, that appropriate security measures, technical and organisational, should be taken to protect personal data from unintended or unauthorised disclosure, destruction or modification.

European countries have generally enacted legislation to attempt to regulate data protection and privacy. In the US the strategy has been to rely more on self-regulation by organisations. This makes it difficult for many multi-national companies to transfer data across the Globe. In order to ease such data transfer the US Department of Commerce and the European Union have created the Safe Harbour Framework. Companies which sign up to this framework are seen as having adequate data protection procedures for cross-border data transfer.

Within the UK, all organisations that maintain personal data must register the data held with the Data Protection Register and are obliged to ensure that their use of such data conforms to the principles established above. Many other countries such as those in Scandinavia have stronger data protection legislation in place.

Personal data and identity

The issue of *data privacy* and the associated idea of data protection are particularly directed at the proper management of personal data. So what makes data personal? Generally, speaking the term personal data is used to refer to data structures composed of three things: personal identifiers, attributes of some person or events in which a person has participated.

In face-to-face communication between business actors personal identity is signified through natural signs such as appearance (how a person looks), behaviour (such as how a person speaks) or names (such as personal names and nicknames). Within forms of mediated communication, such as when a person emails a company, such forms of natural identifier are not available. In substitute, mediated communication tends to use surrogate or artificial identifiers. Examples of surrogate identifiers are codes (such as customer numbers), tokens (such as credit cards) or knowledge (such as PINs and passwords). More recently, there has been increasing interest in biometric identifiers. A biometric is a machine-readable measurement or more readily a series of measurements of some bodily characteristic or behaviour such as an iris scan, a fingerprint or a DNA pattern. These measurements can be used to build a unique profile of an individual and this profile can serve as a strong identifier in situations of remote communication.

Hence, when using an online banking website a customer is likely to be required to enter a range of identifiers to access the services of the website such as a customer number, a password and possibly even aspects of personal knowledge such as the name of a person's father. Certain banks have now started to issue card readers to their online customers. This requires the customer to swipe an identity token such as a debit or credit card through the reader to gain access to the services provided by the website. It is possible for such readers and tokens to eventually store and manipulate biometric data held about the individual.

The banking customer in our example is actually engaged in a process of authentication. *Authentication* involves validating the association between some identifier and the person it stands for. Therefore, the identifier is a symbol or set of symbols that can be used to authenticate an object such as a person. Authentication is a process that involves answering the question – *Am I who I claim to be?* It involves validating the association between the identifier and the person and is a critical aspect of data systems that handle personal data.

Authentication is a prior activity to identification. *Identification* is the process of using an identifier to connect to a stream of data constituting a person's identity. Personal identification in the large involves answering the question *Who am I?* This question is normally answered in terms of attributes of the person such as age, gender, occupation etc., as well as events in which the person has participated, such as having gained a qualification, made an order with a company or submitted a tax return. In this manner, personal identifiers are used to assign identities to individuals within given information systems. For example, a country's public sector agencies frequently have to legitimate somebody as a legal resident or a taxpayer. Within the private sector, financial institutions have to validate the credit-worthiness of a customer before offering a loan.

Organisations authenticate and identify people because these processes determine which persons are entitled to participate in some activity system provided by the organisation. Therefore, a validated identity serves to enrol the individual in some defined activity system. *Enrolment* in this sense involves answering the question – *What am I expected to do and to receive?* Hence, a validated identity such as that of a taxpayer will enrol the individual in a whole range of rights, responsibilities and expected actions in the government activity systems associated with fiscal matters. In some countries it will also entitle the individual to access services provided by the authorities of a particular nation-state such as healthcare.

Hence, personal identity in the modern age is entangled with the operation of a multitude of business or organisational systems. Individuals in the information society use a complex web of identity for existence and action. In our information society an individual may take on a number of different identities, one for each electronic service in the public, private and voluntary sectors with which the individual engages. As a consequence, an individual may accumulate a vast array of personal identifiers for such 'services' and is also likely to accrue a range of physical representations or tokens of such multiple identification such as a credit card, debit card, driving licence, passport, library card, parking permit etc.

The upshot of this is that identifiers and personal data is a critical resource for the accomplishment of everyday existence. Not surprisingly, this valuable resource becomes attractive to criminals. Identity fraud occurs when someone uses personal data gained about another person to impersonate that person. Identity theft occurs when an unauthorised person uses another person's recorded identity to make purchases or engage in other illegal activity. What is interesting is that such issues are a comparatively recent phenomenon. The American sociologist, Michael Poster (2006), for instance, finds no reference to the notion of identity theft before 1995. Indeed, the US government only made identity theft a crime in 2003.

Political environment

The political environment concerns issues of power. Political systems are made up of sets of activities and relationships concerned with power and its exercise. A *polity* is a political system centred on some geographical area in the modern world, such as the nation state, and the shape of a polity will clearly be different depending on the country to which it refers. Some polities such as the European Union may be supra-national polities in the sense that they impose a certain level of communality amongst the political systems of the member states of the union.

Generally speaking a polity will consist of a structure of government, usually some form of parliamentary democracy in the Western world. Polities generate processes of governance through institutions of government. Legislation is the major instrument of such governance processes. In systems terms legislation and agencies of enforcement can be viewed as the major control system within the contemporary nation-state. In such terms, governance is fundamentally the process by which a polity controls a nation state.

Therefore, any organisation, including the business organisation, works within a political environment of legal regulation. Political systems exert considerable pressure on the development and use of ICT systems in organisations. Most polities require that commercial organisations behave in certain ways and enact law to attempt to ensure this. The rise and continued growth of eBusiness has raised the stakes in this process of regulation. A fundamental problem exists in that most legislation is enacted by national governments whereas the phenomenon of eBusiness and particularly eCommerce is a global phenomenon, the activities of which typically cross national boundaries. But eBusiness is not only affected by polities; it has an influence on the shape of the modern polity. In Chapter 9, for instance, we discuss the similarities between issues of relevance to electronic business and their application within the modern domain of electronic government.

Legislation

Political systems can exert significant pressure on the development and use of information systems in organisations. This normally occurs through the requirements of particular aspects of national and supra-national legislation. Most polities require that commercial organisations behave in certain ways. Legislation is enacted to ensure this and the information systems of some organisation as well as the systems of ICT supporting this are normally critically shaped by such legislation.

There are fundamentally two viewpoints on the relationship between eBusiness and legislation. Some legal commentators suggest that the world of eBusiness raises challenging questions about the effectiveness of law, which in the non-electronic world has evolved over centuries to reach its current form. This school of thought argues that although the goals of law remain the same when applied to eBusiness, it often falls short of meeting these goals. Hence, new forms of legislation designed to cope with the practicalities of eBusiness are inevitable. The other school of thought argues that concerns over the role of technology in undermining current legislation are not new. Each new form of remote communication – including surface mail, telegraph, telephone, and fax – has brought with it a new set of legal concerns about, for instance, forming contracts and fulfilling their terms. However, the law has evolved appropriately to cope with the demands of each new technological innovation. Those espousing this view argue that law will evolve as it has done before, and although some new legislation may be required in response to the rapid change in social and business practices brought about by the internet, the existing body of law, perhaps modified in places, will largely be sufficient.

Regardless of the relative merits of the arguments presented by these schools of thought, it cannot be disputed that the rate of development of technologies such as the internet and the web as tools for conducting business have brought challenges to legal systems at a greater rate than previously experienced with the advent of other innovative forms of remote communication. For instance, conventionally law involves a centralised sovereign actor such as a nation-state exerting power within its territorial boundaries. This traditional concept of law is challenged by eCommerce since it lacks geographical boundaries and there is no centralised authority controlling key infrastructure on which it relies such as the internet. Therefore, some of the key areas of concern for eBusiness in the area of regulation include use and enforcement of contracts, use and enforcement of intellectual property rights, laws enacted by nation-states to enforce advertising standards and collection of sales tax from global customers.

Contracts

Contract law defines the use and nature of contracts between individuals and business organisations. A contract is an agreement between parties which is enforceable in law. Such legislation defines valid business activity between customers, suppliers and organisations. Hence, the design of trading systems between customers, suppliers and organisations will be heavily affected by contractual regulation. A contract defines an agreement between parties over business activity. The basic elements of a valid contract in the UK are offer, consideration, intention to create legal relations and acceptance (compared with offer, consideration and acceptance in the USA).

In terms of a sale of goods, for instance, a contract details the precise nature of the sale including the price of goods and delivery conditions. When making a purchase in person, opportunities exist to raise questions about the goods, the price and other concerns. If parties have doubts about the integrity of the product, are concerned about whether the parties have authority to make the transaction, or if the payment is suspect, again opportunities exist to ask questions in order to obtain further information. If anything goes wrong with the sale then either party has recourse to the law.

In the world of eCommerce a number of difficulties emerge with contracts. For instance, because a sale is made through the exchange of electronic messages it is frequently difficult to determine the precise nature of contractual obligation. Some commentators question whether an electronic communication can be considered a 'writing' that will be accepted in a court of law. Also, there is a lack of opportunity for parties to evaluate the goods being sold before purchase and it is frequently difficult for parties to authenticate each other. Finally, because a sales transaction may be conducted across national borders it is frequently difficult to determine which nation's contractual law applies in a particular case. This is expressed as the problem of jurisdiction.

In the UK, commercial contracts do not generally have to take written form and hence the law is generally favourable to electronic contracts. However, some types of contract (particularly those relating to property) do have to be in writing. Interestingly, the content of a website (which may include price information) is not viewed as a contractual obligation, but as an advertisement, the content of which is covered by the code of the Advertising Standards Authority (ASA).

At the international level, there is no consensus on contractual law. However, the United Nations Commission on International Trade Law (UNCITRAL) has, through its Model Law on Electronic Commerce, attempted to establish an international standard. Although this law has no authority until individual countries adopt it through their respective legislative processes, it does represent an effort to bring clarity to electronic contracts in the international environment. The UNCITRAL Model Law adopts a minimalist approach, recognising that contracts may be made and signed in an electronic environment, and that electronic transmissions may satisfy signature requirements. Similarly, the European Union (EU) has issued a Directive on Electronic Signatures (1999/93/EC) that requires member states to enact legislation pertaining to the authentication and recognition of electronic signatures.

Intellectual Property Rights

Another key aspect of the law which has been significantly affected by eCommerce is that of intellectual property rights. The nature of eCommerce is such that it is constantly involved in the production and transfer of data. It is this data-based nature of eCommerce that brings the phenomenon into direct confrontation with intellectual property law. Intellectual property rights emerged as a means of ensuring that creators are able to benefit from their intellectual accomplishments. Two types of intellectual property rights are commonly recognized: those which are protected by patents, trademarks and design rights, and those which are protected by *copyright*.

A trademark is an attempt to distinguish the goods or services of one company from that of another. A trademark is a sign that distinguishes the goods or services of one business from another, and should be registered with the appropriate authorities. A trademark may consist of a company logo, a name or even a sound or tune. Indeed, anything which serves to identify an organisation can be registered as a trademark.

In the UK, trademarks are registered at the *Trade Marks Registry*. Once in possession of a trademark, the owner is in a strong position to prevent a third party from using that mark. Unfortunately, trademarks can be registered only within the realms of a particular country. Hence, protecting a trademark on the internet is made difficult because a user of a trademark registered in one country is not guaranteed use of that trademark in another country.

Within the domain of eCommerce, the issue of trademarks is very much bound up with the technology of domain names. As we have seen in Chapter 6, computer systems are identified on the internet via Internet Protocol or IP addresses. In turn, such IP addresses are mapped to domain names by *domain name servers*. These are computer systems in the inter-network that perform this transformation. Clearly, for such domain servers to work effectively some form of standardisation is needed in the adoption of domain names.

Any domain name is typically made up of three or more parts referred to as domain levels. Levels therefore provide structure to the domain name. In a particular URL, domain levels read from right to left: sub-domain, 2nd level domain, top-level domain. Top-level domains (TLDs), consist of either so-called generic top-level domain names (such as *.com*) and referred to as gTLDs or country codes (such as *.uk*) and referred to as ccTLDs. gTLDs are also referred to as 1st level domain names. 2nd level domains serve to further refine the top-level domain name by typically suggesting the type of provider. For instance, *.ac* indicates an academic institution based in the UK. Sub-domains refer to those domains below the 2nd level and are typically used to refer to a specific content provider. In our example, *cardiff* signifies the website of Cardiff University.

Standardisation of domain names has traditionally been in the hands of the US government. During the late 1980s and early 1990s, the responsibility for allocating domain names was given to the Internet Assignment Number Authority (IANA). Then a company – Network Solutions Inc. (NSI) – was set up and started charging customers for the registration of domain names. In 1997, IANA and a number of other organisations advocated self-governance in the domain name service and a year later the Internet Corporation for Assigned Names and Numbers (ICANN) was created. Its main role is to oversee the allocation of domain names and the distribution of addresses by domain name registrars. Domain name registrars are public and private organisations that exist within countries tasked with maintaining registries (databases of domain names and IP addresses). ICANN therefore have responsibility for a number of naming conventions including gTLDs such as *.com* and *.org* and ccTLDs such as *.uk* and *.fr*. They also have responsibility for sponsored top-level domain names (sTLDs) such as *.coop* and *.museum* and un-sponsored TLDs such as *.biz*.

IANA originally created seven Generic Top Level Domains (gTLDs), consisting of strings of three letters taken from the following list: *.com.* (signifying some form of commercial organisation), *.org* (signifying any type of organisation but typically used to signify public sector or voluntary sector organisations), *.gov* (initially used to signify government establishments generally but now restricted to refer to US government establishments), *.edu* (used generally to signify an educational institution internationally), *.mil* (initially used to signify military establishments generally but now restricted to refer to US Armed Forces establishments), *.int.* (initially conceived for international entities), *.net* (initially used to signify 'networks' and therefore a generic free usage domain).

Therefore, over time the domain system has been gradually extended, sometimes in an apparent piecemeal manner. For instance, the current ICANN namespace contains 21 registered gTLDs all of which are open for use as supporting infrastructure for the internet. At the end of 2006 there were 120 million unique registered domain names in the world and, of these, 80 million were generic TLDs. The most commonly used generic TLD was *.com*, with 62 million domains. There was a 32% increase in domain name registrations in 2006 as compared to 2005. In early 2010 there were 192 million registered domain names with the largest fraction still being in the *.com* TLD.

In the world of eCommerce companies often register their domain names as trademarks in an attempt to prevent what is called cyber-squatting – the use of a popular domain name by another company to attract customers. There have been a number of cases in the UK where domain name registrations have been challenged in court. For instance, the retail store Harrods obtained an injunction requiring the holders of the domain name *harrods.com* to transfer all rights to Harrods.

Perhaps the best known case of this type was the 1998 Court of Appeal decision in favour of British Telecom and others who had mounted a legal challenge to the activities of the One-in-a-Million organisation. One-in-a-Million had registered domain names of a number of well-known entities including marksandspencer.com, sainsbury.com, BT.com, virgin.com and spicegirls.com. These domain names contained the names and/or trademarks of those involved, and were judged to constitute an instance of trademark infringement. The view of the Court was that there was clear evidence of systematic registration of well-known names in order to prevent their registration by their authorised owners, and that even though the names had not been used online, the law had been infringed. The judgement against One-in-a-Million effectively ended the practice of domain name squatting, at least in the UK.

Copyright law enables authors of an intellectual property to prevent unauthorised copying of such material. The law applies to physical transactions of written material regardless of its country of origin. The law applies equally to digital products such as computer programmes and documents published on the internet. The difficulty lies in the enforcement of copyright law between countries. Also, copyright law is unclear over the precise nature of links from websites to other material.

The ease with which digital material placed on the internet may be copied, altered and redistributed poses obvious intellectual property problems. Although copyright laws suggest that use of material is only lawful with the consent of the copyright holder, once material is placed on the internet the copyright holder effectively loses all control of the material. The material may be downloaded, printed, distributed, altered or even sold for profit without the consent of the copy-right holder. The ease in which material may be purloined from internet sources has resulted in numerous legal disputes. The key lesson for business is that careful thought should be given to possible repercussions when any material is placed on a website. This extends to the use of material for which a license is already held, as licenses are generally granted to use copyrighted works for a specific and limited purpose and this purpose may not extend to use of that material in electronic form on a website.

Copyright may also be breached by the use of hypertext links on websites. In a well-known case (Shetland Times vs Wills and Zetnews Ltd), the Outer House Court of Session in Scotland ruled that the defendants' use of hypertext links to point directly to news stories in the plaintiff's website (bypassing the plaintiff's home page), coupled with their copying of the plaintiff's headlines in their website constituted an infringement of the Copyright, Designs and Patents Act, 1988. Part of the settlement entitled the defendants' continued use of the headlines, provided that they displayed the Shetland Times logo on their homepage, and acknowledged that the headlines referred to Shetland Times new stories.

Taxation

The internet facilitates the creation of global electronic marketplaces. This causes key problems in taxation which affects commercial activity such as transactions affecting the sale of goods. The establishment and enforcement of taxation in such areas is typically an issue for a nation-state. However, companies trading over electronic markets can typically choose to set up operation where the costs of taxation are the lowest. For instance, the UK bookmaker William Hill has set up an internet-based betting operation in Gibraltar where there are lower duties on betting than in the UK. Such movement to 'offshore' operations has caused significant loss of revenue to the UK government. Supra-national governments such as the European Union are attempting to establish policy that will cross national boundaries and cope with some of these problems of eCommerce.

Physical environment

Any activity, whether it is performed by individual actors or groups of actors working for organisations, has an impact upon the physical environment. As ICT has become more and more embedded within the activity of the modern business, an increasing focus has been given to the proper management of ICT to mitigate effects upon the ecological footprint of the business organisation.

The idea of an *ecological footprint* is an attempt to measure the impact of human activity upon the physical environment. Any human activity on this planet consumes resources of natural capital such as land, sea and the atmosphere. As a by-product of such activity humans also produce waste which has the potential to contaminate the physical environment, thereby degrading resources of natural capital. As a measure, an ecological footprint is the amount of natural capital (expressed as a planet Earth) that it takes to supply resources for current human activity. In 2006 this was calculated as 1.4 planet Earths. In other words, humanity is consuming physical resources 1.4 times faster than the Earth can renew such resources, clearly an unsustainable and potentially unviable system.

At the level of nation-states and business organisations another related measure is typically used as a measure of environmental impact: that of a *carbon footprint*. This is the total amount of greenhouse gas (GHG) emissions caused by some actor such as an organisation, person, plant or machine. A greenhouse gas is a gas in the atmosphere that absorbs and emits radiation within the thermal infrared range. This property of such gases is the fundamental cause of the greenhouse effect which contributes to global warming. The primary greenhouse gases in the atmosphere are water vapour, carbon dioxide, methane, nitrous oxide and ozone. Greenhouse gases are emitted directly in various ways such as through transport, land clearance or industrial manufacture. Such gases are also an indirect consequence of the production and consumption of food, fuels, manufactured goods and services. For simplicity of reporting, a carbon footprint is typically expressed in terms of the amount of carbon dioxide, or its equivalent, emitted by some activity system.

The ICT infrastructure of an organisation can impact an organisation's carbon footprint in a number of ways. Consider, for instance, the life-cycle of a typical piece of ICT hardware such as a personal computer. To produce a typical PC and its associated monitor over 27 different materials are likely to be used. The extraction and production of these materials causes considerable GHG emissions. These materials then have to be transported to the site of manufacture, frequently from diverse parts of the globe, causing up to 5% of the GHG emissions associated with the entire life-cycle. In the manufacture of a PC, crucial processes such as semiconductor manufacture use more than 1,000 hazardous substances. Once a PC is put into use its lifetime of electricity consumption typically amounts to 50% of its original purchase cost. At some point the hardware is disposed of, meaning that processes have to be devised for recycling as much of the original material as possible. It is currently possible to recycle as much a 75% of such materials.

What has become known as green IT is a collection of IT- or ICT-related initiatives which aim to directly reduce the carbon footprint of some organisation. There are many such initiatives including environmentally-friendly printing, energy-efficient computing, sustainable data storage, virtualisation, cloud computing and use of software as a service.

Environmentally friendly printing

Environmentally friendly printing involves the replacement of standalone printers dedicated to one PC with network-enabled printers that are shared between a number of personal computers. Such printers should also be configured to print in duplex mode (on both sides of the page) and on recycled paper for most internal business uses. Finally, such printers should never be left in standby mode for long periods of time, but turned off.

Energy-efficient computing

One of the most effective ways of improving the energy efficiency of computing infrastructure is through the replacement of desktop personal computers with laptops. Laptop computers are designed as a matter of course with energy efficiency in mind because of the need to prolong battery life. Normally, for instance, such machines can be configured to go into hibernation mode when unused, consuming little energy. In this manner, the typical laptop can, if properly configured, consume as much as 85% less energy than the comparable desktop personal computer.

Sustainable data storage

Data storage devices consume large amounts of energy. Organisations can minimise their use of such a resource by reducing the amount of redundancy in their data resource. This involves actively searching for unnecessary duplication amongst files backed-up to external storage and removing such duplication to reduce the size of stored data and consequently the amount of such storage needed.

Cloud computing

At first glance cloud computing does not appear a good idea in terms of its impact upon the physical environment. For instance, Google is said to operate a global network of approximately 36 data centres needed to run its *search engine*. Microsoft's data centre in Chicago is reputed to need three electrical substations with a capacity of 198 megawatts to run effectively. The Environmental Protection Agency in the US estimates that the 7,000 or so data centres that exist in the country consume 1.5% of the country's electricity consumption.

However, there are a number of environmental advantages proposed for cloud computing. From the point of view of the producer, infrastructure such as data centres can be located in areas with lower property costs, close to water (for cooling purposes) and within easy access of electricity supplies. This centralisation of resources may make it easier to mitigate the environmental impact of ICT infrastructure. For example, from the point of view of the consumer cloud computing has the potential to make applications much more scalable. Hence, if a company expands its activities it does not need to purchase vast new communication and data resources; it merely extends its use of cloud services. Further, the application itself in terms of software and data can be separated from physical resources such as hardware. Hence, if more computing power is required to handle peak loads additional cloud servers can be applied to the task on an as-needed basis. This on-demand use of computing resources may be more energy-efficient than having vast communication and data resource managed by consuming organisations themselves.

Summary

The primary environment of a commercial organisation is the economy. Economies are systems for coordinating the production and distribution of goods/products and services. An economic system is thus a system for the exchange of value between diverse economic actors. Commerce is the term normally used for that process which deals with the exchange of goods and services from producer to final consumer. Commerce of whatever nature can be considered a system or process with the following generic phases of activity: pre-sale, sale execution, sale settlement and after-sale. The economic value of ICT lies in its ability to support communication and activity both internally within the business and externally with other business actors. As such, ICT is particularly promoted within both the public and private sector as a means of improving the performance of the delivery of services and goods to internal and external actors.

There is clear evidence that modern Western societies are now information societies. The definition of the information society relies on a critical mass of the populace using what we have called electronic delivery as their preferred method of accessing the services and products of public and private sector organisations. A number of pre-conditions exist to the successful uptake of electronic delivery: awareness, interest, access, skills, use and impact. The digital divide fundamentally refers to the phenomenon of differential rates of awareness, interest, access, skills and use amongst different groups in society. Evidence suggests that low levels of trust and concerns over data privacy affect the take-up of electronic delivery.

Traditional conceptions of law are being challenged by electronic commerce. Some of the key areas of concern for eBusiness include the use and enforcement of contracts and intellectual property rights. Contract law defines the use and nature of contracts between individuals and business organisations. In the world of electronic commerce a number of difficulties emerge with contracts such as a lack of opportunity for parties to evaluate the goods being sold and it is frequently difficult for parties to authenticate each other. Another key aspect of the law which has been significantly affected by eCommerce is that of intellectual property rights. Two types of intellectual property rights are commonly recognised: those which are protected by patents, trademarks and design rights, and those which are protected by copyright. There is significant overlap between the issue of internet domain names and that of trademarks. A key concern for copyright is the difficulty of protecting creators rights in terms of content published on the web.

Any activity has an impact upon the physical environment. As ICT has become more and more embedded within the activity of the modern business, an increasing focus has been given to the proper management of ICT to mitigate effects upon the physical environment. The ICT infrastructure of an organisation can impact an organisation's carbon footprint in a number of ways. Green ICT is a collection of ICT-related initiatives which aim to directly reduce the carbon footprint of some organisation, such as environmentally friendly printing, energy-efficient computing, sustainable data storage, virtualisation, cloud computing and use of software as a service.

Review test

Commerce constitutes the exchange of goods and services between businesses, groups and individuals	True or False?
True	
False	

The precise form of the process of commerce will vary in terms of...	Choose all that are relevant
The economic actors involved	
The type of technology	
The frequency of commerce	
The nature of the goods or services being exchanged	

Commerce of whatever nature can be considered as a process with four main phases….	Put the phases in descending order with 1 used for the first phase
After-sale	
Sale settlement	
Sale execution	
Pre-sale	

In terms of the types of commerce match the term to the appropriate definition	Match the elements
Repeat Commerce	Where irregular transactions occur between trading partners and the processes of settlement and execution are separated
Credit Commerce	The pattern in which regular, repeat transactions occur between trading partners
Cash Commerce	When irregular transactions of a one-off nature are conducted between economic actors and when the processes of execution and settlement are typically combined

Put the preconditions for electronic service delivery in the correct order	Use 1 for the first precondition, and so on..
Awareness	
Skills	
Impact	
Use	
Interest	
Access	

The digital divide is an issue of social exclusion	True or False?
True	
False	

One of the principles of _____ in the European Union is that personal data should be collected for a specific and declared purpose.	Fill in the blank

_____ is the use of a popular domain name by another company to attract customers.	Fill in the blank

A carbon footprint is the total amount of greenhouse gas (GHG) emissions caused by some actor such as an organisation, person, plant or machine	True or False?
True	
False	

Green ICT is ...	Choose the most relevant definition
The use of energy efficient laptops	
The sustainable disposal of IT equipment	
A collection of ICT-related initiatives which aim to directly reduce the carbon footprint of some organisation	

Exercises

- Consider a commercial transaction you have made such as buying some product over the internet. Run through the stages of the generic commerce model in terms of this transaction.
- Take two access devices such as a mobile phone and a tablet computer. Investigate the degree to which these two devices could be said to be digitally converged.
- Find an example of cyber-squatting.
- Have a conversation with a person over 70 known to you. Assess them in terms their awareness of, interest in and ability to use ICT.
- Take one government service such as housing benefit. Are you able to access such benefits online? Are any people excluded from such access?
- Social networking media have been seen as important to the organisation of political protest in the Middle East. Access some news reporting on this issue and assess their importance for yourself.
- Consider what data you hand over to a company such as a supermarket chain when you sign up for their loyalty card. Ask the company to tell you how they keep your personal data protected.
- Develop a plan to improve the sustainability of your own personal use of ICT.

Projects

- Investigate at least two commerce systems used by a company known to you. Assess what model of commerce is used in each system. How closely does each system follow the model described in this chapter?
- Investigate current copyright law in more detail and evaluate its capability for coping with the increasing demands of digital convergence.
- Digital rights management technology has been proposed as one solution to problems of infringing copyright. Investigate the capabilities of such technology.
- Investigate the prevalence of the activity of cyber-squatting in a particular industrial area.
- In terms of some electronic service known to you use the model of pre-conditions to analyse some of the barriers to effective take-up of such a service.
- Investigate the literature to determine what characteristics of individuals tend to be involved in making them digitally excluded.
- Investigate data protection legislation in two countries: one perhaps within Europe and one outside Europe. Assess the similarities and differences in such legislation. In which state are your personal data the best protected?
- Investigate whether an organisation known to you has a green ICT strategy. If it does not, develop elements of such a strategy.

Critical reflection

How extensive do you think the digital divide is at the moment? What policies might have an impact on the digital divide? Are you personally able to list the benefits of electronic delivery? What strategies are needed to raise the awareness of such benefits? Are low levels of awareness a concern for business and why? How would you persuade a customer of your organisation that there is significant added-value in electronic delivery to your products and services? What is the added-value? At what level do you think that access to the internet will stabilise amongst the general population? Do you think that public internet access points actually increase levels of access? Are there any specific skills associated with using transactional websites? Is it easy to switch between using say one flight booking service on the internet and another?

How concerned are you over the privacy of data held about yourself? How much trust do you place in eCommerce. Do you release your credit or debit card details in eCommerce transactions currently? Have you had any adverse experiences, such as identity theft, with eCommerce?

Which do you think is the most appropriate position – that existing law may be adapted to cope with eBusiness and eCommerce or that new forms of legislation will need to be invented to cope with this phenomenon? Why are trademarks and domain name registration such a significant problem for modern business? Have you ever typed in a web address on the basis of some expected company name and found yourself in a surprising place? What were your reactions to this? How significant do you think is plagiarism from web content in relation to student courseworks? Is this a copyright problem? If the internet became a tariff-free zone what consequences might this have for conventional forms of trade? What consequences would this have for e-Commerce?

Case exploration

Consider the national identity card case or the electoral system case in terms of the issues discussed in this chapter. For instance, assume the UK implemented an electronic voting system. What impact would the digital divide have on the success of such a system. Would this system improve democratic representation? Would the use of this system be more environmentally friendly than the traditional system of voting?

India is undergoing a process of issuing a national identity number to each of its citizens. The idea is that this will help reduce corruption experienced in attempts to distribute aid to the poor. Reflect on this in the light of the UK experience of trying to introduce a personal identifier for UK citizens.

Further reading

Worthington and Britton (2009) provide a review of the economic environment of the business. An overview of the idea of Green ICT is covered in the book by O'Neill (2010). Stevens and O'Hara (2006) review the issue of the digital divide and its links to social exclusion. Cowhey and Aronson (2009) cover some of the issues within the political environment influencing global communication.

References

Cowhey, P. F. and J. D. Aronson. (2009). *Transforming Global Information and Communication Markets: The Political Economy of Innovation*, Cambridge, MA, MIT Press.

ONeill, M. G. (2010). *Green IT: For Sustainable Business Practice*, Swindon, British Computer Society.

Poster, M. (2006). *Information Please: Culture and Politics in the Age of Digital Machines*, New York, Duke University Press.

Stevens, D. and K. OHara, eds (2006). *Inequality.Com: Power, Poverty and the Digital Divide*, Oxford, Oneworld publications.

Worthington, I. and C. Britton. (2009). *The Business Environment*, Harlow, UK, Pearson Education.

8

Forms of eBusiness

Learning outcomes	Principles
Understand the distinction between eBusiness and eCommerce.	eBusiness is a term we use to encompass the entire range of ICT application within business, whether this is to improve internal operations or to extend the organisation into its environment. We restrict the term electronic commerce to the use of ICT within the external activities and relationships of the business with individuals, groups and other businesses.
Describe a number of innovations constituting B2C eCommerce.	Business-to-Consumer eCommerce refers to the support of the organisation's customer chain with ICT and involves the ICT-enablement of key processes in the customer chain. We portray an organisation's experience of B2C eCommerce as moving through a number of distinct stages of increasing complexity.
Describe a number of innovations constituting B2B eCommerce.	B2B eCommerce represents the attempt by organisations to use ICT to improve elements of their supply chains. Considered as a process, a typical supply chain includes activities such as search, negotiate, order, delivery, invoice, payment and after-sale.
Describe a number of innovations constituting C2C eCommerce.	C2C eCommerce represents ICT enablement of the community chain. Public sector initiatives have been interested in enhancing traditional communities with increased ICT use. The private sector has been interested in the community chain as a new revenue source or as a means of adding value to traditional commercial activities.
Describe a number of innovations constituting P2P eCommerce.	Whereas recent interest has been directed at the ways in which networks of consumers generate value there has also been interest in the ways in which networks of businesses can utilise ICT to collaborate as well as compete. Internally, organisations are beginning to manage collaboration across internal units and divisions globally. Externally, digital ecosystems of businesses are emerging.

Introduction

The eminent British scientist Michael Faraday once gave a tour of his laboratory to the then Prime Minister. He was asked what use the discovery of electricity could possibly have. 'I cannot say', Faraday replied, 'but one day Her Majesty's government will tax it'.

Prediction of the impact of technology is an inherently tricky business. For a number of years continuous predictions have been made as to the revolutionary potential of ICT in relation to business. Many such predictions have missed the mark but many others have hit the target. ICT has been applied over the past 60 years as a catalyst for change of internal business practices. More recently innovation within this area has shifted to an external focus and is now focused upon the application of such technology within external activities and in support of relationships with external stakeholders.

Within this chapter we make a clear distinction between these two application areas for ICT. As we have seen in Chapter 2, business can either be considered as an entity or as that set of activities undertaken by a commercial organisation. Electronic Business or eBusiness can be defined as the application of information and communication technologies in support of all activities undertaken by the business. In contrast, and as we have seen in the previous chapter, the term commerce is normally taken to constitute the exchange of products and services between the business and external business actors: other businesses, groups and individuals. Therefore, electronic commerce or eCommerce focuses on the use of ICT to enable the external activities and relationships of the business with such external actors.

Hence, these distinctions allow us to distinguish between the use of ICT to enable communication and coordination between the internal stakeholders of the business such as employees (*intra-business eBusiness*) from the use of ICT to enable communication and coordination with external actors such as suppliers and customers (eCommerce). By definition intra-business eBusiness has been around as long as ICT has been applied within business. Many aspects of eCommerce also have a history of 20 years or so in terms of business application. However, we should not assume that we are at the end of innovation in this area. Both the technical (Chapter 6) and activity infrastructure (Chapter 10) of eBusiness is continually evolving to meet the challenges of an increasingly volatile and global environment within which the modern business must both remain currently viable and sustainable in the longer-term.

eBusiness and eCommerce

Rather ephemerally, traditional businesses have been referred to as *bricks-and-mortar businesses* in the sense that they have a physical presence usually in terms of some offices, factories or retail outlets where they are located. In contrast, traditional businesses that have moved into the world of eBusiness are referred to as clicks-and-mortar businesses. They still maintain a physical presence but also offer services and products accessible via ICT, particularly via websites

(Chapter 6). Businesses that have emerged entirely in the online environment are known as 'clicks-only' businesses. It is clearly in the latter two areas that our interest lies in this chapter. Decisions as to the strategy (Chapter 10) taken in relation to the particular type of eBusiness adopted by a company relies upon an understanding of the ways in which ICT can be used by businesses to innovate within their wider value-network (Chapter 4).

Figure 8.1 provides a framework for understanding the current makeup of electronic business based upon the idea of the organisation as a value-creating system working within a wider value network (Chapter 4). To refresh, the original value-chain model has proven useful as a generic 'business model' for understanding the place of ICT in the business. More recently the value-chain idea has been extended into the idea of the value-network, which is particularly useful as a means of distinguishing between distinct forms of eBusiness. The model in the figure also allows us to place some of the newer application areas for eBusiness (such as social networking sites) in relation to some of the more established areas of eBusiness such as supply-chain management systems.

The traditional view of eCommerce mapped onto the value-network represents the use of ICT to support the external activities/relationships of business with two major stakeholder groups: suppliers and customers. Business to consumer (B2C) eCommerce is sometimes called sell-side eCommerce and concerns the enablement of the customer chain with ICT. Business-to-business (B2B) eCommerce is sometimes called buy-side eCommerce and involves supporting the supply chain with ICT. C2C or Consumer-to-Consumer eCommerce also has a place within this model and is a developing form of eCommerce recently linked to 'new media' services. This is potentially the most radical form of eCommerce since it overlaps with non-commercial activity in the area of community (Chapter 4). C2C

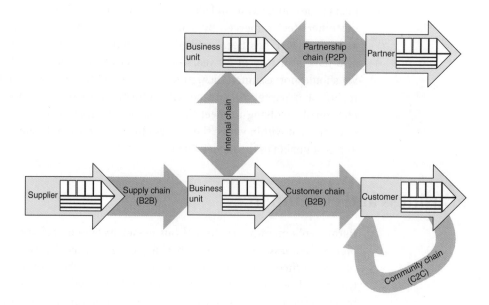

Figure 8.1 Forms of eBusiness

eCommerce is therefore built upon the 'community' chain and a new range of business opportunities emerge within virtual networking as a phenomenon driving new levels of content and services.

But the massive levels of interest in eCommerce over the past decade have tended to devalue the importance of ICT to internal operations. This is a mistake. The model in Figure 8.1 emphasises that eBusiness is as much about internal operations as it is about external operations. It also highlights the increasing importance of integration between the internal and external focus across the value-network. Therefore, Figure 8.1 also includes two areas which extend to both the internal and external forms of electronic business.

First, any contemporary definition of eBusiness must include the growing range of issues associated with providing effective infrastructure for multi-part businesses spread geographically across the globe. The modern eBusiness is likely to be made up of numerous dispersed business units some physically co-located, some mobile. Modern ICT infrastructure acts as a critical backbone for such complex organisations.

Second, any accurate conception of eBusiness must extend the notion of business cooperation and collaboration beyond that of the supply chain. This means that contemporary eBusiness is likely to be evident in a network of business partnerships of varying complexity. Hence, eBusiness involves the application of ICT both in cooperative as well as competitive activity. As we have seen in Chapter 4, a particular business may actually fulfil a number of different roles in the value-network at the same time – such as being both a partner and a competitor. Therefore, some have referred to this phenomenon as co-option.

Goronwy Galvanising

Consider the case of Goronwy Galvanising (Chapter 2). Goronwy was initially a classic bricks-and-mortar business specialising in the manufacture of steel products. But Goronwy is actually one business unit of a large multi-national company, Rito Metals, whose primary business includes the extraction and processing of base metals such as zinc as well as the production of various metal alloys. Rito Metals maintains ten galvanising plants on similar lines to Goronwy situated around Europe. Each plant is relatively autonomous in terms of managing its day-to-day business. Head office at Rito Metals co-ordinates administrative activities such as finance and human resources but each plant manages its own operational activities in areas such as sales, production and logistics.

We established in Chapter 3 that information systems are critical to supporting decisions and action within an activity system. The performance of the activity system itself is hence heavily reliant on the flow of quality data from its associated information system. However, in the case of Goronwy Galvanising in the 1980s, there were a number of problems with the manual data system supporting this information system.

First, data needed to be shared amongst a number of people, particularly inbound logistics operatives, production controllers, shift foremen and outbound logistics operatives. This meant that copies frequently had to be made of documentation, consuming much-needed time and resource. Second, to ensure an effective flow of data, a considerable amount of time was taken in transferring data from one collection of forms (such as delivery advice notes) on to other forms (such as job sheets). Third, human errors in entering the wrong data onto any of the three forms in the data system of Goronwy Galvanising had a number of considerable repercussions for the efficiency of the galvanising process. Valuable time and effort was frequently expended in resolving such errors by staff throughout the company. Fourth, managers in the company found it difficult to utilise the data stored in records for strategic as well as operational purposes. For example, it was difficult for managers at headquarters to collate and analyse data to determine trends such as the throughput of the plant and consequently the productivity of the workforce. In order to conduct such analyses much time and effort had to be expended on the part of both local and headquarters administrative staff.

Problems such as these persuaded both Goronwy and its parent company, Rito Metals, to consider investing in the construction of an ICT system to handle the basic administrative functions of the data system described in Chapter 2. This effectively began the process of implementing intra-business eBusiness within Goronwy.

At Goronwy, this new ICT system continued in operation at the plant for a couple of years. After this time an evaluation was conducted by the parent company, Rito Metals. It concluded that the introduction of this ICT system had been successful in improving the plants' performance in a number of ways. Less documentation was produced and less time was consequently spent in copying data or resolving errors in data handling. This had a positive impact upon the general throughput of material through the plant. It also made it much easier for managers to monitor operations and adjust resource allocation to maintain performance at targeted levels. The results of this evaluation were distributed to executives at headquarters who on the basis of this made the decision to roll-out the ICT system at all ten galvanising plants within the group. The objective of this strategic decision was not only to improve the data-handling across its galvanising plants; it was also to promote a degree of inherent standardisation of both information systems and activity systems across separate plants.

The eventual rollout of the ICT system across the group took a further two years to complete. Some plants found it difficult to change their specific working practices (performative and communicative activities) to the demands of the new ICT system. However, the presence of a standard ICT infrastructure across all its galvanising plants opened up the possibility of creating a management information system at headquarters, fed with data from the individual ICT systems at plants around Europe. To enable this, a dedicated wide-area communication network was created, linking each of the ICT systems within its plants with the new management ICT system at headquarters.

This new management information system enabled Rito Metals to carry out more effective strategic management of its galvanising plants, because it was able to obtain an accurate and up-to-date picture of operations and problems at particular plants, making them easier to identify and rectify. In this sense, the presence of the management information system enabled more effective control of separate business units.

Each of the technological innovations described above contributed to the establishment of an integrated ICT and information systems infrastructure for the company. In a sense, the emergence of this infrastructure moved Rito Metals in the direction of becoming an eBusiness, because the use of ICT became critical to supporting its internal value-chain across Europe. Goronwy Galvanising in the mid-1990s soon realised the potential of providing remote access channels to its ICT system both for its employees and its customers. The first step taken in this direction was the introduction of hand-held devices for inbound and outbound logistics operatives within plant. Through implementation of a plant wireless communication network these handheld devices can now be used to access data from the central plant ICT system and update data from the sections in which material is received and dispatched.

In terms of eCommerce, Goronwy initially invested in a limited corporate website which merely promoted the service it offered and provided contact details for prospective clients. Eventually, however, a companion website was created specifically for repeat customers of the company, such as Blackwalls. On this site, customers entered details of orders and tracked the through-put of their products throughout the process, from receipt through galvanisation to dispatch. This effectively was the company's first step into B2B eCommerce. More recently the Rito group has introduced RFID tracking of batches, which has removed the need for many of the checking processes that used to take place in plant activity systems. For instance, rather than an inbound logistics operative spending much time receiving material sensors, within the receiving yard now automatically update the ICT system with details of goods received.

After ten years of operation a decision was made to upgrade the ICT system onto a new hardware and software base, to make it easier to develop web interfaces and integrate them with a central corporate database system. The system was re-designed and re-written and investment was also made to ensure the privacy of electronic data held in the system and the security of transactions travelling both within Goronwy and between Goronwy and the central ICT systems at Rito Metals.

Electronic Commerce

Electronic Commerce is the use of ICT to enable the external activities and relationships of the business with individuals, groups and other businesses. ECommerce supports supply chains, customer chains and community chains of business (Chapter 4) and has traditionally been conducted in terms of eMarkets or eHierarchies. More recently we have seen the rise of the network as a control mechanism for electronic activity and hence electronic social networks have become important for business activity.

Much hype has always been associated with eCommerce, particularly that experienced during the so-called dot com boom. This refers to the investment bubble that became associated with internet start-up companies during the late 1990s. Many (Cassidy, 2002) have made the analogy between the 'irrational'

Table 8.1 Forms of electronic commerce

	B2C eCommerce	B2B eCommerce	C2C eCommerce	P2P eCommerce
Value-chain	Customer chain	Supply chain	Community chain	Partnership chain
Economic actors	Company/ Consumers	Company/ Suppliers	Consumers/ Consumers	Company/partners
Direction of transactional flow	Consumer – Company	Company – Supplier	Consumer – Consumer	Company – partner
Nature of goods/ services	Standard-priced items	Customised/ High-price items	Negotiated/ Low-price items	Shared goods and services
Form of commerce	Cash/ Credit commerce	Credit/ Repeat commerce	Cash commerce	Credit/repeat commerce
Model of economic exchange	Markets	Hierarchies	Networks	Networks

investment behaviour associated with dot com companies at this time and other financial boom and bust periods, such as the South Sea Bubble that occurred in the 18th century. Much of the dot com phenomenon was directed at B2C eCommerce, probably because it has always been the most visible form of eCommerce. However, a substantial amount of the business conducted electronically over the past couple of decades has been B2B eCommerce. The recent interest in the business opportunities afforded by so-called social networking sites has provided renewed vigour to the phenomenon of C2C eCommerce.

On the basis of much of the material covered in previous chapters, we may distinguish between the three major forms of eCommerce in a number of ways: in terms of the value-chain supported, the economic actors involved, the direction of transactional flow between economic actors, the form of commerce transacted, the nature of goods or services exchanged and the typical model of economic exchange utilised. These distinctions, which build upon our discussion, are summarised in Table 8.1. We examine each of these forms in more detail in the following sections.

Business-to-customer and customer-to-business eCommerce

These forms of eCommerce concern the use of ICT to enable modes of cash and credit commerce between a company and its customers/consumers. Hence, B2C eCommerce generally supports activities within the customer chain in that it focuses on sell-side activities. The primary difference between B2C and C2B eCommerce is in terms of transactional flow. In B2C eCommerce the primary direction of such flow is from business to consumer. In C2B eCommerce the primary direction of such flow is from consumer to business. To avoid confusion, we use the term B2C eCommerce to refer to both directions of flow in this text.

Customers or consumers will typically be individuals, sometimes other organisations. Cash commerce for low- and standard-priced goods typically follows the four stages of the generic commerce model discussed in Chapter 7 quite closely. For medium- to high-priced items some form of credit commerce will operate. Typically, B2C eCommerce will utilise a market model of economic exchange in which economic actors freely exchange goods and services in many-to-many interaction.

Business-to-business eCommerce

B2B eCommerce supports the supply chain of organisations since it focuses on buy-side activities. B2B commerce clearly occurs between organisational actors – public and/or private sector organisations. Hence, this form of eCommerce invariably involves use of ICT to enable forms of credit and repeat commerce between a company and its suppliers or other partners.

For high-priced and customised goods traded between organisations some form of repeat commerce model operates. Hence, typically some form of managerial hierarchy is employed to control the operation of the commercial relationship. In particular, the use of inter-organisational information systems such as extranets (Chapter 6), have become popular as a technological vehicle for supporting B2B eCommerce.

Consumer-to-consumer eCommerce

C2C eCommerce supports the community chain surrounding the organisation and hence can be seen as a commercial extension of community activities. It typically occurs between individuals and where monetary exchange is involved uses forms of cash commerce, generally for low-cost services or goods. In such circumstances it tends to follow a market model for economic exchange. However, as we have seen, other forms of value may be generated in the communities or social networks that engage with C2C eCommerce. Of particular interest is the degree of social capital (Chapter 4) that may emerge in such social networks. Hence, the idea of network forms of economic control is particularly applicable to C2C eCommerce.

Partner-to-partner eCommerce

Organisations are likely to engage in partnerships with other companies in the delivery of goods and services to the customer. This we referred to as the partnership chain within the value-network. P2P eCommerce therefore supports this partnership chain through the sharing of data between the ICT systems of companies. Such electronic commerce will be done on a continuing or repeat basis and managed through the dispersed control of an exchange network.

Amazon

To help illustrate how the different forms of eCommerce described play out within one organisation, consider the case of Amazon.com, an American eCommerce company based in Seattle within the United States of America, but which has global reach. The company was one of the first to sell goods over the internet and was launched on the web in June 1995 by Jeff Bezos who had obtained the backing of venture capitalists in Silicon Valley to start the operation. Bezos chose to name his site after the world's longest river because he believed it was set to become the world's largest bookstore. At the time of Amazon's entry into the market it had no significant rivals and within one year of starting the company was recognised as the web's largest bookstore. However, Amazon was also one of the most prominent traded securities within the late 1990s dot com 'bubble' described above. When this bubble burst over the millennium, many claimed that Amazon's business model was unsustainable in the longer term. It took until 2003 before the company registered its first annual profit but since that time the company has proceeded from strength to strength. The domain *amazon.com* attracts over 600 million visitors annually and consequently, Amazon.com is probably the most cited example of a company that has succeeded at eCommerce. We examine why in the sections which follow.

B2C eCommerce

Traditional business activity systems involving relationships between businesses and customers include sales, marketing and after-sales. All such activity systems have been amenable to ICT innovation for a number of years. However, two trends explain the current renewed explosion of interest in ICT-enablement of the customer chain. First, there has been increasing infiltration of ICT infrastructure into the home and public spaces stimulated by the increasing penetration of the internet and the web as key communication technologies (Chapter 6). This technological innovation has increased the variety of access channels to business products and services open to the potential consumer. Second, postal and telephone services have enabled customers to access services and products remotely for a number of years. Changes to the ICT infrastructure worldwide have opened up increased opportunities for organisations to extend the realms of remote access by implementing efficient and effective electronic delivery systems. It is only comparatively recently with the rise of such technology as the internet that direct (dis-intermediated) and remote connections between customers and businesses have been made possible.

In this section we describe some of the major ways in which the customer chain is being supported and re-structured using ICT. On one level, B2C eCommerce can be seen to be an extension of the customer-facing information systems discussed in Chapter 3. It involves the integration of such customer-facing systems with an increasing range of access devices and channels used by consumers.

B2C eCommerce applications can be used to support the pre-sale, sale execution, sale settlement and after-sale stages of the customer chain. For instance, in terms of pre-sale, product identification can be enabled through banners on websites, inclusion in search engines and personalised marketing based on customer profiling. Online catalogues and portals may also enable product comparison between vendors. In terms of sale execution, websites permit online ordering of products and services. Sale settlement means that online payment can be made through secure B2C sites and integration with back-end information systems such as finance and distribution. After-sale may involve various forms of customer profiling and preferencing and may be used to encourage further purchases from customers. The use of such technology has stimulated interest in integrating information across all the phases of the customer chain. Hence, eCommerce can be used to support the integrative process of customer relationship management.

To get a handle on this phenomenon, we may think of an organisation's experience of B2C eCommerce as moving through a number of distinct stages of increasing ICT infrastructure complexity, which support the various activities of B2C eCommerce. Such stages include engaging in information-seeking and communication, establishing an online marketing presence, creating an online catalogue, conducting online ordering, handling online payment, offering online delivery and performing customer profiling and preferencing.

For example, small- and medium-sized enterprises (SMEs) (those with less than 250 employees) will probably first use a computer and an internet connection to seek out information about potential competitors. They will also probably use this facility to email suppliers. The more sophisticated it gets, and depending upon its business strategy, the SME may eventually reach the stage at which most of its business with customers is conducted electronically.

Each of these stages supports part of the model of commerce described in Chapter 7. Pre-sale activities include information seeking and communication, creating a marketing presence and establishing an online catalogue. Sale execution activities are online ordering and potentially online delivery. Sale settlement activities equate to online payment and after-sales activities equate to customer profiling and preferencing.

Information-seeking and communication

The first stage describes a company which is beginning to engage with the internet, probably using it primarily for *information seeking and communication* via eMail as well as surfing the web (Figure 8.2). The internet and the web have enabled more effective and efficient information-seeking behaviour on the part of individuals. Many software tools exist, such as search engines, to support such behaviour.

A *search engine* allows the user to specify a combination of keywords with logical operators such as AND, NOT and OR. The search engine then looks up the keyword combinations in what is effectively a large index linking keywords to URLs and displays results for the user to select from. Search engines are typically offered by information intermediaries or infomediaries which normally are organisations maintaining *horizontal portals* to the web. The most critical current example is that provided by google.com

Electronic mail is a significant technology for business because it allows asynchronous communication between stakeholders. In association with file transfer protocols it also enables easy transfer of electronic files around computer networks. In terms of B2C eCommerce the availability of an eMail address for a company makes it easy for customers to make enquiries and even to communicate details of an order to the company.

Most companies within Western Europe, including so-called micro-enterprises (those with less than 10 employees), are at least at this stage in the adoption of eCommerce. Such businesses use the internet primarily as a tool for gathering information about organisations in the same market segment as themselves, receiving emails from customers and emailing suppliers.

Marketing presence

Most companies have typically considered establishing a *marketing presence* on the internet through the creation of a corporate website with details of the company profile placed upon it (Figure 8.3). The company profile will most likely include a

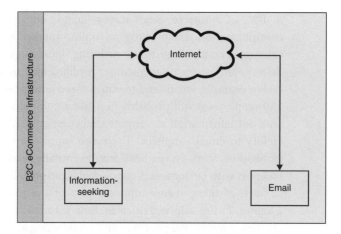

Figure 8.2 Information seeking and communication

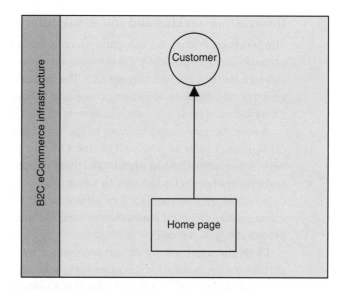

Figure 8.3 Marketing presence

description of the main activities of the company, its location and some contact details. The simplest form of such infrastructure is as a passive website where potential customers may use the site to gain contact details, but will contact the company probably through interaction with email systems.

Online catalogue

The next step up in complexity involves a company providing an *online catalogue* of its products or services available for inspection by potential customers. The catalogue may amount to a series of static web pages or may be dynamic in the sense that it is updated from a database containing product data. More sophisticated sites of this nature will allow dynamic pricing of product data perhaps for different types of market segment such as irregular versus regular customers. Figure 8.4 assumes that customers still have to place orders through traditional channels such as over the telephone, through the post or potentially through eMail.

Suppose, for instance, a music publisher produces an online catalogue of its limited range of specialist publications. The catalogue contains a cover image, a short synopsis of the contents of each publication, details the cost of each publication and delivery charges. To order publications customers still have to ring a telephone line or send an order form through the post with appropriate payment.

Online ordering

The next logical step is to enable customers to place *orders online* for products or services through the website itself. This is a key transition point for most businesses since it involves close integration of websites with back-end ICT systems. In forms of credit commerce the company will invoice the customer for payment

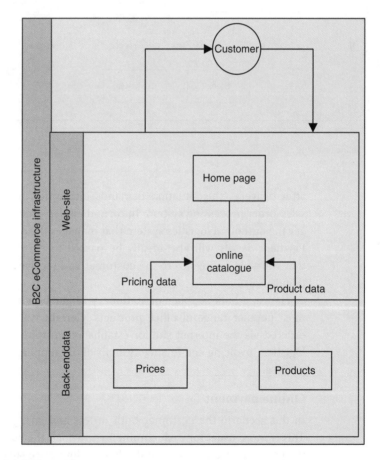

Figure 8.4 Online catalogue

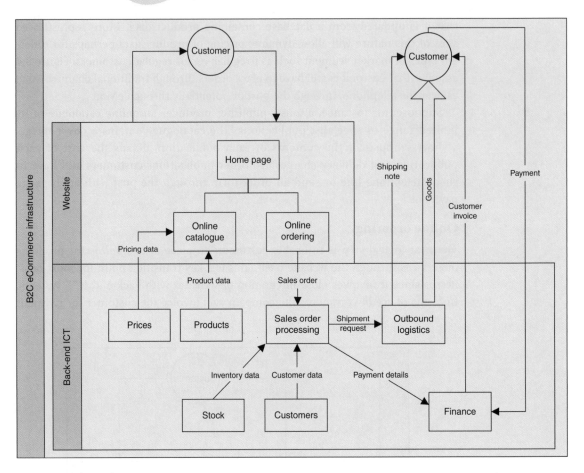

Figure 8.5 Online ordering

after delivery. This situation demands integration between the website and the sales-order processing system. In turn, the sales-order processing system will trigger the outbound logistics system that manages the delivery of goods and services. Payment details will also ideally be passed to the organisation's finance system that will send an invoice to the customer and receive payment from the customer (Figure 8.5).

Hence, a bulk supplier of stationery might provide an online catalogue of its most popular range of office products. Certain volumes of this material can be ordered via the internet site for established customers. The traditional outbound logistics, invoicing and finance systems of the supplier are used to support the B2C process.

Online payment

In this scenario the customer both orders and *pays for goods* using the website. This is more usual for cash commerce in which the customer is an individual and the goods are standardised and relatively low-price such as CDs, DVDs or books. This form of B2C eCommerce demands a close integration not only between an organisation's front-end and back-end ICT infrastructure but also with ePayment systems supplied by other organisations.

Figure 8.6 describes the typical functionality of many sites offering online ordering and payment. Clearly the details of the specific functionality of each site will vary. The customer may first order goods using an electronic shopping facility in the sales system. The shopping facility calculates the total cost of the order for the customer and includes the delivery charge. The customer enters her credit or debit card details to complete the purchase. For such payment details to be entered, the organisation either provides a secure payment system itself, or more likely uses a facility provided by a financial intermediary.

Payment details usually need to be checked with a further financial intermediary such as the customer's bank. If the customer has sufficient funds available the financial intermediary makes an electronic funds transfer to the company's bank account and details of the transfer are recorded in the company's finance system (Figure 8.6).

Within a company which supplies high-quality prints of works of art, the customer is able to search for prints by theme, period, artist and price. Images of

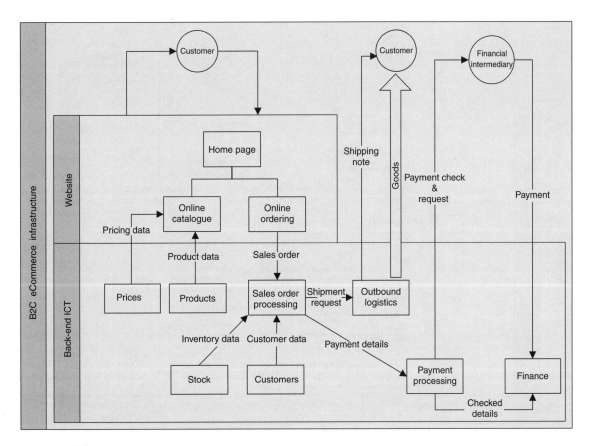

Figure 8.6 Online payment

selected prints can be displayed at various degrees of resolution and prints are also offered in various sizes. The customer can add prints to a shopping trolley and pay online by credit or debit card. The site automatically confirms orders via email to the customer.

Online delivery

As we discussed in some detail in Chapter 4, certain intangible goods or products are converging to a digital standard making the capture, storage and dissemination of media of various types in digital format (Chapter 6). Therefore, for certain intangible goods it is possible to *deliver* such goods online. Hence, in Figure 8.7 the outbound logistics systems are replaced with an online delivery system. This means that there is no need for separate inventory and products databases. Both product descriptions and the intangible products themselves are likely to be accessed from the products database. For certain packaged goods such as software, payment will involve some form of cash commerce. For other products or services such as online newspapers and magazines, the payment method is likely to be based on some monthly, quarterly or yearly subscription paid through credit or debit details.

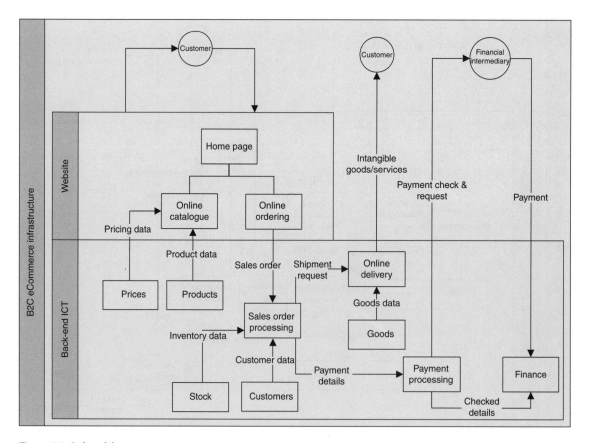

Figure 8.7 Online delivery

For instance, certain companies pay a subscription charge to sites managing the online delivery of software. Subscription entitles the company to download upgrades of key software products such as virus protection. Many online music and movie sites that provide downloading of content for a fee work more with a cash-based model for online delivery. In other words, payments are made per download.

Customer profiling and preferencing

Customer relationship management has become a popular philosophy within recent management literature. Winning new customers and keeping existing customers satisfied is seen to be important to organisational success.

It might be argued that B2C eCommerce in general and CRM in particular are a natural consequence of the increasing customer focus of organisations. As we have seen, Michael Porter (1996) has argued that the value delivered to the customer is the key feature of contemporary business (Chapter 7). Hence, it is not surprising to find companies attempting to re-orient their processes and systems around an overt customer focus as opposed to a traditional focus around business events such as orders and sales. Having an integrated approach to both front-end and back-end customer information systems means that companies can identify repeat customers, identify their behaviour and on the basis of this information offer personalised packages of products and/or services to such customers in the hope that they will continue to conduct business with the company.

To enable this an organisation's information systems need to track all customer interactions with a company from initial enquiries through making orders to the whole range of after-sales services that might be offered to and consumed by the customer. This will also probably involve integration of the customer-facing systems with a *customer profiling and preferencing* system. This information system will dynamically build a profile of a customer and on the basis of this continuously adjust the profile to offer the customer individualised goods and/or services (Figure 8.8).

Many online booksellers such as Amazon now use customer-profiling systems. Stored eMail addresses combined with a previous purchase history enables the site to change aspects of the interface or to eMail customers with details of new products such as books in their area of interest, perhaps offering special discount schemes for established customers.

Customer relationship management

Profiling and preferencing is one aspect of the broader phenomenon of customer relationship management or CRM. In the modern business world with increasing degrees of competition and the associated globalisation of business the customer is a key focus. CRM concerns that set of activities that support the entire customer chain. Hence it is sometimes known as customer chain management. CRM is an attempt to establish long-term relationships with customers and it is useful to consider CRM as a system composed of three inter-related processes or activity systems: customer acquisition, customer retention and customer extension.

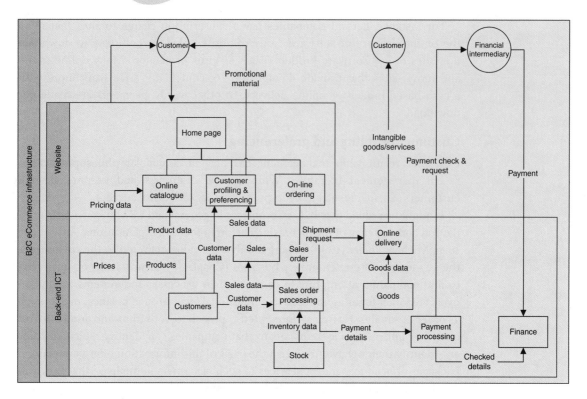

Figure 8.8 Customer relationship management

Customer acquisition consists of that set of activities and techniques used to gain new customers. For eBusiness this clearly involves the process of attracting new customers to websites. Hence, eMarketing is a critical part of this aspect of CRM (Chapter 9). However, customer acquisition also involves attempts to persuade the customer to engage in a dialogue with the company. Through such dialogue the company's systems can construct a profile of the customer in terms of the products/services she is interested in, her demographic profile and her general purchasing behaviour. Hence, many retail websites attempt to open up an online chat with the customer by some sales assistant.

In terms of a high-street bank, for instance, customer acquisition primarily involves persuading people to open bank accounts or purchase other financial products with the financial institution. Online banking has become an expected part of the services offered by such banks and hence forms an important part of attracting new customers.

Customer retention refers to the set of activities and techniques used to maintain relationships with existing customers. In terms of eCommerce customer retention has the related goals of retaining customers (repeat customers) and persuading customers to keep using the online channel of communication (repeat visits). Two factors are critical to retention: customer satisfaction and customer loyalty.

One technique used in customer retention is the personalisation of eMail content. Having captured an eMail address for the customer the company can regularly send personalised alerts of particular products or services which the customer profile indicates to be of potential interest. Such alerts may also offer discounts or other value-added services in a bid to persuade customers to return to a B2C website.

In terms of a high-street bank, customer retention may involve the bank in offering services such as multi-channel access to bank accounts and may also involve the bank in offering aggregated products such as combined bank accounts, insurance and mortgages. Certain products may be targeted at the online customer such as higher interest savings accounts.

Customer extension consists of that set of activities and techniques used to encourage existing customers to increase their level of involvement with a company's products and services. This is made easier in the online environment as more targeted promotions can be offered to the customer.

All these activities are critically dependent on good data: knowing who your customers are, what they are purchasing, how satisfied they are with the company and what they want in terms of future services and products. Hence, there has been an increasing emphasis on the implementation of an increasing range of data and associated information systems to support the CRM process. Data collected about the attributes and behaviour of customers is a critical resource for business intelligence (Chapter 9).

Models of B2C eCommerce

In our discussion of the typical B2C systems of a company provided in previous sections we have focused on one particular business model for B2C e-Commerce which some refer to as an eShop. An eShop is a single firm selling their products or services online. In an eShop, increased revenue is sought through access to a larger market, offering a larger range of products or offering longer 'opening hours' than a traditional offline retailer. Lower costs may result from the use of low-cost warehouses, volume discounts on purchases and improved inventory management.

However, there are a number of other business models for B2C operations, including eMalls, third-party marketplaces, forms of eProcurement, value-chain integrators and providers, information brokerages and other service models. An *e-Mall* is a business model in which a range of businesses share a website for the provision of eServices. Effectively it amounts to a form of inter-organisational information system. Increases in revenue are sought in much the same way as for an eShop. Cost-savings are expected through sharing the implementation and maintenance costs of front-end systems. In the business model of a *third-party marketplace*, a third party firm provides internet marketing and transaction services for other firms. This is frequently used by an established company that wants entry-level exposure in eCommerce without incurring major costs of implementation and maintenance. Revenue generation is typically through membership fees, fees per transaction or a percentage of transaction value. Some forms of *eProcurement*, as we shall see, effectively involve the electronic tendering of goods and services from other suppliers. *Value-chain integrators* are companies that offer a range of services across the value-chain and the value-network. Such services are integrated and companies may outsource major parts of their customer chain or supply chain activities to such companies. *Value-chain service providers* are companies that specialise in a particular function within the value-chain or value-network such as electronic payments, inventory management and logistics. Companies employing such providers save on having to provide such services themselves. Providers of these services normally accrue a fee or a percentage of the services provided from the company. An *information brokerage* is a company specialising in the provision of information to consumers and to businesses: helping such individuals and organisations to make buying decisions or for business operations. Revenue models include membership fees, advertising fees and cross selling. Lastly, some companies authenticate the services and products of other companies provided on the web. Revenue models typically involve some form of membership fee.

Costs and benefits of B2C eCommerce

Implementing B2C e-Commerce is likely to be a customer-chain strategy for the business and as such benefits will be factored into a strategic evaluation of infrastructure change within some organisation. Benefits of B2C e-Commerce can be considered either from the viewpoint of the consumer or from that of the business organisation. From the consumer side, benefits include being able to access goods and services from the home or other remote locations, the possibility of lower cost goods and services and access to a greater variety of goods and services on offer potentially across the globe. From the business side, benefits include lower transaction costs associated with sales, access to global markets and hence to more potential customers, and opportunities for dis-intermediation leading to possibilities for greater customer retention and extension.

However, implementing B2C eCommerce relies upon a sufficient customer base online. There are also significant costs associated with re-engineering back-end ICT infrastructure and associated information systems around a customer-focus, integrating such back-end systems with B2C websites, ensuring the security of online transactions and access to personal data, and making sure that there are sufficient resources to ensure the continuity of the online service over time.

Amazon

Amazon primarily engages in B2C eCommerce and provides a number of levels of functionality through its website such as search features, additional content and personalisation. The site also provides searchable catalogues of books, CDs, DVDs, computer games etc. Customers can search for products such as books using keyword, title, subject, author, artist, musical instrument, label, actor, director, publication date or ISBN.

Therefore, the primary value-stream for Amazon is tangible products such as books and CDs. In recent times, it has attempted to broaden the range of this value by offering a broader range of products including computer software, video games, electronics, clothing, furniture, food and toys. It also provides added-value and intangible services such as a personalised notification service. More recently it has started to offer delivery of intangible products such as eBooks, through its Kindle access device.

In terms of added-value, the company offers a vast range of additional content over and above its products, through its website. For example, cover art, synopses, annotations, reviews by editorial staff and other customers and interviews by authors and artists. The website attempts to personalise the customer experience by greeting customers by name, instant and personalised recommendations, bestseller listings, personal notification services and purchase pattern filtering.

To order from Amazon, customers have to register their details, including payment details. Amazon is able to combine this data with data gathered about customers' browsing and ordering behaviour to progressively update a profile held about each customer. Such customer profiling is used to drive targeted advertisements at the customer, such as suggestions about suitable reading matter to purchase or movie DVDs to buy.

Currently the company is claimed to be the internet's number one retailer. However, although Amazon is a retailer, its key business strategy is based on differentiation in terms of technical infrastructure. For Amazon to keep this competitive differentiation it must continually be at the forefront of internet technology. In such terms Jeff Bezos has indicated that he considers Amazon to be a technology company first and a retailer second. Hence, the key-differentiating factor for Amazon over the conventional retailer is the internet and web. Not surprisingly, the company has to ceaselessly innovate in terms of such technology.

Amazon offers only one access channel to its goods – that of the Amazon.com website. Hence, Amazon is a clicks only company, meaning that all its retail operation is conducted online and that the key access device used by its customers is the internet-enabled PC. In recent times Amazon has been promoting the idea of electronic books as an additional access channel for its customers. After purchasing an eBook reader from the company book material in digital format can be downloaded onto this access device for a charge. Clearly, this form of access enables Amazon to substantially reduce its distribution costs for this type of product.

To maintain its B2C operation, significant investment in front-end and back-end ICT is required by Amazon. For instance, Amazon's service to customers relies on a close integration of its website to back-end information and activity systems. The company uses a streamlined ordering process reliant on previous billing and shipment details captured from the customer. Amazon also utilises secure server software that encrypts payment information throughout its integrated fulfilment process. Most of the company's products are available for shipping within 24 hours. The Amazon website run within each geographical region updates a large sales information system. This sales information system is also integrated with inventory management systems run at each distribution centre.

From this description it is possible to describe briefly some of the gains that Amazon experiences from its engagement with B2C eCommerce, and in particular, through its close integration of ICT infrastructure with its activity infrastructure. First, in terms of efficacy, Amazon has been able to diversify into a vast range of products for retail. Since Amazon is primarily a B2C company it is able to run without any physical retail outlets and can pass on efficiency gains in lower costs to its customers. Finally, in terms of effectiveness, Amazon is able to sell its products across the world, meaning that its potential customer base is huge, and is able to relate to a large range of suppliers to fulfil orders from customers.

B2B eCommerce

Up until quite recently it was argued that B2B eCommerce was even more critical to business activity than B2C eCommerce. B2B eCommerce involves the use of ICT within the supply chain activity of organisations. Much discussion of B2B eCommerce is directed at supporting the repeat commerce model, discussed in Chapter 7. Here a company sets up an arrangement with a trusted supplier to deliver goods of a certain specification at regular intervals (Figure 8.9). Each of the phases of this repeat commerce model may be impacted upon by B2B eCommerce.

In terms of *search*, buyers within organisations will be required to detail features of the product or service required from suppliers by completing online forms. Such forms may then be submitted via web interfaces on the corporate intranet for requisition approval. After requisition approval the purchasing department will issue a request for quote electronically to potential suppliers. This may be conducted through an online bulletin board or B2B hub that connects businesses online as buyers and sellers.

In terms of *negotiate*, after all bids have been received, a vendor is selected probably using some software that ranks bids on the basis of chosen key features of the request for quote. *Order* involves the supplier being notified of a successful bid and a purchase order being electronically transmitted to the chosen supplier. After *delivery* of goods the inventory management system is automatically updated and following receipt of the invoice from the supplier the company arranges an electronic funds transfer (*payment*) with the supplying company. Finally in terms of *after-sale*, supplier relationship management systems monitor all interactions with suppliers and can be used to check on performance of particular suppliers.

This approach to B2B eCommerce is primarily modelled on the economic model of an electronic hierarchy (Chapter 4) and can be considered to be an extension to the supplier-facing information systems described in Chapter 3. More recently, forms of market-based trading are infiltrating the B2B sector leading to an overlap of both B2B and B2C business models and ICT infrastructure.

B2B eCommerce infrastructure

B2B eCommerce is a natural extension of a major part of the internal informatics infrastructure of commercial organisations. In Chapter 4 we referred to such *front-end information systems infrastructure* as supplier-facing information systems. Purchase order processing and payment processing systems normally handle the settlement and execution stages of the commerce cycle. Such information systems are an established part of the information systems infrastructure of most medium to large organisations. The pre-sale and after-sale stages of the commerce cycle have been the most open to innovation in B2B eCommerce. Requisitioning, request for quote and vendor selection are part of what we previously called a supplier

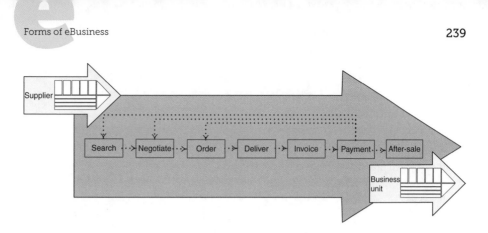

Figure 8.9 The supply chain

relationship management information system (Chapter 4). It is in this area that most of the discussion of B2B eCommerce occurs.

Figure 8.10 illustrates the relationships between the supplier facing systems of supplier relationship management, procurement and purchase order processing and other infrastructure systems such as finance and inventory management. This serves to emphasise that successful B2B eCommerce relies upon integration with back-end information systems.

Supplier relationship management

Supplier relationship management (SRM) is sometimes referred to as supply chain management and involves the coordination of all the supply chain activities of the company. Supply chain management is a generalisation of inbound logistics (Chapter 4), the management of material resources supplied to the organisation. It is also sometimes used to encompass outbound logistics, the management of resources supplied by the organisation to its customers. Just as customer relationship management can be seen to include electronic marketing, supplier relationship management can be seen to include electronic procurement (Chapter 10).

Business models for B2B eCommerce

B2B commerce traditionally relies on trusted relationships between a company and one or more established suppliers. Traditionally, management of the supply chain has been organised in terms of managerial hierarchies. With the rise of the internet and the web there has been an increasing trend for supply chain management to move more closely towards market-oriented models. In terms of pre-sale activity the internet has enabled four distinct models for B2B eCommerce to emerge: supplier-oriented B2B, buyer-oriented B2B, partnership-oriented B2B and intermediary-oriented B2B.

Supplier-oriented B2B is sometimes referred to as sell-side B2B eCommerce and effectively is a mirror-image of B2C or buy-side eCommerce. Typically, supplier-oriented B2B eCommerce involves one supplier and many potential purchasers and will take place for low-cost items and low-volume purchases. One of the most popular forms of supplier-oriented B2B is the eShop which involves the promotion of the suppliers' products or services through the internet.

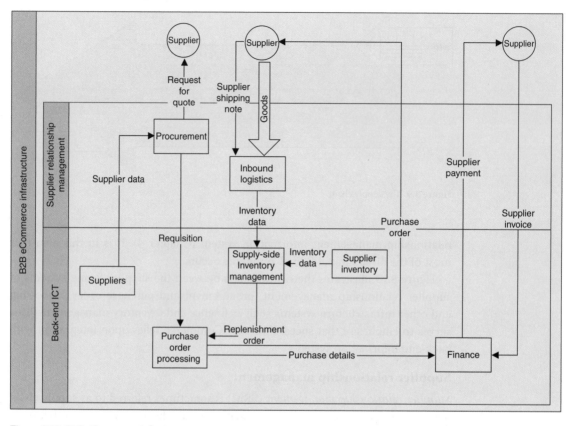

Figure 8.10 B2B eCommerce infrastructure

In *buyer-oriented B2B*, a consumer opens an electronic market on its own servers. It then invites suppliers to bid on the supply information displayed on some website constructed for this purpose. Hence, one buyer tenders for products amongst many potential suppliers. As such buyer-oriented B2B is sometimes referred to as buy-side B2B eCommerce. This scenario can be expanded into full eProcurement in which the later stages in the supply chain are handled electronically (Chapter 10).

In *intermediary-oriented B2B* an intermediary runs effectively a sub-set of some electronic market where buyers and sellers can meet and exchange products and services. As such, this form of B2B eCommerce involves many-to-many exchanges and is also referred to as B2B eMarketplaces or B2B hubs.

The three previous models are all effectively market-oriented in the sense that they are designed for many-to-many exchange. However, the traditional model of B2B eCommerce runs as an electronic hierarchy, sometimes referred to as partnership-oriented B2B. Here an established relationship exists between a company and its supplier. The relationship is likely to be supported by some form of integration of information systems within the business partnership using technologies such as extranets (Chapter 6).

Intermediary-oriented B2B is a key form of re-intermediation in the supply chain and can be conducted in a number of ways. Vertical portals aggregate buyers and sellers around a particular market segment. They produce revenue through subscription, advertising, commission and transaction fees. B2B auction sites enable buyers and sellers to negotiate the price and terms of sales. The seller holds inventory but the auction site handles fulfilment of goods and the exchange of payment. eMalls or eStores are general portals run by third parties offering a range of products/services from suppliers for customers. As we have seen, an *eMall* is effectively a collection of eShops.

Amazon

Although Amazon is frequently seen only as a B2C eCommerce company, much of its success is based upon the efficiency and reach of its B2B eCommerce operations. Two of Amazon's core competencies are clearly to retail books effectively and deliver such books efficiently to its customers. The latter competency relies upon efficient logistics. Amazon maintains a network of large warehouses or distribution centres which rely on ICT integration to perform effectively. Within these warehouses staff use hand-held devices connected to an inventory management system to fulfil customer orders. Inbound logistics involves the management of the purchasing of books and the distribution of books to these distribution centres. The process of operations involves unpacking and storing such shipments as well as picking of books to fulfil customer orders. Outbound logistics involves the distribution of books to the customer. Amazon actually operates separate B2C websites in Canada, the United Kingdom, Germany, France, China and Japan. Although it ships certain selected products globally it also runs a number of fulfilment centres in North America, Europe and Asia. This enables it to meet customer demand quickly.

C2C eCommerce

The internet is a domain not only for business-to-business or business-to-consumer eCommerce, but it is also a domain for consumer-to-consumer eCommerce. We may define *C2C eCommerce* as ICT enablement of aspects of the community chain. In a way it is the most radical form of eCommerce since it overlaps with non-commercial activity in the area of community. Commercial and non-commercial organisations are attempting to incorporate aspects of their community chain into their operations or are attempting to formulate new business models embedded in various social networks external to the organisation.

As a form of exchange, many forms of C2C eCommerce revert to earlier models of markets and trade in which products and services are exchanged between individuals, where the fixed price model of products and services breaks down and where in some instances trade reverts to earlier forms of economic exchange such as barter. In such terms, C2C commerce is a many-to-many commerce model. It typically involves the exchange of low-cost items and monetary transactions. With C2C eCommerce a form of trade that typically survives in local market places is opened up to global access.

In this section we reconsider our definition of a community from Chapter 4 and use this definition to distinguish between three forms of electronic community: an *eNabled community*, *virtual community* and an *adjunct community*. It is to adjunct communities that many businesses are now turning to increase levels of value associated with their products and services.

Electronic community

The two concepts of a social network and social capital, as defined in Chapter 4, help us understand some of the different forms of *electronic community* or *eCommunity*. On the one hand, ICT is seen either as an enabler or disabler of traditional forms of community: an eNabled community. On the other hand, ICT is seen as offering potential for newer forms of community based on communication networks: the virtual community. Virtual communities may exist separate from the organisation concerned or be built upon infrastructure provided by the organisation. The latter is the concept of an adjunct community.

An *eNabled community* is a traditional community enhanced with use of ICT. Community is normally established on the basis of frequent and prolonged interaction between individuals resident in a clearly defined geographical area. This form of community chain addresses the rise of communication networks and considers whether they are vehicles for re-creating community and social capital in local areas. Some argue that communication networks are a threat to existing forms of community, others that they provide a new basis for enhancing social capital.

The internet and the web were initially established for free information exchange between dispersed actors around the globe. Some have begun to consider such dispersed networks of individuals and organisations as examples of electronic communities. In such virtual communities social networks rely upon electronic rather than face-to-face communication. Social networks based upon communication infrastructure may not only be dispersed geographically; they may also have a much more specific area of focus than traditional communities.

As a generalisation, public sector organisations have particularly been interested in making connections between their informatics activities and initiatives in the area of eNabled community. Such forms of eCommunity are seen as offering the potential for the stimulation of local economies, particularly in disadvantaged areas.

In contrast, private sector organisations have particularly been interested in connecting to the second form of eCommunity, that of a virtual community. The idea is that various forms of value produced by the community-chain may support and encourage commerce of various forms. It is only comparatively recently that the internet and web have been used as vehicles for commerce and trade/business purposes. C2C eCommerce mediates between pure forms of trade and pure forms of communication exchange.

Virtual communities

Rheingold (1995) defines *virtual communities* as 'social aggregations that emerge from the Net when enough people carry on those public discussions long enough, with sufficient human feeling, to form webs of personal relationships in cyberspace.'

For example, it could be argued that one of the first virtual communities was the community of academics that started to use the internet in the early 1970s to share data, exchange messages and collaborate together on various research programmes. Tim Berners Lee originally produced the web as a tool for networks of scientists to share documentation easily.

In more recent times the idea of virtual communities has become inherently associated with a range of websites collectively known as social networking sites. A social networking site is a website that provides a number of facilities for constructing and maintaining online relationships between members. Prominent examples of such social networking sites are Facebook, LinkedIn and MySpace. Globally, hundreds of millions of people have become members of these sites.

Virtual communities are founded in social networks and produce social capital just like traditional communities. However, there is still some question as to whether the bonds in the social network of a virtual community are as strong and the social capital produced as great as that produced in traditional communities. This is because there are a number of differences between virtual communities and traditional communities including issues of space, the form of communication used and the general focus of the community.

In terms of space, traditional communities are normally established on the basis of long residence by individuals in a prescribed geographical region. In contrast, virtual communities break geographical boundaries and individuals are effectively nodes in a wide-area communication network. In traditional communities the dominant form of communication between community members will be face-to-face conversation. In virtual communities various forms of remote communication may be employed, using a variety of access devices, such as email, chat, telephone conversation, video-conferencing etc. Finally, the focus of a traditional community will be diverse but all located around a particular geographical area. The focus of virtual communities is likely to be much more specific in nature but span the globe.

It is clearly possible to define various types of virtual communities. For instance, virtual communities can be formed in terms of different types of content provided on websites such as transactions, area of interest, industry or expertise. Many virtual communities are actually established to facilitate the buying and selling of products and services and to delivering data that is related to the completion of transactions. Many community websites focus on areas such as theatre, sports, science fiction or fantasy. Community websites frequently locate around key industrial areas such as accounting or manufacturing. Also, occupational groups may focus around key areas of expertise such as waste management or software engineering.

Virtual communities are now being used to enhance conventional eCommerce activity: what we shall call adjunct communities. Virtual communities also underlie forms of many-to-many eCommerce: what we shall refer to as C2C exchanges.

Social networking sites

Recently, there has been much interest in the growth of so-called *social networking* sites; sometimes referred to as *social networking media, social media* or *digital media*. This is of course a bad name for this phenomenon because most social networks, as we have explained in Chapter 4, are not virtual. This phenomenon is really about using ICTs, particularly Web 2.0 technologies (Chapter 6), to facilitate networking amongst dispersed individuals and hence constitutes a variant of the virtual communities discussed above.

In terms of business the key question is what impact this is having on business or what potential it holds for business. Besides the obvious fact that these sites are in fact businesses themselves there is interest from business more generally in utilising the technologies involved for internal and external use. For example, the Web 2.0 technologies (Chapter 6) on which social networking sites rely may have an internal impact as in the case of fostering and supporting collaborative working and communication in distributed organisations. In an external sense, virtual communities of this form could be used to improve customer relationship management. For example, many companies are exploring the use of blogs and tweets as tools for marketing or improving customer relationship.

Certain social networking sites such as Facebook are attempting to establish themselves as a third application layer on top of the web and the internet. This is because these sites wish to encourage their members to engage in most of their communicative activity through the social networking site, rather than through the more open environment of the World-Wide-Web. For the user of the social networking site this offers a more convenient way of communicating with other members of the social network than through more open standards of communication such as email. This enables the social networking site to gather masses of data about the attributes and activities of its users, which is of great value for business purposes such as marketing. Some commentators worry however about the possible infringements of data privacy that might arise from this and caution of a potential backlash against social media by its users.

Adjunct communities

Certain electronic businesses are attempting to foster and support virtual communities as a means of adding value to their products and/or services. *Adjunct communities* are forms of virtual community that focus around the development of relationships between customers and the business. The key benefits to business are that by creating and supporting such virtual communities businesses will be better able to build membership audiences for their products and services. Certain features of social capital such as increased mutual support amongst members of a virtual community can be particularly beneficial to companies. Enhanced levels of trust between members of a virtual community may support increased levels of trade with a company. These forms of added value may increase customer loyalty and trust.

Timmers (1998) argues that there are two business models appropriate for adjunct communities. A *communication exchange* is a business model which attempts to add value to products and services through support of communications between a network of members. The company provides an environment in which members can partake in unedited communication exchange. Revenue is generated through membership fees, advertising revenue and cross-selling of products and services. In contrast, *collaboration platforms* tend to be much more focused on enabling collaboration between individuals and organisations and typically provide a set of tools and an environment for collaboration with a company.

C2C exchanges

Other business models for C2C focus more precisely on facilitating customer-to-customer relationships of exchange. C2C exchange involves trade of typically low-cost items between complex networks of individual actors. Revenues from C2C communities may be generated through advertising, transaction fees and/or membership fees.

Timmers (1998) argues that there are two main business models appropriate for C2C exchange. *Electronic auctions* constitute the prominent business model underlying C2C eCommerce and are discussed in more detail below. *Information brokerages* are companies specialising in the provision of information to consumers and to businesses. They help such individuals and organisations make buying decisions for business operations. Revenue models in this area include membership fees, advertising fees and cross-selling.

C2C exchanges involve trade between complex networks of individual actors. Although typically the monetary value of each exchange may be low, added together, billions of dollars are traded annually in such forms of C2C commerce. However, C2C exchange is not a new phenomenon. A range of traditional business models have been created for this purpose which includes newspaper classified advertisements, flea markets and auction houses.

Users of newspapers typically list items for sale, normally in newspapers distributed on a local basis. Buyers inspect items before purchase and may collect and pay for the item in person. In a flea market, sellers stock and display items for sale typically at their own homes or at organised markets. Buyers typically browse for artefacts and will negotiate prices and collect and transport items themselves. Within auction houses, sellers take items to specialist organisations for sale. Buyers are able to inspect items before an auction. Buyers will have to pay a registration fee to bid and are required to be at an auction or to nominate a proxy bidder. The highest bidder wins the auction and pays the auction house. The auction house in turn takes a percentage of the sale and pays the balance to the seller.

The value and take-up of a C2C exchange, such as that provided by eBay (see case) is likely to be affected by Metcalfe's law (Chapter 4). The community value of a network grows as the square of the number of users increases. It is likely that the variety in a C2C network will strongly influence the take-up and use of such applications. In other words, the more people available to communicate with and share goods and information the more likely it is that people will participate.

Amazon

From the start Amazon offered a range of value-added services to its customers. A popular feature of the website is the ability for users to submit reviews for each product. As part of their review, users must rate the product on a scale from one to five stars. Such rating scales provide a basic measure of the popularity of a product. Such a reviewing facility has been seen by some as critical to the explosive growth of the company. Other value-added services include a personal notification service for customers requesting particular titles, a recommendations section where customers can recommend titles in various categories to other customers, an awards section which lists books that have won prizes and an associate programme where other sites can link to Amazon to sell their own selections.

At the start Jeff Bezos warned investors that they were unlikely to make a profit in the first five years of operation. However, Amazon has engaged in an aggressive expansion strategy and acquired a number of additional retail outlets such as toys, CDs and has provided a facility for online auctions of small goods. It introduced zShops in 1999, which is a facility that allows any individual or business to sell through Amazon.com – a form of C2C trading. Amazon has also created an online community known as Mechanical Turk. This is an open marketplace in which workers perform tasks for requesters. Amazon receives a percentage of the fee charged for work by a worker.

Intra-business eBusiness and P2P eCommerce

Figure 8.1 details two other forms of eBusiness beyond the forms of eCommerce discussed in previous sections: intra-business eBusiness and Partner-to-Partner eBusiness. *Intra-business e-Business* involves enablement of the internal value-chain with ICT, sometimes across separate business units. *P2P eBusiness* comprises the use of ICT to support the partnership chain: networks of organisations collaborating in the delivery of value to customers.

In a sense, all the material covered in previous chapters of this book is relevant to successful intra-business eBusiness. However, a number of issues are of particular relevance. First, intra-business eBusiness is very much about the importance of re-designing activity systems within organisations with the support of ICT to achieve improvements in efficacy, efficiency and effectiveness. Second, such re-design is based in the central importance of information and data as organisational resources for coordinated action. Third, to achieve performance gain organisations need to develop integrated and inter-operable ICT infrastructure in support of improvements to organisational performance.

The traditional structure of organisations is founded in a functional model. In this view, organisations are structured in terms of functions such as marketing, finance and manufacturing. As a consequence, information systems have been designed to emulate this organisational structure: each functional unit tends to have its own information system to service its needs. This type of organisational model, James Martin (1996) refers to as a series of functional silos and the information systems infrastructure associated with it as one of stovepipe systems. Stovepipe systems frequently use incompatible data, making it difficult for communication across functional silos. They are also systems that are likely to suffer from redundancy and fragmentation.

Fragmentation is the situation in which data are fragmented across information systems because organisational units put up barriers of ownership around key data sets. Fragmentation may also be evident in processing where separate ICT systems communicate through manual interfaces, causing delay and other inefficiencies. *Redundancy* is the situation where large amounts of data are unnecessarily replicated across information systems usually because interfaces do not exist between systems, causing the same data to be entered many times. Redundancy may also be present when separate systems perform the same effective processing on data.

Value-chain models of organisations stress the importance of cross-organisational processes or activity systems. The emphasis is on designing efficient and effective cross-organisational processes that deliver value to the customer. This model of the organisation encourages the design of integrated information systems to support key organisational processes. Martin argues that this form of information systems infrastructure not only provides more utility for organisations, but it also enables the organisation to more easily adapt to changes in the environment.

As we have seen, electronic markets are founded on competition since a market is a network of interactions and relationships by which products and services are negotiated and exchanged. However, business can also be founded on cooperation and collaboration. A key way in which information systems may participate in business cooperation is through the concept of an inter-organisational information system (IOS) (Barrette and Konsynski, 1982). An IOS is an information system developed and maintained by a consortium of companies for the mutual benefit of member companies. Generally such systems provide infrastructure for the sharing of some application. IOS can prove a particularly effective way of sharing the costs of developing and maintaining large and complex information systems. Therefore an IOS is a type of information system directed at collaboration.

The automatic teller machine (ATM) networks run by major building societies and banks in the UK are key examples of IOS. These networks are constructed and maintained by consortia of financial institutions. This enables them to distribute the large costs of running such networks amongst the participating members. Another example is BACS, the clearing system of the major high-street banks in the UK that handles the debit and credit transactions to customer bank accounts.

An inter-*organisational informatics* infrastructure based upon developments in service-oriented software architecture has been proposed as a backbone for fostering what some have referred to as *digital business ecosystems*. The ideal is that businesses may flexibly utilise this backbone to develop new business models based on cooperation with other businesses.

Amazon

Amazon engages in P2P eCommerce. For instance, the websites of Waldenbooks (waldenbooks.com), Virgin Megastores (virginmega.com), CDNOW (cdnow.com) and HMV (hmv.com) are all hosted by Amazon. The company also runs multi-channel access for a number of companies such as Marks & Spencer and Mothercare. Such sites allow the customer to interchangeably interact with the retail website, standalone in-store terminals, and phone-based customer service agents.

Summary

This chapter has introduced the term electronic business or eBusiness to encompass the entire range of ICT application within business, whether this is to improve internal operations or to extend the organisation into its environment. We have restricted the term electronic commerce to the use of ICT within the external activities and relationships of the business with individuals, groups and other businesses.

We have distinguished between different forms of eBusiness in terms of our discussion of features of the value-network discussed in Chapter 7. In terms of eCommerce, we may distinguish between three major forms: B2C eCommerce, B2B eCommerce and C2C eCommerce.

Business-to-Consumer eCommerce refers to the attempt to support the organisation's customer chain with ICT and involves the ICT-enablement of key processes in the customer chain: pre-sale, sale-execution, sale-settlement and after-sale. We have portrayed an organisation's experience of B2C eCommerce as moving through a number of distinct stages of increasing complexity which support these phases of commerce. A company is likely to first use the internet for information-seeking and communication. Eventually, it wishes to establish a marketing presence on the internet and may eventually put an online catalogue of its products and/or services on a website. Online ordering and online payment are two additional levels of functionality likely to be provided on a company B2C site. At the highest level of sophistication, forms of customer relationship management may enable a company to better track its interactions with customers.

B2B eCommerce represents the attempt by organisations to use ICT to improve elements of their supply chains. Considered as a process, a typical supply chain includes activities such as search, negotiate, order, delivery, invoice, payment and after-sale. B2B eCommerce systems are likely to be built on bedrock of sound back-end information systems infrastructure. Supply chain management has arisen as a distinct philosophy within organisations and helps frame the objective of B2B eCommerce for many companies.

C2C eCommerce represents ICT enablement of the community chain or social networks surrounding the organisation. Public sector initiatives have been interested in enhancing traditional communities with increased ICT use. Private sector initiatives have been particularly interested in the community chain as a new revenue source or as a means of adding value to traditional commercial activities.

Whereas recent interest has been directed at the ways in which networks of consumers generate value there has also been interest in the ways in which networks of businesses can utilise ICT to collaborate as well as compete. Internally, organisations are beginning to manage collaboration across internal units and divisions globally. Externally, digital ecosystems of businesses are emerging. This we have referred to as P2P eBusiness.

Review test

eCommerce is a superset of eBusiness	True or False?
True	
False	

There are three main forms of eCommerce	Select all that apply
B2C eCommerce	
B2B eCommerce	
I2I eCommerce	
G2G eCommerce	
C2C eCommerce	

Some of the benefits of eCommerce include	Select all that apply
Cost savings	
Time savings	
Increased security	
Connection improvements	

B2C eCommerce is an extension of customer-facing information systems	True or False?
True	
False	

Place the stages of B2C eCommerce growth in increasing order of complexity	Use 1 for the lowest level of complexity
Marketing presence	
Information seeking and communication	
On-line catalogue	
On-line payment	
On-line ordering	
Customer relationship management	

Customer relationship management is composed of three main processes	Select all that apply
Customer search	
Customer acquisition	
Customer satisfaction	
Customer retention	
Customer extension	

B2B e-commerce is an extension of supplier-facing information systems	True or False?
True	
False	

Match the type of B2B eCommerce to the appropriate definition	
Buyer-oriented B2B	In this approach a consumer opens an electronic market on its own server
Supplier-oriented B2B	In this model, producers and consumers use the same marketplace.
Intermediary-oriented B2B	In this model an intermediary runs effectively a sub-set of some electronic market where buyers and sellers can meet and exchange products and services

C2C eCommerce is ...	Select the most appropriate definition
ICT enablement of the community chain	
Connect to Cardiff	
Competitive e-commerce	

Match the type of community to the appropriate definition	
eNabled Community	A traditional community in which most interaction is conducted off-line – some interaction is supported by communication networks.
Virtual Community	A community in which all interaction between members is conducted via communication networks.
Social Networking site	Using ICTs, particularly Web 2.0 technologies, to facilitate networking amongst dispersed individuals

Exercises

- Find one other example of B2C eCommerce.
- Access a B2C site and attempt to assign the features you find to the phases of the customer chain.
- Consider a company known to you. Determine at what stage it is in as far as B2C eCommerce is concerned.
- In terms of some company determine what information is searched for using the internet.
- Find a website for an SME in your local area. Determine how successfully it markets itself through the internet.
- Find a website with an online catalogue. Describe the features of the online catalogue.
- Make a list of the sort of goods you can order over the internet and what you may not. Reflect on the types of product characteristic of markets and hierarchies.
- Visit the Amazon site and attempt to determine what forms of customer profiling they employ.
- Investigate the range of CRM systems offered by vendors.
- Determine the level of discounting on the price of goods available by ordering via an internet site.
- Find an example of supplier-oriented or buyer-oriented B2B.
- In terms of an organisation known to you investigate whether it uses any forms of B2B e-commerce – even if it is as simple as emailing suppliers with orders. Try to identify

the key benefits of such electronic activity for the company. If the company does not undertake any B2B commerce currently, try to identify the potential.

- Find a company using B2B e-commerce and identify any problems they may be experiencing.
- If you live in what you would class as a community, investigate how much social capital exists in your community. Determine the evidence for such social capital. Identify ways of measuring the social capital in a community. Try to list a number of the social networks within which you participate.
- Try to find an example of a community website and determine what content is provided on this website.
- Find one or more examples of a virtual community. Analyse it in terms of the features described in the section on virtual communities. How would you measure social capital in a virtual community?

Projects

- Investigate the take-up of eBusiness and eCommerce amongst companies in your local area. Attempt to determine the importance of eBusiness to their operations.
- Choose an industrial or commercial sector. Investigate the degree with which B2B and B2C eCommerce has penetrated the sector. As a consequence, how have the value-networks in such a sector been transformed?
- Determine the levels of dis-intermediation and re-intermediation amongst eCommerce conducted in a particular market sector such as travel agencies and high-street banking. In other words, what sort of structural change has been caused to the market through ICT over the past 10–15 years?
- Inter-organisational information systems are important to collaboration between business partners such as high-street banks or major airlines. Determine the benefits associated with such inter-organisational information systems for a particular partnership network. Also determine the costs associated with building and operating such inter-organisational systems.
- In terms of a particular market sector determine the most appropriate organisational form for eBusiness. In other words, can the business be run entirely online or is it important to maintain a physical presence.
- Study the take-up of B2C eCommerce amongst a limited range of companies. Discover the degree to which the evolution of eCommerce in these companies corresponds to the growth model discussed.
- The rise of online trading has caused a parallel increase in online theft and fraud. Investigate the impact this growth has on the issue of consumer trust in relation to the growth of B2C eCommerce. Will trust be a major brake on the continued growth in B2C eCommerce?
- Customer relationship management is now a major philosophy for companies. Determine the degree to which such a philosophy relies on customer relationship information systems. How do such information systems help improve organisational performance and how can this be measured?
- Consider the most effective ways of evaluating B2C systems. In other words, how can companies determine the value that B2C eCommerce provides for them? Does conducting B2C eCommerce inevitably make such measurement easier and why?

- Amongst the various forms of B2B eCommerce described in this chapter, determine the most prevalent form. For instance, determine the level of usage of intermediary-oriented B2B in a market sector known to you such as retail.
- Those companies that survive in the eConomy will be those that integrate effectively their front-end information systems such as their B2B systems with their existing core information systems infrastructure. Investigate the degree to which such integration is critical to the success of eBusiness.

Critical reflection

Michael Porter has recently argued that clicks-and-mortar firms are more likely than 'clicks only' firms to be viable in economic markets long-term. Why should this be the case? In what way is it appropriate to use a growth model such as that for B2C eCommerce to plan eBusiness strategy? How important is customer relationship management as an element of business strategy and how important is it for companies to invest in CRM systems? Does the importance of CRM vary by industry sector? Which is the most significant benefit of B2C e-Commerce for business and why? Which is the most significant problem for modern business in the area of B2C e-Commerce? Is the supply chain as significant for service-oriented organisations? Is B2B e-commerce important for such organisations? What sorts of organisation are likely to benefit from B2B e-Commerce the most? What business potential is there in an eNabled Community? Are virtual communities viable? What value is created in an informal exchange of communication between members of a virtual community? Does the auction model of exchange have potential for infiltrating conventional fixed-price models of exchange with the increasing penetration of the internet?

Case exploration

Most medium- to large-scale organisations can be seen to engage in all the forms of commerce discussed in this chapter. Try to unpack a particular case in terms of the distinctions between the major forms of eCommerce. For instance, what does B2C eCommerce mean in the case of Tesco? How does it engage in B2B eCommerce? Does it have any C2C eCommerce and what sort of P2P eCommerce does it engage in?

Further reading

An alternative vision of the forms of eCommerce can be found in Laudon and Traver (2011). The idea of P2P eCommerce through inter-organisational information systems was first raised by Barrette and Konsynski (1982).

References

Barrette, S. and B. R. Konsynski. (1982). Inter-Organisational Information Sharing Systems. *MIS Quarterly* 6(Fall): 93–105.

Cassidy, J. (2002). *Dot.Con*, London, Allen Lane/Penguin Press.

Laudon, K. C. and C. G. Traver. (2011). *E-Commerce 2011: Business, Technology and Society*, 7th edn. New York, Pearson Education.

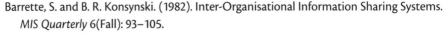

Martin, J. (1996). *Cybercorp*, New York, American Management Association.

Porter, M. E. (1996). What Is Strategy? *Harvard Business Review* Nov-Dec: 59–78.

Rheingold, H. (1995). *The Virtual Community: Finding Connection in a Computerised World*, London, Minerva.

Timmers, P. (1998). Business Models for Electronic Marketplaces. *Electronic Markets* 8(1): 3–8.

9 Further forms of eBusiness

Learning outcomes	Principles
Describe the distinctive features of mobile eCommerce.	Mobile commerce relies upon the use of a growing range of access devices, particularly mobile phones, laptops and tablets, by a range of different business actors to access and interact with the informatics infrastructure of organisations.
Relate the similarities and differences between eBusiness in the commercial sector and forms of eGovernment	*Internal eGovernment* refers to enablement of internal processes within the government body with ICT. *G2C eGovernment* involves supporting the customer-chain of the government body. *G2B eGovernment* concerns electronic enablement of relationships between government bodies and the private sector. *G2G eGovernment* is the use of eGovernment to support intra-government cooperation and collaboration. Finally, *C2C eGovernment* concerns enablement of the community chain of government bodies with ICT.
Understand the importance of eMarketing to B2C eCommerce and the major approaches taken.	Electronic Marketing is the use of electronic channels for delivery of promotional material. Electronic marketing channels are characterized by being pull, aggressive, interactive, time-independent, one-to-many and many-to-many and information-strong.
Describe the relevance of business intelligence to business.	Business intelligence refers to a number of techniques for identifying and analysing patterns in business data. The aim is to use such intelligence for better business decision-making, particularly strategic decision-making.
Understand the importance of eProcurement to B2B eCommerce and the major approaches taken.	Electronic procurement refers to the use of ICT to enable the whole of the procurement process. Significant performance improvement is possible through forms of eProcurement such as eSourcing, ePurchasing and ePayment.

Introduction

Because of the central role ICT plays in supporting communication and activity within organisations, forms of eBusiness as critical innovation continue to multiply. In this chapter we consider a number of such further forms of eBusiness. First, we consider the growing use of informatics infrastructure to support mobile and remote work patterns: people working on the move or from some remote location such as from home. Second, we consider the growing adoption of eBusiness principles amongst public sector organisations, particularly government and its agencies. Third, we consider an important part of B2C eCommerce: that of electronic marketing. As more and more interaction with organisations occurs online, more and more potential exists for using electronic channels for marketing purposes. There is also some overlap between the process of marketing research and that of business intelligence. Business intelligence refers to a number of techniques for identifying and analysing patterns in business data. The aim is to use such intelligence for better business decision-making, particularly strategic decision-making. Finally, we consider a critical part of B2B eCommerce: that of electronic procurement. This form of eBusiness innovation is seen as a means of reducing major supply chain costs to companies and to public sector organisations.

Mobile eBusiness and eCommerce

Mobile eCommerce or mobile commerce is seen to be a significant new avenue for eBusiness. We shall argue that this area is really a logical extension of the model of eBusiness discussed in Chapter 4. The value-network model is particularly useful as a way of understanding the position of mobile commerce within the wider context of eBusiness and eCommerce. Mobile commerce relies upon the use of a growing range of access devices, particularly mobile phones, laptops and tablets, by a range of different business actors to access and interact with the informatics infrastructure of organisations. This may be accessing the B2C and B2B eCommerce websites of organisations while on the move or at a location remote from the organisation. Hence, mobile commerce may involve online delivery of content to such access devices and includes the issue of remote working using such access devices.

Remote/Mobile working

It is possible to identify four major places that remote access devices may be used: from the home, within public spaces, while on the move (mobile) or while in the workplace. Particular access channels will be associated with particular places of access and use. Hence, as a means of improving access to electronic services, governments have been putting more access devices into public places such as schools, libraries, community centres and museums. Also, an increasing range of WiFi hotspots are being offered in private sector cafes and other public spaces.

This technological change supports changes in work and leisure activity. Within countries such as the UK a growing number of people are working outside traditional organisational settings such as offices. Some of these workers are nomadic workers in the sense that they move around or between countries in conducting their work. Some of these workers still work from a fixed location such as from home either on a full-time or a part-time basis and some are working for themselves (their own businesses) or for a larger organisation.

All such workers rely on critical elements of our model of technical infrastructure discussed in Chapter 6. First, they need to have regular access to some access device such a personal computer, laptop and/or mobile phone. Second, they need to connect such access devices easily to ubiquitous broadband infrastructure, whether this is to the conventional telephony network, the mobile cellular network or a growing range of WiFi and WiMax facilities. Third, such mobile actors are likely to need to access organisational services, either in terms of some dedicated services run as part of an organisation's informatics infrastructure, or more widely in terms of software as services run on cloud servers.

Let us just look at one facet of remote working to emphasise some of the costs and benefits associated with this change in working practices. In terms of remote working from home there are a number of held benefits for the individual. Remote working might provide improved access to work for persons who might find it difficult to travel regularly to some place of work, such as carers or the disabled. For certain persons such as parents with young children, working from home might provide opportunity for an improved work–life balance. For many, remote working reduces the need for commuting to work, freeing up more work time and reducing the stress of regular travel.

There are also a number of held benefits for the organisation employing remote workers. For instance, it has been found that remote working generally increases worker productivity while also reducing absenteeism. Remote working means that organisations can easily tap in to a supply of personnel willing to work outside of normal office hours and providing quality customer service. Remote working also can reduce an organisation's overheads, particularly the costs of maintaining expensive office space and associated services. Generally, remote working has also been found to improve staff loyalty and retention. It encourages valuable staff with particular skills but with other commitments to stay within the workforce.

Lastly, there are a number of benefits for the physical environment arising from increased remote working. Less people commuting as a result of increased remote working means that there is reduced congestion on the road network. Reduced road traffic means less CO_2 emissions and less expenditure on maintaining road infrastructure.

However, remote working does raise a number of challenges. First, this style of work does not suit all individuals. Many workers prefer a structured working day; they appreciate contact with other workers and the group support familiar within traditional forms of work. Second, some have argued for the reduced visibility of remote workers, placing them at a disadvantage in terms of work assignment and promotions. From the point of view of the organisation, remote working demands significant investment in and management of ICT infrastructure. Also, increased home working demands a certain degree of culture change. For instance, managers are no longer able to directly observe and control workers from home. This means that more trust has to be invested in the manager–employee relationship and that normally clearer performance management practices need to be established.

Virtual organisation

A key theme of this book is that ICT is an effective tool which supports the design of new activity systems or the re-design of existing activity systems. One of the most radical forms of such re-design is the virtual or network organisation. A *virtual organisation* has one or more of the following characteristics. Physical structures such as offices are reduced in number, or perhaps removed entirely. Workers are provided with electronic work-spaces rather than physical work-spaces. Where office-space is required workers are encouraged to 'hot desk' – to share office facilities on a booking basis. Physical documentation is discouraged; electronic documentation is promoted. Work is organised in terms of loose projects which workers join and leave in a flexible way. The members of the organisation communicate and collaborate using ICT. In these senses, the informatics infrastructure, including the communications network, becomes the organisation.

Virtual organisations such as these have been proposed as viable business models, particularly for knowledge-intensive industries and corresponding sets of knowledge workers. Hence, for instance, the production of content such as magazines or software can be managed as loose sets of project workers, collaborating remotely or in a nomadic manner.

Mobile B2C eCommerce

The term mobile eCommerce is better expressed as mobile B2C eCommerce. This term is now particularly used to refer to a growing range of applications available to the consumer or a range of mobile access devices such as tablets and mobile phones. As we have seen in Chapter 6 it is possible for consumers to access the web via a mobile device. However, the access to such content is typically much slower than through a fixed device connected to the internet through a conventional wide area network. The interface of certain access devices such as the mobile phone is also not ideal in that it does not permit easy navigation of web content. Some organisations specifically produce websites with reduced functionality for mobile access. The growing range of tablet devices offers a more convenient interface to web content through larger, touch-sensitive screens.

The key growth in the mobile B2C eCommerce sector in recent years has been in so-called apps. Apps, short for mobile applications, are small pieces of software developed specifically for the operating systems of handheld devices such as mobile phones, PDAs and tablet computers. Mobile apps can come preloaded on such handheld devices or can be downloaded by users from app stores over the internet. The most popular operating platforms that support mobile apps are Windows Mobile, Android, Symbian, Java ME and Palm. There were something like 17 billion downloads of mobile apps in 2011. However, the technological standards supporting such apps are frequently closed or proprietary leading many to question the long-term viability of this business model.

eGovernment

As a term, eBusiness is normally used to refer to the ICT-enablement of activity systems within private sector organisations. But the redesign of activity systems is also of importance to the public sector, particularly within government and its agencies. Government typically fulfils three major functions: enabling and supporting democracy, developing and implementing policy, delivering services. Electronic government to date in most countries around the world has traditionally focused on the last of these functions, perhaps because of the ease with which a model of service delivery has been adapted from the commercial sector.

As we have seen in Chapter 7, we may also view government in system's terms as the major control process in a political system; this provides meaning to the concept of governance. In the modern Western world it has been argued that governance is now undertaken by a network of stakeholders not all of which are traditional political organisations or even public sector organisations. In this view, the disaggregation of the government value network which this implies demands an increasingly sophisticated web of technology to support communication and coordination between a diverse network of actors.

Foundations of eGovernment

Fundamentally, it is possible for eGovernment to be conceptualised around the value-network idea. For instance, a government body's delivery of a service can be considered as a process of producing value for a number of different stakeholders. Each stakeholder will participate at different points in the value-network and therefore will interact with different government systems. Each government service will use given inputs of resources such as finance, staffing, equipment and property and will produce outputs in terms of units of service delivered to customers or citizens.

The customer focus and service delivery ethos characteristic of the description above is based largely in the approach to public sector service provision founded in the philosophy of the *New Public Management*. In the early 1990s Osborne and Gaebler (1992) published an influential examination of US government entitled *Reinventing Government*. This book consisted of a call to build more effective public administrations based around ideas of results-based and customer-focused government. This collection of ideas is often referred to as the New Public Management (NPM) or alternatively as Public Sector Modernisation. The fundamental features of NPM include a focus on process, management, markets, monitors and customers.

First, NPM maintains that the public sector should be interested in the process of governance, not in the structures of government. This is expressed in the belief that government bodies should be interested in 'steering' not in 'rowing' – 'rowing' can be outsourced to other agencies. Therefore, this philosophy advocates disaggregation of the public sector value network through the separation of the purchaser and provider functions in government. Second, NPM proposes a focus on public sector management rather than public sector administration. It emphasises the importance of strategic management for government and the introduction of rational planning processes into government organisations. Third, NPM promotes a drive towards greater competition in the public sector, implicitly introducing a market-based model for control into this sector. This typically involves improving performance through government functions facing market tests. It also involves reducing government functions through privatisation and contracting out services to other bodies. Performance is compared with other providers through benchmarking and engaging in partnerships and projects with the private sector. Fourth, as a consequence of its focus on markets, NPM promotes the drive towards more explicit standards of performance. Government agencies are expected to establish key service delivery targets against which their performance will be assessed to see if continuous improvement is being achieved. This means extensive use of contracts in public administration. Coordination of a nexus of contracts with providers creates huge demands for efficient data handling. Finally, government bodies are required to orient their activities around a customer focus: an empowering of citizens by pushing control out of the bureaucracy, into the community. They also feel that the focus of government organisations should be not merely on providing public services but in catalysing all sectors (public, private and voluntary) into action to solve community problems.

However, the New Public Management is not without its critics. Key differences are highlighted between public and private sectors which means that the activity systems infrastructure of government organisations is significantly different from private sector organisations both in terms of overall purpose and structure of processes. For instance, the purpose of the typical public sector organisation is much more diffuse than that in the private sector. In terms of process, the position of citizen as 'customer' of government services has also been subject to challenge since the customer of many government services is usually not in the position to switch to another service provider as is possible in the private sector.

Electronic government can be seen to be very much an instrument of the public sector modernisation agenda in that it typically frames public sector institutions and their activities in terms of the NPM philosophy of process, management, markets and monitors. However, the definition of what eGovernment means is in continual flux and has been subject to some change over the years, both in the UK and internationally. Curtin *et al* define eGovernment as 'the use of any and all forms of information and communications technology (ICT) by governments and their agents to enhance operations, the delivery of public information and services, citizen engagement and public participation, and the very process of governance' (2004). In this definition, eGovernment is seen as a lever for modernisation. It is particularly seen as a lever for process change amongst government administrations with significant potential for performance improvement in the public sector. The definition also includes consideration of interaction with external actors particularly through the use of ICT to enable and enhance democratic

AQ1

participation. Hence, electronic democracy or eDemocracy is considered a part of e-Government alongside electronic administration or eAdministration.

History

The electronic government agenda is normally seen to have originated within President Bill Clinton's Administration in the US during the early 1990s. At this time, Vice-President Al Gore associated the development of the Information Super-highway with the reinvention of Government. Since the 1990s many major nation-states internationally have instituted programmes for eGovernment. Consulting organisations which report on international progress in eGovernment, consistently has placed the governments of the US, Canada and Singapore at the top of the list, closely followed by a raft of European nations.

Within the UK, eGovernment can be seen to have originated out of the Modernising Government White Paper, and is clearly coupled in this document with the idea of public sector modernisation. This paper outlined a strategy for Information Age Government with the initial aim of e-enabling all government's services by 2008. It focused on better services for citizens and businesses and aimed to make more effective use of government's information resources. The strategy challenged all public sector organisations to innovate and implement eBusiness methods and it challenged the centre of government to provide common infrastructure. In addition, in March 2000 the Prime Minister moved forward this White Paper and committed the UK government to getting all government services online by December 2005 and ensuring that everyone who wanted it had access to the internet by end of 2005.

A number of researchers and commentators on the eGovernment agenda have however cast doubt on the leverage potential of ICT in the government domain. Fountain (2001), for instance, argues that initiatives in e-Government, at least in the US, display very little evidence of deep process change. Instead, the use of ICT is patched on to existing government structures with the aim of making them more efficient. However the efficacy and effectiveness of government administrations is left largely unchallenged and consequently unchanged.

Forms of electronic Government

It is possible to identify at least five major forms of eGovernment in terms of the value-network idea. These forms are located around the major value-chains within the network and hence typically involve different stakeholders.

Internal eGovernment refers to the enablement of internal processes within the government body itself with ICT. The major stakeholder involved is the employee of the government body and the value-chain supported is the internal value-chain. In this area the significant innovation is the integration of back-office systems and processes within government.

G2C or government-to-citizen eGovernment is a form of external eGovernment since it is particularly involved in supporting the customer-chain of the government body. Since the major stakeholder involved is the citizen, many of the so-called customer chain issues in eBusiness also exist in G2C. However, many distinct issues arise located in the public sector nature of service provision such as diffuse sometimes conflicting goals characteristic of government bodies and the difficulties inherent in the distinction between citizen and customer. The key promise of eGovernment in this area is particularly seen as the process of dis-intermediation – providing direct contact between citizen and government agency.

G2B or Government-to-Business eGovernment concerns electronic enablement of the relationships between government bodies and the private sector. One of the major forms of such relationship involves management of the supply chain and the government agency. Hence, many of such supply chain issues are held to be similar in nature to eBusiness issues in this area. However, many features of the context of public sector procurement shape the relevance of technological solutions in this area.

Much of eGovernment success is predicated on delivering what has been referred to as 'joined-up' government. This is the key issue for G2G e-government – the use of eGovernment to support intra-government cooperation and collaboration. This can be seen to be an internal value-chain issue for the super-system of government. Significant issues in this area include inter-operability of systems and data sharing between government agencies.

C2C eGovernment concerns enablement of the community chain of government bodies with ICT. C2C interaction is not traditionally seen to be a part of government. However, it is likely to be an important part of future governance, particularly in the way it links with two of the other functions of government – democratic accountability and policy-making.

Lenk and Traunmuller (2002) argue that it is important to include all these forms within an extensive definition of eGovernment. Definitions of eGovernment should also include conceptions of eDemocracy – the use of ICT to support informed deliberation among citizens and help them to participate in decision-making. Hence, eDemocracy can be seen to be a component part of eGovernment along with eAdministration. Forms of eDemocracy can also be seen to mirror forms of eAdministration as described above.

In narrow terms, eDemocracy can be used to refer solely to the enablement of democratic processes between members of some political grouping and their governmental representatives. This is clearly a form of *external* eDemocracy and mirrors external forms of eAdministration such as G2C. On the other hand eDemocracy can serve to refer to the way in which ICT can be used to improve internal democratic processes within government. This is a form of *internal* eDemocracy which closely mirrors both forms of internal e-Government and G2G. There is also the notion of *local* eDemocracy. Local eDemocracy occurs where local groups use ICT to create democratic forms, forums and processes to facilitate political interaction within the community itself. It hence has a close relationship to C2C eGovernment.

Electronic government in the UK

In terms of the UK context, historically internal eGovernment has been the most significant type of eGovernment change. Large central government agencies such as the Inland Revenue (Beynon-Davies, 2005) have been subject to considerable computerisation, many such projects being financed by a mix of public and private sector investment. Some 4 million people work in local government, central government and public administrations such as the National Health Service in the UK. It is therefore not surprising to find much of the rhetoric surrounding the expected benefits of eGovernment within Britain to be focused around efficiency and effectiveness improvements associated with the re-organisation and re-deployment of staff supported by integrated ICT systems.

Since the formulation of an explicit eGovernment agenda in the UK in 2000, G2C eGovernment has assumed some significance. For example, large-scale investment has been made in promoting electronic service delivery amongst local authorities in England. More recently, G2B (particularly in the area of eProcurement) and G2G eGovernment have assumed significance attached to efficiency-oriented public sector reform. In the UK, C2C has not really assumed any significance whatsoever although e-Democracy initiatives such as piloting of electronic voting and promotion of electronic consultation at the local government level has been on-going.

However, eGovernment change over the past decade in the UK has focused primarily on a G2C model of eGovernment. Such a model relies on a particular informatics infrastructure, which we referred to in an earlier chapter as electronic service delivery. For instance, much of the effort made by the Inland Revenue (now Inland Revenue and Customs) has been devoted to re-engineering key aspects of its customer chain. The department's eServices strategy identifies a number of core customer-facing services that it sees as common to its major customer groups.

Central government in the UK issued guidance to government bodies, encouraging them to develop channel strategies in 2002. These strategies were described as a set of choices about how, and through what means, services will be delivered to the customer. Government organisations have been encouraged to 'reflect customer preferences in their channel strategies to promote social inclusion, so that cost, skill and lack of confidence are not impediments to use' (Beynon-Davies, 2005). Critical to this are plans for supporting different access mechanisms for different customer segments. Also important is consideration of the use of intermediaries such as the Post Office and the Citizen's Advice Bureau (CAB).

For effective eBusiness and eGovernment people must trust electronic delivery. A major part of such trust is reliant on ensuring the privacy of electronic data held in ICT systems and the transactions flowing between ICT systems, particularly payments. As a key example, in the UK a government secure intranet is used for internal and G2G communications within and between major government bodies.

Much emphasis is made in the UK central Government literature of so-called joined-up thinking (Beynon-Davies, 2007). In eGovernment terms this translates into sharing data with key government partners and providing 'one-stop shops' for key government services. It also refers to the use of intermediaries both in the public and private sector as a means of delegating key aspects of service delivery and hence of disaggregating the customer chain of government. For example, voluntary sector agencies are particularly attractive as intermediaries in the government customer chain. A key example of such change in the role of the voluntary sector is that of the Citizen's Advice Bureau. This organisation is seen as an important customer-sponsored intermediary in the UK G2C area. It is seen as fulfilling a key role in tiered access to government services.

The technical innovations possible with ICT are predicated on changes to organisational processes and structures. Hence, eGovernment change is organisational as well as technical change. A key example here is the way in which service efficiencies expected with the increasing use of ICT by UK central government departments such as the Inland Revenue is expected to enable reductions in back-office functions and a consequent movement of staff to front-office activities.

eMarketing

Marketing can be defined as the process of planning and executing the conception, pricing, promotion and distribution of ideas, goods and services to create exchanges that satisfy individual and organisational goals. This definition emphasises that marketing is not just an activity that occurs after a product has been produced or after a service has been formulated. In modern business practice, marketing input is important in the design of a product and in the after-sales process: it is important to the design of the so-called value proposition of a company's business model. The internet and ICT generally offer innovative ways of engaging in pre-sale activity with the customer. One of the most significant of such activities is the electronic marketing of goods and services. In terms of customer relationship management, eMarketing is particularly directed at customer acquisition but is also relevant to customer retention and extension. Not surprisingly, marketing strategy is typically an important part of organisational strategy and eMarketing strategy is likely to be a critical component of any eBusiness strategy.

Marketing channels

Advertising products and services is a substantial part of marketing and can be seen in our terms as a form of communication or information system between organisational actors and customers. Advertising involves attempting to transmit certain messages to particular customer segments in the hope of persuading people to buy products and/or services. Messages frequently take the form of assertions about particular properties of organisational value such as its quality or price. But many other messages consist of what we called expressives: communications which express people's feelings about particular forms of value. The intention is to attempt to build some form of emotional attachment to particular products or services.

Traditionally marketing has focused on the transmission of messages to potential customers through channels such as television, radio, newspapers, magazines and more recently through direct-selling approaches using the telephone. Such approaches to marketing are characterised by being push, passive, linear, event-driven and information-weak. A company disseminates (*pushes*) the material to a perceived market of potential customers. Traditional modes of advertising require potential customers to find an advert either through browsing or through some more directed search. They are hence *passive*. The marketing material is scripted and is expected to be delivered in some *linear* sequence as a package. The material is *event-driven* in that it tends to be delivered at a specific point in time and the material is typically 'broadcast' from one source to many potential customers.

Because of such characteristics, it is typically difficult to gather direct data on the impact the distribution of a traditional marketing product has on a given population (*information-weak*).

Take an advertisement placed in relevant newspapers and magazines to promote a new type of car produced by an automobile company. The company pays to have the advertisement produced by a graphics company (scripting) and is likely to make a key decision on the types of newspapers and magazines to place the advertisement in on the basis of the intended customer-base for the car (push). For a multi-national automobile manufacturer it will probably decide to run separate marketing campaigns in each of the countries it sends to (location-dependent). These decisions will be predicated on the assumption that potential customers will come across the advertisement while reading their newspaper or magazine (passive). The company will pay print companies to place the advertisement for a particular day, perhaps timed to coincide with some launch event for the car (event-driven). Since it appears in all copies of the particular newspapers and magazines it is effectively a broadcast of the advertisement. Advertising agencies have to engage in a number of post-hoc techniques to attempt to capture evidence of the impact of particular advertisements such as interviewing a sample of customers (information-weak).

In contrast, *electronic marketing* uses electronic delivery and thus tends to be characterised by being pull, aggressive, interactive, time-independent and information-rich. Potential customers themselves access the material using channels such as websites (*pull*). Such advertising also involves actively seeking out customers through technologies such as email and initiating some form of contact with them (*aggressive*). The potential customer can communicate with the company about its products and services using channels such as email and there is also potential for customising the material for particular customers (*interactive*). The marketing material can be accessed 24 hours a day, 365 days a year (*time-independent*). The material can also be accessed in different contexts in a one-to-one or one-to-many relationship between the potential customer and the business or in a many-to-many way between the customer audiences themselves. Because of the transaction-based nature of B2C eCommerce sites a vast amount of data can be captured which relates customer searching with eventual purchase (*information-rich*). Finally, marketing via the internet can be achieved on an international scale from one location.

However, a website will not prove effective as a marketing tool without sufficient numbers of people accessing it. Hence, eMarketing cannot be divorced from traditional promotional activities. Such promotional activities have to be undertaken over and above the creation of a website to achieve sufficient levels of traffic to the site. Once a sufficient level of traffic has been produced then a number of eMarketing techniques may be applied.

eMarketing strategy

Good marketing is reliant on good planning and planning for eMarketing will be an important part of general eBusiness planning. Such planning will include an analysis of the environment for eMarketing, an assessment of current internal infrastructure available to the company for eMarketing, establishing a vision for eMarketing, specifying an eMarketing strategy, implementing such a strategy and evaluating the contribution eMarketing makes to the business.

Market analysis will involve determining the demand for eCommerce in particular segments of the market. It will also involve close attention to the behaviour of competitors and partners such as intermediaries in this area. Market or customer segmentation is the process of identifying the characteristics of different segments of the population to which a company sells or wishes to sell its products or services. Customer segmentation is a concept frequently used within marketing strategy. The assumption is that a customer population can be distinguished in terms of a number of key dimensions. Different customer segments are likely to have different behaviour patterns with an organisation and potentially have different expectations of eCommerce.

Some key dimensions as far as segmentation is concerned are socio-economic group, age, sex and ethnicity. Customer segmentation may be an important part of a channel strategy for organisations. Different customer segments will have different profiles of interaction with an organisation. Different access channels may also be needed to be maintained for different customer segments. It is also likely that different customer segments will need different content on such websites.

On the basis of an analysis of such segments it becomes possible to determine particular marketing requirements for each customer segment. There are five key questions companies should ask themselves in relation to customer segmentation: 'who are our customers?' 'how are their needs changing?' 'which do we target?' 'how can we add value?' 'how do we become first choice for the customer?'

Assessment will involve evaluating the performance of the current infrastructure and determining the feasible options available to a company in terms of extending its eMarketing infrastructure.

Establishing a vision will involve setting clear objectives for the use of eMarketing in terms of online contribution to company performance and the marketing mix of product, price, place and promotion. As a *product*, companies will be looking to offer added-value associated with using electronic channels. Value could be added to products within electronic delivery channels by improving searching facilities to online catalogues or providing more personalised products.

Pricing strategies for products and services should reflect the capabilities of electronic channels. In terms of pricing companies may offer discounts for using online ordering or differentiate pricing more dynamically in terms of time of purchase or customer segment. For instance, EasyJet.com, like most low-cost airlines, operate a dynamic pricing policy for its ticketing based on advanced booking to its flights and on customer demand.

Due consideration should be given to the most appropriate *place* to promote goods and services through electronic channels. Placing decisions will involve consideration of whether to dis-intermediate or re-intermediate in particular markets. It will also involve decisions as to the degree of integration between a company's promotional strategies with that of its partners.

Finally, *promotion* will involve consideration of the integration of electronic promotional channels with conventional promotional channels. It will also concern decisions about the appropriate mix of online with conventional promotion.

Promotional decisions will critically concern the amount of investment to be made in eMarketing as opposed to traditional marketing. Low cost airlines such as RyanAir, for instance, have used newspapers to offer discounts for advanced booking. Potential customers collect tokens from the newspaper and then contact the company via telephone or the web.

Specifying an eMarketing strategy will involve detailing the part that eMarketing plays in general eBusiness strategy. *Implementing an eMarketing strategy* will involve building a technical infrastructure for eMarketing and putting the associated human activity systems in place. *Evaluating eMarketing contribution* will involve monitoring the performance of eMarketing in terms of defined objectives such as online contribution.

The techniques of web-based eMarketing

Websites are now the primary approach for eMarketing. The main techniques of web-based eMarketing include, amongst others, banner adverts, target adverts, the use of domain names and email, and more recently the use of viral marketing.

Banner adverts are so-called because they are usually displayed across the top of some web-page. These are one-to-many passive advertisements that are encountered by the user merely by accessing a web-page. *Target advertisements* are one-to-many active advertisements in the sense that the user must click on something in order to be taken to the particular advertisement page. Certain banner advertisements may also be click-through. *Email* or other forms of remote communication such as SMS texting and instant messaging can also be used to directly contact existing customers with offers or promotions. Use of direct email is a one-to-one aggressive promotion strategy. Email or texting can also be used to contact potential customers from purchased customer databases.

Banner advertisement campaigns may involve placing such adverts on many different forms of website such as portals, generalised news services and special interest sites. Certain large online companies may utilise a large-scale network of affiliates. Affiliates will place small target advertisements on their websites encouraging users to re-direct to the home page of the major company for certain products and services.

Companies are likely to make charges for advertisements on their websites and this may form an important revenue stream for a web-based intermediary such as a web portal or affiliate. Generally there are four main ways of charging for online advertising: flat fee, CPM, Click Through and CPA. *Flat fee* is a traditional model for advertising revenue. Here a set fee is charged for placing the advertisement for a set time-period. Cost per thousand Presentation Model or *CPM* is a method of billing based on the number of advertisements viewed. *Click through* is relevant to target advertisements and involves billing on the basis of the number of consumers who click through to the particular advertisement. Many companies offering advertisements on the web, such as Google, are now using a Cost Per Action/Acquisition (*CPA*) revenue model. Cost per action is when an advertiser pays for each specified action such as a purchase or a form submission achieved through an online advert. Cost per acquisition is a related type in which the advertiser pays for new acquisitions such as new customers, prospects or leads achieved through online adverts.

Search engines provide an increasingly important gateway into products and services for consumers. Since Google is the most prominent example of such a gateway into the web it is not surprising to find that most of its multi-billion dollar revenue is generated from banner and targeted advertisements on its website. Such revenue is generated in two major ways under its AdWords programme. First, advertisers bid for a series of keywords that they think should trigger an advertisement from their company on the Google web page. If they are successful in their bid such keywords, when typed into the search engine, generate a sponsored link placed in some position on a list displayed on the right hand side of the Google web page. Where the link is placed upon the list depends on an algorithm based upon factors such as the level of bid paid by the advertiser and a historical analysis of the rate of previous click-throughs for particular advertisements.

One other important tool in the eMarketing armoury is the use of *branding* in *domain names*. Brands are classic examples of signs. The logo or brand-name of some company is an example of a symbol. Generally speaking such symbols signify certain referents such as particular products or the whole of company activity. However, particular logos or brand-names are also associated with a range of other connotations or concepts such as perceived company values and behaviour. In the online world it is particularly important to ensure that a brand is used to maximum effect. This may involve copyrighting the brand, registering an existing and well-recognised brand name as a domain name, registering the domain name with the most well-used search engines, ensuring that the domain name returns high in the lists of returned results to users of search engines and monitoring access from search engines and adjusting strategies to maintain presence.

One of the much discussed marketing techniques in recent times is that of viral marketing. This is the idea of using pre-existing social networks to produce an increase in brand awareness or to achieve other marketing objectives, such as increases in product sales. In traditional social networks these marketing objectives would be achieved through normal face-to-face communication between actors. The idea is to get ideas such as product referrals to spread throughout a social network in a similar manner to the way in which a virus might spread through a population – hence the name, viral marketing. As we argued in Chapter 4 this is fundamentally reliant on the level of social capital generated in a social network. In more recent times viral marketing relies particularly upon the growth in social media and the transmission of various forms of content such as video clips, images or text messages through such technologically enabled social networks.

Three other technologies are also mentioned as relevant to marketing through social media: blogs, podcasts and tweets. Blogs were covered in an earlier chapter. A *podcast* or webcast is a series of digital media files such as audio or video files that are released episodically to users. The word podcast has replaced the more accurate term webcast in common usage following the success of the Apple iPod. The mode of delivery differentiates podcasting from other means of accessing media files over the internet, such as direct download, or streaming. Normally, a list of all the audio or video files currently associated with a given series is maintained centrally on the distributor's server as a web feed. The listener or viewer then employs special client application software that can access this web feed, check it for updates and download any new files in the series. This process can be automated so that new files are downloaded automatically. Web or podcasting is normally achieved with *RSS, which* stands for Really Simple Syndication and consists of a family of web feed formats used to publish frequently updated content such as blog entries, news headlines or pod-casts to subscribers. Twitter is a social networking site which enables its users to send and read text-based posts of up to 140 characters, informally known as *tweets*. Many business organisations are now using tweets as an advertising channel.

Channel strategies

There is a clear relationship between eMarketing and the issue of channel strategy, in the sense that eMarketing has to be tailored to particular channel strategies. To refresh, an access channel is a means for an organisation to deliver goods and/or services to its customers. Traditional access channels include voice and face-to-face contact. There are also a range of remote access channels of which telephone contact is the most familiar. Goods and services can either be delivered directly by an organisation or indirectly using intermediaries.

A *channel strategy* is a set of choices for the organisation about how, and through what means, services and goods will be delivered to the customer. This typically means deciding upon which access channels will be made available to which customer segments. Different levels of interactivity and content may be required to meet the needs of differing customer segments. The capability of a particular access channel to cope with demand is a critical part of any channel strategy as is the necessary integration between different access channels.

For example, in terms of the delivery of local government services a channel strategy will involve deciding what proportion of services, if any at all, will be delivered remotely to PCs or through interactive digital TV. It will also involve determining the degree to which delivery of services are to be managed via contact centres and to ensure that seamless service delivery is possible across multiple access channels.

Channel strategies typically may involve tiered access to products and services. At least three tiers of access are offered by most large-scale private and public sector organisations. Each of these tiers has a different cost and availability implication for the organisation. The first tier is remote direct access through a sub-set of the access devices discussed in Chapter 6. The second tier is through a multi-channel access centre. Here, contact centre staff manages delivery through computer integrated telephony. The third tier involves direct contact with employees through face-to-face communication or letter. This is illustrated in Figure 9.1.

Adoption of a particular channel strategy will have a critical impact on overall informatics strategy. For instance, providing tiered access to services implies a unified view of the customer information across different access channels. This probably implies adoption of a customer relationship management system which collects data from face-to-face contact, interaction with the contact centre as well as remote interaction with the customer. This means either purchasing and installing such a system as a package or building such a system in-house, perhaps using existing ICT infrastructure such as customer databases as a platform.

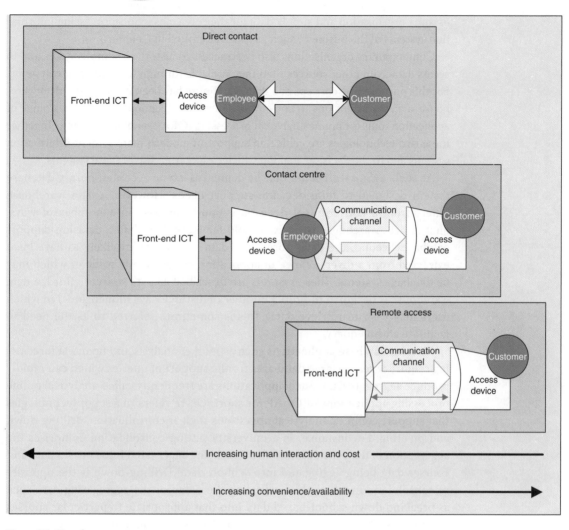

Figure 9.1 Tiered access

Business intelligence

There is a close association between market research and business intelligence. Business intelligence, sometimes referred to as business analytics, more broadly refers to a number of techniques for identifying and analysing patterns in business data. The aim is to use such intelligence for better business decision-making, particularly strategic decision-making. A number of critical technologies support business intelligence. These include *data warehousing*, OLAP and data mining.

Conventional database applications, such as those described in Chapter 6, are normally designed to handle high volumes of business transactions such as orders, payments and sales. As such, this type of database system is frequently referred to as an online transaction processing (OLTP) system. As we have seen, the data available in such applications are important for running the day-to-day operations of some organisation and supply data for the core transaction-processing information systems of the business, such as those described in Chapter 7.

Contemporary organisations also need access to historical, summary data and to access data from other sources than that available through OLTP database systems. For this purpose, the concept of a data warehouse has been created. The data warehouse requires extensions to conventional database technology and also a range of application tools for online analytical processing (OLAP) and data mining. Together these two technologies are critical in support of modern management information systems and to the decision-making which results from use of these systems.

As such, a *data warehouse* may be defined as a type of contemporary database system designed to fulfil decision-support needs. However, a data warehouse differs from a conventional decision-support database in a number of ways. First, a data warehouse is likely to hold far more data than a decision-support database. Second, the data stored in a data warehouse are likely to have been extracted from a diverse range of application systems, only some of which may be database systems. These systems are described as data sources. Third, a data warehouse is designed to fulfil a number of distinct ways (dimensions) in which users may wish to retrieve data. This is sometimes referred to as the need to facilitate ad-hoc query.

Modern database applications such as market analysis and financial forecasting require access to large databases for the support of queries which can rapidly produce aggregate data. Such applications are frequently called analytical online processing applications or OLAP for short. *OLAP* refers to a set of technologies that support complex analytical operations such as consolidation, drilling-down and pivoting. For instance, in a university setting consolidation comprises the aggregation of data such as modules data being aggregated into courses data and courses data being aggregated into schools data. Drilling-down is the opposite of consolidation and involves revealing the detail or dis-aggregating data such as breaking-down school-based data into that appropriate to particular courses or modules. Pivoting, sometimes referred to as 'slicing and dicing', comprises the ability to analyse the same data from different viewpoints, frequently along a time axis. For example in the university domain, one slice may be the average degree grade per course within a school. Another slice may be the average degree grade per student age-band within a school.

Data mining is the process of extracting previously unknown data from large databases and using it to make organisational decisions. Data mining is concerned with the discovery of hidden, unexpected patterns within data and usually works on large volumes of data typically held in a data warehouse. To gain benefit from a data warehouse the data patterns resident in the large data sets characteristic of such applications need to be extracted. As the size of a data warehouse grows the more difficult it is to extract such data using the conventional means of query and analysis. Also, large volumes are frequently needed to produce reliable conclusions in relation to data patterns. Data mining is useful in making critical organisational decisions, particularly those of a strategic nature. For instance, in retail chains data mining has been used to identify the purchasing patterns of customers and associating such data with demographic characteristics such as the age and class profile of customers. Such patterns are useful in making decisions such as what products to sell in which retail stores and when. Also, in the insurance industry data mining has been used to analyse the claims made against insurance policies and hence feed into actuarial decisions such as the pricing of particular insurance policies.

A consequence of the trend for moving much business communication online has been that much of this communication has become accessible to intelligence gathering and analysis purposes. Much of this is now referred to as web analytics, which can be seen to be a sub-set of business analytics. Broadly, web analytics refers to a battery of techniques employed to measure website traffic. Techniques include measuring the number of visitors to a website, the number of page views and how users navigate around a website through clicks. Web analysis such as this is typically performed in association with advertising campaigns and is used as one means of assessing the success of such promotions.

eProcurement

The pre-sale activity of search, negotiate and order in the supply chain is frequently referred to under the umbrella term of procurement. Sometimes the term procurement is used to refer to all the activities involved in the supply chain. Hence, *procurement* is an important business activity system in the value-chain and involves the purchasing of goods and services from suppliers at an acceptable quality and price and with reliable delivery.

Electronic procurement (eProcurement) refers to the use of ICT to enable the whole of the procurement process. EProcurement is a specific and important feature of B2B eCommerce. In this section we consider some of the key differences between conventional procurement and eProcurement. In terms of this distinction we examine some of the key areas of performance improvement possible with this form of eCommerce. This leads us to examine various forms of eProcurement and suitable technologies for supporting this form of process strategy (Chapter 10) for eBusiness.

The conventional procurement process

It is possible to distinguish between two types of procurement performed by companies: production-related and operating procurement. *Production-related procurement* is designed to support manufacturing operations. As such, procurement must be geared to fulfilment of long-term needs, generally involves the procurement of customised items and is frequently undertaken through established and regular relationships with suppliers. As such, procurement for production-related activities tends to be organised as managerial hierarchies. Non-production or *operating procurement* is conducted to support all the operations of the business. Such procurement is designed to fulfil immediate needs typically for commoditised items. As such relationships with suppliers tend to be irregular and temporary. Hence, operating procurement is frequently organised in terms of a market-based model of economic exchange.

Historically, procurement has been a human-intensive process involving activities such as requesting quotations, submitting purchase orders, approving and confirming orders, shipping, invoicing and payment. Traditionally, procurement has been performed by a specialist-purchasing department typically employing many people using paper documentation, the telephone and fax to communicate with suppliers. An activity systems model of this traditional procurement process is illustrated in Figure 9.2.

Employees first search for a product matching a particular need. Details of the product are then entered on a requisition form, which is sent for authorisation to the purchasing department. This department receives the requisition, authorises production of a purchase order and then produces the purchase order which is sent to an established supplier. The supplier dispatches goods to the company with an attached shipping note. When the goods have been checked a payment authorisation is issued to the accounting department which pays the supplier. The goods are then dispatched internally to the originating department.

It is possible to analyse the performance of this activity system in a number of ways. One approach is to analyse the average time taken to conduct each of the activities in this process. These are indicated on the diagram as annotations and Table 9.1 provides us with a total lead time for the procurement process.

It is important to recognise that this estimate of the average duration of the procurement process is large because of inherent delays, lags or waiting times

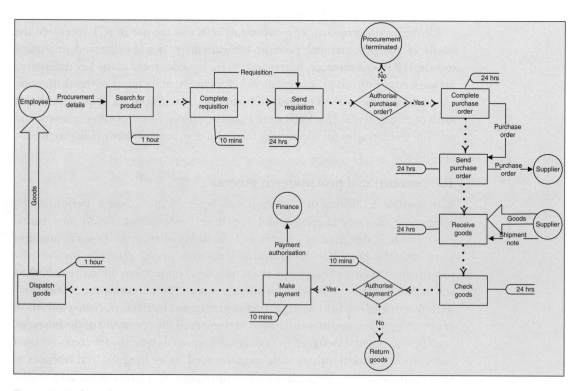

Figure 9.2 Traditional procurement process

Table 9.1 Activities and timings for a traditional procurement process

Activity	Average Time
Search for product and product identified	1 hour
Complete requisition	10 minutes
Send requisition	24 hours
Receive requisition	12 hours
Authorise and complete order	24 hours
Send order	24 hours
Delivery from supplier	24 hours
Receive goods	24 hours
Check goods	24 hours
Authorise payment	10 minutes
Despatch goods	1 hour
Total	6 days 2 hours and 20 minutes

embedded within the current activity system. Key delays are evident in the receipt of paper work and goods. For instance, items of documentation such as requisitions may sit in a person's in-tray for up to 12 hours before receiving attention.

Figure 9.3 illustrates an activity system that has been re-designed with the use of ICT. We are assuming here that employees are able to order directly from supplier websites. It therefore represents a model of a typical eProcurement process.

The same sort of analysis may be conducted for this electronic procurement process. The analysis is presented in Table 9.2.

It is evident that the speed of procurement is significantly increased using this activity system. This is because there is more automation of activities and more electronic transmission and storage of data. Consequently, certain activities are no longer required and there is less waiting time in the process.

Forms of eProcurement

It is possible to distinguish between three broad categories of eProcurement, roughly corresponding to the inter-dependent activities found in all procurement processes: electronic sourcing, purchasing and payment.

Electronic sourcing typically involves the use of electronic tendering systems that enable organisational agents to create requests for quotation (RFQ). Electronic RFQs can then be issued to suppliers. Forms of electronic auction may then be utilised to source best-priced contracts with suppliers.

Once a contract with a given supplier is awarded then a number of tools may be used to search catalogues, select desired goods or services, place them in an electronic shopping basket and automatically raise a requisition or purchase order. This is *electronic purchasing*.

Invoices may be issued in XML-format from a supplier once goods have been dispatched. Also, once the buyer has received the goods an invoice can be

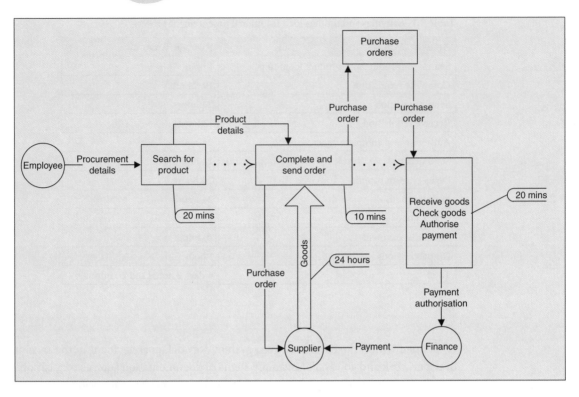

Figure 9.3 An eProcurement process

Table 9.2 Activities and timings associated with a re-engineered procurement process

Activity	Average time
Search for product and product identified	20 minutes
Complete order	10 minutes
Delivery from supplier	24 hours
Receive goods, check goods and authorise payment	20 minutes
Total	1 day 50 minutes

automatically matched to the purchase order for price and to the goods received for quantity. Various *electronic payment systems* may then be used to transfer payment to the supplier.

To facilitate standardisation of data and hence effective analysis for management information, many forms of eProcurement will use standard commodity classification coding. Such standard coding schemes may also enable faster searching for a particular item amongst a range of possible suppliers. Commodity coding is the assignment of standard codes to item records (at the part number level) and to purchase orders (at the purchase order line item level).

There are various coding schemes available. The common procurement vocabulary (CPV) is used in the EU within public procurement to group together products of similar producers. The European article number (EAN) is widely used in association with a standard for bar-coding. The United Nations Standard Product and Services Code (UN-SPC) provides a hierarchically organised product classification system. For example, a UN-SPC code for a mobile phone would be 43.17.15.12. The 43 stands for *Communications and Computing Equipment*; 17 stands for *Hardware and Accessories*; 15 stands for *Telephony equipment*; *12 stands for Mobile Telephone.*

Summary

The value-network model is particularly useful as a way of understanding the position of mobile commerce within the wider context of eBusiness and eCommerce. Mobile commerce relies upon the use of a growing range of access devices, particularly mobile phones, laptops and tablets, by a range of different business actors to access and interact with the informatics infrastructure of organisations. It is possible to identify four major places that remote access devices may be used: from the home, within public spaces, while on the move (mobile) or while in the workplace.

It is possible for eGovernment to be conceptualised around the value-network idea. For instance, a government body's delivery of a service can be considered as a process of producing value for a number of different stakeholders. Each stakeholder will participate at different points in the value-network and therefore will interact with different government systems. It is possible to identify at least five major forms of eGovernment in terms of the value-network idea. Internal eGovernment refers to enablement of internal processes within the government body itself with ICT. G2C eGovernment is involved in supporting the customer-chain of the government body. G2B eGovernment concerns electronic enablement of the relationships between government bodies and the private sector. G2G e-government is the use of eGovernment to support intra-government cooperation and collaboration. Finally, C2C eGovernment concerns enablement of the community chain of government bodies with ICT.

Electronic Marketing is the use of electronic channels for delivery of promotional material. Traditional marketing channels are characterised by being push, passive, linear, event-driven, one-to-many and information-weak. In contrast, electronic marketing channels are characterised by being pull, aggressive, interactive, time-independent, one-to-many and many-to-many and information-strong. Techniques for web-based eMarketing include the use of banner advertisements on websites and the use of email to contact potential customers. Revenue in the area of eMarketing can be achieved through schemes such as flat fee, CPM or click-through.

There is also some overlap between the process of marketing research and that of business intelligence. Business intelligence refers to a number of techniques for identifying and analysing patterns in business data. The aim is to use such intelligence for better business decision-making, particularly strategic decision-making.

The pre-sale activity of search, negotiate and order in the supply chain is frequently referred to under the umbrella term of procurement. Sometimes the term procurement is used to refer to all the activities involved in the supply chain. Electronic procurement (eProcurement) refers to the use of ICT to enable the whole of the procurement process. Significant performance improvement is possible through forms of eProcurement such as eSourcing, ePurchasing and ePayment.

Review test

_____ commerce relies upon the use of a growing range of access devices, particularly mobile phones, laptops and tablets, by a range of different business actors to access and interact with the informatics infrastructure of organisations.	Fill in the blank

It is possible to identify four major places that remote access devices may be used.	Select the most relevant
From the home	
From university	
Within public spaces	
While on the move	
While in the workplace	

Electronic government refers to the ICT-enablement of activity systems within private sector organisations.	True or False?
True	
False	

_____ can be used to refer solely to the enablement of democratic processes between members of some political grouping and their governmental representatives.	Fill in the blank

Match the type of eGovernment to the appropriate definition	
Internal eGovernment	Involved in supporting the customer-chain of the government body.
G2C eGovernment	The enablement of internal processes within the government body itself with ICT.
G2B eGovernment	The use of eGovernment to support intra-government cooperation and collaboration
G2G eGovernment	Concerns electronic enablement of the relationships between government bodies and the private sector.
C2C eGovernment	Concerns enablement of the community chain of government bodies with ICT.

Market or customer segmentation is the process of	Select the most relevant definition
Identifying different segments of the population to which a company sells or wishes to sell	
Offering differing discounts to different customers	
Personalising the delivery of goods and services to customers	

A channel strategy is a set of choices about how, and through what means goods and services will be delivered to the customer.	True or False?
True	
False	

Techniques for web-based eMarketing include ...	Select all that apply
use of banner advertisements on websites	
use of email to contact potential customers	
use of cookies	
use of popups	

Business intelligence broadly refers to a number of techniques for identifying and analysing patterns in business data.	True or False?
True	
False	

_____ refers to the use of ICT to enable the whole of the procurement process.	Fill in the blank

Forms of eProcurement include ...	select all that apply
eSourcing	
ePurchasing	
ePayment	
eShopping	

Match the type of procurement to the appropriate definition	
Production-related procurement	Procurement designed to support manufacturing needs, typically for customised goods and consequently organised as a hierarchy.
Operating procurement	Procurement designed to fulfil immediate business needs for commoditised items and hence typically organised as a market.

Exercises

- If you have a mobile phone try to identify what forms of mobile commerce you can conduct using this access device.
- Try to identify the sort of services provided electronically by a particular government agency, such as a local authority.
- See whether you can identify two practical examples of G2G eGovernment.
- Produce a brief statement of the characteristics of a traditional promotional channel such as a television advert.
- Produce a brief statement of the characteristics of an eMarketing promotional channel such as a banner advertisement.

- Generate a list of the efficiency improvements relevant to a particular organisation's use of eMarketing. Generate a list of the effectiveness improvements relevant to a particular organisation's use of eMarketing.
- Access a particular web portal and determine what eMarketing techniques are used.
- In terms of some particular eMarketing technique try to determine the revenue model used.
- Pick some organisation known to you and speculate as to whether it uses business intelligence in any way.
- Examine and analyse the whole of or part of some procurement process known to you in terms of the time taken to complete activities.
- Identify key ways in which the procurement process may be re-engineered through ICT.
- Determine what forms of e-Procurement are suitable for operational as opposed to production-related procurement.
- Detail the forms of eProcurement used by an organisation known to you.

Projects

- Investigate the idea of mobile computing and its relevance for organisational informatics. How much of a nation's workforce now works on the move and how many workers are likely to do so over the next decade? What practical problems will organisations face in managing a mobile workforce and what consequences has this for informatics infrastructure?
- Choose two nation-states. Determine what stage they are at in terms of eGovernment. Use the forms of eGovernment discussed in this chapter to help compare the two nations.
- Access an eGovernment website known to you. Try to determine when first this site was created and for what intended purpose. How has the website changed since its inception? Are there any plans to change the website in the future?
- Find an organisation and determine the degree to which it uses electronic marketing. What sort of eMarketing techniques does it use. Develop a plan for improving its utilisation of eMarketing.

Critical reflection

In what respect may large-scale product design projects be organised in terms of virtual or networked organisations?

Will the traffic to websites ever reach a position where it will become possible to replace conventional channels of marketing solely with e-Channels? In what ways is the marketing mix likely to be different for intangible as opposed to tangible products and services? What type of business is likely to have a high online revenue contribution? How does cyber-squatting damage the potential for eMarketing?

Besides the time it takes to complete tasks in the process, what other measures of the efficiency of the procurement process might be employed? Is it possible to identify the most important efficiency or effectiveness improvement produced through eProcurement? What forms of market models are most appropriate for electronic sourcing?

Attempt to access one of the many government websites. What did you think of the content? Do you regard it is useful? How might it be improved? To what degree is the modern welfare state dependent on information systems? Could the modern welfare state operate effectively without ICT? Can you provide examples?

Case exploration

Electronic government is a significant facet of eBusiness. Consider the case of the UK customs and revenue in terms of the types of eGovernment discussed in this chapter. For instance, consider what G2C eGovernment means in the light of this case?

Mobile commerce particularly relies on customers using the growing range of applications on smartphones. Most people use such access devices to engage with organisations such as Facebook and Twitter. But what about interacting with the traditional bricks-and-mortar companies? In terms of one of the case organisations discussed at the end of the book, such as Tesco and IKEA, consider how you can currently interact with the organisation using a mobile phone or a tablet computer.

Further reading

Chaffey *et al.* provide a thorough coverage of eMarketing approaches (2009). Although dated in terms of its portrayal of technology, the analysis of the advantages of mobile commerce by Barnes (2002) is still relevant. Farrington and Lysons (2012) cover forms of electronic procurement within the general context of supply chain management. Business intelligence is explored in Sabherwal and Becerra-Fernandez (2011). The various models for eGovernment are discussed in my paper (Beynon-Davies, 2007).

References

Barnes, S. J. (2002). The Mobile Commerce Value Chain: Analysis and Future Developments. *International Journal of Information Management* 22(1): 91–108.

Beynon-Davies, P. (2005). Constructing Electronic Government: The Case of the UK Inland Revenue. *International Journal of Information Management* 25(1): 3–20.

Beynon-Davies, P. (2007). Models for eGovernment. *Transforming Government: People, Process and Policy* 1(1): 1–24.

Chaffey, D., R. Mayer, K. Johnston and F. Ellis-Chadwick. (2009). *Internet Marketing.* 4th edn. Harlow, UK, Pearson Education.

Curtin, G. C., M. H. Sommer and V. Vis-Sommer. (2004). *The World of e-Government,* New York, Haworth Press.

Farrington, B. and K. Lysons. (2012). *Purchasing and Supply Chain Management,* London, Financial times/ Prentice Hall.

Fountain, J. E. (2001). *Building the Virtual State: Information Technology and Institutional Change,* The Brookings Institution.

Lenk, K. and R. Traunmuller. (2002). Preface to the Focus Theme on E-Government. *Electronic Markets* 12(3): 147–148.

Osborne, D. and T. Gaebler. (1992). *Reinventing Government: How the Entrpreneurial Spirit Is Transforming the Public Sector,* Reading, MA, Addison-Wesley.

Sabherwal, R. and I. Becerra-Fernandez. (2011). *Business Intelligence,* New York, John Wiley.

10 Activity infrastructure for eBusiness

Learning outcomes	Principles
Understand the notion of eBusiness strategy and how it differs from organisational strategy.	Organisation strategy is a detailed plan for future action. Planning is the process of formulating strategy; management is the process of implementing strategy. Business strategy should drive informatics strategy: a detailed plan for future informatics activities. Organisation strategy should determine what information is relevant. Information strategy should determine what information systems are important. Information systems strategy should determine which information technology is relevant.
Describe the process of eBusiness management.	eBusiness management concerns both general business management and informatics management. Three levels of informatics management are important: information management, information systems management and information technology management.
Relate the key activities of eBusiness development.	The process of eBusiness development can be seen as being made up of a number of generic phases: conception, analysis, design construction, implementation and maintenance. Development is normally organised in terms of projects. To undertake any development effort the information systems developer needs a toolkit: methods, techniques and tools for supporting the activities of the development process.
Relate the forms of eBusiness evaluation.	Evaluation involves assessing the worth of something. An information system may be assessed in terms of its functionality, usability and utility. There are three main processes associated with information systems evaluation: strategic evaluation, formative evaluation and summative evaluation.

Chapter outline

Introduction

As well as the conventional competencies in areas of business activity such as finance, sales and production, the eBusiness must develop and maintain competencies in informatics if it is to survive in a marketplace dominated by technological innovation. Hence, this is a reflection of the socio-technical nature of eBusiness: eBusiness is about the convergence of activities, communication and technology. The eBusiness has to continually adapt not only to changing market demands but also to changes in technologies. Within this chapter we consider those activities which support eBusiness as infrastructure. These include competencies in eBusiness planning, management, development and evaluation.

eBusiness strategy

The term strategy has its roots in military operations. According to the Oxford English Dictionary, strategy is the art of a commander-in-chief, the art of projecting and directing the larger military movements and operations in a campaign. Strategy is seen to differ materially from tactics. Tactics belongs only to the mechanical movement of bodies set in motion by strategy. The term strategy is now very much used in the same sense in which it is used in the military but directed towards organisational and particularly business activities.

Igor Ansoff (1965) defines strategic decisions as being primarily concerned with external rather than internal problems of the firm and specifically with selection of the product mix which the firm will produce and the market to which it will sell. In such terms, strategic decisions are concerned with establishing an 'impedance match' between the firm and its environment, or, in more usual terms, it is the problem of deciding what business the firm is in and what kinds of business it will seek to enter. In systems terms strategy concerns issues surrounding the viability and sustainability of organisations: how organisations can maintain their existence and seek to continuously adapt to changes in the environment.

According to Johnson et al (2007) the formulation of business strategy involves three inter-dependent activities. Figure 10.1 represents these activities in a linear sequence. First, *strategic analysis* involves analysis of the environment, expectations, objectives, power and culture in the organisation and organisational resources. Strategic analysis involves determining the organisation's mission and goals and involves answering the questions 'what should we be doing and where are we going?' Second, *strategic choice* involves generating strategic options, evaluation of such options and the selection of a suitable strategy to achieve the selected option. Strategic choice involves answering the question 'what routes have we selected?' Finally, *strategic implementation* involves organising resources, re-structuring elements of the organisation, and providing suitable people and systems. Strategic implementation comprises determining policies, making decisions and taking action as well as answering the questions of 'how do we guide our collective decisions to get there', 'what choices do we have and how shall we do it?'

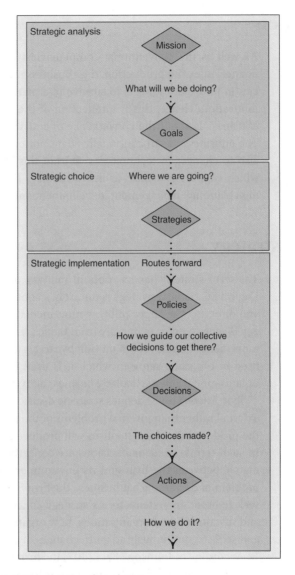

Figure 10.1 The activities of strategy formulation

Strategic thinking as exemplified in the activities described above is normally documented in terms of an organisation's mission statement, which typically consists of a limited number of statements of future intention. In terms of each statement of intention a number of goals may be formulated. For each such goal a number of strategies or routes forward may be planned. Each strategy has to be made operational in a series of policies or plans. Plans, in turn are collection of decisions that involve a series of actions. Hence strategic planning involves constructing a hierarchy of goals, strategies, policies, decisions and actions.

An organisation's mission statement at various levels of the hierarchy consists of a limited number of objectives stipulated as a guide to future intention. Such objectives should be SMART objectives: Specific, Measurable, Achievable, Realistic and Timely. Specific: meaning that each objective should be clear and focused. Measurable: meaning that the objective should clearly include means by which achievement will be measured. Achievable: meaning the objective should be achievable with organisational resources. Realistic: meaning the objective should be realistic in terms of organisational constraints. Finally, timely: meaning the objective should contain details of the duration of achievement.

Consider the case of the UK Ambulance Service, first discussed in Chapter 3. Two national targets are set for response-times to category A and B calls. Within the UK, ambulance services are required to reach 75% of category A calls within eight minutes and 95% of category B calls within 19 minutes. These objectives are effectively written into the mission statement of the Ambulance Service. They are specific objectives, can be measured, are deemed to be achievable and realistic within resource constraints and are timely in the sense that data on performance to target are collected on an annual basis.

Over the past 20 to 30 years managers within organisations have become very much concerned with developing explicit organisation strategy and with initiating effective ways of planning and implementing such strategy. The eBusiness literature has followed this trend and concerns itself with how strategies for information, information systems and ICT can be developed which aligns itself with organisation strategy in the sense of supporting planned changes to activity systems.

Forms of eBusiness strategy

There is no one correct view of what eBusiness strategy represents. Indeed, we would argue that there are at least three different viewpoints as to what eBusiness strategy constitutes: the appropriate viewpoint being defined by organisational context. In other words, eBusiness strategy will depend on what business models are felt appropriate for eBusiness within a particular organisation. eBusiness strategy will particularly reflect responses to the changing value-network of the organisation.

The first viewpoint on strategy is that eBusiness strategy is *organisation/corporate strategy*. In this viewpoint there is little or no distinction between organisation strategy and eBusiness strategy. This viewpoint is appropriate if the eBusiness is effectively the entire corporation. In practice it may be applicable only if a traditional bricks-and-mortar company attempts to establish a complete re-engineering of its processes around ICT or a new green-field eBusiness is established – a clicks-only strategy. Another viewpoint is that eBusiness strategy is *business unit strategy*. In many companies the eBusiness strategy may be applicable only to a particular business unit. For example, some companies run their eBusinesses as separate but parallel operations. Finally, eBusiness strategy may be seen as a process strategy. A key organisational process or activity system, or perhaps an integrated set of such processes may be chosen for radical re-design with ICT innovation. For example, a company may decide that it wishes to concentrate on re-designing its supply chain or customer chain processes with ICT innovation. We would argue that this is the most common form of eBusiness strategy if only because eBusiness is normally an incremental and continuous strategy for most organisations.

Take University Short Courses, which we considered in Chapter 1. This company is in the business of providing short technology courses to industry. Being a traditional company that has grown into eBusiness, USC is best described as a clicks-and-mortar company. As a result its strategies, as we have already seen, have tended to be process strategies. ICT has been particularly used to improve aspects of its B2C, B2B and C2C operations, as well as of course its internal operations. Hence, a major strategy of the company has to improve its customer chain activities through the provision of a B2C website. This website has enabled the company to improve customer acquisition and customer retention.

Competitive position

In commercial environments an organisation takes up a particular position in relation to its competitors. This we might define as the *competitive position* of the organisation. The development of organisational strategy in terms of the business has normally its prime objective as being the improvement of this competitive position and probably the sustainability of the business long-term. This is normally expressed as the attempt to gain competitive advantage.

According to Michael Porter competitive advantage can be gained by engaging in one or more of three generic organisational strategies. First, there is *cost advantage*. This essentially aims to establish the organisation as a low-cost leader in the market. The organisation aims to sell its products or services cheaper than its competitors. This may be achieved in a number of ways such as concentrating on areas involved in improving overall efficiency via better planning. Second, there is *differentiation*. The organisation undertaking this strategy aims to differentiate its product or service from its competitors. The aim is probably to establish amongst customers in the marketplace the perception that the organisation's product or service is better in some way than its competitors. This may be through improving quality and reliability relative to price, better market understanding, image promotion etc. Finally, there is *location*. A location strategy involves the organisation attempting to find a niche market to service. A niche market is one where no other organisation currently has an established presence. This may be achieved in a number of ways: by producing innovations in products or services or by placing distribution, marketing and information outlets in areas not utilised currently.

These three generic strategies have to be implemented in terms of organisational changes, normally supported nowadays through some form of ICT innovation. Hence, lower-level organisational strategies have to be put in place to achieve cost advantage, differentiation and/or location improvements. Modern organisations may be subject to a number of such lower-level organisational strategies. For instance, low-cost production is an efficiency strategy generally directed at cost advantage. Alternatively, there is a focus on quality and service, which is an effectiveness strategy directed at differentiation.

Dell (see case) has implemented many elements of a cost advantage strategy. It utilises B2C eCommerce to deliver low cost computer products to customers. This it achieves particularly through effective utilisation of informatics infrastructure to manage its supply chain and inventory management. In contrast, many aspects of the business of Apple (see case) rely upon a differentiation strategy. Through design Apple has continuously attempted to innovate and establish a reputation for distinctiveness and quality amongst its product offering. Amazon (see case) achieved its dominance as the largest internet bookstore initially through a location strategy. It was the first dot com company to offer customers significant access to published material on the web.

Informatics strategy

It should be apparent from this discussion that eBusiness strategy is subtly different from but inter-dependent upon informatics strategy. An *informatics strategy* defines the structure within which information, information systems and information technology is to be applied within an organisation over some future timeframe. Such an informatics strategy can be divided into three major layers and supports organisational or activity strategy. The *information strategy* details the information needs of the organisation. The *information systems strategy* consists of a specification of the information systems needed to support organisational activity. Finally, the *ICT strategy* consists of a specification of the hardware, software, data, communication facilities and ICT knowledge and skills needed by the organisation to support its information systems.

In classic models of informatics strategy formulation the ideal of alignment between organisation strategy and informatics strategy is attempted. Ideally, the four layers of strategy mutually support the other. A strategy for activity systems in the organisation (organisation strategy) will be supported by the three layers of informatics strategy. The information needed by the organisation will determine the information systems it requires. In turn, the information systems needed determine the ICT infrastructure required.

The notion of alignment suggests that business strategy formulation should come ideally before informatics strategy formulation, as is illustrated in Figure 10.2. Organisation planning is the process of formulating organisation strategy, while informatics planning is the process of formulating an informatics strategy. An organisation strategy will critically affect the direction of an informatics strategy. However, in the modern business world organisational and informatics strategy are typically in a mutual cycle of reinforcement. The formulation of an informatics strategy is likely to critically affect the formulation of future business strategy.

Organisations may also choose to develop a global focus for its products and/or services. In different ways organisations may utilise globalisation strategies for cost advantage in terms of their supply chains and for differentiation or location advantage in terms of their customer chains. As we have seen previously B2C and B2B eCommerce are particularly important to such global reach. An organisation may also choose to focus on customer intimacy – building better relationships with customers – in order to differentiate itself. It may also attempt supplier intimacy – building better relationships with suppliers, which is a possible cost advantage strategy. In terms of intimacy customer relationship management systems and supplier relationship management systems might prove critical. Finally, the manufacturing organisation may employ a strategy known as just-in-time manufacturing, which involves keeping inventory levels at a minimum through efficient supply chains.

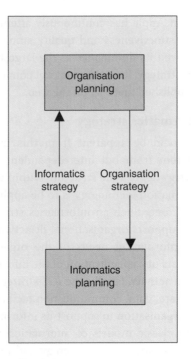

Figure 10.2 Business and informatics strategy

This is primarily a cost advantage strategy, which, as we have seen, relies on effective inventory management and logistics systems.

Many informatics projects are closely linked to organisational strategy; many are not. In ideal terms business or organisational strategy should be a key driver of informatics strategy. One of the proposed benefits of having an explicit informatics strategy is to encourage a closer fit between an organisation's activities and its information systems. The question remains: 'how do we measure this fit or alignment?' Four aspects of an organisation's informatics infrastructure that may be measured and which can be used to determine elements of fit are the levels of fragmentation, redundancy, *inconsistency* and inter-operability in the informatics infrastructure.

Poor fit is evident in the situation in which data are fragmented across information systems usually because such information systems emulate structural divisions within the organisation and because organisational units put up barriers of ownership around data sets. Fragmentation may also be evident in processing where separate ICT systems communicate through manual interfaces. Poor fit is also evident when large amounts of data are unnecessarily replicated across information systems usually because interfaces do not exist between systems causing the same data to be entered many times. Redundancy may also be present when separate systems perform the same effective processing on data.

A lack of fit is evident when the same data is held differently in different systems or processed differently by different systems leading to inconsistencies in the ways in which information is produced, stored and disseminated. The property of inter-operability is related to the other three problems of fitness. Generally speaking those systems that are fragmented, redundant and inconsistent are likely to suffer from poor levels of inter-operability. This refers to the level to which systems communicate and cooperate within the infrastructure.

Situations subject to fragmentation, redundancy and inconsistency create a series of 'islands' of data, communication and activity within the organisation. The existence of such islands makes it difficult to model the organisation in terms of its data. Hence, operational managers find it difficult to plan effectively on a day-to-day basis and strategic managers find it difficult to plan for the medium and long-term future.

eBusiness management

Planning is the process of determining what to do over a given time-period. Managing is the process of executing, evaluating and adapting plans in the face of contingencies. In systems terms, planning provides the key parameters for control, while management constitutes the exercise of control.

Just as we have done in the previous section in terms of strategy it is possible to distinguish between eBusiness management and *informatics management*. We may distinguish between the general management of the activity systems of some organisation and the specific management of the informatics infrastructure of some organisation. eBusiness management bridges between general business management and informatics management (Figure 10.3).

Activity management

In terms of general business management the focus on organisational change through ICT is critical. A key emphasis has been on the re-design of activity systems or business processes with ICT. Such re-design is likely to involve the activities of mapping, selecting, designing, specifying and implementing business processes.

Process mapping involves constructing a high-level map of organisational processes and indicating on such a map key process boundaries. Some form of modelling notation, such as the one we have used in previous chapters, is normally used for this. From the process map particular processes or sub-processes need to be prioritised in terms of the importance of re-design to them. Three sets of criteria may be used to rank processes for re-design: the health of the process, its importance to organisational performance and the feasibility for re-design. Process design will involve the identification of problems with the existing process, challenging assumptions about ways of doing things and brainstorming new approaches to organisational activity. Design workshops will be held in which various stakeholders will participate. Process specification involves modelling both existing processes and the design of new processes using some agreed way of representing systems. Finally, process implementation is probably the most difficult phase of *process re-design* and involves introducing new work practices and associated technologies into the organisation.

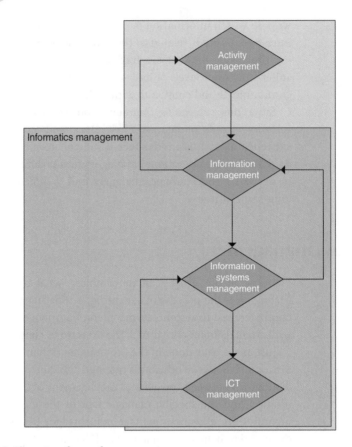

Figure 10.3 The various forms of management

The first three stages constitute *unfreezing* activities in the sense that they involve studying current inadequacies in organisation activities and generating plans for new ways of doing things. The last two stages constitute *freezing* activities in the sense that they involve specifying a new process in some detail and implementing the new process within the organisation.

Consider the case of the inbound logistics at Goronwy Galvanising. If you remember from Chapter 2, this involved a series of activities such as receiving delivery, unloading batches and checking batches. These performative activities were supported by a large amount of communicative activity such as directing operatives to unload batches and commitments to do as ordered. The precise nature of this process was therefore mapped using models such as those used in Chapters 2, 3 and 4. Key problems were then identified with this process such as the excessive amount of communication involved and the potential for errors this introduced. As a result of this it was decided, in consultation with their major customer, that they would introduce a system of tagging batches with RFID tags. This removed cumbersome processes of inspection and record-keeping, reduced the amount of manpower needed and speeded up the throughput of material through delivery, galvanisation to eventual dispatch.

Informatics management

In terms of informatics management Michael Earl (1989) distinguished some time ago between three forms of such management: *information management*, information systems management, and ICT management. *Information Management* is concerned with the overall strategic direction of the organisation and the planning, regulation and coordination of information in support of this direction. *Information Systems Management* is concerned with providing information handling to support organisational activities. *ICT Management* is concerned with providing the necessary technical infrastructure for implementing desired information handling. For many organisations information, information systems and ICT services will be organised in one function. This function, service or department will be particularly involved in setting up and managing development projects. It will also be critically involved in evaluating ICT systems for the organisation in various ways.

Rather confusingly, the term information management is used in a number of different ways and overlaps with a number of other closely related terms of concern to informatics management: data management or administration, records management, content management and knowledge management.

Data administration is that function concerned with the planning, management, documentation and operation of the data resource of some organisation (Gillenson, 1991). Data administration is concerned with the management of an organisation's meta-data, that is, data about data. It is a function which deals with the conceptual or business view of an organisation's data resource. Data administration inherently assumes an interest in both the physical and electronic records of organisations and as such subsumes records management within its domain (DAMA, 2007). *Records management* is defined by the International Standards Organisation as 'the field of management responsible for the efficient and systematic control of the creation, receipt, maintenance, use and disposition of records, including the processes for capturing and maintaining evidence of and information about business activities and transactions in the form of records'.

Let us refresh why data, particularly in the form of records, are such a critical resource for organisations. Consider the case of a university. Without data such as what students it has, what students are taking which modules and what grades students have achieved a university is unable to operate effectively. However, consider the case in which different university departments or schools maintain their own distinctive collections of data with their own distinctive definitions for data items. As a consequence, data are frequently missing or incomplete, are frequently out of date and there is incomplete knowledge amongst staff as to what data are collected, and where data are kept.

Since the turn of the millennium it has been argued that knowledge is a significant resource for organisations, because increased knowledge leads to increased capability to perform effectively (Davenport and Prusak, 2000). Knowledge is hence seen as one of the major assets of an organisation. Knowledge is also complex and usually difficult to imitate. Therefore it has the potential to generate long-term and sustainable competitive advantage for organisations. Loss of personnel with significant amounts of knowledge through retirement, downsizing etc. is a significant loss to the organisation. Hence, there has been much emphasis on capturing, storing and sharing knowledge throughout the organisation to mitigate against staff turnaround.

Knowledge is frequently defined as networked information. This implies that both data and information are necessary prerequisites to effective knowledge. In such terms, *knowledge management* can be considered as being the top-most layer of management processes in organisations reliant on effective information management.

Individuals clearly acquire knowledge that improves their performance in specific fields. The question is to what degree is it appropriate to speak of human groups and in particular organisations as having knowledge? One useful concept is that of organisational memory. This is what an organisation knows about its processes and its environment. The knowledge in an organisation's memory is a critical resource for organisations in that it enables effective action within economic markets.

Knowledge management effectively consists of three key processes. *Knowledge creation* involves acquisition of knowledge from organisational members and the creation of new organisational knowledge. *Knowledge codification* and storage consists of the representation of knowledge for ease of retrieval. *Knowledge transfer* involves the communication and sharing of knowledge amongst organisational members.

Knowledge management is frequently discussed in the context of maintaining content on corporate websites by employees and making such content available across the organisation, typically over some intranet. *Content management* is the organisational process that manages the maintenance of web-based material.

Two dimensions are critical to establishing the case for content management within some organisation: the volatility of content and the visibility of content. Consider the case of a website designed for the electronic delivery of services and products to customers. Such a website is likely to be highly volatile. In other words, the content on such sites is updated on a continuous and regular basis and is likely to include products, prices and promotions. B2C sites are also likely to be highly visible. The prime purpose of such sites is to attract and keep customers. In contrast, consider a website designed for use by sub-contractors of a company; perhaps forming part of an extranet. The information on such a website is likely to be less volatile as the content will be less subject to change. The content on such sites tends to remain constant for a reasonable period of time in the sense that the content is updated on a less regular basis and is likely to be less visible than a customer site. The more volatile and visible the website the more important it is for an organisation to establish a content management process. Such a process will ensure that updated content is accurate, relevant and timely. To ensure this a content management process needs to be put in place.

Any content management process is likely to include activities such as the following. First, the content itself as well as its proposed presentation has to be created. This will be conducted by a team of content producers including technical staff and representatives of business units. Second, the content has to be reviewed by stakeholders such as the web manager, marketing manager and legal department. Such stakeholders will ensure that the content adheres to web-based and marketing standards for the company as well as ensuring that the content does not infringe any laws. Third, the content is tested running upon a site which is not live. Ideally, content should not be released until it has been thoroughly tested. This is the reason for using some test machine. Fourth, the approved and tested content is published to a live site. The release of content should occur only after full review and testing. The organisation may also wish to ensure that the release is planned to coincide with other organisational activities and that time-scales are established for the content management process. The time-scales may vary depending on the type of content to be released.

eBusiness development

eBusiness development is that activity concerned with the design, construction and implementation of key aspects of the e-Business infrastructure of some organisation. The key inputs into the system are ICT resources and developer resources. The key output is some information system. A number of key activities are involved in the *development process* including conception, analysis, design, construction, implementation and maintenance. A specialist organisation is normally required to undertake development and a toolkit of methods, techniques and tools is required by the developer to engage in these activities.

Development process

Development is that socio-technical system concerned with the design, construction and implementation of key aspects of eBusiness infrastructure for some organisation. This critical activity system for modern business is represented in Figure 10.4. The key inputs into the system are ICT resources and developer resources. ICT resources may comprise systems construction tools or software packages. Developer resources include not only people but also a toolkit that includes methods, techniques and tools available to the developer.

The key outputs are an ICT system and its associated activity system. We use the term information system to incorporate both these constructs. Information systems in themselves are socio-technical systems since they include both an ICT system and a system of use. Ideally the activity system and the ICT system should be designed in parallel. The ICT system produced may be a bespoke system or a configured/tailored software package.

Three key types of organisational stakeholder are critical to the development process: clients, users and developers. Clients are frequently managerial groups involved in setting the major parameters for a development project – costs, benefits and constraints. They are critical in providing budgets for projects, used for funding ICT and developer resources. The eventual users of an information system are likely to be involved in the development process. They will provide important detailed requirements for the functionality and usability of the system. Developers are the persons tasked with analysing, designing, constructing and implementing the information system. They may also have a key part to play in delivering the information system into its context of use.

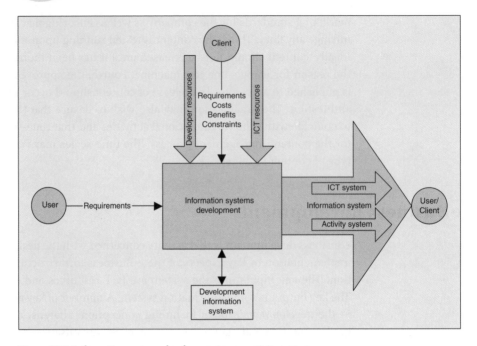

Figure 10.4 Information systems development as an activity system

Development activities

The process of development involves the following activities (Figure 10.5): conception, analysis, design, construction, implementation, and maintenance.

Conception is the first phase in the development process and will follow on from eBusiness planning. Conception is the phase in which the development team produce the key business case for an information system. This is a form of evaluation of the system in strategic terms. The team also attempt to estimate the degree of risk associated with a project to construct the proposed system. Finally, they consider the feasibility of the IS project in terms of organisational resources. A project that succeeds the strategic evaluation, risk analysis and feasibility exercise will pass on to a process of systems analysis.

Information systems *analysis* involves two primary and inter-related activities – *requirements elicitation* and *requirements specification*. Both sets of activities demand different techniques. Requirements elicitation demands approaches for identifying requirements. Requirements specification demands techniques for representing requirements. Systems analysis benefits from forms of stakeholder participation, especially in the elicitation phase.

Systems analysis provides the major input into systems design. *Design* is the process of planning a technical artefact to meet requirements established by analysis. Design involves the consideration of requirements and constraints and the selection amongst design alternatives. Design also benefits from the participation of system stakeholders. Such a design or system specification acts as a blueprint for systems construction.

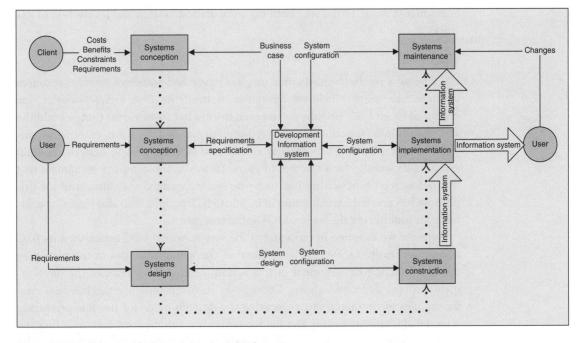

Figure 10.5 The activities of information systems development

Construction involves building the information system to its specification. Traditionally ICT system construction involves the three related processes of programming, testing and documentation. This may either be conducted by a team internal to the organisation or undertaken by an outside contractor (a form of construction known as outsourcing). Many information systems are now also bought in as a package and tailored to organisational requirements.

The process of systems *implementation* (sometimes called systems delivery) follows on from systems construction. Systems implementation involves delivering an information system into its context of use. Since an information system is a socio-technical system, implementation of such systems involves the parallel implementation of both an information system and some form of activity system. Once a system is delivered into its context of use it will be subject to the process of operation and the process of systems maintenance.

Systems *maintenance* follows on from systems implementation. Maintenance is the process of making needed changes to the structure of some information system. Maintenance activity may stimulate suggestions for new systems. Hence, it may act as a key input into the process of systems conception and thus provides a form of feedback to the process of information systems development.

It must be acknowledged that information systems rarely stand still. They may change for a number of reasons. For instance, in the process of using information systems errors may be found in such systems or changes may be proposed. Fixing errors (bugs) and changing systems is normally classed as maintenance. At some point in time a system may be abandoned or need to be re-engineered to fit new organisational circumstances. Changes also occur over time in terms of adjustments made to the way both the information system and its context of use works.

USC

USC, being a medium-sized company, has never had sufficient internal resource to undertake much eBusiness development itself. Its first, simple website was produced by an USC employee. However, it soon became evident that to build the sort of additional functionality they required demanded the use of external suppliers. Therefore, USC has contracted a dedicated ICT supplier to design, maintain and host its website for a number of years. However, the company recognises that this outsourced relationship has to be carefully managed over time and for this purpose has created a small group of in-house ICT people, who also have responsibility for monitoring the internal ICT infrastructure.

Suppose we examine in more detail the way in which USC established its B2C eCommerce website. We can map some of the actual activities in the plan they produced for the development of this system against the phases of the development process described above. Conception involved building the business case for the new eCommerce site, registering the domain name for the site, producing a tender document, issuing the tender, reviewing submissions and awarding the contract. Analysis involved the web developers in eliciting key requirements for the site from clients (USC managers) and users (USC administrators and customers). It also involved producing key content and presentational requirements for the website. Design involved producing key prototypes of content and presentation. It also involved considering changes to work practices and reviewing this with users. Construction consisted of producing the final HTML pages and graphics, implementing any integration with back-end systems, testing the pages individually and as an integrated set and setting up new organisational structures and processes. Implementation consisted of producing a marketing campaign to accompany release of the website, updating stationery and registering the site. It also consisted of publishing the site on its appropriate server and putting new organisational processes into action. Finally, maintenance involved measuring the performance of the site, managing the content over time and reviewing organisational structures and processes.

Approaches to information systems development

There are a number of distinct approaches to information systems development. Here we consider alternatives in terms of two major dimensions: type of information systems product and form of sequencing of activities.

In terms of information systems product we may distinguish two main types of development activity: bespoke development and package development. In *bespoke development* an organisation builds an information system to directly match with the requirements of the organisation. This may involve programming the entire system or the organisation may build a system out of pre-established components. Bespoke development normally offers the organisation the opportunity to closely match some information system to organisational processes. The main disadvantage is that the organisation must make a considerable investment in developing the information system in terms of particularly maintaining a suitably skilled internal informatics service. In *package development* an organisation purchases a piece of software from a vendor organisation and tailors the package to a greater or lesser extent to the demands of a particular organisation. A software package is a software application designed to encapsulate the functionality necessary to support activity in some generic business area and may be customisable to a specific organisation's needs. Hence, package development introduces a reversal of the place of organisational process. Generally speaking organisational processes have to be adapted to the requirements of some package.

As we have seen in the case of USC, for small companies development of systems from scratch is not normally a feasible option because of lack of sufficient resources. Hence, such companies will either buy in some package or will employ the services of an external contractor to produce a system. However, even for these alternative approaches to development, the key phases above have to be followed. For instance, it is critical that companies make a business case for the purchase of a package just as they would if they were proposing to construct the system themselves.

By sequencing we mean the way in which the various phases of the development process are organised. We may distinguish between two broad forms of sequencing: linear and iterative. The linear model of the development process is indicated in Figure 10.6. Here the phases discussed above are strung out in a linear sequence

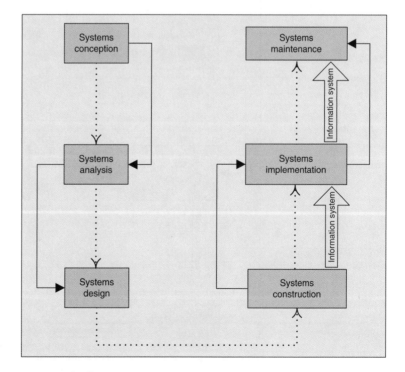

Figure 10.6 Linear development

with outputs from each phase triggering the start of the next phase. In the first three phases the key outputs are forms of system documentation. In the last three phases the outputs are elements of some information system.

The linear model has been particularly popular as a framework for large-scale development projects. This is mainly because a clear linear sequence makes for easier project planning and control (see below). The major disadvantages of the approach lie in the difficulties associated with changing early analysis and design decisions late into a project.

The iterative model of the development process is illustrated in Figure 10.7. In this model systems conception triggers an iterative cycle in which various versions of a system (prototypes) are analysed, designed, constructed and possibly implemented.

The iterative approach to development is popular amongst agile computing approaches. Agile computing refers to development approaches which emphasise, amongst other things, iteration, the construction of prototypes (*prototyping*) and significant amounts of user involvement. Such approaches are frequently referred to as 'lightweight' in contrast to the 'heavyweight' approaches which generally adopt a linear model of development. Agility in development is seen to reduce the risk associated with ICT innovations and generate stronger commitment from system stakeholders. Agile approaches are also seen to be particularly suitable for

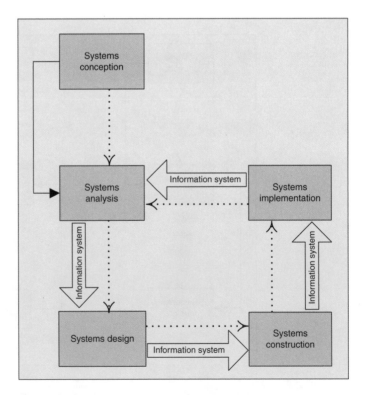

Figure 10.7 Iterative development

development work in small- to medium-scale projects, such as the development of a B2C eCommerce website. However, because it is frequently uncertain in an iterative approach how much resource will needed to be devoted to the project at the start, iterative approaches generally appear to suffer from more difficult project planning and management. This is particularly true for medium to large-scale ICT development projects are concerned.

The distinction made above between the forms of development make clear that no one approach to development is applicable to all types of circumstance. Hence, eBusiness projects are likely to use a range of approaches depending upon development resources, the scale of the project and whether the systems work impinges on the front-end or back-end ICT infrastructure.

Generally speaking large-scale back-end projects perhaps implementing a large corporate database system are likely to use a linear, bespoke model of development. In contrast, major modules within an ERP system are likely to be developed using a linear, package approach. Front-end ICT systems, particularly those that are web-based are likely to adopt iterative approaches because of the time-pressures associated with such projects as well as the high-levels of interactivity required from such systems.

Development organisation

As discussed in previous sections, development is normally organised in terms of projects. A project is any concerted effort to achieve a set of objectives. All projects comprise teams of people engaging in the achievement of explicit objectives usually within some set duration. Most informatics work in organisations is structured in terms of projects and thus planning, management and development will normally be conducted as projects. In this chapter we focus on development projects. A development project is any concerted effort to develop an information system.

The initiation of development projects will be done as part of an organisation's e-Business planning and management processes. Project management will interact with the development process in the sense that it acts as the major control process for development (see Figure 10.8).

Project control is a type of formative evaluation. The aim of project control is to ensure that schedules are being met, that the project is staying within budget and that appropriate standards are being maintained. The most important objective of project control is to focus attention on problems in sufficient time for something to be done about them. This means that continual monitoring of progress must take place. This is normally achieved through the provision of regular progress reports from the development process.

Figure 10.8 illustrates the need for two major forms of information in support of development. The actual process of development itself needs documentary support to enable collaboration between the development team. The process of managing a project also needs its associated information system. This will store not only project plans but also data concerning progress against plans.

Prior to the initiation of the development process a development team is assembled. A number of development roles will be critical to particular phases of the development process. The business analyst undertakes organisational analysis and

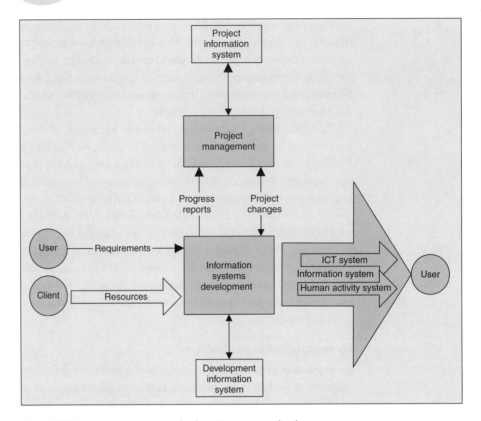

Figure 10.8 Project management and information systems development

systems conception activities such as cost/benefit analyses and risk analysis. The systems analyst role undertakes feasibility study, analysis and design activities. The project manager is concerned with managing the development process as a unit. Programmers undertake construction and maintenance activities. Finally, the change manager undertakes implementation activities. Various representatives of other stakeholder groups, particularly clients and end-users, are also likely to form part of the development team, either throughout the development process or at key points in the life of the information system.

The development or project organisation may utilise native employees of the organisation or outsource the development to an external organisation in various ways. In general terms we may distinguish between a number of distinct types of informatics outsourcing. *Body shop outsourcing* is a type of outsourcing in which contract programmers are brought in to supplement informatics personnel in the organisation. *Project outsourcing* involves outside vendors developing a new system for some organisation. *Support outsourcing* is the type of outsourcing in which vendors are contracted to maintain and support a particular application system. Organisations may also choose to outsource hardware operations, disaster recovery and network management. Finally, *total outsourcing* is 'keys to the kingdom' outsourcing implying outsourcing of the entire informatics service – the development, operation, management and control of informatics processes for a company.

A *development information system* is essential to ensure the effective operation of the activity system that is the development process. Any reasonable-sized development project will need a consequent information system to support communication between teams of developers, to feed up into a project management and an eBusiness management process and to communicate with other stakeholder groups such as users and business managers. Such an information system consists of both system documentation and project documentation. System documentation acts as a model of the developing system; project documentation acts as a model of the development process. The key point here is that all information systems in a sense model elements of other systems. Such elements may be artefacts or organisational activities.

Development toolkit

Humans are Homo Habilis – man the toolmaker. We make tools in order to aid in the construction of artefacts and to extend our physical and mental grasp. Therefore, to undertake any development effort the information systems developer needs a toolkit. Such a toolkit will consist of methods, techniques and tools for supporting the activities of the development process – conception, analysis, design, implementation and maintenance. Methods, techniques and tools are what we might call supporting 'technology' for information systems development. The term technology is used here in its broadest sense to refer to any form of device that aids the work of some person or group of persons.

Methods constitute frameworks which prescribe, sometimes in great detail, the tasks to be undertaken in a given development process. Methods are used to guide the whole or a major part of the development process. Techniques form the component parts of methods in that they constitute particular ways of undertaking given parts of the development process. By tools we primarily mean here available hardware, software, data and communication technology for engaging in some part of the information systems development process or its set of associated external activities. Tools are also frequently used to support the application of particular techniques.

As a key example, a variety of tools are available to support the work of web-based systems development. Generally speaking such tools support the phases of construction, implementation and maintenance of websites. For instance, text and graphic editors are general-purpose packages for the editing of text and graphics files, such as Microsoft Notepad and Microsoft PhotoDraw. They may be used to edit HTML documents and associated graphics files in various formats. Modern word processing packages generally have ways of producing HTML tags from document formatting. Usually however such facilities are not as flexible as those found in specialised tools for the production and maintenance of HTML documents. Hence, specialised HTML editors are frequently used (such as Microsoft FrontPage Express), accompanied by graphic tools used to produce high-quality graphics and animations (such as Adobe Photoshop, Macromedia Flash and Director-Shockwave). Site maintenance tools provide advanced HTML editing facilities such as style templates combined with functionality that makes for easier tracking of changes and testing, such as ColdFusion and DreamWeaver. Front-end/

Back-end Integration Tools provide means of connecting web pages to back-end systems, particularly DBMS. Finally, eCommerce site tools constitute packages for the development of site functionality such as electronic shopping baskets, such as Lotus Domino Merchant Server and Microsoft Site Server Commerce.

The complexity of web-based development

The development of websites for B2C, B2B, C2C or intra-business purposes is one of the major forms of eBusiness development undertaken by contemporary organisations. Therefore, it maps onto the model of the development process described above, must be conducted by some form of development organisation, must be project-managed suitably and produces both an information system and an associated activity system as its output.

A website is fundamentally a front-end ICT system for some organisation. It is also likely that there will be significant degrees of integration between this front-end ICT system and the back-end ICT infrastructure. Hence, much *web-based development* presupposes the existence of an efficient and effective back-end ICT infrastructure.

The development of ICT systems is an innovation process based on three sets of actor or agent: producers, the ICT system itself and its consumers. Each of these actors is arranged in a triangle of dependencies. The ICT system depends on the producers, the producers depend on consumers and the consumers depend on the ICT system. The ICT system requires the efforts and expertise of the producers to sustain it; the producers are heavily dependent on the provision of support in the form of material resources and help in coping with contingencies from agencies of consumption; consumers require benefits from the ICT system (Figure 10.9).

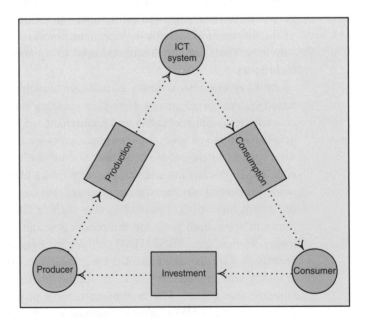

Figure 10.9 Development as an innovation process

The three exchange relations between these agents are fundamentally processes of production, consumption and investment. Organisations usually cycle around these relations in various degrees of rapidity depending on the scale of the system being developed. Sauer (1993) uses this model to understand and explain the ways in which development projects frequently terminate or fail. This occurs when the level of perceived flaws in some developing ICT system triggers a decision to remove levels of investment in a development project.

However, the development of web-based systems is far from straightforward because the network of actors and relations is more complex and uncertain than for 'conventional' ICT systems.

Firstly, the actors in web-based development are less easy to define. Producers of web-based ICT systems are frequently teams of people with an array of different skills. Such skills may range from film production and graphic design through to programming and database design. Consumers of such technology are much less easily 'configured'. In other words, it is much more difficult to decide as to how to design websites that meet the needs of a range of possible user groups including suppliers, customers, employees, partners and regulators. Web-based ICT systems consist of integration of complex content and structure. Many organisational websites act as effectively front doors to the organisation. As such the system becomes the visible representation of the organisation and must continually reflect changes in organisational structure and practice.

Secondly, the relations in the network also are more complex. The process of producing web-Based IT systems is subject to rapidity and increasing levels of uncertainty. The typical life cycle for an eCommerce site is of the order of a few months. The requirements of such systems are also likely to change rapidly as organisations attempt to adapt to the rapid changes in the eBusiness environment. The process of consumption is much more diverse. Consumers of web-based ICT systems may not only be internal stakeholders such as employees. They may include partner organisations such as suppliers. The processes by which systems are planned for, financed and managed is much more fluid. Since much web-based development is outsourced, management processes have to be established with external suppliers and service agreements negotiated for the maintenance of such systems.

Development at USC

Let us consider the process by which USC established a B2C eCommerce website for itself in more detail. Conception involved the company in building the business case for the new eCommerce site. In particular, the costs of establishing the new website were balanced against the expected benefits the website would provide for the company. Convinced it should go ahead it first needed to register a domain name for the site and first suggested www.usc.co.uk for this purpose. Unfortunately, this domain name was already registered and so a compromise – www.trainict.co.uk – was chosen. A tender document was then drawn up and issued to an agreed list of web development companies. Submissions from these companies were reviewed and one particular supplier was awarded the contract to produce the website.

A period of analysis then occurred between the contracting company and both managers and potential users within USC. As we have seen in previous chapters, web pages can be used both to display data and as sophisticated data entry and query interfaces to ICT systems. Therefore, in many ways web page design is a hybrid activity. On the one hand the design of web pages can be considered to be in many ways similar to the design of physical media such as newspaper pages or magazine pages. Hence web page design demands an appreciation of the principles of good graphic design. On the other hand web pages are now used as interfaces to both the front-end and back-end ICT systems of the organisation. As such, an understanding of good user interface design is required.

The analysis conducted by contractors therefore involved determining not only the key content that should appear on the website but how this should be structured and presented. Figure 10.10 illustrates a high-level map of the key requirements for this website.

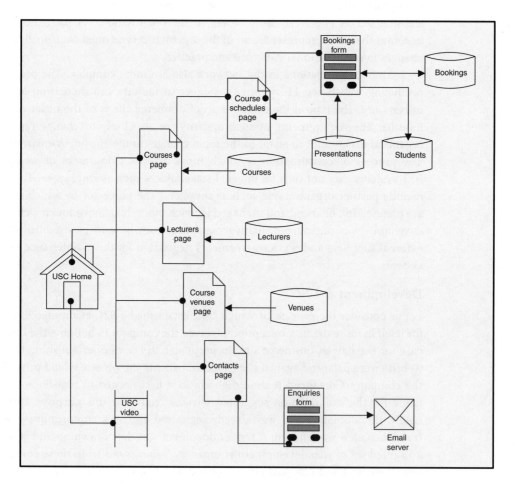

Figure 10.10 Conceptual map of the USC website

From the home page four key web pages were planned: a page detailing the courses provided by the company, a page listing the qualifications of its teaching staff, a page describing the major course venues used by the company and a page providing key contact details for customers. The Courses, Lecturers and Course Venues page were all envisaged as dynamic pages, in the sense that content on the particular page would be updated from the appropriate back-end table in the company's database. The courses page was to contain a set of links allowing the user to access details of the appropriate course schedule and also to book onto a particular course via a bookings form. The contacts page was to allow enquiries via an enquiries form, which would fire off an email message to the email server of the company.

Once the overall structure of the website had been agreed a number of prototype web pages were produced to confirm more detailed functionality for the system. For instance, Figure 10.11 illustrates a mock-up of the home page of the website, produced in this manner. Under a prominent banner heading a collage of appropriate images would be displayed. Underneath these images a short piece of text would describe USC and what it provides. Down the right-hand side of the page a series of hot-spots would allow navigation to other parts of the website. Finally in the lower right-hand corner of the scheme the user could access a short piece of video which described the company in audio-visual terms.

The design stage also involved considering changes to work practices within USC and reviewing this with users. Hence, for instance, key responsibilities had to be assigned for maintaining accurate data in course schedule files. Also, appropriate persons had to be nominated for handling both bookings and enquiries received from customers.

Construction consisted of producing the final HTML pages, including any graphics and video. It also involved implementing the integration of pages with

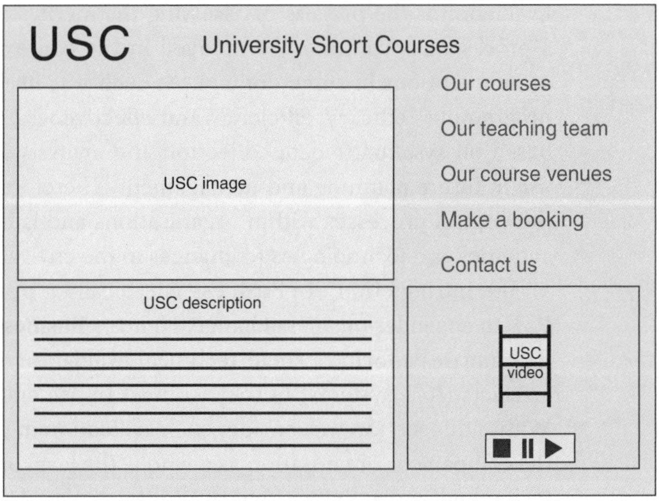

Figure 10.11 USC Home page

back-end database tables. Each page within the website was tested both individually and as an integrated set. Finally, any new organisational structures and processes were established within USC.

Implementation involved not just releasing the website on an appropriate server. It also involved production of both a tradition and an electronic marketing campaign to accompany release of the website. All stationery and public relations material had to be updated with the new URL for the company. Once all this was ready the website was published on its appropriate server and new organisational processes were put into action.

But a website, just like any ICT never stands still. The performance of the website was monitored on a continuous basis and this data was used in decisions for refreshing both the content and presentation of the website. Over time, additional functionality was also added to the website to accommodate changes to the work of USC. For instance, a link was eventually added to the home page of the website to the eLearning system provided by the company.

eBusiness evaluation

This section considers the critical question of how we determine that our infrastructure for eBusiness is successful. To answer this question we must evaluate our systems at various levels. In this chapter we distinguish between a number of distinct forms of eBusiness evaluation. First, we consider evaluating some of the distinct features of an information system. Then we consider three processes of evaluation closely aligned with the model of the development process discussed in a previous section. At the end of the section we focus on the critical problem of evaluating the worth of websites and consider the relevance of some of the approaches discussed.

Evaluation

Evaluation is the process of assessing the merit, value or worth of something. As a process it is commonly employed in the context of a coordinated programme of interventions in some domain. As such it is likely to make judgements about a programme's efficacy, efficiency and effectiveness. Evaluation should normally be based on systematic data collection and analysis and is likely to be designed for use in future planning and management. Therefore, evaluation is critically part of the control processes within organisations and is important for adjusting internal activities and technologies to changes in the environment.

The introduction of eBusiness is typically a programme of intervention using ICT to engender business change. Hence, eBusiness evaluation is difficult because it comprises a form of socio-technical evaluation. It involves evaluating technical artefacts (ICT systems) in their context of use and application (activity systems). Within this section we consider such evaluation in terms of three levels: the level of the company or organisation as a whole, the level of the mediating system between technology and activity – that of an information system –and the level of a specific website.

eBusiness maturity

One way of evaluating eBusiness is in terms of the idea of the growth of technological adoption in an organisation. This is frequently known as maturity assessment and is a well-used idea in other areas such as software process improvement and ICT governance. Ideas of plotting stages of growth in relation to ICT adoption date back to at least the early paper of Nolan (1979). Much work has also been done in building models which attempt to encapsulate eCommerce and eBusiness growth (Jones *et al.*, 2006). However, a number of limitations are evident in such stages of growth models. First, they assume that companies adopt ICT and progress such adoption in a linear manner. Second, the assumption is that adoption is a uniform phenomenon that one size of adoption fits all. In our experience both these assumptions are suspect in that they cannot deal with the complexity of the modern eBusiness. We see eBusiness maturity assessment as being better formulated upon the platform of an eBusiness framework. Since eBusiness is a socio-technical phenomenon any framework must cover both the social and technical aspects. Within knowledge transfer work we have therefore used a value-chain and value-network approach for key processes and technologies (the technical). However, we have also included aspects of social infrastructure (capability/the social). We are particularly interested in the capacity of a company to engage in strategic eBusiness thinking and process innovation.

Clearly any effective maturity framework needs to provide answers to questions such as 'what is eBusiness?' 'what is it composed of?' 'what elements of eBusiness relate to what other elements?' We have represented such knowledge packages and their relationships as a hierarchical set of kiviat diagrams. Figure 10.12 represents a top-level view of elements from this eBusiness framework. To turn the eBusiness framework into a maturity assessment tool we need some way of scoring a company's experience against a particular knowledge package. In other words, for each dimension on any particular kiviat diagram we need some way of translating a company's experience of a technology/process mix into a score between 0 and 9. We may then aggregate 'scores' against topic areas. This allows us to plot a profile for a particular company against the hierarchical set of kiviat diagrams; the profile being represented by the area under each polygon formed on a kiviat diagram. This can then be used to benchmark the eBusiness profile of a particular organisation against that of others in a particular organisational sector. In turn, this can be used as a tool to guide the formulation of eBusiness strategy.

Functionality, usability and utility

Any given package of socio-technical innovation, driven perhaps by an assessment of maturity, can be considered an information system. An information system may be evaluated in three ways: in terms of its functionality, usability and utility. We may also consider three evaluation processes that lie at different points in the development life-cycle: strategic, formative and summative evaluation.

Conventional approaches to evaluation focus on the evaluation of information systems or components. We can distinguish between three dimensions on which an information system should ideally be assessed. *Functionality* involves asking the

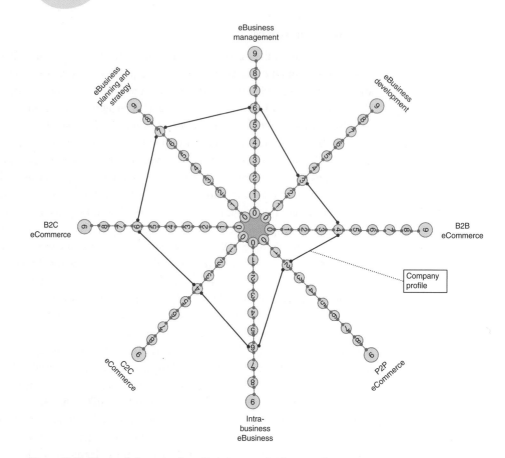

Figure 10.12 Top-level elements of an eBusiness maturity framework

question: 'does the information system do what is required?' Assessing the degree to which a system is functionally complete and consistent is a classic concern of systems development. In general system terms functionality is normally an efficiency concern. *Usability* involves asking 'is the information system useable by its intended population?' Assessing the usability of systems has become important with the continuing progress and use of graphical user interfaces and multi-media interfaces popular within web-based systems. In general system terms usability is normally an efficacy concern. *Utility* consists of asking: 'does the information system deliver business benefit for the organisation?' Assessing the utility of an information system is something which most organisations conduct at the pre-implementation stage of a project but seldom thereafter. However, this form of evaluation is becoming increasingly important because of the greater pressure being placed on the management of eBusiness to account for its activities. In general system terms utility is normally an effectiveness concern.

In terms of the development cycle discussed in previous sections, functionality, usability and utility can be seen to relate to the key processes of production, consumption and investment (Figure 10.13).

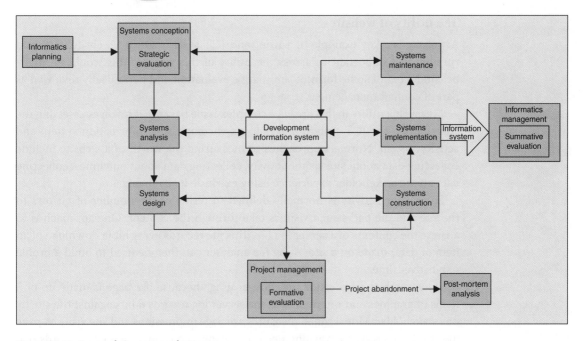

Figure 10.13 Forms of eBusiness evaluation

Functionality is a feature or guiding principle for the process of producing ICT systems. Usability is primarily an assessment made by the consumers of some ICT system. The assessment of the utility of some ICT system investment must be made both prior to construction and after delivery of some system.

Strategic, formative and summative evaluation

It is possible to distinguish critical forms of evaluation aligned with the model of the development process. Figure 10.13 makes a distinction between three types of evaluation activity in this way: strategic, formative and summative evaluation.

Strategic evaluation, sometimes referred to as pre-implementation evaluation, is that type of evaluation which involves assessing or appraising an information system investment in terms of its potential for delivering benefit against estimated costs. This is fundamentally part of the systems conception process and is primarily concerned with assessing utility.

Formative evaluation involves assessing the shape of an information system whilst in the development process itself. Traditionally, formative evaluation will be part of the project management process. Within iterative approaches to development, formative evaluation may be used to make crucial changes to the design of an information system. Formative evaluation is primarily concerned with assessing both the functionality and usability of an information system.

Summative evaluation occurs after an information system has been implemented. For this reason it is sometimes referred to as post-implementation evaluation. Ideally, summative evaluation involves returning to the costs and benefits established in strategic evaluation after a period of use of the information system. It is a critical activity within effective eBusiness management.

The utility of websites

A website is a key example of a front-end ICT system. Once a website is up and running it is important to assess the utility of this system. This would normally be conducted in some form of summative evaluation and periodically reviewed as part of content management strategy.

Measuring utility in this area is a complex issue because it involves assessing the contribution the ICT system makes to its encompassing information system and activity system. Normal approaches to measuring the worth of a website include collecting data about site visitor activity, collecting data about outcomes, collecting data on the stakeholder experience using extrinsic instruments.

Site visitor activity is normally defined in terms of the number of visitors to the site and the paths such visitors take through the content. One approach is to analyse the contents of a server log file. This file records every hit (a download of an item of data) made on a site. A log file analyser can then be used to build a profile of hits over time.

However, hits are a crude measure of usage because if a page is made up of 5 items of graphics and 1 item of text, the server log records 6 hits against the site by one stakeholder. More refined measures are page impressions and site visits. A page impression records a hit as one person viewing one page. A site visit records one hit on one website by one person. Such statistics can be produced by log analysers. Yet another approach is to use a browser-based approach. Here a short piece of code is inserted into a web page. When accessed by a user the programme runs within the browser and records access to each web page by the user.

Outcomes are the key transactions that affect the business such as online enquiries, orders and payments. Even if a site is used merely for marketing purposes the company is likely to want to know what contribution a site is making to outcomes. Outcome measures clearly call for a close integration between front-end and back-end ICT systems. An integrated ICT infrastructure should be able to begin to provide answers to questions such as 'how many initial online enquiries turn into eventual sales?' 'what affect does the website have on online sales?' 'how many customers purchase online that also purchase within our stores?'

Extrinsic instruments are the conventional tools of marketing research and include questionnaire surveys and focus groups. The fundamental purpose of such research is to build profiles of customers and establish their attitudes to the eBusiness experience provided by a company. This might also include some attempt to measure the 'quality' of some website in terms of an established instrument. An external company specialising in 'auditing' websites may frequently conduct such an approach.

Strategic and summative evaluation of ebusiness

Assessing the utility of some website is one part of the process of evaluating the efficacy of eBusiness. Evaluation of eBusiness is normally expressed in terms of projects and is normally undertaken in terms of an analysis of costs and benefits associated with such projects. The costs of some information system concern the investment needed in the information system. The benefits of some information system concern the value that the organisation gains from having an information system. Simplistically, if benefits outweigh costs then the project and system are regarded as successes. If costs outweigh benefits then the system and project are classed as failures.

It is useful to make the distinction between two types of costs and benefits associated with information system projects: tangible or visible costs/benefits and intangible or invisible costs/benefits. Tangible costs or benefits are frequently referred to as visible costs/benefits because they are reasonably straightforward to measure. Intangible costs or benefits are frequently referred to as invisible costs/benefits because most organisations experience difficulty in assigning actual measurable quantities to such costs and benefits.

In terms of the development of some website tangible costs may be the salary costs associated with the development team. Intangible costs may be the user and management involvement in development. A tangible benefit may be increased numbers of sales for particular product lines. An intangible benefit might be an increase in customer satisfaction.

The important point to make is that the costs of an information system must be taken into account over its entire life, not solely in terms of its development cost. Frequently organisations forget that the initiation of an information system means a permanent commitment to costs in terms of continuing resources being committed to the operation and maintenance of the information system. Producing and publishing a website is not the end of the matter for some organisation. A company must make a continuous commitment to manage the content on the site and upgrade it periodically with the latest technologies.

Some form of *cost–benefit analysis* is therefore critical to assessing whether or not the process of developing an information system is a worthwhile investment. Most of the established techniques for evaluating information system investments focus on tangible costs and benefits and thus are directed primarily at assessments of efficiency gain. Two of the most popular are return on investment and payback period.

The return on investment (RoI) associated with an information system project is calculated using the following equation:

RoI = average (annual net income/annual investment amount)

Hence, to calculate a RoI one must be able to estimate the income accruing from the introduction of an IS and the cost associated with an IS for a period into the future. The average of this ratio of annual costs to benefits is then taken to indicate the value of the IS to the organisation.

Payback period still assumes that one is able to estimate the benefit of the introduction of an IS to the organisation for a number of years ahead. Benefit is measured in terms of the amount of cash inflow resulting from the IS. Payback is then calculated on the basis of:

Payback = Investment – cumulative benefit (cash inflow)

The payback period is equal to the number of months or years for this payback figure to reach zero. Clearly the assumption here is that those systems that accrue financial benefits the quickest are the most successful.

For example, typical tangible costs associated with the development of some B2C eCommerce website and that might be used in some RoI or calculation of payback period include: hardware costs, software costs, the costs of the development team, costs of project management, training costs, promotional costs and maintenance costs. Typical tangible benefits associated with the development of some B2C eCommerce website and that might be used in some RoI or calculation of payback period include: reduction in costs associated with marketing such as catalogues, reduction in costs associated with support materials such as leaflets, forms etc., lower number of inaccurate orders, staff savings and reduction in number of complaints.

Summary

Within this chapter we considered those activities which support eBusiness as infrastructure. These include competencies in eBusiness planning, management, development and evaluation.

Strategic decision-making is focused on the future and the environment of the organisation. Organisation strategy is a detailed plan for future action. Planning is the process of formulating strategy; management is the process of implementing strategy. Business strategy should drive informatics strategy: a detailed plan for future informatics activities. Organisation strategy should determine what information is relevant. Information strategy should determine what information systems are important. Information systems strategy should determine which information technology is relevant.

The management of electronic business concerns both general business management and informatics management. Three levels of informatics management are important: information management, information systems management and information technology management. Rather confusingly, the term information management is used in a number of different ways and overlaps with a number of other closely related terms of concern to informatics management: data management or administration, records management, content management and knowledge management.

The process of eBusiness development can be seen as being made up of a number of generic phases: conception, analysis, design, construction, implementation and maintenance. A development information system is essential to ensure the effective and efficient operation of the activity system that is the development process. Development is normally organised in terms of projects. A development project is any concerted effort to develop an information system. To undertake any development effort the information systems developer needs a toolkit. Such a toolkit will consist of methods, techniques and tools for supporting the activities of the development process. Sustained and invasive web-based development is likely to be more complex than conventional development because of the variety of actors and the diversity and rapidity of relations between actors.

Evaluation involves assessing the worth of something. An information system may be assessed in terms of its functionality, usability and utility. There are also three main processes associated with information systems evaluation: strategic evaluation, formative evaluation and summative evaluation. Strategic evaluation involves assessing or appraising an information systems investment in terms of its potential for delivering benefit against estimated costs. Formative evaluation involves assessing the shape of an information system whilst in the development process itself. Summative evaluation involves returning to the costs and benefits established in strategic evaluation after a period of use of the information system.

Review test

Distinguish strategy from tactics.	Write two sentences

An informatics _____ is the major output of informatics planning	Fill in the blank

An informatics strategy comprises three levels – what are they?	Select all that apply
ICT Strategy	
Information Strategy	
Computing Strategy	
Information Systems Strategy	

What is meant by alignment in terms of information systems?	Write two sentences

_____ mapping involves constructing a high-level map of organisational processes and indicating on such a map key process boundaries.	Fill in the blank

Informatics management can be broken down into three related forms of management.	Mark the three most relevant.
Information systems management	
ICT management	
Content management	
Information management	

Distinguish between the linear and iterative models of the development life-cycle.	Write two sentences

Place the phases of the information systems development life-cycle in the correct sequence	Mark the 1st phase with a 1 and so on
Maintenance	
Design	
Analysis	
Construction	
Conception	
Implementation	

A developer's toolkit consists of methods, techniques and tools.	True or false?
True	
False	

Conception is the phase in which we develop the key business case, analyse risk and assess the feasibility of an information system.	True or false?
True	
False	

Evaluation involves assessing the _____ of something	Fill in the blank

There are three types of information systems evaluation - what are they?	Select all that apply
Strategic Evaluation	
Technical Evaluation	
Formative Evaluation	
Summative Evaluation	

_____ analysis involves the summative evaluation of some failed IS project	Fill in the blank

Exercises

- Find two examples of a strategic decision made by some organisation. Find two examples of a tactical decision made by some organisation.
- In terms of some expressed goal, determine some other strategies, policies, decisions and actions that might be formulated in terms of this goal. Determine whether there may be any information strategies that might contribute to this goal.
- In terms of an organisational goal such as improving worker productivity, determine what other strategies, policies, decisions and actions that we might have in terms of this goal.

- List two SMART informatics objectives.
- In terms of some organisation known to you, attempt to delineate some of the differences between activity systems management, information management, information systems management and ICT management.
- Try to identify some piece of development work and identify the key inputs and outputs for this process.
- Find some past information systems development project. Determine how closely the project undertook activities similar to the phases described in the life cycle.
- In terms of some development project known to you determine whether it used a linear or an iterative approach.
- In terms of some development project known to you determine whether it used a bespoke or a packaged approach.
- Determine whether there are any specific methods for web-based development. Determine the range of web development tools available.
- Choose an information system known to you. Attempt to estimate the benefits associated with the system and the costs associated with its development.
- Attempt to calculate RoI and Payback Period for some web development project known to you.
- Find and describe one example of strategic evaluation. Find and describe one example of formative evaluation. Find and describe one example of summative evaluation.

Projects

- Informatics planning is important but do organisations engage in such planning? Investigate the degree to which a small sample of organisations conducts systematic informatics planning. Determine the forms of informatics planning undertaken.
- Consider outsourcing as part of an informatics strategy. In terms of an examination of some of the literature on this topic, determine the critical success factors for successful outsourcing of informatics?
- The management of informatics is likely to be organised differently in different organisations. Try to investigate such differences amongst a small range of organisations. For instance, how closely do organisations distinguish between information, information systems and ICT management?
- Earl argues that informatics management demands different competencies. In terms of some organisation try to examine the extent to which the management of informatics is distributed through the technical and business sides of the organisation.
- Agile development is seen by many as a solution to development problems. Investigate the degree to which organisations utilise a linear or *iterative development* process. For what sorts of application are these different approaches used?
- In terms of eBusiness projects, determine the degree to which they truly are examples of socio-technical design. For instance, do job considerations such as job satisfaction play a part in analysis activities. Does design constitute both design of activity systems as well as ICT systems?
- Investigate the degree to which strategic, formative and summative evaluation is used in an organisation known to you.

Critical reflection

Why are good definitions of performance critical for compelling change in organisations? What is the relationship between a business model and a business strategy? What potential problems exist in adopting a top-down approach to strategy-making? What is the relationship between customer intimacy and customer relationship management? What is the relationship between supplier intimacy and supplier relationship management? Is it possible to develop measures of the fit between an organisation and its information systems? What sort of knowledge and skills does an eBusiness manager require as compared to a general business manager? Are three types of role required in organisations to manage information, information systems and ICT? Large companies seem particularly attracted by package development. What sort of advantages do you think are seen to lie in package development for such companies? What sort of problems do you think might emerge in outsourcing informatics in organisations? Many commentators would argue that organisations are not very good at evaluation. Why do you think this might be the case? What barriers must be overcome for successful evaluation? Many information systems have failed to return satisfactory levels of benefits to costs. Why should this be the case? Many commentators have argued that the benefits of ICT are frequently intangible in nature. What consequences does this have for effective evaluation of ICT?

Case exploration

Consider a major ICT project such as the attempt to introduce a national identity card for every UK citizen. If you were given the brief of planning the project how would you go about it? What sort of activities would be important in terms of conceiving this project? What would be involved in the analysis and design of this project? This project could be considered a major eBusiness or eGovernment failure. Attempt to evaluate why it failed?

Further reading

Ward and Peppard (2002) discuss strategic planning of informatics infrastructure. The distinction between various types of informatics management is originally due to Earl (1989). Avison and Fitzgerald (2006) discuss information systems development in more detail. Baskerville *et al.* (2010) discuss appropriate development approaches for current website developments. The application of the maturity assessment framework is described in more detail in Beynon-Davies, 2010. The application of the types of evaluation discussed in this paper to an actual case is discussed in Beynon-Davies *et al.*, 2004.

References

Ansoff, H. I. (1965). *Corporate Strategy*, New York, McGraw-Hill.
Avison, D. E. and B. Fitzgerald. (2006). *Information Systems Development: Methodologies, Techniques and Tools.* 4th edn. McGraw-Hill.
Baskerville, R., J. Pries-Heje, *et al.* (2010). Post-Agility: What Follows a Decade of Agility? *Information and Software Technology*, 53(1): 543–555.
Beynon-Davies, P. (2010). eBusiness as a Driver for Regional Development. *Journal of Systems and Information Technology* 12(1): 17–36.

Beynon-Davies, P., I. Owens and M. D.Williams. (2004). IS Failure, Evaluation and Organisational Learning. *Journal of Enterprise Information Management* (formerly *Logistics and Information Management*) 17(4): 276–282.

DAMA (2007). *DAMA-DMBOK Functional Framework*, Data Management Association.

Davenport, T. H. and L. Prusak. (2000). *Working Knowledge: How Organisations Manage What They Know*. 2nd edn. Boston, MA, Harvard Business School Press.

Earl, M. J. (1989). *Management Strategies for Information Technology*, Hemel Hempstead, Prentice Hall.

Gillenson, M. L. (1991). Database Administration at the Crossroads: The Era of End-User-Oriented, Decentralised Data Processing. *Journal of Database Administration* 2(4): 1–11.

Johnson, G., K. Scholes and R. Whittington. (2007). *Exploring Corporate Strategy: Text and Cases*. 8th edn. Englewood-Cliffs, Prentice-Hall.

Jones, P., E. Muir and P. Beynon-Davies. (2006). The Proposal of a Comparative Framework to Evaluate E-Business Stages of Growth Models. *International Journal of Information Technology and Management* 5(4): 249–266.

Nolan, R. L. (1979). Managing the Crises in Data Processing. *Harvard Business Review* 57(2) (March–April).

Sauer, C. (1993). *Why Information Systems Fail: A Case Study Approach*, Henley-On-Thames, Alfred Waller.

Ward, J. and J. Peppard. (2002). *Strategic Planning for Information Systems*. 3rd edn. Chichester, John Wiley.

11 eBusiness futures

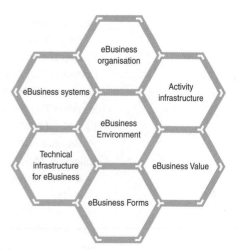

Introduction

Predicting the future is by its very nature prone to error, particularly in the area of technology and its impact. For instance, in 1949 ENIAC, an early computer, was equipped with 18,000 vacuum tubes and weighed 30 tons. It was predicted at the time that computers in the future may have only 1,000 vacuum tubes and perhaps weigh 2 tons. In 1977 the president of Digital Equipment Corporation predicted that no one would ever want to have a computer in their home. These are key examples of how it is possible to be spectacularly wrong about the future of technology and its use.

However, there are a number of trends which it is possible to extrapolate from. This enables us to provide a picture of some of the issues that are likely to arise over the next decade or so and impact upon the continuing shape of electronic business. We organise this discussion in terms of the model of eBusiness we first presented in Chapter 1.

Business signs, patterns and systems

The key principles upon which eBusiness are built will remain over the coming decades. Humans will still need to organise themselves to achieve collective goals, and to do so will need to establish systems of performance, communication and representation.

As we have seen in Chapter 2, the term organisation is normally associated with the social world, particularly with human institutions. People world-wide now spend a substantial proportion of their life either working within or interacting with organisations of various forms. Since the 1950s much of the sense of modern-day life is made significant as organisational life.

But organisation is also a term that has importance in the physical sciences. The late Tom Stonier argued for information to be treated as a basic property of the universe as are matter and energy (Stonier, 1994). Just as energy is defined in terms of its capacity to perform work, so information is defined in terms of its capacity to organise a physical system. Organisation, in such terms, is a sign of negentropy within an entropic universe. Within the physical theory of thermodynamics the natural state of the universe is one of disorder – known in more formal terms as *entropy*. Systems (or more specifically open systems such as human organisations) are islands of order – negative entropy or *negentropy* – in a universe of disorder.

Hence, when we say a system, whether physical or social, is organised, we are actually flip-flopping between organisation considered as a noun and organisation considered as a verb. As a noun, organisation is evidence of pattern in some aspect of the 'world'; organisation is another word for the emergent effect of patterning. As we discussed in Chapter 2, the patterning of performance, communication and representation amongst a group of human actors is what we mean by human social organisation. However, such patterning is evident only in action. We speak of organisation when patterns of performance, communication and representation are enacted and reproduced. In this sense organisation is best treated as a verb – as a process of continual re-production.

In this light, the ideas presented in the first few chapters of the book can be used as 'tools' to help breakdown established conceptions of organisation and the place of information and communication technology within organisation. We would argue that on the one hand eBusiness is a way of thinking about organisations differently; it is also a way of conceptualising some key elements that co-exist in all forms of organisations both now and in the future. Figure 11.1 acts as a composite illustration of the elements and inter-relationships of the three facets of our conceptual framework: business signs, business patterns and business systems.

We take signs to be important because of the way they act as conceptual 'glue' which inter-connect various levels of system, meaning that signs take their shape within systems of various forms. We also take systems broadly to constitute some continuing patterning of order or organisation in the world. Hence, we use the term system to refer not only to the patterning of signs, but also to denote the patterning of activity, communication and representation. This continuous and entangled patterning we take to constitute organisation.

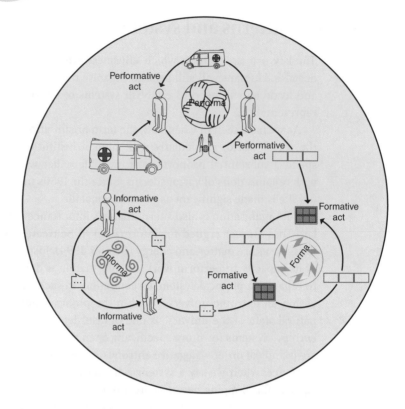

Figure 11.1 Our conceptual framework

Organisation is created and re-created in a continuous process in which signs interrelate between and within three different patterns of order which we have referred to in previous chapters as forma, informa and performa. Forma constitutes the substance or representation of signs, informa the content or communication of signs and performa the use of signs in coordinated action. The patterning of order characteristic of human organisation is enacted through three inter-related forms of action. Formative acts amount to the enactment of forma: acts of data representation and processing. Informative acts constitute the enactment of informa: acts of communication involving message-making and interpretation. Finally, performative acts constitute the enactment of performa: the performance of coordinated action amongst a group of actors.

These patterns of order and action have allowed us to more clearly define three levels of system which inter-relate to form what we mean by human organisation: activity systems, information systems and data systems. Activity systems consist of the patterning of performa: of regular and repeating patterns of performative acts. Information systems consist of the patterning of informa: of regular and repeating patterns of informative or communicative acts. Finally, data systems consist of the patterning of forma: of regular and repeating patterns of formative acts.

Consider the ambulance service in such terms. Performative action in this situation includes call-takers taking incident calls, health-care professionals driving to the scene of some incident in ambulances and paramedics administering emergency health-care at incidents. Or consider the case of Goronwy Galvanising. Performative action here consisted of receiving black material, checking black material, galvanising conforming black material and dispatching white material back to customers. Activity systems in both cases consisted of the pattern of inter-relations between collections of such performative acts.

Informative action supports the coordination of performative action. Informative action in the case of Goronwy consisted of actors asserting things that were happening such as *15% of all the black material we received over the last year was non-conforming,* issuing directives such as *please ensure that all conforming black material is galvanised on its day of delivery* and making commitments such as *we promise to turnaround all products within a three day period.* In the case of the ambulance service informative acts consisted of assertives such as *a medical emergency has taken place at location X on person Y,* directives such as *this type of resource X needs to be sent to incident Y* or commitments such as *an ambulance will respond within 8 minutes.* Information systems consist of patterns of such communication which continuously repeat in organisations such as these.

Any informative action utilises formative action. We have particularly focused on persistent formative action: the making of records. In the case of the ambulance service, formative acts include creating incident records, updating incident records and reading such records. In the case of Goronwy formative acts include reading delivery advices, updating job sheets and creating dispatch advices.

The reason we have spent considerable time explaining such theory is to demonstrate a number of features of organisation that will not change over the coming decades. Any form of human organisation will still involve this entanglement of performative, informative and formative action. However, the way in which technology enfolds in these patterns of organisation will undoubtedly change.

Value-chain and value-network

In 2007 Floridi (2007) argued that the threshold between online and offline would break down in the near future. As a result, he claimed that we would all become what he refers to as information organisms. What he means by this is that ubiquitous informatics infrastructure within civil society will cause a fading between face-to-face and remote or mediated communication. The transition between the off-line and online worlds will therefore become almost invisible to the average citizen and consumer. There is certainly evidence of this happening. Consider a normal day which you spend – how much of this day is spent in communication with humans and how much with machines of various forms? In terms of human communication, how much of this communication is conducted face-to-face and how much remotely using technology?

This communication shift will be fuelled by the increasing penetration of what has been referred to by some as ubiquitous or pervasive computing. In one guise, ubiquitous computing involves a future in which small, inexpensive, processors are distributed throughout everyday activities. For example, within the home ubiquitous computing might mean the interconnection of utilities such as lighting and heating with personal biometric monitors woven into the clothing of occupants. This would mean that that illumination and heating conditions throughout a home or office would be adjusted continuously and imperceptibly. Another example might be a smart refrigerator that is able to sense food items stored within its confines. On this basis it might be able to communicate to its users to warn them of impending stale or spoiled food.

On another level ubiquitous computing means access to communications infrastructure anywhere and at any time. This will need to be facilitated by better communications infrastructure but also technological developments such as wearable computing devices. Such changes to technological infrastructure will make possible a range of new applications such as the pervasive marketing seen in the film *Minority Report*.

To support ubiquitous and pervasive computing one should expect increasing demand for penetration of even higher-bandwidth broadband into the home, into the office and into public spaces. Hence, high-bandwidth will be needed to support multiple and sophisticated use by households both for leisure and work purposes. This is likely to be a critical driver for increased levels of home/remote working. There is predicted growth in number of workers who work from home at least one day per week over the next decade. This will be paralleled by a probable greater rise in the number of workers who work on the move or nomadically. The growth in employee remote access channels and the convergence of access devices coupled with the consequent growth in nomadic working will need to be supported by a reliable, efficient and ubiquitous communication infrastructure (Economist, 2008). Much more communications traffic is likely to be loaded onto this network as traditional telephony moves onto the network supported by internet protocols. A growing range of collaborative applications supporting nomadic working will also rely on increasing connectivity of different access devices (particularly) mobile devices.

The way in which value is produced, distributed and consumed will undoubtedly be affected by such technological innovation. Production of tangible products has already been impacted by technological innovation, through areas such as the use of robotics within manufacturing plant. Perhaps in the relatively near future the distinction between production, distribution and consumption of certain forms of value may start to break down.

Consider the notion of content. Many predict that much of the new generation of online content will be produced outside of commercial and public sector organisations. Content delivery channels will multiply leading to a continued increase in user-generated content. With this explosion new approaches to ensuring the quality control of content will develop. A new generation of content will be targeted at the person not the place or the device. A mixed economy model of delivery of content is already evident and is likely to develop in the future. Narrow-casting of content will become the norm, although a considerable proportion of content delivered will still be from broadcast organisations where the 'quality' of content is assured.

We made great play in earlier chapters of the distinction between tangible and intangible products and made the inference that electronic delivery is particularly suited to intangible products such as content. This might change significantly in the future with the increasing penetration of technologies such as 3D printers, sometimes referred to as additive engineering. Unlike the current range of two-dimensional printers which produce two-dimensional artefacts such as printed documents on demand, a three-dimensional printer can be instructed to build a three-dimensional object. Such printers are already being used to produce proto-type objects within design settings. Eventually, with developments in such printers and the lowering of their cost it might prove feasible to bridge the traditional gap between the production of a product and the consumption of the product. Hence, for instance, suppose you need a particular automobile part. Currently, you either have to go to some retail outlet or order delivery of such a part with a supplier. But suppose you had a general purpose 3D printer in your home. Now you only need to pay for the instructions to be sent over a communication channel to your access device, which you can use at home to instruct your printer to build the part for you.

Environment

The increasing penetration of informatics infrastructure world-wide is seen by many as contributing to the process of globalisation. This term is typically used to describe the process by which regional economies and societies become more closely integrated through greater inter-communication, transportation and trade. On the downside many see globalisation as a cultural process in which Western norms, values and ideas replace indigenous ideologies and value-systems. On the upside globalisation increases inter-dependencies between countries and as such may act to reduce inter-national conflict.

The internet and web have certainly helped form a global communications infrastructure. The downside of such technological globalisation may mean that local industries find it increasingly more difficult to compete within a global market. On the upside, the existence of such a global communications infrastructure improves the capability of people around the world to organise political protest. Some have suggested that this capability may imbue such infrastructure with the status of a human right in the near future. Access to communication infrastructure will be a necessary prerequisite for free speech.

Hence, it is reasonable to expect that communication infrastructure, particu-larly the provision of broadband communication channels, will further strengthen its position as a ubiquitous utility over the next 10 years, over major parts of the world. As a result, an increasing range of social, economic and political activity will rely on the provision of efficient and effective ICT infrastructure. Ubiquitous communication infrastructure will become increasingly important to the economic performance of companies. It will also be critical for the consumer/ citizen in supporting their interactions with organisations, particularly entertain-ment content and the electronic delivery of private, public and voluntary sector services.

It is reasonable therefore to expect there to be an increasing range of eGovernment services offered to citizens. Indeed, in many countries it might become expected that citizens by default will interact with government agencies through electronic service delivery. But this of course assumes that all citizens have access to informatics infrastructure and know how to use it. Hence, increasing eGovernment places more demands on attempts to erode digital divides, if aspects of social exclusion are not exacerbated by this process of technological innovation.

Part of the reason that governments are interested in eGovernment initiatives is the efficiency gain that is envisaged in this process. But initiatives such as eGovernment may have an important part to play in encouraging more sustainable activity. For instance, electronic procurement need not just focus on issues of getting the cheapest product from the largest supplier. eProcurement can be used as a way of encouraging interaction between more local SMEs and government agencies. In such ways, and if planned appropriately, ICT infrastructure can have a significant impact upon sustainability. It is likely that ways will be found to produce and use ICT in more energy efficient ways. ICT will also prove important in improving management of finite resources such as in the recycling of material.

Technological infrastructure

The convergence of technologies around standards will become critical, making content accessible from a range of different devices and fostering easy coordination between devices. This will also foster an increasing range and sophistication of content, applications and services available to the consumer/citizen. In turn, this will lead to greater demands on communication channels in terms of bandwidth.

The range and functionality of access devices will undoubtedly increase allowing ubiquitous access across public, home and work settings through high-bandwidth data communication infrastructure to a host of new applications, services and content. Convergence of devices such as mobile phones, tablets and digital television will be driven by increasing adoption of common technical standards. The role of the 'television' itself is changing from a passive receiver to a significant platform for accessing and delivering electronic content of various forms.

As far as the consumer is concerned, growth will continue in conventional applications such as web surfing and music downloading. Alongside this growth an increasing range of applications will develop supporting an increasing range of content, much of this personalised. The key applications driving the increased provision of broadband to the home are likely to be Voice over Internet Protocol, video download, IPTV and HDTV. IPTV along with HDTV will emerge as a major delivery platform for the delivery of broadcast content. Such a platform, along with the delivery of commercial content, could be a significant channel for the introduction of public sector applications such as electronic medical monitoring and care.

In terms of the ICT infrastructure one should expect the interoperability of components to rely on increased adoption of service-oriented architecture. The increasing migration of infrastructure to web services should enable greater integration of ICT systems. This will act as continuing impetus to the distribution of data and processing around wide area networks through technologies such as cloud computing.

In terms of web developments we should expect a continued movement to the application of Web 2.0 technologies. Web 1.0 was characterised by static web content; Web 2.0 has been typified by a range of technologies that encourage inter-active content. The most prominent consequence of this has been the rise of social networking sites and systems.

Current predictions are that over the next decade the major trend will be one of providing greater control to the web. What some people have called Web 3.0 will involve limits being placed upon the openness of the web. Increasing fears over data privacy will lead to greater embedding of privacy enhancing technologies within the architecture of the web. Media companies are also likely to introduce greater restrictions around the distribution of content.

eBusiness and eCommerce

In Chapter 1 we made the claim that in the early years of the 21st century socie-ties are moving from industrial societies to information societies. It is therefore not surprising to predict that the provision of informatics infrastructure will have a significant impact on economic growth world-wide. Many new industries will be reliant on ubiquitous informatics infrastructure. The competitive advan-tage of businesses will be reliant on effective and efficient data communication infrastructure as business activity is increasingly designed around location-independence.

Currently an increasing range of services in the private, public and voluntary sectors are delivered electronically in an increasing number of areas of life. This trend is likely to continue. In terms of the home the integration of communication between domestic devices such as fridges and cookers and access devices such as the mobile phone is forecast to lead to the possibility of remote operation of devices in the home. The growth of the use of ICT in schools will continue with an increased range of educational content available online and an increased use of eLearning as a delivery mechanism to pupils. In the public sector, there will be an increased range and penetration of government services available online and an increased range and penetration of eHealth applications.

The sophistication of electronic delivery will demand intra-organisational data sharing between back-end and front-end information systems. Increasingly we should also expect increased inter-organisational sharing of data, particularly in the public sector. This is likely to occur not only between public sector organisa-tions such as health bodies and social services but also between a growing range of private and voluntary sector intermediaries. Data sharing in this context demands forms of inter-organisational records management.

The key issue of identity management occurs in forms of intra-organisational data sharing but particularly inter-organisational data sharing. The information economy is likely to see an increasing need for identity registers of various forms, not only of persons but also land, buildings, products and potentially services.

As levels of remote interaction between individuals and organisations increase, situations in which the management of the personal identity become important multiply. We would therefore expect that the management of personal identity will assume increasing significance both in terms of internal organisational activity and particularly in cross-organisational infrastructure. This will act as an impetus to an increasing range of socio-technical activity aimed at embedding personal identity management within organisations themselves and between organisations. Successful attempts at this are likely to further enable growth in levels of remote interaction.

Personal data are extremely valuable to organisations, particularly for such activities as business intelligence and reality mining. Reality mining can be seen to be an extension of traditional business intelligence work which involves the collection and analysis of machine-sensed data about human social behaviour, the goal being to identify predictable patterns amongst such behaviour. Reality mining tends to utilise data gathered about the usage of wireless devices such as mobile phones and GPS systems. This enables applications to develop accurate models of what people do, where they go and with whom they communicate. Applications such as this may enable private sector organisations to better plan activities, such as the positioning of retail outlets and marketing. In the public sector, much interest is shown in using patterns identified to better plan public health policy.

As more and more activity moves online, securing data and systems will become increasingly critical for organisations both in the public and private sectors. Deviant activity associated with remote electronic delivery such as identity fraud and theft is likely to continue to be a problem. Ensuring the privacy of personal data and transactions will become critical to the trust invested in both public and private sector organisations. Protecting ones' identity and data will also become an increasing area of concern for individuals in everyday activities.

Networking effects created by increased connectivity to informatics infrastructure is likely to create space for new organisational forms. So-called channel applications may be key drivers of a 'network' effect in the private, public and voluntary sectors. A key aspect of organisational strategies will be finding spaces for organisational innovation within the wider value-network through application of ICT.

Over the past few years interest has grown in so-called virtual organisations, also referred to as network organisations. A virtual organisation is one built on an informatics infrastructure that enables collaborative, remote and nomadic working amongst members. Such organisations are also characterised by flat organisational hierarchies and work is typically organised in terms of team-working within transitory projects. Hence, virtual organisations do not utilise traditional physical infrastructure such as office space. People will work out of their homes or from wherever they can access communication infrastructure.

However, the inertia embedded within existing organisational structures and cultures will act as a brake on such transformation through ICT. This means that traditional organisational forms will persist and the conventional support and supplant strategies for the application of ICT will continue to be evident into the near future.

Generally within business we would expect the continued embedding of information systems and ICT within organisational life. This will involve continued attempts to informate aspects of the value-chain distributed over internal communication networks. It will also increasingly involve attempts to integrate the wider value-network with the internal value-chain.

Once used solely for business-to-business purposes, today nearly everyone has made at least one purchase using an eCommerce platform. A tipping point has therefore already been reached in relation to B2C eCommerce for a number of reasons: it is convenient, offers access to a wide range of goods and services, at any time and from anywhere. We can therefore expect an increasing penetration of traditional B2C eCommerce such as online retail within the economy. We should also expect an increasing range of information-based corporations supplying content of various forms for the consumer.

However, one should not expect the demise of the bricks-and-mortar organisation. Such organisations will merely change to meet the requirements created in new business models in different value-networks. Some have predicted that the change in consumer behaviour caused by online shopping is reshaping the offline shopping experience. Within the next ten years we are likely to see many clicks-and-mortar businesses reshape their offline operations to better match customer expectations. For many organisations the high-street store is likely to change into a B2C hub where customers can collect goods ordered online or obtain added-value services associated with online purchases. Such stores will also provide internet access points where customers can browse products or provide free Wi-Fi services to attract customers.

We can also expect that B2B eCommerce will merge with P2P eCommerce over the longer term. Some have referred to the development of a digital business ecosystem in which both competition and cooperation activity is supported through ICT. The Digital Business Ecosystem (DBE) is an internet-based software environment in which business applications can be developed and used. Effectively, the hope is that this will provide a common supporting infrastructure for the wider value network.

The community chain is likely to assume greater levels of significance over the next decade. Companies are already interested in using Web 2.0 technologies to build communities of interest. The use of technologies such as wikis and blogs within the commercial context is therefore likely to increase.

Conclusion

In this book we have attempted a number of things. First, we have attempted to demonstrate that eBusiness is in a sense nothing new. eBusiness is founded on three types of inter-related action which entangle together and produce organisation. This means that eBusiness is business; in fact the principles of eBusiness underlie all organisational form. Second, we have attempted to show how modern information and communication technology has inherently developed as it has because it helps to better enable activity, communication and representation within organisation. This provides the key value of ICT: such technology as data systems support information systems which in turn support activity systems. Third, we have attempted to show how considering organisations as value-creating systems working within a wider-value network provides a useful lens for understanding the importance of technology to current activity but also more importantly as a key agent in organisational change. But such change has to be planned for and managed effectively: that changing data systems must necessarily involve changes to information systems and associated activity systems. This book is an attempt to provide you the reader with a new vocabulary for both understanding and debating with the nature of eBusiness.

References

Economist. (2008). Nomads at Last: A Special Report on Mobility. *The Economist*. 75–76. 12 April.

Floridi, L. (2007). A Look into the Future Impact of ICT on Our Lives. *The Information Society* 23(1): 59–64.

Stonier, T. (1994). Information as a Basic Property of the Universe. *Biosystems* 38(2): 135–140.

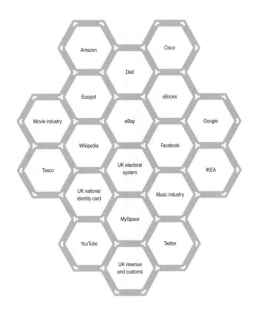

eBusiness cases

Case matrix

Case study	Activity System	Information System	Data system	Electronic delivery	B2C eCommerce	B2B eCommerce	C2C eCommerce	P2P eCommerce	mCommerce	eMarketing	eProcurement	eGovernment	Strategy
Amazon	X	X	X	X	X	X		X	X	X			X
Apple									X				X
Cisco	X	X	X	X	X	X	X			X	X		X
Dell	X	X	X	X	X	X	X			X	X		X
easyJet	X		X	X	X	X				X			X
eBay	X		X	X	X	X	X	X		X	X		X
eBooks									X				X
Facebook													X
Google	X		X	X	X	X			X	X	X		X
IKEA	X	X	X	X	X	X			X		X		X
Movie industry								X	X				X
Music industry								X	X				X
MySpace			X	X	X	X				X			X
Tesco	X	X	X	X	X	X	X			X	X		X
Twitter									X				X
UK Revenue and customs	X	X	X	X								X	X
UK Electoral System	X	X				X						X	
UK National ID Card				X	X	X	X			X		X	
Wikipedia	X		X	X	X					X			X
YouTube	X			X	X				X				X

Amazon.com

Case description

Amazon.com is an American eCommerce company based in Seattle, Washington State, US. The company was one of the first major companies to sell goods over the internet. It was also one of the most prominent traded securities of the late 1990s dot com 'bubble'. When this bubble burst, many claimed that Amazon's business model was unsustainable. The company made its first annual profit in 2003. Consequently, Amazon.com is probably the most cited example of a company that has succeeded at B2C eCommerce (Saunders, 2001). The domain amazon.com attracts over 600 million visitors annually.

Amazon.com was launched on the web in June 1995 by Jeff Bezos. Bezos obtained backing of venture capitalists in Silicon Valley to start the operation. He chose to name his site after the world's longest river because Amazon according to Bezos was set to become the world's largest bookstore. At the time of Amazon's entry into the market it had no significant rivals. Within one year the company was recognised as the web's largest bookstore.

At the start Bezos warned investors that they were unlikely to make a profit in the first five years of operation (Brandt, 2011). However, Amazon has engaged in an aggressive expansion strategy since its inception. It has acquired a number of additional retail outlets such as toys, CDs and has provided a facility for online auctions of small goods. It introduced zShops in 1999 which is a facility that allows any individual or business to sell through Amazon.com – a form of C2C trading. It also has invested in a number of dot com companies such as Pets.com and Drugstore.com and has opened a number of distribution centres and operations around the world.

The primary value-stream for Amazon is tangible products such as books and CDs. As primarily a books retailer the major transformation of its value-creating system is distribution and sales. It offers a vast range of such books for sale to customers and delivers them to customers. In recent times, it has attempted to broaden the range of this value by offering a broader range of products including computer software, video games, electronics, clothing, furniture, food and toys. It also provides added-value services such as a personalised notification service.

From the start Amazon has also offered a range of value-added services to its customers. A popular feature of the website is the ability for users to submit reviews for each product. As part of their review, users must rate the product on a scale from one to five stars. Such rating scales provide a basic measure of the popularity of a product. Such a reviewing facility has been seen by some as critical to the explosive growth of the company. Other added-value services include a personal notification service for customers requesting particular titles, a recommendations section where customers can recommend titles in various categories to other customers, an awards section which lists books that have won prizes and an associate programme where other sites can link to Amazon to sell their own selections.

Currently the company is claimed to be the internet's number one retailer. However, although Amazon is a retailer, its key business strategy is based on differentiation in terms of technical infrastructure. For Amazon to keep this competitive differentiation it must continually be at the forefront of internet technology. Bezos has indicated that he considers Amazon to be a technology company first and a retailer second. Hence, the key-differentiating factor for Amazon over the conventional retailer is the internet and web. Not surprisingly, the company has to ceaselessly innovate in terms of technology. Having said this Amazon must ensure that back-end systems managing its supply, sales and distribution processes work effectively. To be continuously able to upgrade its informatics infrastructure the company employs a vast range of software developers situated in a number of centres around the world. Amazon's main software development outfit is now based in Seattle, US.

Amazon played a significant part in the development of cloud computing. An analysis of the performance of its data centres in the early 2000s found that they were utilising only 10% of their capacity at one time. Introducing aspects of cloud architecture such as data virtualisation allowed it to operate its data centres far more efficiently. This led to the development of an effort to provide cloud computing to external customers. Amazon Web Service was launched in 2006.

Amazon primarily engages in B2C eCommerce but as described has recently started a C2C operation in support of its B2C site. For instance, Amazon created an online community known as Mechanical Turk. This is an open marketplace in which workers perform tasks for requestors. Amazon receives a percentage of the fee charged for work by a worker.

Amazon has separate websites in Canada, the UK, Germany, France, China and Japan. However, it ships certain selected products globally. It also runs a number of fulfilment centres in North America, Europe and Asia. The company provides a number of levels of functionality through its website such as search features, additional content and personalisation. The site also provides searchable catalogues of books, CDs, DVDs, computer games etc. Customers can search for titles using keyword, title, subject, author, artist, musical instrument, label, actor, director, publication date or ISBN. In terms of added-value, the company offers a vast range of additional content over and above its products. For example, cover art, synopses, annotations, reviews by editorial staff and other customers and interviews by authors and artists. The website attempts to personalise the customer experience by greeting customers by name, instant and personalised recommendations, bestseller listings, personal notification services and purchase pattern filtering.

Amazon's service to customers relies on a close integration of its website to back-end information and activity systems. For instance, the company uses a streamlined ordering process reliant on previous billing and shipment details captured from the customer. Amazon also utilises secure server software that encrypts payment information throughout its integrated fulfilment process. Most of the company's products are available for shipping within 24 hours.

Amazon requires a range of integrated back-end systems in place. Inbound logistics involves the management of the purchasing of books and the distribution of books to large warehouses. The process of operations involves unpacking and storing such shipments as well as picking of books to fulfil customer orders. Outbound logistics involves the distribution of books to the customer. Marketing and sales involves the advertisement of books on its web catalogue and handling the purchasing of books through its website. After-sales service involves the handling of customer enquiries and complaints.

It is possible to describe briefly some of the gains that Amazon experiences from its engagement with B2C eCommerce and in particular, the close integration of its ICT infrastructure with its activity infrastructure. First, in terms of efficacy, Amazon has been able to diversify into a vast range of products for retail. Since Amazon is primarily a B2C company it is able to run without any physical retail outlets and can pass on efficiency gains in lower costs to its customers. Finally, in terms of effectiveness, Amazon is able to sell its products across the world and is able to relate to a large range of suppliers.

Since the mid-2000s Amazon has engaged in a strategy of attempting to build upon its core business model of online retail as a basis for engaging in two major forms of B2B eCommerce: providing order fulfilment and web services for external business actors.

Fulfilment allows small and large companies to pay to use Amazon's order fulfilment infrastructure for their own purposes. Amazon stores the company's inventory in their own warehouses and provides product picking, packing and shipping to the customer once an order is received by the company.

In 2006 the company launched Amazon Web Services. This developed from a major revision of its ICT infrastructure which separated its back-end from front-end functions. This initially enabled the company to manage its websites more effectively. Eventually it was realised that a new business offering could be built upon this technological change. Now Amazon offers not only base utility functions such as cheap online storage to external businesses but also the ability to run complete applications for companies on Amazon servers.

This infrastructure has also enabled the company to engage in forms of P2P eCommerce. For instance, the websites of Borders (borders.com, borders.co.uk), Waldenbooks (waldenbooks.com), Virgin Megastores (virginmega.com), CDNOW (cdnow.com) and HMV (hmv.com) are all hosted by Amazon. The company also runs multi-channel access for a number of companies such as Marks & Spencer and Mothercare. Such sites allow the customer to interchangeably interact with the retail website, standalone in-store terminals and phone-based customer service agents.

Reflection points

- Amazon obtained dominance in online book retail by being the first into a niche market. This raises the question of the importance of niche strategies in the online world.
- It took a considerable while for Amazon to make a profit. Many dot com companies created in the same period as Amazon now no longer exist. What caused Amazon to survive and other companies to go under?
- Dot com companies such as Amazon rely on a critical mass of people having access to the internet and prepared to order and pay for goods and services

online. What affect does the digital divide have on the customer-base of companies like Amazon?

- Online retail of low-cost, packaged goods such as books, CDs and DVDs now outstrips physical retail of these items in many countries. How has online retail affected consumer behaviour generally?
- Amazon relies on effective management of a supply and distribution (customer) chain to make a profit. How effectively does Amazon engage in B2B eCommerce?
- Amazon.com does not publish a customer service number on its own website. Customers are instead asked to submit written service requests (which are answered by e-mail) or to use a click-to-call service to be connected by phone to an available service representative. Despite the perceived difficulty in reaching customer service by phone, Amazon.com remains high in customer satisfaction surveys. Why do you think this might be?

Reference

Brandt, R. (2011). *One Click: Jeff Bezos and the Rise of Amazon.com*, London, Viking.
Saunders, R. (2001). *Business the Amazon.com Way*, Oxford, John Wiley.

Apple

Case description

Based in Cupertino, California, Apple is a multi-national company that designs and markets a variety of products, including personal computers, software and consumer electronics. Apple, which was created in 1977, has established a unique reputation in the consumer electronics industry for the aesthetic principles exercised in its design work and its distinctive advertising campaigns (Moritz, 2009).

The range of Apple hardware products has evolved over time: from the Macintosh line of personal computers to the iPod, the iPhone and – most recently – the iPad. The Mac OS X operating system, the iLife suite of multimedia and creativity software , the iTunes media browser and the iWork suite of productivity software are well-known examples of Apple software.

The company operates a number of retail stores in number of countries worldwide as well as an online store. In mid-2010 Apple was reported as one of the largest companies in the world. It was also reported as the most valuable technology company in the world, having surpassed Microsoft in this regard.

Part of the secret of the company's continued success is ceaseless innovation. In 2001, Apple introduced the iPod digital music player. This was not the first of the so-called MP3 players, but in 2003 the company introduced the iTunes music store, which was closely integrated with the iPod. This online store essentially connected various music providers directly with a large market of music consumers and soon made Apple the world's largest online music retailer. It also made the iPod the market leader in portable music players.

In 2007 the company announced the iPhone, a product that integrated an internet-enabled smartphone with an iPod. In 2008 the company launched its App store for the iPhone, which enabled users to directly download applications and install them on their iPhones. Apps are created in large part by external software producers, but Apple takes a 30% royalty on all apps sold through its app store.

In 2010 Apple announced their tablet computer the iPad. As well as offering much of the functionality of the iPhone it allows access to a wider range of media content through a device controlled by a touch-sensitive screen interface.

Apple develops software to support its increasing range of devices. It has always used its own operating system Mac OS X for its personal computers and laptops. The company also independently develops its own productivity software, which is normally installed on Apple computers. Software applications such as iDVD, iMovie, iPhoto, iTunes, GarageBand and iWeb, for example, are bundled together in the iLife software package. The Apple package for presentation, page layout and word processing is iWork. Sometimes Apple software can be downloaded for free – this is the case of the QuickTime media player or the Safari web browser, which can be used on both Mac OS X and Microsoft Windows.

Apple has sourced the production of much of its technology, such as the iPod, from Chinese manufacturers such as Foxconn and Inventec. In 2006, a number of media outlets reported that sweatshop conditions existed in some of these factories in China, with employees regularly working in overcrowded conditions for more than 60 hours per week and for little pay. Apple reacted to these allegations launching an investigation and introducing yearly audits of all its suppliers regarding worker's rights. However, there is much debate over the success or otherwise of such initiatives. In 2010, it was revealed that the workers making iPads and iPhones in a Foxconn facility in China had to sign a legally binding document in which they pledged that they would not commit suicide; apparently, this was due to the high number of suicides among the company's employees. In 2011 Apple recognised that some of the factories of its major suppliers in China had employed a growing number of child workers.

Reflection points

- Apple has a large and loyal customer base for its products. Reflect on how this loyalty is maintained.
- How does Apple compete in terms of software with other established suppliers such as Microsoft?
- Apple has demonstrated the power of what some refer to as a digital ecosystem business model. It did this with the iPod and iTunes store and the App store and the iPhone. Reflect on the similarities and differences between the business model of Apple and Amazon in these terms.
- Many hardware suppliers, such as Apple, rely on production facilities based in the Far East. Reflect upon the pros and cons of this strategy.

Reference

Moritz, M. (2009). *Return to the Little Kingdom: Steve Jobs, the Creation of Apple, and How It Changed the World*, Oxford, Gerard Duckworth.

Cisco

Case Description

Cisco systems was founded in 1984 at Stanford University by husband-and-wife team Leonard Bosack (who developed early router technology) and Sandra Lerner and three colleagues (Kraemer and Dedrick, 2002). Cisco is generally regarded as the leader in the market for inter-networking equipment. It is generally seen as the company which commercialised the router – a device which determines the optimal path along which packets of data should flow on a computer network. The growth of Cisco is also attributed to its setting of standards for networking equipment through its proprietary Internet Operating System (IOS). Both routers and IOS are key technologies supporting the internet and enables customers of the company to build large-scale, integrated computer networks. Growth of the company has been driven by the surge in data traffic on the internet. The company initially targeted universities, aerospace and government facilities relying on word-of-mouth and contacts for sales. The market for routers opened up in late 1980s and Cisco became the first company to offer reasonably-priced, high-performance routers. It went public in 1990 and soon after initiated an acquisitions strategy to broaden the range of products offered. Originally focusing on corporate data networking it began to target both Internet Service Providers and the home networking market.

The primary value-stream for Cisco is products, particularly routers. It has attempted to broaden the range of this value by offering a wider range of products. It also provides traditional added-value services such as its after-sale service. However, Cisco also provides value by managing its wider value-network with a range of partners. These include resellers that sell and support Cisco products, service specialists providing network integration and operations and component manufacturers that provide most of the company's actual manufacturing capability.

Cisco's main transformation is the assembly of inter-networking equipment such as routers. The key inputs for Cisco consist of parts from a vast range of suppliers as well as a vast range of data associated with this supply. The key outputs from Cisco are completed products. The competitive environment for Cisco consists of companies producing comparable products in support of the infrastructure of the internet. Control in the case of Cisco means ensuring that it has sufficient information about its internal operations to ensure the efficient and effective delivery of goods to its customers (regulation). It also needs to ensure effective monitoring of its competitive environment to ensure that it develops new products for its marketplace (adaptation).

Cisco engages in B2C and B2B eCommerce. In terms of B2B eCommerce it has integrated its ERP systems with key suppliers through an extranet. In terms of B2C eCommerce it has built a web portal which enables its customers to order and configure products online.

It is possible to describe briefly some of the gains that Cisco experiences from its engagement with eBusiness. In terms of efficacy, Cisco is able to relate to a large range of suppliers and assemble a vast range of parts to produce its technical products. In terms of efficiency, Cisco uses B2C and B2B eCommerce as well as intra-business eBusiness to lower its costs. In terms of effectiveness, Cisco maintains that eBusiness has allowed it to grow quickly and allows it to more quickly adapt to environmental changes. It is therefore better able to compete in its key markets.

Cisco has implemented an e-Business strategy to enable fast integration of its supply-chain with key business processes. The supply chain is critical to the business as Cisco's manufacturing operation globally consists of 34 plants, only two of which are owned by the company. Suppliers make up to 90% of the subassembly of Cisco products and 55% of the final assembly. This means that suppliers regularly ship finished goods directly to Cisco customers.

A key component of Cisco's B2B eCommerce strategy is integration of its ERP systems with the information systems of its key suppliers. Suppliers use their ERP systems to run their Cisco production lines, allowing them to respond to demand from Cisco in real-time. This is enhanced by the introduction of Cisco Manufacturing Online, an extranet portal that allows partners to access real-time manufacturing information including data on demand forecasts, inventory and purchase orders.

Such a technical infrastructure means that changes in parts of the supply chain are communicated almost instantaneously to the company. For instance, if one supplier is low on a component then Cisco can analyse its supply chain for excess supplies elsewhere. Changes in forecasted demand are also communicated in real-time, enabling suppliers to respond immediately to requests for products or materials.

Payments to suppliers are triggered by a shop-floor transaction in the ERP system indicating that production is complete. The transaction initiates an analysis of inventory to determine the value of components sold by suppliers and triggers an electronic payment to suppliers. Annual benefits from the use of this ERP system integration are estimated to be in the realm of millions of dollars of savings per year.

Cisco has also engaged in B2C eCommerce innovation. It has introduced a web portal known as Cisco Connection Online which consists of a dynamic online catalogue, a facility for ordering and configuring products online, a status agent which allows customers and retailers to track orders, a customer service section, a technical assistance section and a software library. The company currently estimates to earn 75% of its $20 billion sales through its portal. The portal is also indicated as contributing to a 20% reduction in overall operating costs.

Cisco has created an internal online community within its emerging technologies group called the Idea Zone or I-Zone. Within this space anyone can propose ideas for new products, processes or markets. Ideas are critiqued by others and filtered for further development.

In 2009 Cisco is reported as having revenues of $36 billion and employing over 66,000 people. This revenue was driven largely by its core business which consists of sales of hardware devices such as routers and switches, software such as its network operating system and the provision of associated services such as network management. More recently however, Cisco has diversified into a large range of associated businesses such as optical networks, wireless equipment and internet telephony. It is also particularly diversifying in technologies associated with supporting the increase in video traffic via the internet. As part of this strategy it has produced a technology known as TelePresence, which provides a high-quality videoconferencing facility.

Cisco has organised its structure around key functions rather than customer segments. To manage innovation in new markets it has introduced an elaborate system of committees made up of managers from different functions. Such committees are supported by fluid working groups. This form of matrix organisation is supported by collaborative working using online tools provided by the company itself, such as TelePresence.

Reflection points

- Cisco does have a general internet website. Could this be regarded as a form of B2C eCommerce? Who are the typical customers of Cisco?
- How much of Cisco business is P2P eBusiness? Does it maintain partnership networks and what role does ICT play?
- Cisco uses an extranet to ensure integration of external relationships with suppliers. Consider the benefits as well as costs of extranets in managing the supply chain.

Reference

Kraemer, K. L. and J. Dedrick. (2002). Strategic Use of the Internet and e-Commerce: Cisco Systems. *Journal of Strategic Information Systems* 11(1): 5–29.

Dell

Case description

The US-based technology company Dell Inc. has its headquarters in Round Rock, Texas. The core business of Dell is the development, production and support of personal computers, servers, data storage devices, network switches, software, televisions, computer peripherals, and other technology-related products. As of 2008, the company employed more than 95,000 people world-wide.

Michael Dell, the founder of Dell Computer Corporation, is often credited with creating a revolution in the personal computer industry. Dell's business model built around direct selling to the customer and managing its inventory and distribution processes effectively is credited with a rapid growth in the business (Holzner, 2008).

The idea for the company originated in a business run from Michael Dells parents' home when he was a teenager. From here he originally sold memory chips and disk drives for IBM PCs. Michael Dell was able to sell his products through newspapers/magazines at 10–15% below retail prices. He dropped out of college in 1984 and started assembling his own IBM clones selling direct to customers at 40% below retail price. In 1988 his company went public. Having experienced some problems in 1990 the company re-established its position through selling its PCs via mail order through soft warehouse/compUSA superstores. In 1994 the company abandoned superstores to return to its mail-order/direct retail roots. Dell is now a worldwide business based around integrated manufacturing and supply of hardware.

The primary value-stream for Dell is tangible products such as computers and peripheral equipment. A certain degree of other intangible items such as software are also provided to customers. It attempts to provide added-value services such as customisable configuration and online help and support. Dell originally started its internet initiative in the late 1980s to attempt to increase its level of customer support. The company traditionally provided such customer support using a call-centre. At the call-centre Dell customer care representatives normally advised customers to obtain software updates either sent on disks or as software downloads from a site run by Compuserve. By 1989 Dell began online distribution of software updates.

Dell's main transformation is the assembly of computing equipment. The key inputs for Dell consist of parts from a vast range of suppliers as well as a vast range of data associated with this supply. The key outputs from Dell are completed products. The competitive environment for Dell consists of hardware companies producing comparable products. Control in the case of Dell means ensuring that it has sufficient information about its internal operations to ensure the efficient and effective delivery of goods to its customers (regulation). It also needs to ensure effective monitoring of its competitive environment to ensure that it develops new products for its marketplace (adaptation).

Dell engages in both B2C and B2B eCommerce. It has also integrated its internal information systems to become an effective intra-business eBusiness. In terms of efficacy, Dell has been able to diversify into a vast range of hardware products for retail. In terms of efficiency, Dell has been successful at lowering its internal costs and is able to pass on lower costs to its customers. In terms of effectiveness, Dell is able to sell its products across the world and is able to relate to a large range of suppliers.

In 1996 the company launched *www.dell.com* to provide technical support online. Initially, the website was used to provide technical information to customers. Later, customers were able to order through a website that provided an online catalogue of products. Customers can now also enter details of specific configurations of hardware they require and hence configure systems online. Dell routes technical support queries according to component-type and to the level of support purchased. For instance, there are five levels of support offered for business customers. For individual consumers the company offers 24 × 7 telephone and online troubleshooting.

Dell engages in supply-chain innovation including customisation of hardware and direct retailing to customers. Customers may order a personal computer through a website that provides an online catalogue of products. Customers can also enter details of specific configurations of hardware they require through this website. Such build-to-order retail requires assembly plants around the world (Austin, Texas; Limerick, Eire; Penang Malaysia) close to suppliers such as Intel (Chips), Maxtor (Hard drives) and Selectron (Motherboards). Order forms follow each PC across the factory floor. As well as online customer support the Dell site provides order and courier-tracking and pages of technical support related to the tagging of machines. Dell associates a Service Tag, a unique alpha-numeric identifier, with most of its products.

Traditionally, Dell has sold all its products whether to individual consumers or to business customers using a direct-sales model via online and telephone channels. The company receives payments for products before it has to pay for the materials and practices just-in-time (JIT) inventory-management. This means that Dell builds computers only after customers place orders and by requesting materials from suppliers as needed. Dell advertisements have used several channels including television, the web, magazines, catalogues and newspapers. Marketing strategies include lowering prices at all times of the year, offering free bonus products (such as Dell printers) and offering free shipping. Dell also runs its own online community site in which members can access and contribute to fora and blogs on the use of latest technology. Dell introduced a customer community known as IDEAStorm. The aim was to allow users of Dell products to help each other with problems such as software installation. One aim of IdeaStorm was to take pressure off the company's helpdesk. IdeaStorm also enabled the company to gather information about use of their products and what their customers thought.

Reflection points

- Would you describe Dell as engaging in customer relationship management through its website?
- Dell uses just-in-time inventory management and manufacturing. How important is ICT to this business philosophy?
- How important is tracking of products to the Dell business, not only in terms of the supply chain but also in terms of its customer chain?

Reference

Holzner, S. (2008). *How Dell Does It*, New York, McGraw-Hill Professional.

easyJet

Case description

Cost-savings through use of online booking helped to establish the business model for low-cost airlines such as easyJet. Other re-engineering of processes associated with commercial airline travel has enabled further efficiency gains. For instance, the seating on many aircrafts have been changed from the standard configuration and seats are not pre-allocated to customers before flights. Many airlines have also begun introducing forms of automatic check-in relying on ICT.

In 1994 Stelios Haji-Ioannou launched easyJet as a low-cost air-carrier and in 1998 he created EasyGroup as a holding company for a number of additional high demand/low margin businesses. easyJet is one of the largest low-fare airlines in Europe, operating domestic and international scheduled services on over 300 routes across over 100 European and North African airports. easyJet has seen rapid expansion since its creation, having grown through a combination of acquisitions and base openings fuelled by consumer demand for low-cost air travel (Jones, 2007).

It is reported that the company has a typical profit margin of only one pound sterling or so per customer. Initially, in order to keep running costs low, the company used a single sales channel of the telephone. The group now uses the internet as a low-cost sales channel but it is also significant to the branding of the company as being focused on eCommerce.

easyJet offers high-frequency services on short and medium-haul routes within Europe. It sees itself as a no-frills airline and has designed its business processes to avoid complexity. For example, it maintains single fares on flights, only offers fares one way, offers no in-flight refreshments, operates out of less used and consequently less congested airports and does not issue tickets but relies on booking numbers. To achieve this, the company relies heavily on close integration between its front-end sales systems and its back-end revenue management systems.

easyJet's aircraft cabins are configured in a single class, high-density layout. The airline's Boeing 737–700 aircraft carry 149 passengers plus three cabin crew, and its Airbus A319 aircraft carry 156 passengers plus four cabin crew. A typical Airbus A319 carries approximately 140 passengers in a single class configuration, but as easyJet does not serve meals the airline opted for smaller galleys and had a lavatory installed in unused space at the rear of the aircraft. The airline's 29-inch seat footprint allowed for the installation of 156 seats. Due to this high-density seating arrangement, easyJet's Airbus A319 aircraft have two pairs of over-wing exits, instead of the standard one pair configuration found on most Airbus A319 aircraft, to satisfy safety requirements.

easyJet does not provide complimentary meals or beverages on board its flights. Instead, passengers may purchase items on board the aircraft. Products include sandwiches, toasted sandwiches, pizza slices, chocolate, snacks, hot drinks, soft drinks and alcoholic drinks. On-board sales are an important part of the airline's ancillary revenue, so easyJet also sells gifts such as fragrances, cosmetics and easyJet branded items on board, as well as tickets for airport transfer services.

easyJet's early marketing strategy was initially based on 'making flying as affordable as a pair of jeans' and urged travellers to 'cut out the travel agent'. Its early advertising consisted of little more than the airline's telephone booking number painted in bright orange on the side of its aircraft. Initially booking was by telephone only since there is no incentive for travel agents to sell easyJet bookings because there is no commission, a standard practice for the low-cost carriers.

In December 1997, one of the company's Adverting Agencies, suggested to Stelios that he should consider trialling a website for direct bookings. Haji-Ioannou originally pronounced that the internet was for nerds. However, the company's marketing director saw the potential and approved a website trial. This involved placing a different telephone reservations number on the website, to track success. Once Stelios saw the results he changed his mind, and easyJet commissioned the development of an eCommerce website capable of offering real-time online booking from April 1998 – easyjet.com. easyJet was the first low-cost carrier to do so in Europe. Internet bookings were priced cheaper than booking over the phone, to reflect the reduced call centre costs and the aircraft were repainted with the web address.

By August 1999 the site accounted for 38% of ticket sales. This meant that the company had exceeded its target of 30% of sales online by 2000. Within a year of its launch over 50% of bookings were made using the website. By April 2004 the figure had jumped to 98%. Now, flights can be booked only over the internet except during the two weeks immediately before the flight when telephone booking is also available.

The transition to running the website proved relatively smooth. This was because easyJet was a 100% direct phone sales company and as such it was reasonably straightforward to integrate the website with its booking system. The savings the company makes through online booking have enabled the company to offer discounts to customers who book online.

easyJet varies the mix of its promotional campaigns. It frequently runs internet-only campaigns in newspapers designed to improve online sales. It ran the first of this type of promotional campaign in February 1999 with impressive results. 50,000 seats were offered to readers of *The Times* at discounted prices. Within the first day 20,000 of the seats had been sold, 40,000 within three days. The website is also used as a public relations facility. For example, journalists wishing to learn about changes to company policy or strategy are referred to the website. This saves the company employing a specialist PR company.

Reflection points

- easyJet, just like most low-cost airlines, has introduced charging for certain added-value such as priority boarding and baggage. Consider other ways in which low-cost airlines now make money from their online channels.
- The usability of websites is critical to the volume of bookings for companies such as easyJet. Assess the usability of easyJet's website as compared to its major competitors.

- The easyJet website, like many others allows customers the ability to create a profile of details which they can use to speed bookings. Consider this facility in relation to issues associated with the security of personal data.
- Since easyJet relies so much on its website for bookings, the continuity and availability of the site is critical to its success. Consider the ways in which such continuity is assured.

Reference

Jones, L. (2007). *easyJet: The Story of Britain's Biggest Low-Cost Airline*, Aurum Press, London.

eBay.com

Case description

eBay is one of the foremost examples of C2C eCommerce (Cohen, 2002). Its dominance is due to early entry into what was a niche market at the time. Its business model relies on that used in familiar *exchange and mart* catalogues that have existed for decades. The competitive edge for the business lies in the way in which eCommerce enables mass customers to trade low-cost items efficiently through an auction process across the globe. eBay uses what is known as a Dutch auction model for its business. In this form of auction the seller places one or more identical items for sale at a minimum price for a set period. When the auction ends the highest bidder gains the item at their bid price. eBay now also offers the ability for customers to pay for certain items offered through its website at a fixed price.

Pierre Omidyar created eBay in September 1995, using a website hosted by Omidyar's internet service provider, and running the company in his spare time from his apartment. In its early guise eBay was little more than a simple marketplace where buyers and sellers could bid for items. The company took no responsibility for the goods being traded and gave no undertaking to settle disputes between parties.

By February 1996 so many people had visited the site that Omidyar decided to introduce a 10 Cent listing fee to recoup ISP costs. By the end of March 1996 eBay showed a profit. Eventually the volume of traffic to the site persuaded his ISP to ask him to move elsewhere. Omidyar decided to transfer the operation to a one-room office with his own web server and he employed the services of a part-time employee. He also developed software capable of supporting a robust, scalable website as well as a transaction processing system to report on current auctions.

By August 1996 Omidyar had established one of his friends as the first president of eBay. In June 1997 the company approached venture capitalists for funding and secured $5 million. This enabled the company to establish a more extensive management structure for planned expansion. By the end of 1997 more than 3 million items (worth $94 million) had been sold on eBay amounting to revenues of $5.7 million and an operating profit of $900,000. eBay had an operating staff of only 67 employees at the time.

In its early days eBay undertook only limited marketing and relied on the loyalty of its customer-base and word-of-mouth referrals for its increased business growth. Eventually the company began to employ cross-promotional agreements including banner advertising on web portals such as Netscape and Yahoo! as well as providing an auction service for AOL's classified section. This evolved into a conventional marketing campaign through traditional print and broadcast media in 1998.

In 1999 the company expanded internationally by creating communities in Canada and the UK. This was followed by expansion into Germany, Australia, Japan and France. During this year and into 2000 the company successfully held its position against strong new entrants into the online auctions market such as Amazon.com. The company also moved into the bricks-and-mortar area with the purchase of a San Francisco-based auction house. eBay used this acquisition to move into the higher-price antiques sector of the market. By the end of June 1999 eBay had 5.6 million registered users and had conducted 29.4 million auctions during the previous three-month period. In the third quarter of 2000 $1.4 billion worth of goods were traded on eBay in 68.5 million auctions and which generated $113.4 million in revenues.

Millions of people join eBay each month from around the world and thousands of people around the Globe earn a living as an eBay trader. Essentially, eBay's business model is a simple one of providing C2C auctions online. Much of such activity relies on collectors trading small-price items such as coins, stamps, militaria etc. Although the average item sold through these markets constitute no more than tens of dollars, as a whole, billions of dollars are traded every year in the US in C2C trading of this nature.

The concept is to provide a website where anyone wishing to buy or sell on eBay must register by providing personal and financial details. Every user of eBay is given a unique identifier. eBay offers a virtual tour of its services but people can start buying and selling straight away.

Sellers list items for sale by completing an online form. They pay a small listing fee for this privilege. The size of the fee depends on where and how the listing is presented and whether a reserve price is required for the item. Sellers also choose the duration they wish buyers to bid for the item. At the end of an auction, eBay notifies the seller of the winning bid and provide details of the successful bidder to the seller. The buyer and seller then make their own arrangements for payment and delivery of the goods usually through email. Payment can be made by cash, cheque and postal order or electronically through a payment service or financial intermediary such as PayPal (paypal.com), now a subsidiary of eBay. eBay charges a percentage of the final value of the transaction. For instance, suppose a seller listed a collection of stamps for sale at £24.00. The seller might pay approximately 50 pence to eBay to list this collection as a standard item on the website. If the collection was sold then the seller would pay 5% of the final sale price to the company.

Since buyers pay sellers before they receive items the business model runs on trust. The eBay feedback system is used to indicate problems with particular users. Users can file feedback about any user on the feedback site. This discourages trade with rogue participants. The only costs to eBay therefore amount to the costs of computing infrastructure and expenses associated with customer services. eBay keeps no inventory, has no distribution network and does not have to maintain a large amount of staffing to make the company viable.

Most of eBay's sellers were serious collectors and small traders who used eBay as their shop-front. eBay enabled them to access a global marketplace for trading of collectibles. For such a community eBay set up the eBay Café. This comprised a chat room where users of the site could communicate and exchange information. Such a facility proved useful to the company in being able to monitor customer reaction to various company initiatives. For instance, changes in pricing were frequently adversely commented on in such fora. eBay also used its customers to post answers to frequently answered questions (FAQs) on its bulletin boards and even employed some active and knowledgeable users of its site to provide email help to its new customers.

In an attempt to develop trust and loyalty amongst its customer community eBay established SafeHarbour in February 1998. SafeHarbour offered certain verification and validation of customers, insurance associated with the selling and buying process and certain regulation of sales activity. The company also created My eBay, a tool that customers could use to personalise the site in terms of keeping track of their favourite categories, view items they were selling or bidding on or check their account balance.

Following a number of outages in 1999 the company decided to outsource its backend infrastructure to an external supplier. It outsourced its web servers, database servers and routers to these companies with the expectation of having excess capacity for preserving its service. Hence, periodic overhaul of the technical infrastructure of the company is critical to its success.

Reflection points

- Consider the issue of trust in relation to eCommerce transactions and how eBay attempts to build trust with its customers.
- How are electronic payments managed within eBay?
- Examine the issue of auction types. Try to identify the model for electronic auctions applied in eBay.
- Can eBay be considered a serious eProcurement hub?
- Investigate other ways of running auctions and search for any sites that run alternative auction models.
- eBay has been successfully sued by a number of companies for allowing traders to offer fake versions of their products through the website. Are problems with the trade in fake goods through eBay affecting eBay's long-term business model?

Reference

Cohen, A. (2002). *The Perfect Store: Inside eBay*, Little, Brown and Co, New York.

eBooks

Case description

The book is one of the most remarkable inventions of mankind and the format of this artefact has changed relatively little since Gutenberg produced his bible in 1450. For hundreds of years it has consisted of a collection of sheets, made of paper, parchment or some other material on which are printed various media such as text and illustrations. Usually the pages are bound together at one side to enable convenient access. ICT has impacted the book industry in various ways over the past few decades. Authors now typically produce content using software tools such as word-processors. The publisher then formats the book using other software tools such as publishing software and transfers this onto the physical page using printing technology heavily supported by ICT. More recently ICT in various forms has also affected both the way in which books are distributed as well as the ways in which books are consumed. This change is generally referred to as the electronic book or the eBook. Some see the eBook as overtaking what they refer to as the 'legacy media' of the printed book.

eBooks rely on the publishing of books in some digital format and the distribution of such books through various electronic intermediaries. Such books are accessed by consumers from such intermediaries and consumed with the aid of various forms of access device such as personal computers. Some specialist devices, known collectively as eBook readers or eReaders, have grown in popularity as an access device to this type of content. More recently tablet computers such as the Apple iPad have also been used as an access device for eBooks. Some eBooks distribute free through outlets such as Google books or project Gutenberg. Conventional publishers are experimenting with many other forms of charging model for distribution of eBooks, particularly for new books in digital format.

Specialist eReaders

It is possible to speak of at least three generations of specialist eReader. The first wave of these devices consisted of first entrants that were generally regarded as being difficult to find, buy and use to read eBooks. For instance, SoftBook Press offered the first commercial eReader in 1997 and the unit weighed over three pounds and cost $599. The second generation of eReaders were more consumer-friendly in generally being lighter, cheaper and easier to use. Sony, for instance, launched its ebook reader – the PRS 500 – in 2006 and Barnes and Noble also offered an eReader called the Nook. This second generation technology generally demanded that the user select and download titles to their PC and then transfer them to their eReader. The latest or third generation of eReaders enables the user to select and download titles direct to the eReader using wireless networks. One of the most prominent of these is Amazon's Kindle.

Amazon launched the Kindle in November 2007, the name being devised to suggest the 'crackling ignition of knowledge'. This early device, which measured approximately six inches on the diagonal, had a four-level grey-scale display and an internal memory of 250MB. It also used technology from e-ink corporation which purportedly greatly improved the eReading experience. This first generation Kindle allowed something like 250 titles to be stored on the device at any one time and viewed without the need for backlighting of the image. The device was also innovative in allowing users to download titles wirelessly direct to the device. The hardware retailed initially at $399. A few hours after its launch, the device was sold out, and remained out of stock until April 2008.

The Kindle 2 was launched in February 2009 and included an expanded memory to store up to 1200 titles and an enhanced battery life. Three months later yet another version – the Kindle DX – launched which included a 9.7-inch screen and larger memory allowing around 3500 books to be stored on the device. Amazon maintains an electronic book store of hundreds of thousands of titles that can be downloaded direct to the device through a proprietary wireless network known as Whispernet. The kindle uses proprietary formatting and digital rights management technology that limits eBook reading to the Kindle device.

The predicted next battleground in this hardware market will be eBook readers that handle colour. In September 2011 Amazon launched the Kindle Fire – this not only offers colour presentation of book content but most of the features offered on the iPad. Such convergent devices mean that eventually stereo audio and full-frame video may be incorporated into books, challenging the concept of the book itself as being purely an artefact made up of textual, graphical and image content. There is also a growing range of competition to eReaders from software-based devices that allow users to view books on other devices such as smart phones. Not surprisingly, some have spoken of eBooks as saving the publishing industry. Others have predicted the death of the high-street bookshop because of the growing adoption of eReaders.

Palgrave

Palgrave Macmillan are a major academic publisher delivering material in print and, more recently, digital formats. The company was formed in 2000 through the merger of St. Martin's Press Scholarly and Reference (US) and Macmillan Press (UK). In 2002 it became Palgrave Macmillan when it reacquired rights to use the Macmillan name internationally. The company focuses mainly on publishing work in the Humanities, the Social Sciences and Business and offers this content in four main ways: as textbooks for higher education, books for the professional market, scholarly and reference works (such as monographs and conference publications) and through a number of academic journals.

Palgrave Macmillan publish a growing range of its material as ebooks. The company began experimenting with eBook provision in the early years of the century. Since this time it has taken the strategy of releasing a portion of its catalogue as ebooks in a controlled manner. The eBook programme primarily consists of books from the company's Scholarly and Reference team, which have libraries as their main market, and by 2009 scholarly titles were released in both print and digital formats as a default, unless electronic publishing rights were unavailable for some reason. Books are provided as PDF files both via library suppliers and via the company's own eBook platform: Palgrave Connect.

Palgrave Connect is a specially created platform which offers access to more than 10000 titles from the company's Scholarly and Reference division, back to 1990. Some 650 new scholarly ebooks are offered each year and the catalogue is updated monthly, with titles publishing simultaneously in print and digital formats. Both backlist and recent books are available to purchase for a one-time fee, this fee guaranteeing access in perpetuity to the content. Palgrave Connect offers institutions the opportunity to purchase a site license to Palgrave Macmillan's complete eBook collection or to any number of subject collections, including Business & Management, History, Literature & Performing Arts, Religion & Philosophy, Economics & Finance, Language & Linguistics, Political & International Studies, Social & Cultural Studies. On Palgrave Connect, titles have no technical digital rights management (DRM) constraints, and many are also available in ePub format. Many of the Scholarly and Reference eBooks are also available from other suppliers, including Amazon, Dawson, Ebooks.com, Ebrary, Gardners, Myilibrary, Netlibrary, Waterstones.

To support the delivery of eBooks, a strategic development team has been established at Palgrave Macmillan consisting of business analysts and project managers. This team is broadly tasked with developing strategy for eBook publishing, and with investigating and supplying different routes to market.

Palgrave Macmillan currently offer a more limited selection of textbooks as eBooks. There are a number of reasons why the strategy is different for textbooks than for scholarly and reference works. First, there appears to be less demand from students to have textbooks as eBooks than for research monographs to be available electronically, particularly in areas such as mathematics in which students value the ability to annotate a physical copy. Second, direct sale of textbooks as eBooks to individuals increases the potential for digital piracy (illegal distribution of copies of such material) and the approaches and technologies in the area of digital rights management have yet to stabilise sufficiently for the company to decide on the most appropriate way forward. Third, some of the formats for eBooks required by eReaders are not suitable for the complex typesetting applied to many of the textbooks produced by the company. This means that conversion to these formats causes loss of many presentation features, such as those associated with illustrations and images. Most eReaders are currently limited in their ability to display effectively colour and complex illustrations. They are hence more suitable for content such as novels where colour and the use of illustrations are not normally necessary (although a growing range of tablet devices such as the Apple iPad and the Kindle Fire open up a growing range of possibilities). Fourth, eTextbooks throw up complex commercial questions for publishers, particularly when considering library relationships. The print business relies on lecturer recommendations for multiple sales year-on-year, while a digital library copy (if available for all students to access in perpetuity) would need a high price point to offset this risk – and that is not sustainable for many institutions. Finally, eBooks attract VAT within Europe – this is difficult to manage in relation to global distributors, and is a new cost to factor in (print books are exempt from VAT). VAT affects textbooks as well as monographs.

Because of these reasons, the strategic development team is working to identify appropriate outlets for their textbook content, including investigating what they refer to as 'born digital' products. 'Born digital' refers to products which do not necessarily come from a print book, but which have been created specifically for the digital environment. Producing content in this manner could mean the creation of flexible content similar in nature to a website. As such, the content would not be 'published' in one go but is likely to be continuously and dynamically updated.

However such an approach demands more investment than the traditional textbook. It is likely that this new way of delivering textbook content will require new models of production, with Palgrave Macmillan providing support to the author from project idea through to completion. It will also demand changes to both human resource and technical infrastructure in order to be successful. The skills of Palgrave Macmillan staff, and the means of managing and distributing book content will need to adapt to the new environment.

This approach has some obvious advantages for the consumer, such as access to more up-to-date textbooks with richer content. From the producer end this approach may also help to reduce digital piracy: when eBooks become available as flexible content that is continuously and dynamically updated then the incentives of pirating such content reduce. Depending upon demand the company might also be able to reduce pricing of such content by introducing levels of subscription to such content.

Reflection points

- As in the case of textbooks are certain other types of book likely to change significantly in eBook form?
- Will the widening availability of the eBook mean the death of the printed book over time?
- Will the idea of the bookshop as a physical outlet diminish because of the rise of the eBook?
- Academic publishers such as Palgrave Macmillan currently find it difficult to persuade academics to produce textbooks. Will eBooks make this more or less difficult?

Facebook.com

Case description

Facebook was launched in February 2004 as a social networking website by Mark Zuckerberg along with his fellow computer science students Eduardo Saverin, Dustin Moskovitz and Chris Hughes (Kirkpatrick, 2011). The name of the company is taken from the name applied to a book commonly given to university students within the United States at the start of the academic year.

All Facebook users have their own personal profile. A Facebook profile usually consists of a profile picture, contact information, lists of personal interests, photos, notes and other personal data. To this profile other users may be added as 'friends'. Facebook friends can interact in different ways: writing on profile walls, exchanging public or private messages or using a chat feature. They may also receive automatic notifications when one of the friends in their network updates their profile. An additional facility for Facebook users is the creation of public or private groups formed around common interests. Public and private organisations can maintain their own pages (the so-called like pages) as a form of advertising.

The entry requirement for all Facebook users is to have a user's name and a profile picture that can be viewed by all the other users. The extent to which a profile can be accessed by other Facebook members, however, can be controlled through a number of specific privacy settings. For example, all Facebook profiles have their own Wall – that is, a space on which Facebook users can write short messages and post hyperlinks; however, Facebook users can decide who can see (and write on) their wall, and who cannot. One of the most popular applications in Facebook is the *Photos* application, that allows Facebook users to upload and share albums and photos.

Originally, Facebook was intended as a social network for Harvard students only. The website was later expanded to other colleges in the Boston area, the Ivy League and Stanford University. Over time, students at other universities as well as high school students were gradually admitted to Facebook. Nowadays, membership is open to anyone aged 13 and over.

Facebook eventually became a company in the summer of 2004. The first president of the company was Sean Parker, the creator of Napster. At the same time Facebook moved its base of operations to Palo Alto, California. The domain name facebook.com was purchased in 2005 for $200,000. In October 2008 Facebook set up its international headquarters in Dublin, Ireland. Facebook now has over 3,200 employees and offices in many countries.

The majority of the company's revenue comes from advertising, with Microsoft being the company's exclusive partner for serving banner advertising. In September 2009 the company first began to make a profit. Companies can create a page on Facebook with the aim of getting members to 'like' their products or services. Clicking on the like button enables the company to add an advertisement not only to the member's page but all friends of this member.

In 2010 Facebook reshaped the way in which its users can interact introducing a new Facebook Messages service. This is a combination of text messaging, instant messaging (chat), emails and regular messages. In terms of privacy policies, Facebook Messages is very similar to the other Facebook services. In 2011 the company announced a timeline feature which allows members to build an online record of their life-history. Millions of websites now integrate with Facebook through social plug-ins that allows people to share things such as songs listened to or articles read with other Facebook users.

It was estimated that Facebook reached 500 million users in 2010 and had 845 million users as of early 2012 (Economist, 2012). This trajectory suggests that 1 billion users will be achieved in 2013. Facebook ranks as the most popular social networking site in several English-speaking countries, including Canada, the United Kingdom and the United States. However, it has failed to penetrate countries such as China.

In February 2012 the company announced an initial public offering in an attempt to raise $5 billion dollars for further investment. In 2011 the company generated $3.7 billion in revenue and $1 billion in net profits. Yet market analysts value the company as worth between $75 to $100 billion. This valuation is primarily based upon on its vast user-base and the data Facebook has about its user-base. It is hoped that the size and penetration of this social network will be a substantial platform for creating new business opportunity in areas such as social or s-commerce: the buying and selling of goods through social networking sites.

Some commentators caution that Facebook's strength is also a potential weakness and that the company will need to walk a tightrope over the next few years to strike the right balance (Economist, 2012). The key strength of the company is reliant on the network effect – the value that members gain from having access to a large social network. In return for the free service which Facebook provides users implicitly provide the company with masses of data about themselves. This data are very valuable as a platform for commercial services such as advertising. But users may feel that certain uses of such personal data invade their personal privacy. At such a point users may decide to switch away from the service, removing the key value that the company provides to the market.

Reflection points

- Several governments have tried to block or even ban Facebook – this has happened in the People's Republic of China, Vietnam, Iran, Uzbekistan, Pakistan, Syria and Bangladesh. Within certain Islamic states, claims have been raised that Facebook would include anti-Islamic content. Are sites such as Facebook a form of cultural imperialism?
- Sites such as Facebook are claimed to have played a major role in the organisation of political protest around the world, such as in the case of the Arab uprising in Egypt and elsewhere. Investigate the role of such sites in political activity worldwide.

- Many young persons now prefer to use Facebook messaging over other forms of communication such as email. What are the long-term consequences for email and what do users of Facebook lose when they use such messaging?
- Use of Facebook has been banned within many workplaces in an attempt to prevent time-wasting. But how does this gel with professional social networking sites such as LinkedIn?
- Difficulties of maintaining the privacy of content produced by Facebook users has been a continuing issue. The safety of user accounts has been compromised a number of times over the history of the site. Reflect upon this in terms of current thinking on data protection and data privacy.
- Some people have questioned the advertisement policy of Facebook. Should friends of a member who likes a company be advertised to by that company automatically?
- Facebook use has successfully moved onto mobile devices such as the smart-phone. What part does a growing range of such mobile devices play in the growth of the company? What part will Facebook play in mobile commerce in the near future?

References

Economist. (2012). A Fistful of Dollars. *The Economist*. 402. 8770. 9 February.

Economist. (2012). The Value of Friendship. *The Economist*. 402. 8770. 20–22 February.

Kirkpatrick, D. (2011). *The Facebook Effect: The Inside Story of the Company That is Connecting the World*, London, Virgin Books.

Google.com

Case description

In a sense although it developed merely as a search engine, Google, as a company is now the most prominent example of an information brokerage on the web. To *google* is becoming established as a verb in the English language and is becoming synonymous with searching for information on any particular topic. As such, the company is in an unprecedented position as a gatekeeper to information on the global scale.

Google Inc. is the most well-known of the companies specialising in internet search and online advertising (Vise, 2005). The company is based in Mountain View, California, employing many thousands of full-time workers. Google's mission statement is 'to organize the world's information and make it universally accessible and useful'.

Google was co-founded by Larry Page and Sergey Brin while they were students at Stanford University, US on the back of research they were conducting on improvement to the algorithms underlying search engines. Traditionally, search engines worked in terms of matching a series of search terms entered by the user against the terms found in web pages. The ranking of sites provided to the user was typically based on the number of times the searched-for terms exist in the pages of the site.

Page and Brin produced an algorithm called PageRank which analyses the links emanating from and pointing to web documents and then assigns a numerical weighting to each element of a set of such documents with the purpose of measuring each document's relative importance within the set. In this sense, the PageRank algorithm treats links in a similar manner to academic citations. Generally, the larger the number of citations of an academic paper the more important the paper is considered by the academic community.

Google uses web crawlers (also known as web spiders or web robots) to build and maintain its representation of links between web documents. A *Web Crawler* is a type of software agent, a program or automated script which browses the World Wide Web in a methodical, automated manner. Web crawlers are mainly used to create a copy of all the visited pages for later processing by a search engine that indexes the downloaded pages to provide fast searches for users.

Google is best known for its web search service, which now gives it a dominant market share of the search engine market. Google indexes billions of web pages through the process described above. Users search for web content through the use of keywords and logical operators such as NOT and AND. The search engine ranks hits on the basis of the number of links a page receives as well as the importance of the web documents sourcing the links.

The company was first created in 1998 and went public in 2004. Through a series of new product developments, acquisitions and partnerships, the company has expanded its initial search and advertising business into other areas, including web-based email, online mapping, office productivity and video sharing, among others. Google has also employed its search technology in other services, including

Image Search, Google News, the price comparison site Google Product Search, the interactive Usenet archive Google Groups and Google Maps.

As a value proposition, Google relies on the network effect: namely, that many people use its search engine to look for products and service. Google's application AdWords allows web advertisers to display advertisements alongside Google's search results and the Google Content Network, through either a cost-per-click or cost-per-view scheme. This means that the company generates most of its revenue by displaying advertisements from the AdWords service that is tailored to the content of the email messages displayed on screen. The service is attractive to advertisers because it allows them to tailor eMarketing campaigns to specific searches and user profiles. The related service, Google AdSense, is also a key revenue stream. This allows website owners to also display Google adverts on their own site, and earn money every time ads are clicked. Advertisers don't directly buy advertising space on Google. They bid on keywords associated with key terms and website content. The bidding occurs through an AdWords auction service. Hence, the more popular a keyword, the more money an advertiser has to pay for it.

In 2004, Google launched its own free web-based email service, known as Gmail, which provides the capability to use Google technology to search email. Google has also developed several applications for the desktop, the most well-known being Google Earth. This consists of an interactive mapping programme powered by satellite and aerial imagery that provides precision images of detail covering the vast majority of the planet. More recently, the application Picasa allows users to maintain an online photo album.

In an attempt to foster a culture of innovation Google encourages its employees to be creative. Personnel are allotted 20% of their time to pursue their own ideas. Several high visibility Google products such as Gmail and Google Earth emerged in this way. New ideas, at whatever stage of development are posted to the company's intranet, where they are evaluated and ranked by other personnel. Those ideas that collect the highest community ranking are pursued in more depth.

However Google's sometimes aggressive expansion strategy has sometimes met with controversy. For example, in January 2006 Google agreed to censor its search service within China. Google.cn was highly regulated by the Chinese authorities and restricted access to thousands of terms and sites. As an instance, the BBC news website was made unavailable and searches for the banned Falun Gong spiritual movement produced only articles denouncing it. In January 2010 Google threatened to stop its censoring of search results in China and even to shut down its site completely in the country. This was in response to apparent hacking attacks on the company's Gmail service, targeting Chinese human rights activists.

Google introduced an application known as Street View in May 2007. This is a feature of Google Maps and Google Earth that provides panoramic views from a row of positions along a street. In March 2009, the service was launched in the UK amongst much controversy. Civil liberty groups cited it as a potential invasion of privacy. A number of images were taken off the site after requests from various people and organisation. These included an image of Number 10 Downing street, an image showing some nude children playing in a garden, an image of a man drunk in the street and an image of a man leaving a sex shop.

In 2008 Google reached agreement with representatives of authors and publishers in the United States to make millions of books in America searchable online. Under the terms of the agreement, Google is free to digitise most books published in America, including those that are out of print. It then makes chunks of text available through its search engine, sells individual eBooks and offers libraries subscriptions to its entire database. Google keeps approximately one-third of resulting revenue and gives the rest to a book-rights registry that pays copyright holders.

In February 2010 Google launched a social networking service known as Buzz. This service is closely integrated with the company's email offering Gmail, allowing users of Gmail to easily create a social network from their email contacts. This is seen as a direct attempt to move into ground currently held by social networking sites such as Facebook.

Reflection points

- Concern has been expressed over the dominance of Google in both the search engine market and the wider information brokerage market. As a reaction Microsoft proposed an alliance with the search engine Yahoo!, which came to nothing. What difficulties might ensue if Google becomes the monopoly player in this market?
- For online businesses the issue of optimising chances of the company website being retrieved early in the list of hits by search engine's such as Google is critical to online orders. This area of search engine optimisation is a specialist component of website design. How important is this optimisation to electronic marketing?
- Google has come under fire for implicitly allowing censorship of web content for users of the search engine in countries such as China. How healthy for individuals and organisations is the reliance on Google as a dominant gatekeeper to web content?
- In its Google books application the company eventually intends to make all of the world's material published in English available in digital form. What are the pros and cons of this development?

Reference

Vise, D. A. (2005). *The Google Story*, Random House, New York.

IKEA

Case description

IKEA is a low-cost retailer of home furnishings that seeks to provide quality products to its customers. It achieves this in three ways. Firstly, it outsources costly processes such as production, as well as outsourcing final product assembly to the customer. This requires data relating to product specifications and assembly instructions to be carefully managed. Secondly, it engages in collaboration with suppliers to develop innovative design, production and distribution solutions. Thirdly, it encourages the analysis and redesign of business processes throughout the value-chain and the wider value-network to meet not only efficiency object-ives but also the company's declared strategy on corporate social responsibility. IKEA has a clearly defined business vision to which all its activities are aligned. It is founded on strong cultural values, and despite having stores worldwide, it makes minimal adaptation to accommodate local culture.

IKEA was founded by Ingvar Kamprad in 1943. The name IKEA is formed by the founder's initials (IK) followed by the first letter of the village and farm where he grew up Elmtaryd (E) and Agunnaryd (A). This reflects the identity of IKEA, embedded in the characteristics and values of the Swedish farming community. Ingvar Kamprad sold a range of products door-to-door and it was in 1948 that IKEA started selling furniture produced by local manufacturers in the forests in Sweden. In 1951, the first IKEA catalogue was published enabling furniture to be sold on a larger scale with the first retail furniture showroom opening in 1953 in Älmhult, Sweden. IKEA is reported to be the world's largest home furnishings retailer and currently has 231 retail stores in 24 countries.

IKEA's business strategy stems from its mission 'to create a better everyday life for the many people'. It has a clearly defined business idea 'to offer a wide range of well designed, functional home furnishing products at prices so low that as many people as possible will be able to afford them'. This informs and directs all business processes from product design and manufacture through to distribution and home assembly.

The IKEA range comprises 9500 products. The design process is rooted in the IKEA ethos and supports the business strategy by focusing on form, functionality and low price. Product design starts with an agreed selling price for the finished item. This influences the resources to be used in the product and requires consider-ation to be given to optimising manufacturing techniques. Consideration also has to be given to how the design and packaging of the product will impact warehous-ing, distribution and final assembly of the product. Product designers work closely with suppliers to find innovative cost-effective solutions to ensure that products are economical in their use of resources, recyclable and easy to transport.

IKEA has 45 trading officers in 31 countries which work with 1350 suppliers. Collection, processing and distribution of information are critical across the supply chain. Product Information Assistance (PIA) is one of IKEA's central ICT systems introduced in 1998. It runs on a series of databases which support the manage-ment of product information, product range structures, technical specifications and drawings. PIA is a key resource for business units both within IKEA and for its suppliers. It supports the main milestones in the project management of product development from requirements specification, through agreeing the technical specification with suppliers to making the product available for IKEA retail stores to order.

Product designers, manufacturers and technical experts regularly engage in face-to-face meetings working together to find ways of reducing costs. Meetings usually take place on the factory floor, reflecting IKEA's social values of respect, informality and equality. For example, a product developer was challenged to reduce the production costs of the LACK table, one of IKEA's bestselling products. The table veneer accounted for a third of the total production costs. The challenge was therefore to find a way of retaining the look and feel of the veneer for the consumer, whilst reducing production costs. This involved meetings with production managers and suppliers of different veneer and lacquering techniques. Working together, a technique for creating an artificial veneer was developed. Such innovative solutions have enabled the selling price of the LACK table to remain the same for over 20 years.

IKEA Components is a wholly owned division responsible for wholesale product distribution. It supplies raw materials for customers to build the furniture, the assembly kits needed for the flat-packed furniture and the packaging materials. Flat packed products enable cost-effective product distribution to the retail stores. Reducing the air being transported within product packaging is an important factor in reducing distribution costs.

It is reported that analysis and redesign of distribution processes against key performance indicators (KPI) has resulted in a 30% improvement of product availability, 85% reduction in customer claims due to damaged, incomplete or incorrect components and 30% reduction in product handling costs (Green, 2008).

In 1990, IKEA developed its environmental policy to ensure that the company and its co-workers take environmental responsibility for all activities conducted within its business. All suppliers are required to adhere to a code of conduct: the IKEA Way on Purchasing Home Furnishing Products (IWAY). This defines what suppliers can expect from IKEA and specifies what IKEA expects from its suppliers in terms of legal requirements, working conditions, active prevention of child labour, the external environment and forestry management.

IKEA's social responsibility is further demonstrated by its aim to reduce emissions of greenhouse gases generated through its operations by using renewable energy and by improving energy efficiency at its suppliers. It aims to improve the energy efficiency of all its stores by 25% and develop sustainable customer transportation to and from its stores.

The website *www.ikea.com* was launched in 1997. Three years later, customers in Sweden and Denmark were the first to be able to shop online with the store. The website seeks to convey the ethos underlying the IKEA experience. It includes a number of online planning tools to assist customers in improving their homes. The website also has an important role in cost reduction. Cost-effective customer support is provided by *Anna*, an automated customer service chat character driven by artificial intelligence. For example, if a customer finds that a part of the flat-pack they are assembling is missing, Anna will arrange for the part to be sent to them, or arrange for them to collect the part from their local store. It was reported that in 2006, Anna provided support to UK customers generating cost savings of 10 million euros. The 'ask Anna' facility is now part of the company's websites in other countries.

Reflection points

- IKEA is committed to addressing environmental issues and using sustainable resources. How can information systems and ICT contribute to improving the energy efficiency of its operations?
- Consider how the planning and development of information systems and ICT can be aligned with IKEA's business strategy. How can the strong cultural values of the company be reflected in its ICT infrastructure?
- Effective collaboration with suppliers to support product development is a key factor in IKEA's success. Consider the extent to which information systems and ICT can support collaboration, beyond the transactional processes of eBusiness.
- Innovation in product design, manufacture and distribution enables IKEA to achieve its vision. What opportunities are there for information systems and ICT to contribute to innovation within IKEA's value chain?
- Consider the roles and interactions between technology and activity systems in product development projects at IKEA.

Reference

Based on an earlier case written by Sharon Cox of Birmingham City University. www.ikea.com

Movie industry

Case description

A number of websites now offer thousands of the latest movies for download over the internet for as little as a couple of dollars. Such content can be downloaded onto personal computers and then burned to DVDs. It is also possible to download content to mobile devices such as iPads. The problem is that many such websites are pirate sites (Economist, 2008). The growing presence of such sites is symptomatic of changes that are impacting upon the entire movie industry. The movie industry has been comparatively slow to react to the potential offered by the web and the internet. However, business analysts predict that the movie industry is likely to undergo fundamental change over the next decade because of the way in which ICT changes fundamental business models within the sector.

Changes in the movie industry are all founded on the technological innovation of digital movie content. Such content is one example of the more encompassing phenomenon of digital convergence. The availability of technologies for managing movie content in digital form is leading to changes in the value network for this industry: the production, distribution and consumption of movies.

The conventional method of making a movie involves a sequence of three processes: pre-production, shooting and post-production. Pre-production involves activities such as establishing production schedules, establishing budgets, obtaining permits, hiring staff and purchasing equipment. Shooting involves the actual capture of images using filming on and off set. Post-production involves the editing of movie content including adding effects, music and other audio.

Production is normally a costly exercise because production staff, actors, studio space and equipment used is traditionally expensive. Filming certain scenes such as action and stunt scenes can prove very costly. For instance, Spiderman 3, the top box office taker in 2007, cost $258m to produce. In terms of production, the cost of producing movies potentially decreases with digital format. For instance, the equipment required to produce high-quality movie content in terms of capture and editing has decreased substantially. The use of computer generated imagery (CGI) has particularly reduced the costs of producing action and stunt scenes. This means that potentially barriers to entry are lowered to production in the movie industry.

Traditionally, distribution involves printing the film, shipping and marketing the film. These processes traditionally cost distribution companies many millions of dollars. The release of movie content is also tightly controlled in a windowing sequence of cinemas first, then DVD for rental and release to pay-per-view television channels, then DVD for purchase and finally release to broadcast television. The introduction of digital projection equipment into cinemas has been undertaken not only to improve the quality of the projection itself but also to reduce distribution costs. Digital content can be transmitted electronically to cinemas around the world for a fraction of physical distribution costs. Potential supply-chain savings of $2bn have been estimated in digital content submission to cinemas. The cost of storage of film in reels is also much reduced. However, the movie companies themselves have made heavy investment in digital projection equipment in cinemas. It is thus felt by the industry that this money needs to be recouped from the conventional delivery channels of cinema release before any new access channels are considered.

Successful films such as Spiderman 3 clearly allow the film industry to recoup such investment. Gross takings in the US alone for this film reached $336m and the film was shown to nearly 49m cinema goers. DVD sales reached 2.7m in the US by end of 2007 with sales revenue of $116m. However, the film industry point to a vast number of other films that made considerable losses.

The movement of movies onto digital format opened up new avenues for distribution of this content, particularly distribution via DVD. It is a short step to offering access to such content via electronic delivery channels over the internet. There is every reason to expect that consumers will want access to movie content online just as they access music, newspapers, television and radio currently. Some have argued that once the majority of people are able to easily buy or rent films on demand, the chances are they will pay for and watch more movie content.

Currently, however the content available from legal download sites is patchy. Hollywood has been slow to adopt new business models because of both the risk it takes in film production and in there being little incentive to move from a currently lucrative DVD market. However, some believe that DVD sales have reached their peak and that the movie industry will need to investigate new ways of making revenue. One key advantage of online distribution is that movie producers and distributors can release their whole back-catalogue of content for the consumer to access.

Some have argued the importance of new access channels to movie content. These include direct to home/movies on demand via conventional satellite/cable, online content downloading (video on demand, P2P sharing, IP television), content download to video devices, digital cinema. They also point to the potential that digital movie content has in providing an added-value service to the consumer such as increased interactivity and personalisation of such content. Some have estimated, perhaps conservatively, that the online digital movies segment constitutes 3% of all home movie entertainment revenues in 2011.

Others have raised the difficulties posed to the distribution of movie content over the internet particularly the increasing potential for digital piracy. Some reckon that digital piracy cost the film industry $858.5m in 2004 and that this rose to some $1.7in 2010. Currently, online piracy is seen to cost the movie industry less than physical copying of DVDs. However, the gap is seen to be diminishing and some see this trend undermining key revenue models for movie producers. It is even seen by some as possibly contributing to the demise of the movie industry as we know it.

The digital nature of movie content and the potential this has for opening up access channels is matched by potential for marketing such content. Movie companies have started experimenting with the release of snippets of movie content on social networking sites such as YouTube as a means of stimulating interest. For instance, the movie Iron Man was heavily promoted on YouTube. Some producers have even experimented with the use of such sites to allow possible consumers to

AQ2

engage in the design of the eventual content, such as in gaining feedback on the attractiveness of particular plot-lines. It is therefore no surprise to find big players in the movie value network investing in these new marketing channels. For instance, News Corporation which owns the major movie company Fox Interactive Media has bought MySpace as the perfect vehicle for Fox to promote its movies.

However, there are a number of technological constraints that are holding back the electronic delivery of movies. First, movie files are large. The typical size of low quality movie file is of the order of 750 MB. This means that the typical download time on a 2Mb/sec internet connection is 50 minutes; on a 8Mb/sec connection it is approximately 12 minutes. However, a DVD quality movie file consumes as much as 4 GB in storage. This means a download time on a 2Mb/s connection of the order of 4 hours or on a 8Mb/sec connection around 1 hour. Although the bandwidth in countries such as Korea and Japan has significantly improved beyond those found in countries such as those in Europe, there are major problems with rolling out higher bandwidth within these countries over the next few years. Second, most people want to watch movies on televisions rather than personal computers because of the wide screens, better audio and potential for high definition. Products that connect PCs and televisions are currently available but difficult to install and use. Hence, the technology is not domestic enough currently for widespread adoption. However, digital convergence has made possible the recent rollout of internet-enabled televisions that allow such access. Third, the lack of standards in the area of online digital movie content halts widespread uptake. For instance, each download site currently sells different usage rights. Attempts to develop common transportable standards are still on-going. Legal film downloads accounted for just $250m in 2009. The Digital Entertainment Content Ecosystem (DECE) that includes five of the six largest film studios (excepting Disney) agreed a common format for digital film and has named a single organisation to keep track of purchases. This is seen to be an attempt to prevent a dominant player in digital markets tying content to specific technologies, such as in the case of Apple with iTunes and Amazon with its eBook reader, the Kindle.

Commentary

Movies are modern examples of digital content and hence are classic intangible goods. This makes their transmission over a number of distinct access channels and to a range of difference access devices possible.

The case demonstrates the way in which ICT is starting to re-structure a major industry. Any technology has opportunities as well as threats for the industry. Technology adoption is likely to change business models because of the ways in which it affects the wider value network. The traditional value network in the movie industry consists of major film producers, major global distributors and mass consumers. The control of the content (value) along such a network has typically been heavily controlled. Movies are traditionally released at different times within cinema chains in different parts of the world first. They are then released onto DVD to the rental network. Finally, they are released for DVD sale. Traditional DVD rental occurred through physical rental stores. More recently online rental operations have emerged.

New channels of access include online downloading of movie content and video streaming of such content. Online access to movie content can be considered a form of dis-intermediation. Problems in upgrading the tele-communications infrastructure of particular nation states may hinder the rapid deployment and adoption of these access channels.

The high cost of DVDs has been traditionally rationalised in terms of the high costs associated with film production and the high risk of failure. Technology such as low-cost camera equipment and PC-based editing reduces the costs of movie production which means that barriers to entry to the production side of the industry are lowered.

Reflection points

- A key concern for the movie industry is how do they protect against digital piracy?
- Digital rights management is a key issue affecting many forms of digital content. How do the producers of such content get a return on their creative investment?
- Investigate the business model underlying online DVD rental. Is this business model sustainable long-term, particularly in the context of electronic delivery of movie content?

Reference

Economist (2008). Coming Soon. *The Economist* 85–87, February.

Music industry

Case description

The key change to the music industry is generally attributed to the creation of an application known as Napster. The software application Napster is an important example of the way in which ICT impacts economic structures in an established industry. In Porter's terms such applications have begun to affect the competitive structure of the music industry.

This technology was created by Shawn Fanning when he was a freshman student at the NorthEastern University in Boston, Massachusetts in the summer of 1999. It was initially produced as a fun application and Fanning originally released it to 15 fellow students swearing them not to release it to others (Menn, 2003). Effectively Napster is a software application that enables users to locate and share digital music in MP3 format. It combined features of existing programs such as search engines, file-sharing systems and instant messaging and is generally regarded as a pioneer in what has become known as P2P (peer-to-peer) internet software.

By August 2000 Napster had been used in a total of 6.7 million homes. By February 2001 Napster had 45 employees and by September 2002 it had 60 million devotees worldwide. Napster threatened the traditional value-chain and business model of the music industry. The music industry encompasses many music-related businesses and organisations and is dominated by the major record groups or labels. Each of these record groups consists of many smaller companies and labels serving different regions and markets.

The traditional business model operated by the music industry involves musical artists recording for a recording company who then mass produce and market the musical material on media such as compact disks (CDs). Such material is then sold by a number of retail outlets. The consumer has to purchase material from the retailer plus an appropriate means of playing the material such as a CD player. In this value network artists get paid royalties on the sale and use of their musical material and therefore get a return on their creative investment.

One of the most significant forms of intangible good to benefit from digitisation is therefore music. The digitisation of music is most readily associated with a file format known as MP3. Developed by the Fraunhofer Institute in Germany in 1992 MP3 stands for Motion Picture Experts Group-1 Level 3. This format employs an algorithm to compress a music file, achieving a significant reduction of data while retaining near CD-quality sound. This means that a three-minute song, which would normally require 32MB of disk space, can be compressed to 3MB without significant reduction in sound quality. Hence, using a standard 56K modem the song can be transmitted over the internet in a matter of a few minutes rather than the hours required if the file had not been compressed.

MP3 is not the only compression format available for digital music but it has become something of a de-facto standard. Its success is frequently attributed to the fact that it is open source and non-proprietary. The algorithm also employs an extremely efficient method of data compression. MP3 technology enables individuals to download and upload music to and from servers over the internet efficiently and effectively. Individuals can 'rip' (duplicate) MP3 files from CDs easily and can exchange such files using technology such as email or more sophisticated peer-to-peer applications. Hence, it is relatively easy for users to build virtual libraries of music and listen to it either from their hard drives on their PC or from a growing range of portable MP3 players.

The recording of music in digital form means that it can be produced and distributed at much lower cost. The convergence of access devices and communication channels around IP-based standards means that it can also be delivered over a wide variety of access channels. Hence, using MP3 and Napster individuals could by-pass recording companies and retailers. This is essentially a form of disintermediation in the customer chain on the music industry. Essentially Napster in its original form and similar offerings could be considered as a form of C2C eCommerce. Initially networks of enthusiasts used the application to share music at no cost.

Music can be quickly copied from CDs and stored as MP3 files. Such files can then be freely distributed around the internet using the Napster application. The music industry responded to digital music in general and Napster in particular on two fronts. First, the Recording Industry Association of America (RIAA) created the Secure Digital Music Initiative (SDMI). This was an industry group which attempted to create a secure form of digital music format. The intention was to attempt to prevent copying of digital music from CDs. Second, litigation was undertaken by various actors within the music industry which attempted to prove that the existence of Napster infringed US copyright law.

In 2002 Napster had to close down because of a judicial ruling in favour of the music industry. However, many P2P applications are still impacting sales of CD music. Napster was re-launched as a legally licensed download site in the US in 2003.

Apple Computer also launched its iTunes online music store in the same year. This stimulated the major record companies to begin to embrace digital downloading as the future of the music industry. Both Napster and iTunes, with the support of the major record labels are promoting digital music subscription as an attempt to reduce digital piracy.

Spotify is a Swedish company which was created in 2008 to offer streaming of Digitally Rights Managed music content from a set of major and independent recording companies. Users can register to listen to the music free, in which case they are targeted with visual and audio advertising. Alternatively, they pay a subscription using credit/debit cards or PayPal.

Reflection points

- Bands such as Metallica have fought back against peer-to-peer programs such as Napster. The issue of digital rights management is a controversial reaction to such trends.
- The introduction of digital downloading is likely to cause a fundamental change in the way music is consumed. It becomes a utility that flows to a consumer rather

than as a commodity that is bought one-by-one. Hence, music may well become purchased like other utilities such as water. People might have a meter for their music or people may pay for their monthly consumption of music. Are any of these things happening and how will it affect music production?

- On-going developments in the music industry have been proposed as a model for the future of other so-called content industries such as the movie industry. What are the similarities and differences between the movie and music industry in the respect?

Reference

Menn, J. (2003). *All the Rave: The Rise and Fall of Shawn Fanning's Napster*, New York, Crown Business.

MySpace.com

Case description

MySpace was founded in July 2003 by Tom Anderson, Chris DeWolfe and a small team of programmers. It was partially owned by Intermix Media, which was bought in July 2005 for $580m by Rupert Murdoch's News Corporation. MySpace is thus now a commercial operation that employs 300 staff. It has its headquarters in Santa Monica, California, USA, while its parent company is headquartered in New York. It describes itself as an 'online community that lets you meet your friends' friends'. It is pitched as a tool for creating or growing a private community or social network in which members can share content such as photos, journals and interests.

MySpace relies on the strength of the network effect. For instance, professional content producers such as musicians load content onto MySpace with the aim of attracting a larger potential consumer-base for their products. The attractiveness of MySpace lies in the size of its user network and the number of visits made to the site. Companies are interested in building upon this network effect and have also started using the site to promote their goods and services. The revenue model is driven by advertisements via the site. However, concerns have been expressed over the viability of this business model long-term.

To use MySpace you create a profile then invite persons to join your network. The profile can range from a simple list of preferences through to a comprehensive list of attributes, attitudes and opinions. The site also supports email and blogging as well as browsing other people's networks with the aim of inviting people to join your network. MySpace is home to various musicians, filmmakers, celebrities and comedians who upload songs, short films and other work directly onto their profile. These songs and films can also be embedded in other profiles, an interconnected-ness which adds to MySpace's appeal.

There are three main components of MySpace profiles: blurbs, blogs and multimedia, friend spaces and comments. Every profile contains two standard sections or 'blurbs': namely, 'About Me' and 'Who I'd Like to Meet'. Optional sections include an 'Interests' section and a 'Details' section. In addition, MySpace users can write their own blogs with standard fields for content, emotion and media. Another facility that MySpace supports is uploading images. Every user can choose one picture as the lead image on their profile. The site has also added the option to upload videos via the MySpace Videos service. The user's Friends Space contains a count of a user's friends, a 'Top Friends' area and a link to view all of the user's friends. Users can choose a certain number of friends to be displayed on their profile in the Top Friends area. By default a Comments section is placed below the User's Friends Space. Within this area, a user's friends may leave comments for all viewers to read. MySpace users have the option to delete any comment and/or require all comments to be approved before posting.

When YouTube was created in 2005, MySpace users very quickly started embedding YouTube videos in their profiles. This practice, however, was perceived as a competitive threat by MySpace, which was concurrently launching its own MySpace Videos service. The subsequent decision of MySpace to ban YouTube videos sparked widespread protest from MySpace users. In the end, MySpace re-enabled the feature shortly thereafter.

Reflection points

- Concerns have been expressed over data privacy issues involved with creating a user profile on MySpace. People posting personal details such as images of themselves, their job, address and telephone number can be used to enable identity fraud. Suggestions are that people's job prospects have also been compromised by material posted about themselves on MySpace. What details would you post on sites such as MySpace and what would you not post in relation to this problem?
- Concerns have been raised over the use of social networking sites for unacceptable behaviour. For instance, since users of MySpace can be as young as 14 concerns have been expressed over the use of the site by paedophiles wishing to 'groom' victims. Also, many schools and public libraries in the United States have restricted access to MySpace because they believe it has become a haven for malicious gossip particularly about teachers. Are social networking sites such as MySpace always likely to experience such problems?

Source

www.myspace.com

Tesco

Case description

History

Tesco PLC is an international grocery and general merchandising retail chain. Founded in the UK it is the largest British retailer and globally it is the third-largest retailer after Wal-Mart and Carrefour. Tesco now controls just over 30% of the grocery market in the UK. In 2007, the supermarket chain announced over £2.55bn in profits. Its declared mission is to 'create value for customers to earn their lifetime loyalty' and its declared strategy is based on offering a range of different types of stores, understanding its customers and treating its employees well.

The company originally specialised in food retail. It has now diversified into other retail areas such as discount clothes, consumer electronics, consumer financial services, selling and renting DVDs, compact discs and music downloads, internet service provision, consumer telecoms, consumer health insurance, consumer dental plans and budget software.

The name Tesco was introduced in 1924, when the founder of the company Jack Cohen bought a shipment of tea from T. E. Stockwell. The product was branded Tesco Tea, merging the first three letters of the supplier's name (TES), and the first two letters of Cohen's surname (CO). In 1929 Cohen opened the first Tesco store in Burnt Oak, Edgware, Middlesex; the first self-service store opened in St Albans less than 20 years later, in 1947, and the first supermarket store in 1956, in Maldon. Meanwhile, the company was floated on the London Stock Exchange in 1947, as Tesco Stores (Holdings) Limited.

The 1950s and the 1960s were years of growth for Tesco: by the end of this period, there were more than 800 Tesco stores. In 1973 Jack Cohen resigned and was replaced as Chairman by his son-in-law Leslie Porter. Porter and managing director Ian MacLaurin changed the strategy of the company from a 'pile it high sell it cheap' philosophy which had left the company stagnating and with a bad brand image. In 1977 Tesco abandoned offering the discount savings scheme, Green Shield stamps, to its customers and implemented price reductions and centralised buying for all its stores.

During the 1970s and 1980s the company continued its strategy of acquiring new stores through takeover of existing food retail chains. During the 1990s the company began diversifying in terms of its product range, its operating area and its delivery channels. Acquisition of Associated British Foods gave the company a major presence in Northern Ireland and the Republic of Ireland. A business alliance with the Esso Petroleum Company allowed the leasing of petrol stations under the Tesco Express format. Key developments in this period were the introduction of a loyalty card and an internet shopping service. Tesco was one of the first UK retailers to be able to make a profit out of online shopping.

This process of diversification and expansion continued during the early 2000s as Tesco started to become a major international food retailer. In October 2003 it launched a UK telecoms division, comprising mobile and home phone services, to complement its existing Internet Service Provider business.

In the UK, there are four major formats for Tesco stores, depending on size and the range of products sold. The largest stores are called Tesco Extra – they are usually located out-of-town and offer the complete range of tangible products. A smaller range of non-food goods is available in Tesco superstores, that can be described as standard large supermarkets, stocking mainly groceries. Tesco Express stores cater to the 'convenience' segment of the market (that is, small neighbourhood stores), while Tesco Metro stores are sized between Tesco superstores and Tesco Express stores and are mainly located in city or town centres.

Informatics infrastructure

Tesco uses ICT and information systems more generally in a number of ways within its business. The company chairman, Terry Leahy, claimed in 2007 that if the firm's ICT failed the firm would fail.

In terms of its customer chain, Tesco introduced its loyalty card for customers, 'which it refers to as clubcard' over a decade ago. To get such a loyalty card must supply a range of personal details to the company. The customer can then use the clubcard in all interactions with the company. Swiping the clubcard through the EFTPOS terminals at checkouts associates purchase of items against details held about the customer. For the customer regular use of the card accrues points which can be redeemed via a voucher scheme in discounting of goods. Eleven million loyalty card customers were reported in the UK in 2007. Capture of this data has become critical to company operation. Aggregation of this data in data warehouses allows the company to identify purchasing patterns and plan product and store operations accordingly (Hunt et al., 2006).

In common with most other large retailers, Tesco draws goods from suppliers into regional distribution centres, for preparation and onward delivery to stores. RFID technology is taking an increasing role in the distribution process.

Within the stores themselves the company's 'one in front' initiative, introduced in 1994, has been heavily reliant on ICT. The company uses thermal imaging technology to measure and predict customer's arrivals at checkouts. This enables store managers to ensure that the right number of checkouts are open for every customer to receive a one in front service.

In 2008 Tesco announced its intention to overhaul its ICT infrastructure. It planned to replace a number of separate voice and data networks with a single communication network, which was eventually outsourced to Cable and Wireless. It intends to use this network to standardise its key ICT systems in areas such as finance, human resources, payroll, in-store management, distribution and sales.

The intention is to manage these ICT systems centrally across the entire network from its ICT services centre in Bangalore, India. Informatics professionals based in particular countries of operation will supply only front-line support. This standardisation is built upon an earlier effort by the company initiated in 2005, known as 'Tesco in a box'. This was a programme of standardisation based upon an Oracle ERP system, which was implemented in all countries of operation.

The rollout of these standard ICT systems is seen as a key enabler for standard business processes and standard management information across the Tesco group.

This allows stores newly opened in Malaysia and Japan to operate and be managed in exactly the same way as a store in the UK.

B2C eCommerce

Tesco made its major push into B2C eCommerce with a strategic move into online grocery retail. The tesco.com domain name and associated website was formally launched in 2000. Soon afterwards, in July 2001, the company attempted to become involved in internet grocery retailing in the USA, when it obtained a 35% stake in GroceryWorks, a joint venture with the American Safeway Inc., operating in the United States and Canada. However, GroceryWorks did not expand as fast as initially expected and Tesco sold its stake to Safeway Inc in 2006.

Having said this Tesco now claims to be the world's largest online grocery retailer. Tesco is reported as having 45.1 per cent of the sales of online grocery sales followed by Sainsbury's (14.1%) and Asda (13.7%). Estimates of the percentage of online groceries within the British Grocery market has placed this as much as 5%, with a doubling of growth over the next five years. On 2010 as much as 13% of grocery shoppers are reported as shopping online for their groceries regularly.

In 2006 Tesco was reported as having picked up two-thirds of all online grocery orders in the UK and had over 750,00 regular users of its online grocery service, generating over 22,000 orders per week. This rose to 1 million active users in 2008 and a growth of 50% in online sales over the previous year. Internet sales were reported as contributing 4.2% of profits and 3.1% of overall sales. Tesco claimed in its 2005 annual report to be able to serve 98% of the UK population from its 300 participating stores. In the financial year ended 24 February 2007 it recorded online sales up 29.2% to £1.2 bn and profit up 48.5% to £83m, with over 250,000 orders per week.

Not surprisingly other online retailers have begun to look seriously at online grocery retail as a profitable market to explore. Amazon, for instance, announced in July of 2010 that it intended to compete with the major British supermarkets in offering online groceries. Of the available 22,000 products available to customers, 2,000 will be stocked in its normal warehouses such as in Swansea. The additional products will be delivered direct from other suppliers. However, established online grocery retailers such as Tesco have a two hour delivery window for their groceries. This might prove difficult for Amazon to compete with given its current business model.

Grocery sales made online through the website are available to customers for delivery within a defined range of selected stores. Goods for each customer are hand-picked from goods held within each store. This is in contrast to other business models which pick items from the warehouse. The pick-from-store model allows rapid expansion with limited investment, but has can lead to a high level of substitutions when stock becomes unavailable.

Through its website, Tesco now offers a wide range of other products, including electronic goods, books, broadband and financial services. The company uses a content management system to maintain the content on its website, restricting content production itself to a limited range of users. More recently, Tesco have introduced the option within a limited range of stores of customers picking up their crate of groceries from the store and thus deferring the delivery charge. Tesco launched its first home shopping catalogue in autumn 2006, as another channel for sales of its non-food ranges. This is integrated with the internet operation, with both channels being branded as Tesco Direct. Tesco has also launched an advertising campaign for its VoIP product, marketing the service to customers by offering free calls to all other Tesco internet phone customers.

Commentary

Organisation

From an institutional perspective Tesco would be considered in terms of a large multi-national company, producing goods and services and competing within a number of markets. We would also be interested in the strategy of the organisation and ways of designing its activities in areas such as its supermarket operations to improve its performance. This would lead us to examine the place of information in support of activities such as decision-making about what products to stock where.

Considered from an action perspective we would be interested in how employees of Tesco PLC perform their work. Hence, for instance we would be interested in the experience of working as a checkout person for the company. We would be interested in the established procedures for doing things such as operating checkouts, stocking shelves and receiving goods into the supermarket store. Some of the knowledge about how to do things will be formalised in the sense of being written down. Many other aspects of the everyday work of employees of the company will rely on tacit knowledge. We would also be interested in how such knowledge is communicated and how it is acquired.

System and environment

Tesco PLC can be considered in systems terms. As a food retailer the inputs to the organisation are the foodstuffs it receives from its suppliers. Outputs consist of foodstuffs sold on to customers. Its key transformation consists of those activity systems involved in supporting the sale of foodstuffs. These activity systems can be considered in a hierarchical fashion. Hence, the company will have systems of supply, supermarket operation and financial management that all contribute to the overall purpose of the organisation, which is making a profit for its shareholders.

The environment of the organisation consists of the retail industry generally and specifically supermarket retail. Within food retail in the UK the dominance of big supermarkets means that they have enormous power in determining pricing levels for key foodstuffs from their suppliers. However, the food retail industry is subject to quite heavy degrees of regulation in such areas as environmental health legislation. The food retail sector is still growing in the UK. In recent years the major supermarkets have increased their levels of technological deployment quite dramatically and have utilised their information systems in new areas such as financial services. The basis of competition has traditionally been on matters of pricing although other bases such as the quality of foodstuffs (particularly in relation to organic foodstuffs) have recently come into play.

Value-chain and value-network

The value produced by Tesco is primarily the sale of foodstuffs to customers. Its declared mission is to 'create value for customers to earn their lifetime loyalty'. Tesco introduced its loyalty card for customers a number of years ago. Value might therefore include the additional value services available to loyalty card customers such discounting of goods.

It is possible to consider the performance of Tesco in terms of the three Es of performance. Tesco efficacy measures are likely to include sales for product groups across different supermarkets. Efficiency measures are likely to include profit margins against product lines or measures of stock fulfilment against orders in warehouses. In terms of effectiveness measures might include the degree to which new customers are attracted to stores, old customers continue to come to their stores and the levels of satisfaction expressed by customers with the level of service they receive.

Consider a supermarket chain in terms of the concept of the value-chain. It is possible to map some of the key processes from the internal value-chain onto this type of business. Inbound logistics involves the management of the purchasing of foodstuffs and the distribution of foodstuffs to warehouses. The process of operations involves the unpacking of bulk deliveries and the presentation of foodstuffs on supermarket shelves. Outbound logistics involves the distribution of bulk foodstuffs from warehouses to supermarket stores. Marketing and sales involves the advertisement of product lines and the purchasing of foodstuffs from stores. After-sales service involves the handling of customer enquiries and complaints.

Tesco operates a number of information systems which contribute both to operational control through single-loop feedback and to strategic control through double-loop feedback. For instance, sales of products within their stores are recorded at checkouts and update information about stock levels in the service area of the store. This information triggers replenishment of products from stock held in the inventory area of the store. This is an example of operational control. Sales to loyalty card holders provide valuable information to the company which is used for determining which products to sell at which stores at which times of the year. This is an example of strategic control.

eBusiness and eCommerce

Tesco is what we would refer to as a clicks-and-mortar company. It is primarily a physical operation but it has an online service as well. Tesco has made eCommerce work successfully and integrated it with its core business.

Tesco as a food retailer has relationships with its customers and suppliers. Revenue flows into its value-chain from its customers and on to its suppliers. Customers are mainly attracted to supermarkets by a combination of low prices and a large variety of goods on offer. Supermarket chains typically sell large volumes of their products and hence their business strategy is typically one of low-cost/high-volume operations with typically low margins on each product. Costs are minimised in a number of ways such as buying in bulk from suppliers and letting customers bear the costs of selecting products from shelves, packing products and transporting such goods to their homes. The critical success factor for a supermarket chain is therefore attracting sufficient customers to its store. This means that location of stores is critical. Stores need to be placed within easy reach of a sufficient catchment area of willing customers.

The provision of an eCommerce site such as Tesco.com changes the business model of a supermarket chain. Relationships with customers and suppliers change, as do costs and revenue. For example, if a supermarket fulfils online orders by having a member of staff walk around the store and picking and packing goods followed by transportation to customer's homes using delivery vans then the costs of the operation can substantially increase. Hence, many supermarkets pass on this cost directly to the customer through a charge for delivery as does Tesco.

An alternative business model is to do away with stores entirely. Goods may then be stored in and delivered from low-cost warehouses. Hence, additional order fulfilment costs (picking, packing and transporting) can be balanced by lower operational costs (larger range, reduced inventory, larger volume, lower margins).

Technology clearly has had and continues to have impact on organisational practices. The introduction of bar-code scanners and electronic point-of-sale terminals at checkouts has rapidly improved throughput of customers. Tesco, like many other large retail companies, has also introduced automated self-service checkouts with the longer-term aim of reducing staffing cost. It is experimenting with the use of RFID tagging in its supply chain and intelligent trolleys in its stores.

Reflection points

- Supermarket chains such as Tesco have been criticised for the control they exercise over both their customer chain and their supply chain. Within food retail in the UK the dominance of big supermarkets means that they have enormous power in determining pricing levels for key foodstuffs from their suppliers. Criticism has also been voiced over the way in which companies such as Tesco have led to the decline in traditional smaller retail outlets on the high street. Examine this issue in greater detail.
- The food retail industry is subject to quite heavy degrees of regulation in such areas as environmental health legislation. This raises significant barriers of entry to the industry. How does Tesco's adoption of eBusiness act as a barrier to entry in such terms?
- The food retail sector is still growing in the UK. In recent years the major supermarkets have increased their levels of technological deployment quite dramatically and have utilised their information systems in new areas such as financial services. How successful has this strategy been and how reliant is it upon technology?
- The basis of competition has traditionally been on matters of pricing although other bases such as the quality of foodstuffs (particularly in relation to organic foodstuffs) have recently come into play. The value network in food retail shows signs of changing subtly. For instance, within the UK there has been significant growth in organic suppliers selling direct to customers through the web – a form of dis-intermediation. Is this a challenge to a major online grocery retailer such as Tesco?

- Tesco has used information systems in a number of ways to help build customer loyalty and retention. Through use of its loyalty card scheme the company captures a lot of information about the behaviour of its customers. Concerns have been raised over the potential dangers of using such transactional data and the questions it raises in areas of personal privacy. Examine the data stored on such cards and the uses to which they are put.

Reference

Hunt, T., C. Humby and T. Phillips (2006). *Scoring Points: How Tesco Continues to Win Customer Loyalty*, Kogan Page, London.

Twitter.com

Case description

Twitter is a website that was launched in July 2006 by Jack Dorsey. Dorsey came across the definition of the word 'twitter' as a 'a short burst of inconsequential information' and felt that this was a perfect description of the type of product that his company wanted to create. The website is based in San Francisco, California, but Twitter also has offices and servers in other US cities including San Antonio, Texas and Boston, Massachusetts.

Twitter is a social networking and micro-blogging website: Twitter users can write and read short text-based messages (up to 140 characters), the so-called tweets; these messages are shown on the user's profile page. By default, tweets are visible to all. However, users can change their privacy settings and restrict delivery of tweets to their followers – that is, those users who subscribe to a particular user's tweets. Twitter users can mention or reply to other users by using the @ sign. In addition, the use of hashtags (#) as a prefix allows Twitter users to group tweets together.

Users send and receive tweets as posts via the website, through external applications such as those available on smartphones or through the short message service (SMS). The messages were initially set to the 140-character limit for compatibility with SMS messaging. This caused users to use shorthand notations in tweets in a similar manner to that used within SMS texts. For this reason, the company is sometimes described as the 'SMS of the Internet'. It is estimated that Twitter has 190 million users, generating 65 million tweets a day and handling over 800,000 search queries per day.

In late 2010, Twitter began rolling out a new interface for the site with some additional aspects of functionality. Such functionality includes the ability to access images and videos by clicking on links embedded within individual tweets. Such links direct to content held on a variety of supported websites such as YouTube.

Twitter displays no advertising. Nonetheless, personal data about Twitter users are collected by the company. These data can be shared with third parties. This means that advertisers can target users analysing their tweets and may also quote tweets in ads directed specifically to the user.

Reflection points

- Twitter has suffered in the past from a number of security vulnerabilities causing a number of security breaches. What are the implications of this for data protection?
- Supporters of the site feel it is a good way to keep in touch with busy friends. Critics maintain that you can be 'too' connected and that following the day-to-day activities of persons described on Twitter is part of the increasing cult of celebrity in modern societies. In this sense, is tweeting or following tweets a good or bad thing?
- Companies have started using tweeting as a form of organisational communication. Examine the pros and cons of this technology for business communication.

UK electoral system

Case description

The UK is a parliamentary democracy and hence is reliant on an effective electoral system (Jones and Norton, 2010). General elections are held after Parliament has been dissolved either by Royal proclamation or because the maximum term of office of five years for a government has been reached. The decision as to when a general election is to be held is taken by the Prime Minister.

For parliamentary elections the UK is divided into 659 constituencies – 18 in Northern Ireland, 40 in Wales, 72 in Scotland and 529 in England. For so-called general elections to Parliament the UK currently employs a first-past-the-post system, sometimes described as a single member plurality system. In this system each voter uses a single poll card to cast a single ballot for one constituency candidate and each constituency elects a single MP on the basis of the majority of the votes cast. Each candidate in the general election generally represents a single political party and the party with the most seats in Parliament (not necessarily the most votes) will usually become the next government of the nation.

Figure C.1 comprises a system diagram of this electoral system. The key inputs into the electoral system are ballot poll cards and ballot papers provided by the key agents, voters. The key outputs are a set of election results provided for each constituency. The key control process is one of electoral monitoring, which establishes guidance on expected electoral practice and monitors the actual election to determine any deviation from such practice. The environment of the electoral system is the overall political system of the UK.

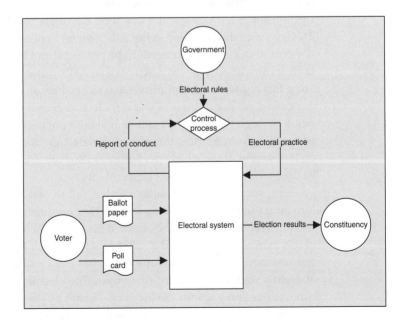

Figure C.1 The UK electoral system

One can argue that a number of emergent properties result from the UK employing this form of electoral system. Some of such properties may be viewed as advantages to the democratic system of the UK; some might be conceived of as disadvantages. The electoral system is relatively simple to implement, use and understand. The system generally provides a clear choice between two main political parties and tends to promote strong single-party governments with a coherent government opposition. A consequence of the system is that political parties tend to be broad churches of political opinion in order to satisfy the demands of various shades of the electorate. This means that the system tends to exclude not only extremist parties but also minorities from fair representation. It also means that party government can maintain in control in the face of a substantial drop in popular support. The electoral system is also susceptible to manipulation of electoral or constituency boundaries.

The British electoral system can be modelled as a highly data-intensive activity system. Interestingly the system has remained relatively unchanged since the ballot act of 1872 and hence relies on very little modern ICT. The key activities in the current system are as follows.

First, candidates and voters need to be registered. Candidates in a UK general election must be over 21 and must register for election for a given constituency. Voter registration used to be done only at set times during the year. Nowadays a person can register to vote at any time prior to the conduct of an election. To vote in a UK general election a person must be a citizen of the UK, be over the age of 18 and not excluded on grounds such as being detained in a psychiatric hospital or a member of House of Lords. Normally voters would be expected to attend in person at a specified polling booth to vote. If they are able to supply a valid reason a person may be entitled to appoint a proxy (some other person) to attend for them. Postal voting was introduced for the first time in the UK general election of 2001. In this election some 1.4m people out of a total electorate of 44m voted in this manner. This has more than doubled in the 2010 general election.

Second, an electoral list needs to be produced and ballot cards issued to voters. Each local authority in the UK is tasked with maintaining an electoral register. From this register each authority needs to produce an electoral list for each of the designated polling stations in its area. Electors receive various items of documentation through the post, the main item being a polling card detailing the name and address of the voter plus the date of the election and address of the designated polling station. Interestingly the poll card also contains a serial number, which can be used to track voters against electoral lists.

Third, voters need to be authenticated and to cast their votes. Voters typically turn up at their indicated polling station. They produce their poll card for inspection and this is checked against the electoral list. If the elector is correctly authenticated in this manner she is handed a ballot paper on which the list of candidates for the constituency is listed. To indicate that it has been issued appropriately a member of polling staff stamps each ballot paper. The elector enters a polling booth and chooses one entry against the list of candidates by placing an 'X' in an appropriate box. The ballot paper is then folded and posted in a sealed ballot box.

Fourth, votes are counted and results declared. Most elections in the UK are held during a weekday (typically a Thursday) and voters are allowed to vote only during the set period of 0700 to 2200 hours on that day. At the end of voting period all ballot boxes are collected and taken to a central counting centre. A team of workers then count the ballots by hand into piles of 50 by candidate. Recounts are normally only ordered if candidate totals are close. Only then the bundles are normally counted unless candidates request that bundles be checked.

Fifth, voting must be validated and results declared. Before announcing a result a constituency offer must confirm a true and proper election. To ensure this, the total number of persons crossed off against the electoral list is usually cross-checked against the total number of ballots cast for each ballot box/polling station. Assuming satisfactory validation, results are announced at each constituency counting centre and communicated to national electoral headquarters.

The activity of electing governments can be modelled as a system and all activity systems demonstrate equifinality. In this case this means that there is more than one way of organising an electoral system. Figure C.2 represents this institution as a sequence of activities. Activities are conducted with the support of much data. Any particular 'design' for a system of elections has emergent effects: some intended, some unintended.

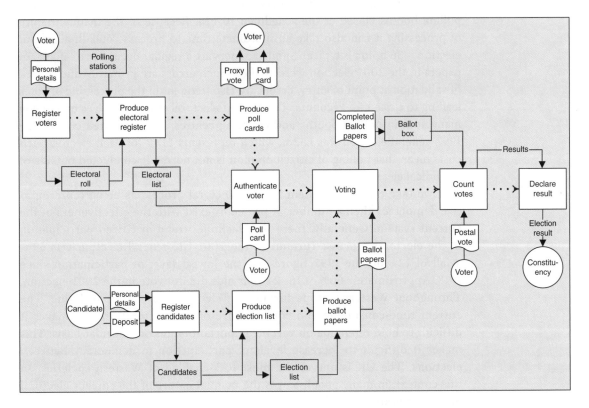

Figure C.2 Voting as an activity system

The performance of the current activity system

The activity system underlying the current approach to electoral voting in the UK experiences a number of problems, many of which are associated with the traditional way in which its associated information system is organised. It is possible to categorise these problems as issues of performance: of efficacy, efficiency and effectiveness.

If we take the key transformation of the electoral system to be the processing of votes a number of problems exist with the efficacy of the current system. Ensuring that a person is registered on one and only one register is a difficult process given social mobility. Ensuring that all persons are registered is even more difficult. It is estimated that as much as 9% of the UK population (3 million people) were not registered for the 2001 election. Frequently people are allowed to vote without an appropriate polling card. Supplying a valid name and address is frequently used as the only form of authentication. There is hence potential for fraudulent activity.

The requirement to visit a polling station during a set period frequently disadvantages certain groups such as the elderly, disabled and shift workers.

If we take the efficiency to be concerned with the balance of inputs to outputs, then the efficiency of the system can be seen to be problematic in a number of ways. Currently voting occurs only on week-days between 0700 and 2200. This can lead to queuing at peak periods at polling booths. During the 2010 election a number of people who queued to vote were denied their vote because the polling booths closed at the scheduled 10 PM. Because of the manual nature of processing it can also take an inordinate time to process votes in a general election – 36 hours is typical. Spoiled papers are a regular occurrence –0.26% of papers in the 2001 election were spoiled. Such errors are primarily due to lack of validation at point of entry. Errors are also frequent in the processing of votes leading to a need for recounts. The current electoral system involves employing many staff in polling booths and counting centres. The estimated cost of the 1997 general election was £52m, which represents £1.19 for each elector. Such costs mean that polling of citizen opinion is not normally conducted outside of periodical elections.

If we take the super-system for the electoral process as being representative democracy then a number of problems exist with the effectiveness of the current system. Generally, there is a declining trend of citizen participation in the electoral process. Turnout in the 2001 UK general election was 59%, a fall of 12% on the 1997 figure and the lowest level of participation since 1918. Approximately 60% of 18–24 year olds did not vote in the 2001 election. Throughout Western Europe turnouts at elections have been declining. The current time-consuming and costly nature of the electoral process makes it difficult to hold referenda on various important issues on a regular basis. This makes it difficult to increase levels of participation in democracy between elections. The UK is one of the most ICT-enabled of Western societies. In this context, in many people's eyes the manual nature of the current electoral process appears arcane.

Electronic voting

Like many other activity systems the UK electoral system is ripe for the application of ICT. Significant cost savings and other benefits might arise from automation of key aspects of the process. The information systems infrastructure supporting voting currently comprises an information system for registering people entitled to vote – the so-called electoral register. The current register is organised on constituency lines and each local authority is tasked with maintaining the register(s) in its area. The basic data held within the register comprises personal details of electors such as name, address and date of birth. From this data store an edited register is produced which may be sold on for commercial purposes. Most local authorities in the UK have instituted the Local Authorities Secure Electoral Register (LASER), which provides electronic electoral registers that are joined up, maintained and managed locally. Such registers will then be accessible on a national level to authorised users.

The problems with the current system of voting considered above have led many to propose the introduction of forms of eVoting. Figure C.3 illustrates how the voting system might be changed with the introduction of ICT infrastructure.

This ICT infrastructure presupposes that different stakeholders will interact with the infrastructure via given access devices running particular interfaces. For instance, consider the process of voting itself. This could be managed in a number

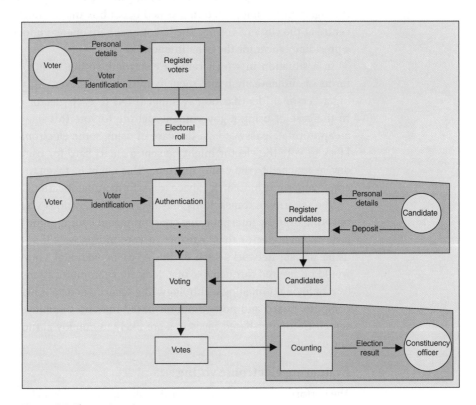

Figure C.3 Electronic voting system

of different ways. First, specialised electronic voting machines could be placed within polling booths. These might record votes as records locally and then transmit such records across public or private WANs after voting closes. Alternatively, specialised voting kiosks might be placed within public spaces such as libraries and supermarkets. Again, transfer of data may occur through physical transfer or over WANs. Voting might also occur from personal computers based in the home. Here the communication channel is likely to involve the use of modems and the public telephony network. Again, in the home, Interactive Digital Television might be used to cast votes. On the move, mobile devices such as WAP-enabled mobile phones might be used, the communication channel being the cellular radio network. Finally, commercial access devices such as lottery machines and ATM machines might be exploited. These devices are already hooked up to dedicate private WANs.

However, the concept of electronic democracy has been slow to take off because of concerns over authentication, data security, particularly data privacy and the potential of fraud. Authentication of electors in the current human activity system of voting consists of the production of a valid polling card by the elector. This is used to check-off elector details such as name and address against an electoral list by a polling officer. Security of voting transactions is assured through the following manual procedures. A line is drawn through the elector details on the electoral list to indicate that a ballot paper has been issued to the elector. The ballot paper is stamped to indicate that a polling officer has issued it and voting is undertaken in a booth under the supervision of the polling officer. Security of voting date is assured through votes being posted in a sealed ballot box that is transferred to a counting centre at the close of voting. The ballot boxes are opened under the supervision of a presiding officer for the constituency.

In a situation in which remote electronic voting is introduced various other forms of authentication and security must be employed. This might include posting a Personal Identification Number (PIN) to each elector on the electoral roll. In the case of using a government website to vote this may be accompanied by an appropriate password. In the case of using some electronic voting machine or kiosk to vote the elector might be sent a smart card for use in an authentication device attached to the voting machine. This might be taken to its logical extreme in employing some biometric device to perform authentication.

The security of transactions may be assured in various ways such as in the case of voting over the internet using encryption and issuing some form of digital certificate to each elector that registers to vote in this way. If voting were conducted using private networks such as the ATM or National Lottery network security would be assured through use of a dedicated communications network or possible by employing tunnelling technology. The security of data is likely to involve various computer-based and non-computer-based measures employed against the voting server. Computer-based measures are likely to employ authorisation control lists and use of firewalls.

Evaluating electronic voting

The performance of electronic voting will depend on the technologies involved and the changes made to the activity system. Let us assume that the UK government decides to implement a version of remote electronic voting providing the following access mechanisms to a remote voting server: personal computers from the home with internet access, WAP-enabled mobile devices, voting kiosks provided in public places such as libraries and supermarkets. Clearly the implementation of such a technical infrastructure will have a major impact on the activity system of electoral voting.

We may strategically assess some of the costs and benefits of such a change. Typical benefits might include a number of tangible cost savings such as a reduction in personnel needed to run polling stations and to count ballots. There is also likely to be a reduction in the number of spoilt ballots and a reduction in time taken to produce results. For instance, an extensive eVoting pilot during the 2002 local elections in St Albans produced a result within four minutes of the polls closing. The intangible benefit of increased convenience for the potential voter is also likely to result. Votes may be cast from any location in the UK or the World thus making it easier for groups such as the disabled, the elderly and overseas voters. Also, the period of voting might be extended to 24 hours or perhaps even a week.

On the downside, there are tangible costs associated with building and managing effective ICT infrastructure in support of such voting. Such costs would include the cost of producing suitable levels of authentication through such measures as PINs, passwords and smart cards, the cost of creating a secure back-end infrastructure for the collection and storage of votes on a national scale and ensuring availability of such infrastructure throughout the period of the election. Such costs will also include employing a suitable level of technical personnel support to operate and administer the technical infrastructure, and the associated cost of creating a secure front-end ICT system accessible from various access devices for the casting of votes.

In the short to medium term the costs of creating a suitable technical infrastructure for remote eVoting may outweigh the tangible benefits. This is particularly the case if the investment in specialised devices such as voting kiosks is made purely for general and local elections. Clearly if double-loop thinking is employed enabling a re-design of certain aspects of the democratic process then eVoting becomes a much more practicable option. For instance, if regular referenda/consultations are required for major policy-making then the importance of an effective technical infrastructure for voting becomes critical to the democratic process.

Reflection points

- Consider whether electronic voting will ever be introduced into a country such as the UK.
- Would the introduction of eVoting improve participation in democracy?
- Would regular referenda be feasible on the platform of eVoting?
- What effects would the introduction of eVoting have on the activity systems of democratic institutions?

Reference   Jones, B. and P. Norton (2010). *Politics UK*. Longman, Cambridge.

UK national identity card

Case description

In September of 2001 the UK Home Secretary, David Blunkett, was facing pressure to do something constructive to combat the threat of increased terrorism. He indicated that the introduction of identity cards was one of a series of measures that the government was considering in the wake of the terror attack on the US. But he acknowledged that there was a balancing act between increasing security and personal liberty. This led him to launch in 2002 a consultation process on the introduction of a proposed national identity token (Beynon-Davies, 2011).

Such an identity card had existed in the UK during the First and Second World Wars but was repealed in the 1950s. For various reasons, a number of Home Secretaries had proposed re-introducing such a card, but these intentions were met with continuous opposition from a range of different stakeholder groups. Like its predecessors, the introduction of a national identity card scheme into the UK did not have a smooth passage. Different stakeholders held differing perspectives as to what constituted the 'problem' and whether technologies for personal identity management were an appropriate solution to such problems. The UK government of the time and its agencies saw an identity card as a 'tool' contributing to the battle against terrorism, illegal working and identity fraud. Therefore, it created an Identity Cards Act and produced a strategic plan for an identity cards scheme. This scheme was intended to create a national identity management infrastructure for the UK. The law enforcement agencies and the private sector (particularly the financial institutions) were generally supportive of the government's intentions and were keen to use aspects of the identity infrastructure to help combat identity-related crime. The ICT sector generally saw significant work opportunities in the programme. They also relished the prospect that building the proposed infrastructure might provide for raising the skills profile of the UK in the area of personal identity management technologies.

However, there was significant opposition to the UK government's intentions on the part of a number of other stakeholder groups. Various civil liberty groups perceived the identity card as a major threat to data privacy and civic freedom. This was supported by the watchdog appointed by the UK government to control data protection (Information Commissioner). A report it commissioned particularly viewed the identity card as a symptom of increasing surveillance in UK society. Not surprisingly, opposition political parties in the UK during the period 2006–2010 indicated their intention to scrap the identity cards scheme if they came to power at the next general election. They promptly announced their intention to do so following their election victory in May 2010.

Following introduction of the idea in 2002, draft legislation was produced which described the intention to create a national identity management infrastructure for the UK. This draft legislation was consulted on for two years. In the original consultation document, what was then described as an 'entitlements card', was seen as having four main purposes. First, it was to provide people who are lawfully resident in the UK with a means of confirming their identity to a high degree of assurance.

Second, it was to establish for official purposes a person's identity so that there was one definitive record of an identity which all government departments could use, if they wished. Third, it was to help people gain entitlement to products and services provided by both the public and private sectors, particularly those who might find it difficult to so do at present. Fourth and finally, it was to help public and private sector organisations validate a person's identity, entitlement to products and services and eligibility to work in the UK.

UK government ministers particularly described the identity card as a weapon against identity theft and identity fraud. This was seen as a growing threat to the public and private sector and to be costing the economy many billions of pounds sterling per annum. Government ministers believed that an identity card, in association with associated processes of identification, would prove a significant weapon against criminals in areas such as preventing fraudulent benefit claims or the fraudulent use of the health service in the UK by non-residents – so-called health tourism. Related to this, the UK government maintained that an identity card would prove a critical tool in the fight against illegal immigration. It maintained that the UK's lack of an identity card acts as a magnet to illegal immigrants who believe that they can work and access state benefits with impunity. An identity card, it was claimed, would make it more difficult for employers to claim evidence of entitlement to work from a vast range of documentation currently used for this purpose.

Implicitly, many commentators suspected that the key rationale for the proposed introduction of the identity card was related to the attempt to combat terrorism following the events of 9/11. A major part of the public debate associated with the national identity card idea in the UK has, since its inception, been associated with benefits provided to security agencies such as MI5 in identifying and tracking suspects of terrorism. It has been particularly seen by such agencies as a way of better managing the cross-border flow of personal identity data. More recently, the identity card was discussed in terms of supporting the electronic government (eGovernment) and transformative government agenda in the UK. In government policy documentation, a clear relationship was drawn between citizenship, national identity and the possession of a personal identifier embodied in a national identity card. Possession of this card was therefore proposed as a 'key' to enrolment in a range of activities associated with citizenship such as work, social welfare, healthcare, taxation and voting. Not surprisingly, an effective and embedded national identity management infrastructure was expressed as having many potential benefits for both the citizen and for government organisations.

But UK Information Commissioner Richard Thomas was worried about the implications of identity cards and related technologies: the introduction of a National Identity Card within the UK was therefore not without its critics. Concerns were expressed by various groups including general civil liberty groups such as Liberty and groups specifically set up to combat the ID cards scheme such as NO2ID, established in 2004. Such groups bolstered their opposition to the scheme with key arguments focused on the technical complexity of the scheme and its associated cost. Also, considerable debate occurred over the data integration and data sharing potential of introducing such a card and the adverse consequences this may have for data protection, data privacy and infringement of civil liberties.

Opponents of its introduction argued that the considerable financial cost expended on the introduction of a national identity management infrastructure was excessive. Estimates by the UK government of the financial cost involved were initially of the order of £454m. However, this figure did not include the substantial costs to government itself of system development and integration. It also did not include the costs to public and private sector bodies which would have to adapt their information systems to meet the needs of a common national identifier. Hence, a revised figure of £3bn was mentioned as the total cost of introducing national identity cards in the original consultation document. However, the Identity Project at the London School of Economics claimed that even this figure substantially under-estimated the likely costs of the scheme. Evidence gradually began to support the claims of the group having produced this report in that the UK government continuously revised the costs of implementing the scheme upwards.

Concerns were also expressed over the potential insidious use of identity data in association with other data gathered about transactions the individual makes in everyday life such as telephone calls, bank credits and retail purchases. The increase in the capture and use of this transactional data has potentially negative effects. Personal identity data combined with historical and transactional data held about the individual would make it theoretically possible for government to build behavioural profiles of its citizenry.

The existence of a national identifier and the government information systems that may be built around it, therefore raised fears that potential future authoritarian governments in the UK might use it as a weapon of mass control. A national identifier would make it easier for government to build a profile of its citizens, and on this basis, government agencies could make decisions about awarding benefits, employing people or issuing fines. Hence, the existence of a national identity management infrastructure was criticised for its potential for data or function creep. Various civil liberties groups such as NO2ID claimed that what starts as an identity management infrastructure may end up as an all-purpose system for monitoring and controlling the UK population.

The rise of transactional data stored as digital records has brought to the fore the issue of ensuring the privacy of data held about an individual. Not surprisingly, a number of data protection concerns were raised in relation to the proposed national identity card. The UK government already holds a vast amount of personal data about citizens, whether it is health records, tax returns, welfare benefit forms, criminal records, local government records or driving license data. But the underlying principle remains that personal data supplied for one purpose are not used for another. In practice, this principle is enforced by maintaining separate data registers with separate personal identifiers for each government agency with which the citizen interacts.

The new purposes described in the draft legislation raised the possibility of the integration of diverse data-sets of personal data held by different government agencies around a common identifier. This raised fears amongst many pressure groups, particularly in relation to the potential for exercises in 'social sorting'. Concerns were also raised that a large central registry of personal identity data would prove extremely difficult to maintain. This raised questions of the consequences of inaccurate data held on the citizen. Also, if possession of an identity card is the only way of accessing public services then not having a card, if only temporarily, may cause appreciable exclusion of individuals from activity important to their economic and social well-being. For instance, people might be denied access to health services while they wait a replacement for a lost or stolen card. Access may also be compromised by temporary inaccuracies in personal data held such as a change of address or marital status.

As information systems become more and more a part of everyday economic, social and political activity, one would expect that the volume of criminal behaviour experienced in relation to such systems is likely to increase. One would also expect that various reactions would be made in the area of information security to counter this increase in technology-related crime. The value of access to a central registry of personal identity data is likely to be enormous for criminals and terrorists. Concerns were therefore raised over the importance but also the difficulties of securing such a large central register.

Some groups expressed the view that a national identity card could potentially contribute to an increase in identity-related crime rather than a reduction in this form of deviance. If an identity management infrastructure was not secure then it was suggested that its existence could actually lead to increased levels of fraudulent activity, as counterfeiting of cards would have greater potential benefits for criminals. The wider scope of use opened up by such a card would enable criminals at one stroke the possibility of multiple interactions with a vast range of public and possibly private sector organisations.

The claims made by the UK government of the time that a national identity card would prove a significant 'weapon' in managing identity issues associated with illegal immigration and working as well as terrorist activity were also questioned. For instance, the proposed correlation between the existence of national identity cards and the prevalence of terrorist activity was contested by many civil rights groups such as Liberty. They raised the case of Spain, which although having a National Identity card suffered terrorist attack.

David Cameron, the shadow leader of the House of Commons at the time, who became leader of the Conservative/Liberal Democrat coalition government in the UK in May 2010, remained unconvinced of the need for identity cards. Despite such opposition, a draft bill for an Identity Cards Act was first introduced through Parliament in the autumn of 2004. But this bill failed to reach its second reading before Parliament was dissolved for a general election in April 2005. A slightly revised second bill was therefore introduced to both houses of the UK Parliament in the autumn of 2005. Much debate ensued and a number of amendments to the Identity Cards Act were included in the final bill that became law on 30 March 2006.

The Identity Cards Act provided the legal framework required to establish a National Identity Register (NIR) and to issue identity cards to those on the register. The identity cards scheme envisaged issuing cards to every person registered as entitled to remain in the UK for longer than three months. This also included powers to designate existing forms of identity such as passports as documents with which the identity card would automatically be issued. Any person applying for a designated document would simultaneously need to apply for an identity card unless he or she already had one. However, individuals could choose to opt out of this arrangement until 1 January 2010. The act included powers to allow personal identity data to be captured and recorded. However, identity cards would have a limited validity depending on the category of individual. For instance, an elderly person might have an identity card issued for the rest of her life. In contrast, foreign European nationals who reside in the UK for less than three months but who regularly visit and work in the UK would have a much more limited period in which their identity card was deemed valid. The act made provision for biographical checks to be made against other databases to confirm an applicant's identity and guard against fraud. Such checks could also be made in relation to the issuing of British passports.

The NIR was conceived as holding core data about the individual such as name, residential address, date of birth, place of birth, sex, nationality and two or three forms of physical characteristics of the individual. Interestingly the act excluded the recording of any identifier on the register that would reveal sensitive personal data such as a Police National Computer reference number. However, the act provided for every person entered on the register to be assigned a unique number to be known as the National Identity Registration number. It also allowed storage of other 'personal reference numbers' such as a driver number or a national insurance number. Other information such as emergency contact details would be included only at the request of the person applying to be included on the register.

A personal identification number would be stored against the record of the individual in the NIR to allow verification against the register by individuals and organisations in service transactions. This included powers to link future access to specified public services with the production of an identity card and suitable checks against the NIR. This effectively established the possible use of the identity card as a way of gaining access to key public services.

Events in 2007 raised questions over the competence of government departments in the administration of personal data and in particular the efficacy of building a National Identity Register. In October 2007, for instance, the records of 25 million individuals dealt with by Her Majesty's Revenue and Customs in relation to the provision of child benefits were lost. Shortly after, a number of agencies such as the Driver and Vehicle Licensing Agency reported loss of substantial amounts of personal data. As a consequence, opposition leaders in the House of Commons at the time questioned the wisdom of the UK government going ahead with the National Identity Card scheme, given its proven difficulties in ensuring the privacy of citizen data.

Despite such continuing concern, the Identity Cards scheme continued. In late 2008 biometric visas in the form of smartcards started to be issued to students from outside the UK and to people with marriage visas. Opposition continued both within and outside Parliament. The Conservative and Liberal Democrat parties both indicated that they intended to scrap the identity cards scheme if they gained power. Following this, the NO2ID campaign suggested that the government would struggle to find private firms willing to bid for elements of the identity card scheme contract, since the expectation was that it would be cancelled by any new government administration. Two firms shortlisted to implement the NIR eventually withdrew from the competitive dialogue process with the UK Government.

In November of 2009 a trial scheme open to the public was launched in Greater Manchester. However, the crisis in public sector finances in the UK following the 'credit crunch' put the identity cards scheme at the forefront of discussion concerning public sector funding cuts. During the summer and autumn of 2009, discourse from central government did not directly mention any potential close-down of the scheme. However, government ministers, including the UK prime minister, indicated that forcing all UK citizens to purchase identity cards would not be part of future government policy.

In May of 2010 a Conservative/Liberal Democrat coalition government was formed following a general election. As part of the coalition's policy pledge the new Home Secretary Theresa May announced plans to introduce a bill (Identity Documents Bill) through the Houses of Parliament by September to scrap the identity card for UK citizens and its associated National Identity Register. So after over eight years of great effort and many millions of pounds in expenditure the UK National Identity cards scheme was abandoned. However, even though UK national identity card will not be implemented, the issues embedded within or arising from this case, particularly issues surrounding personal identity and its management, are likely to remain a significant part of the modern problematic for some time to come. There are many recent examples we could quote. For instance, in July 2008 the UK introduced an eBorders system allowing the transfer of passport data associated with journeys held by the airlines to the borders and immigrations service; the modern generation of mobile phones allow easy identification and tracking of individuals; in 2010 the majority of UK citizens thought they could be at greater risk of identity theft due to the impact of the global recession; the new Conservative/Liberal Democrat coalition plan in 2011 to resurrect plans to require internet service providers working in the UK to hand over envelope data of web and email communications undertaken by UK citizens to the security services.

Reflection points

- As the case of the UK national identity card demonstrates, much modern policy-making relies upon a technological dimension. Such policy-formation tends to be fluid not only in terms of competing claims about the nature and potentiality of the technology itself but also the uses to which it can or should be put. Reflect on the subtle ways in which the policy-space for the identity card scheme changed on the part of the UK government over the period 2002–2010.
- National identity cards exist across the globe. Such cards store different forms of data and are used in different ways in different countries. Some countries such as India have decided not to implement an identity card, only a unique number for each individual. Why do some countries have such cards and others not?
- Identity tokens are prevalent in other situations such as in support of financial transactions. How do such identity tokens relate to issues such as identity theft and identity fraud?

- Identity tokens are particularly used as ways of authenticating the individual. Reflect more widely on the issue of how do I normally establish who I claim to be in various walks of life? In what contexts do I need to establish my identity, and for what purpose? Do I use one or multiple identifiers for such purposes?
- There is an undoubted recent trend world-wide of introducing biometric identification into authentication processes. For instance, many passports internationally store forms of biometric identifier. Investigate which forms are used in which passports and consider why these particular forms of biometric identifier are chosen. Are biometrics necessarily fool proof?
- Document the sources of personal identity you carry around and which are needed to conduct your daily life. Why do such cards take the form that they do? How much data do these tokens disclose about yourself as an individual to organisations?

Reference

Beynon-Davies, P. (2011). The UK National Identity Card. *Journal of Information Technology (Teaching cases)* 1(1): 12–21.

UK revenue and customs

Case description

Large central government agencies such as the Inland Revenue have been subject to considerable computerisation, many such projects being financed by a mix of public and private sector investment. Some 4 million people work in local government, central government and public administrations such as the National Health Service in the UK. It is therefore not surprising to find much of the rhetoric surrounding the expected benefits of eGovernment within the UK to be focused around efficiency and effectiveness improvements associated with the re-organisation and re-deployment of staff supported by integrated ICT systems (Beynon-Davies, 2005).

In April 2000 the UK e-Government Strategic Framework was published requiring all central government departments to produce eBusiness strategies. These were intended to show how each department planned to implement eGovernment and to achieve electronic service delivery targets. The first draft was required in October 2000. From July 2001 departments were required to report progress against eBusiness strategies to the Office of the e-Envoy every six months. The Inland Revenue was until recently the UK government department responsible for collecting and administering taxation. This government department has attempted to be at the forefront of eGovernment in the UK by transforming its performance using ICT. This is evident in much of the strategic thinking emanating from the leadership within the organisation.

For instance, at this time the organisation indicated four indicators that it would use to determine how well it has transformed itself. First, the receipt of clean data from customers would allow the Inland Revenue to remove work that added little value to the organisation and consequently release people to work at the front line of customer care. Second, increasing the organisation's capability to deliver services electronically and increasing the take-up of such services by customers. Third, it intended to increase use of knowledge management so that its staff had better guidance which in turn enhanced its customer service capabilities. Finally, information and data management would enable it to progress towards the 'joined up government' vision of developing seamless, quality services and making best use of the data it receives.

The department set out its first eBusiness strategy in 2000. The key feature of the strategy at this time was the development of a number of access channels for different customer groups with clear incentives to encourage use of such channels. As part of this strategy the organisation intended to offer improved e-services to the UK taxpayer, thus reducing the burden of compliance on individuals and organisations. The revenue also planned use of intermediaries such as the National Association of Citizens Advice Bureau, the Post Office and software suppliers to provide bespoke services to the customers of the organisation. This transformation was predicated upon greater integration of its services with that of other departments and the provision of its services through commercial and government portals. It also required transformation of staff roles to focus around support for the customer through use of electronic tools.

In 2001 the Inland Revenue revised its strategy, keeping the fundamental principles above but making two additions: a transformation of the organisation around a focus on the customer and a philosophy based in customer relationship management, creating a technical framework that would deliver e-services in a modular but integrated fashion. Within this strategy, the Inland Revenue established three targets. First, that 50% of services would be available electronically by 31 December 2002. By this time the organisation aimed to offer basic secure e-services and have developed plans for organisational change based on such services. Second, it intended to have 50% take-up of its services by 2005. Third, all of its services would be available electronically by 31 December 2005. By this date the Inland Revenue aimed to have achieved significant business transformation with most customer transactions being conducted electronically.

However, subsequent to publication of the strategy, the Inland Revenue merged with Customs and Excise in 2006 to form Her Majesty's Revenue and Customs (HMRC). This was part of a wider attempt at improving the efficiency of UK government departments stimulated by a review of activity.

However, the newly formed HMRC soon came into the spotlight in 2007 for its failings in data management.

In October of 2007 a junior official from Her Majesty's Revenue and Customs based in Washington, Tyne and Wear sent two compact disks (CDs) containing government records to the National Audit Office (NAO) based in London. The data was requested by the NAO in order to enable them to run their own independent survey of child benefit payments. The disks were password-protected but the data was unencrypted. The package was sent unrecorded and un-registered using a courier company. The records on the disks contained the names, addresses, birth dates and national insurance numbers of all 25 million individuals dealt with by the HMRC in relation to child benefits. The records also contained details of partners, the names, sex and ages of couple's children as well as bank/savings account details for each claimant. This meant that details of 7.25 million bank accounts associated with families were stored on the disks.

The disks failed to arrive at the offices of the NAO and following notification of this a second package was sent by registered post and arrived safely. In November of 2007 senior managers at the HMRC were told that the first package had been lost. A week later the Prime Minister and other government ministers, most notably the Chancellor of the Exchequer were informed of the loss. Initially, government ministers were told that the CDs would probably be found but when HMRC searches for the lost disks failed the Metropolitan Police were called in to investigate.

This data loss led the Chancellor to consult with the Information Commissioner, the person responsible for overseeing the implementation of data protection in the UK, and they agreed that consultation with UK financial institutions was required. At the request of these financial institutions the public was not informed of the data loss for some days in order to allow these institutions to monitor potential suspicious activity. Banks and other financial institutions tracked transactions back to the date at which the data was lost in an attempt to identify suspicious activity.

As a consequence of this data incident the HRMC Chairman resigned and the Chancellor made an announcement to the House of Commons. It was claimed that a junior civil servant at the HMRC had broken *data security* procedures in downloading the data to disks and sending these via unrecorded postal delivery. The Chancellor reassured the public that the police had no reason to suspect the data had got into the 'wrong hands'. However, the public was urged to keep a close eye on their bank accounts for any unusual activity.

The possibility of criminals gaining access to the data and hence engaging in mass identity theft and identity fraud was raised in numerous quarters. This included not only criminals using data to gain access to existing bank accounts but also the possibility of such deviant groups using personal identity data to open new bank accounts or other financial products such as credit cards in the name of individuals. The issue of paedophile rings gaining access to the data on children and using such data for 'grooming' activities was also raised as a possibility.

A report into this incident was published in June 2008. The report concluded that the HMRC was woefully inadequate in its handling and managing of corporate data. It made a series of recommendations for tightening of data security and improving data management practices across UK government.

Reflection points

- Managing channels of access is a significant issue for eGovernment. How is this issue relevant to the current case?
- In what ways do you think strategy in this area for private sector organisations differs from that for public sector organisations?
- The case highlights the importance of good data security and data management for organisations. With increasing concern over identity theft and data privacy the reputation of organisations is increasingly reliant on good practices in this area. Investigate what the private sector is doing to ensure this.

References

Beynon-Davies, P. (2005). Constructing Electronic Government: The Case of the UK Inland Revenue. *International Journal of Information Management* 25(1): 3–20.

Jones, B. and P. Norton. (2010). *Politics UK*. 7th edn. Cambridge, Longman.

Wikipedia.org

Case description

Wikipedia is cited as the pre-eminent example of the use of Web 2.0 technologies in collaborative production. The content is user-generated by a network of authors around the world for no financial gain. It thus has similarities with the production of open source software. Wikipedia was created by Larry Sanger and Jimmy Wales and launched as an English language project on 15 January 2001 and is now operated by the not-for-profit Wikimedia Foundation (Poe, 2008). Wikipedia is a multi-lingual project which offers a free encyclopaedia on the World Wide Web: the name Wikipedia being a combination of the words wiki and encyclopaedia. Wikipedia uses a type of software called a wiki which handles the construction of shared content that can be updated using easy to use tools through a web browser.

Registered users of Wikipedia are able to create new articles. However, once an article is present on the site anyone with access to it can change its content and changes made to pages are instantly displayed. The consequence of this is that Wikipedia does not declare any of its articles to be complete or finished. This process of so-called collaborative content production is built upon the premise that collaboration among users will improve articles over time, in much the same way that open-source software develops. Some of Wikipedia's editors have compared this process to Darwinian evolutionary processes where the 'fitness' of content improves over time.

However, this collaborative content production model means that so-called vandalism and disagreements about content are common. Some take advantage of Wikipedia's openness to add nonsense to the encyclopaedia. Collaboration also sometimes leads to 'edit wars', which consist of prolonged disputes when editors do not agree.

Controversy has surrounded the project since its inception. Much criticism centres around the reliability and accuracy of the content on the site. Such content has been criticised for uneven quality and inconsistency, systemic bias and preference for consensus or popularity over credentials. The content of particular articles has been accused as being sometimes unconfirmed and questionable, lacking proper sources. The authors of articles need not have any expertise or qualifications in the subjects that they edit, and users are warned that their contributions may be edited mercilessly and redistributed at will by anyone who wishes to do so.

Interestingly, a 2005 comparison performed by the science journal *Nature* of sections of Wikipedia and the Encyclopædia Britannica found that the two were close in terms of the accuracy of their articles on the natural sciences. However, this study was challenged by Encyclopædia Britannica, who described it as fatally flawed.

It is argued that there is a battle for the future of Wikipedia. Inclusionists would like all to have access to making content on whatever people choose to add to the encyclopaedia. The ideal would be to have as many articles on as many subjects as its contributors are able to produce. Deletionists believe that Wikipedia is more likely to be successful if it maintains both a relevance and quality threshold for its content. This implies a certain level of editorial control over content. Currently deletionists have the upper hand. Decisions as to whether to keep or delete articles are made after deliberation by some 1000 or so of Wikipedia's most ardent contributors. If a member of this group believes that your article fails to meet notability criteria it may be nominated for immediate deletion or to be removed after five days if no one objects. Notability criteria consist of a host of ever-changing rules. For instance, in terms of citations articles in journals have a higher notability than an article in a newspaper, ten matches on Google is better than one match and so on. Not surprisingly, debates about the merit of articles can drag on for weeks.

Some believe that the governance bureaucracy surrounding collaborative production deters people from contributing to Wikipedia. This is because to ensure that an article survives authors have to make sure their article is deletion-proof. This raises the threshold for writing articles to a level which deters many.

Currently Wikipedia has more than 5m articles in many languages, including more than 1.4m in the English-language version. There are 250 language editions of Wikipedia, and 17 of them have more than 50,000 articles each. Wikipedia runs on a cluster of dedicated Linux servers located in Florida and four other locations around the world. It uses its in-house created software, known as MediaWiki, which is an open source wiki system written in PHP and built upon MySQL.

Reflection points

- The Wikimedia foundation relies upon donations for its continuous operation. Is this a sustainable business model?
- Academics generally discourage students from citing Wikipedia articles. Is this justified?
- In what sense is the collaborative production model of Wikipedia applicable to other domains? For instance, could you write a magazine in this way or even a textbook?

Reference

Poe, M. T. (2008). *Everyone Knows Everything: Wikipedia and the Globalization of Knowledge*, New York, Random House.

YouTube.com

Case description

Founded in February 2005, YouTube is a popular free video sharing website which lets users upload, view and share video clips. YouTube content is extremely diverse, ranging from movie, TV clips and music videos to amateur content such as video blogging. YouTube.com was founded by Chad Hurley, Steve Chen and Jawed Karim, who were all former employees of PayPal: a micro-payments provider. The birth of the website can be dated to 15 February 2005, when the domain name YouTube.com was activated; the website was developed over the following months. In August of 2005, Macromedia released FlashPlayer 8, which provided a large increase in video quality compared to FlashPlayer 7 and has a very small download size, decreasing download time. For the first time ever, users did not have to use a separate video player such as Windows Media Player or RealPlayer. Claims have been made that without the capabilities of Flashplayer 8, it is unlikely that YouTube would have grown as fast as it did in such a short time.

On 9 October 2006, it was announced that the company would be purchased by Google for US$1.65bn in stock. YouTube continues to operate independently, and the company's 67 employees and its co-founders continue working within the company. Before being bought by Google, YouTube stated that its business model is advertising-based. Industry commentators have speculated that YouTube's running costs may be as high as US$1m per month. This fuelled criticisms that the company, like many internet start-ups, did not have a viable business model. Advertisements were launched on the site beginning in March 2006. Given its traffic levels, video streams and page views, some have calculated that YouTube's potential revenues could be millions of dollars per month.

In March 2009 Youtube took the decision to block music videos to UK users of the site. This followed failure to reach agreement with the Performing Rights Society over a licensing arrangement. The Performing Rights Society collects royalties on behalf of a large number of music producers, many of which are small-scale. Google, which owns YouTube, apparently wanted to pay lower royalties to performers of such music. The Performing Rights Society was fighting this decision.

The presence of YouTube has stimulated a number of controversies. For instance, YouTube policy does not allow content to be uploaded by anyone not permitted by United States copyright law to do so. The company frequently removes uploaded content infringing such legislation. However, a large amount of copyrighted content continues to be uploaded. Generally, unless the copyright holder reports them, YouTube only discovers these videos via indications within the YouTube community through self-policing.

In June 2006, British media reported that YouTube and sites like it were encouraging violence and bullying amongst teenagers. Teenagers were filming so-called happy-slapping fights on their mobile phones and then uploading them to YouTube. While the site provides a function for reporting excessively violent videos, news reports stated that communication of such content with the company was difficult.

Reflection points

- YouTube is considered a pre-eminent example of a social networking site. It uses income from advertisements as its main revenue stream. How viable is this revenue model longer-term?
- What place does YouTube play in the eMarketing strategies of the major companies?
- How can sites like YouTube ensure that its content is ethical?

Bibliography

Ansoff, H. I. (1965). *Corporate Strategy*, New York, McGraw-Hill.

Avison, D. E. and B. Fitzgerald. (2006). *Information Systems Development: Methodologies, Techniques and Tools*. 4th edn. McGraw-Hill.

Barnes, S. J. (2002). The Mobile Commerce Value Chain: Analysis and Future Developments. *International Journal of Information Management* 22(1): 91–108.

Barrette, S. and B. R. Konsynski. (1982). Inter-Organisational Information Sharing Systems. *MIS Quarterly* 6(Fall): 93–105.

Baskerville, R., J. Pries-Heje and S. Madsen. (2010). Post-Agility: What Follows a Decade of Agility? *Information and Software Technology* 53(1): 543–555.

Berners-Lee, T. (1999). *Weaving the Web: The Past, Present and Future of the World Wide Web by Its Inventor*, London, Orion Business Publishing.

Beynon-Davies, P. (2004). *Database Systems*. 3rd edn. Houndmills, Basingstoke, Palgrave Macmillan.

Beynon-Davies, P. (2005). Constructing Electronic Government: The Case of the uk Inland Revenue. *International Journal of Information Management* 25(1): 3–20.

Beynon-Davies, P. (2007). Models for eGovernment. *Transforming Government: People, Process and Policy* 1(1): 1–24.

Beynon-Davies, P. (2009). *Business Information Systems*, Houndmills, Basingstoke, Palgrave Macmillan.

Beynon-Davies, P. (2010). eBusiness as a Driver for Regional Development. *Journal of Systems and Information Technology* 12(1): 17–36.

Beynon-Davies, P. (2011). *Significance: Exploring the Nature of Information, Systems and Technology*, Houndmills, Basingstoke, Palgrave Macmillan.

Beynon-Davies, P. (2011). The UK National Identity Card. *Journal of Information Technology (Teaching cases)* 1(1): 12–21.

Beynon-Davies, P., I. Owens and M. D. Williams (2004). IS Failure, Evaluation and Organisational Learning. *Journal of Enterprise Information Management (formerly Logistics and Information Management)* 17(4): 276–282.

Brandt, R. (2011). *One Click: Jeff Bezos and the Rise of Amazon.com*, London, Viking.

Bratton, J., M. Callinan, C. Forshaw and P. Sawchuk. (2010). *Work and Organisational Behaviour*. 2nd edn. Houndmills, Basingstoke, Palgrave Macmillan.

Cassidy, J. (2002). *Dot.Con*, London, Allen Lane/Penguin Press.

Chaffey, D., R. Mayer, K. Johnston and F. Ellis-Chadwick. (2009). *Internet Marketing*. 4th edn. Harlow, UK, Pearson Education.

Checkland, P. (1987). *Systems Thinking, Systems Practice*, Chichester, John Wiley.

Checkland, P. (1999). *Soft Systems Methodology: A Thirty Year Retrospective*, Chichester, John Wiley.

Christakis, N. and J. Fowler. (2010). *Connected: the Amazing Power of Social Networks and How They Shape Our Lives*, New York, Harper Press.

Coase, R. H. (1937). The Nature of the Firm. *Economica* 4(16): 386–405.

Cohen, A. (2002). *The Perfect Store: Inside eBay*, New York, Little, Brown and Co.

Cowhey, P. F. and J. D. Aronson. (2009). *Transforming Global Information and Communication Markets: The Political Economy of Innovation*, Cambridge, MA, MIT Press.

Curtin, G. C., M. H. Sommer and V. Vis-Sommer (2004). *The World of e-Government*, Haworth Press.

DAMA (2007). *DAMA-DMBOK Functional Framework*, Data Management Association.

Davenport, T. H. and L. Prusak. (2000). *Working Knowledge: How Organisations Manage What they Know*. 2nd edn. Boston, MA, Harvard Business School Press.

Dietz, J. L. G. (2006). *Enterprise Ontology: Theory and Methodology*, Berlin, Springer-Verlag.

Earl, M. J. (1989). *Management Strategies for Information Technology*, Hemel Hempstead, Prentice Hall.

Economist. (2008). Coming Soon. *The Economist*. 386. 8568. 85–87. February.

Economist. (2008). Nomads at Last: A Special Report on Mobility. *The Economist*. 75–76. 12 April.

Economist. (2012). a Fistful of Dollars. *The Economist*. 402. 8770. 9. February.

Economist. (2012). The Value of Friendship. *The Economist*. 402. 8770. 20–22. February.

Farrigton, B. and K. Lysons. (2012). *Purchasing and Supply Chain Management*, London, Financial Times/Prentice Hall.

Floridi, L. (2007). A Look into the Future Impact of ICT on Our Lives. *The Information Society* 23(1): 59–64.

Fountain, J. E. (2001). *Building the Virtual State: Information Technology and Instituional Change*, The Brookings Institution.

Gillenson, M. L. (1991). Database Administration at the Crossroads: The Era of End-User-Oriented, Decentralised Data Processing. *Journal of Database Administration* 2(4): 1–11.

Graham, I. (2006). *Business Rules Management and Service Oriented Architecture: A Pattern Language*, London, John Wiley.

Granovetter, M. (1973). The Strength of Weak Ties. *American Journal of Sociology* 78.

Hay, D. C. (1996). *Data Model Patterns: Conventions of Thought*, New York, Dorset House.

Holwell, S. and P. Checkland. (1998). *Information, Systems and Information Systems*, Chichester, UK, John Wiley.

Holzner, S. (2008). *How Dell Does It*, New York, McGraw-Hill Professional.

Hunt, T., C. Humby and T. Phillips. (2006). *Scoring Points: How Tesco Continues to Win Customer Loyalty*. 2nd edn. London, Kogan Page.

Jackson, M. C. (2003). *Systems Thinking: Creative Holism for Managers*, Chichester, John Wiley.

Johnson, G., K. Scholes and R. Whittington. (2007). *Exploring Corporate Strategy: Text and Cases*. 8th edn. Englewood-Cliffs, Prentice-Hall.

Jones, L. (2007). *easyJet: The Story of Britain's Biggest Low-Cost Airline*, London, Aurum Press.

Jones, B. and P. Norton. (2010). *Politics UK*. 7th edn. Cambridge, Longman.

Jones, P., E. Muir and P. Beynon-Davies. (2006). The Proposal of a Comparative Framework to Evaluate E-Business Stages of Growth Models. *International Journal of Information Technology and Management* 5(4): 249–266.

Kirkpatrick, D. (2011). *The Facebook Effect: The Real Inside Story of Mark Zuckerberg and the World's Fastest Growing Company: The Inside Story of the Company That is Connecting the World*, London, Virgin books.

Kraemer, K. L. and J. Dedrick. (2002). Strategic Use of the Internet and e-Commerce: Cisco Systems. *Journal of Strategic Information Systems* 11 (1): 5–29.

Laudon, K. C. and C. G. Traver. (2011). *E-Commerce 2011: Business, Technology and Society*. 7th edn. New York, Pearson Education.

Lenk, K. and R. Traunmuller. (2002). Preface to the Focus Theme On e-Government. *Electronic Markets* 12(3): 147–148.

Malinowski, B. (1922). *Argonauts of the Western Pacific: An Account of Native Enterprise and Adventure in the Archipelagoes of Western New Guinea*, London, Routledge Kegan Paul.

Malone, T. W., J. Yates and R. I. Benjamin. (1987). Electronic Markets and Electronic Hierarchies. 30(6): 484–497.

Martin, J. (1996). *Cybercorp*, New York, American Management Association.

Maslow, A. (1954). *Motivation and Personality*, Cambridge, MA, Harper and Row.

Menn, J. (2003). *All the Rave:Tthe Rise and Fall of Shawn Fanning's Napster*, New York, Crown Business.

Morgan, G. (1986). *Images of Organisation*, London, Sage.

Moritz, M. (2009). *Return to the Little Kingdom: Steve Jobs, the Creation of Apple, and How It Changed the World*, Oxford, Gerard Duckworth.

Nolan, R. L. (1990). Managing the Crisis in Data Processing. *The Information Infrastructure*. Cambridge, MA, Harvard Business Review.

O'Neill, M. G. (2010). *Green it: For Sustainable Business Practice*, Swindon, British Computer Society.

Osborne, D. and T. Gaebler. (1992). *Reinventing Government: How the Entrpreneurial Spirit Is Transforming the Public Sector*, Reading: MA, Addison-Wesley.

Osterwalder, A. and Y. Pigneur. (2010). *Business Model Generation*, Hoboken, New Jersey, John Wiley.

Paolini, C. (1999). *The Value Net: a Tool for Competitive Strategy*, Chichester, John Wiley.

Pierce, C. S. (1931). *Collected Papers*, Cambridge, Mass., Harvard University Press.

Pinker, S. (2001). *The Language Gene*, Harmondsworth, Middx, Penguin.

Poe, M. T. (2008). *Everyone Knows Everything: Wikipedia and the Globalization of Knowledge*, New York, Random House.

Porter, M. E. (1985). *Competitive Advantage: Creating and Sustaining Superior Performance*, New York, Free Press.

Porter, M. E. (1996). What Is Strategy? *Harvard Business Review* Nov–Dec: 59–78.

Porter, M. E. (2001). Strategy and the Internet. *Harvard Business Review* 79(3): 63–78.

Poster, M. (2006). *Information Please: Culture and Politics in the Age of Digital Machines*, New York, Duke University Press.

Putnam, R. D. (2000). *Bowling Alone: the Collapse and Revival of American Community*, New York, Simon and Schuster.

Rheingold, H. (1995). *The Virtual Community: Finding Connection in a Computerised World*, London, Minerva.

Sabherwal, R. and I. Becerra-Fernandez. (2011). *Business Intelligence*, New York, John Wiley.

Sauer, C. (1993). *Why Information Systems Fail: A Case Study Approach*, Henley-On-Thames, Alfred Waller.

Saunders, R. (2001). *Business the Amazon.com Way*, Oxford, John Wiley.

Sawhney, M. and D. Parikh. (2001). Where Value Lies in a Networked World. *Harvard Business Review* 79(1): 79–86.

Schneiderman, B., C. Plaisant, M. Cohen and S. Jacobs. (2009). *Designing the User Interface: Strategies for Effective Human-Computer Interaction*, New York, Pearson.

Searle, B. J. R. (1970). *Speech Acts: An Essay in the Philosophy of Language*, Cambridge, Cambridge University Press.

Searle, J. R. (2010). *Making the Social World: The Structure of Human Civilization*, Oxford, Oxford University Press.

Senge, P. M. (1990). *The Fifth Discipline: The Art and Practice of the Learning Organisation*, New York, Doubleday.

Shannon, C. E. (1949). *The Mathematical Theory of* Communication, Urbana, University of Illinois Press.

Stevens, D. and K. OHara, Eds. (2006). *Inequality.Com: Power, Poverty and the Digital Divide*, Oxford, Oneworld publications.

Stonier, T. (1994). Information as a Basic Property of the Universe. *Biosystems* 38(2): 135–140.

Tapscott, D. and A. D. Williams. (2006). *Wikinomics: How Mass Collaboration Changes Everything*, London, Atlantic Books.

Timmers, P. (1998). Business Models for Electronic Marketplaces. *Electronic Markets* 8(1): 3–8.

Tsitchizris, D. C. and F. H. Lochovsky. (1982). *Data Models*, Englewood-Cliffs, Prentice-Hall.

Vise, D. A. (2005). *The Google Story*, New York, Random House.

Ward, J. and J. Peppard. (2002). *Strategic Planning for Information Systems*. 3rd edn. Chichester, John Wiley.

Worthington, I. and C. Britton. (2009). *The Business Environment*, Harlow, UK, Pearson Education.

Glossary/Index

Term	Definition	Pages
Adjunct Community	An eCommunity fostered by some commercial operation.	11, 242, 318–319
After-Sales Service	A primary process in the internal value-chain. These are services that maintain or enhance product value by attempting to promote a continuing relationship with the customer of the company. It may involve such activities as the installation, testing, maintenance and repair of products.	26, 105, 127, 141, 196, 233, 331, 373
Amazon	The largest eTailer in the world.	118, 225–226, 233, 236–237, 241, 245–247, 285
Analysis	A phase of the development process involving requirements elicitation and requirements specification.	294
Apple	Apple is multi-national corporation that designs and markets consumer electronics, computer software and personal computers.	164, 267, 284–285, 333–334
ASDL	Asynchronous Digital Subscriber Line. A broadband communication channel for the local loop.	163, 166
Assertive	Communicative acts that explain how things are in a particular part of some universe of discourse.	49–50, 83, 88, 319
Auction	A form of commercial exchange involving bidding.	241, 245–246, 273
Authentication	The process of identifying some actor to a system.	204, 207, 380
Awareness	A pre-condition of electronic delivery. Stakeholders must be aware of the potential benefits of electronic delivery.	23, 200–201
B		
B2B	Business to business. See also *Supply Chain.*	4
B2B eCommerce	The use of eCommerce in the supply chain.	5, 26–29, 33, 35, 223–225, 238–241, 248, 255, 271, 285, 325
B2C	Business-to-customer/consumer. See also *Customer Chain.*	4
B2C eCommerce	The use of eCommerce in the customer chain.	27, 33, 35, 224, 226–227, 230, 233, 235–237, 241, 248, 255, 257, 264, 284, 294, 297, 301, 310, 325

Term	Definition	Pages
Cloud computing	Cloud computing is not one technology but a series of technologies including: client-server computing, software as a service, data centres and virtualisation.	184–185, 212, 330
Commissive	Communicative acts that commit a speaker to some future course of action such as promises, oaths and threats.	49–50, 83, 88
Communication Channel	The medium along which messages travel.	17, 32, 70, 154–161, 174, 185, 198, 321–322, 365, 382
Communication Subsystem	Layer of an IT system concerned with communications. That part of an ICT system enabling distribution of the processing around a network.	172
Communication Technology	Technology used for communication. This forms the inter-connective tissue of information technology. Communication networks between computing devices are essential elements of the modern ICT infrastructure of organisations.	186, 299, 317, 325
Community Chain	The community chain is based on informal social networks of individuals and is a major force underlying C2C e-Commerce.	14, 22, 26–27, 33, 108, 120, 223, 225, 241–242, 261, 275, 325
Comparator	A mechanism that compares signals from sensors with control inputs.	73, 76, 81, 90
Competitive Position	An organisation takes up a particular position in a market defined by its activities and relationships with its competitors, suppliers, customers and regulators.	117, 284
Competitor	A key type of organisational stakeholder. Key organisations in the same industrial sector or market that compete with an organisation.	284
Conception	A phase of the development process. Determining the costs and benefits associated with a proposed information system.	291–294, 296, 298, 299, 301, 307, 310
Construction	A phase of the development process. Traditionally ICT system construction involves the three related processes of programming, testing and documentation.	19, 195, 222, 291–294, 296, 298, 299, 303, 307, 310

Term	Definition	Pages
Consumer	An actor (individual, group, organisation) which consumes a good or service. See also *Customer*.	41, 62, 89, 99, 104, 106–107, 109, 111–112, 115, 118, 160, 184, 319, 321, 325
Content	Originally applied to web-based content, the term is now used for all digital content.	163, 171, 175, 257, 323, 354
Content Management	Content management is the organisational process that manages the maintenance of web-based material.	175, 289–291, 308, 310, 371
Contract	An agreement between actors which is enforceable in law.	22, 24, 112, 206–207, 213, 259, 273, 294, 301
Control	Control is the mechanism that implements regulation and/or adaptation in systems.	12, 22, 27, 29, 32, 41–45, 52, 67, 72–78, 81, 83, 87, 90, 113–119, 137–138, 173, 185, 202, 205, 225, 257–259, 287, 296–298, 304
Control Inputs	Special types of input to a control process that define levels of performance for some system.	12, 32, 73, 75–77, 81
Control Process	See *Control Subsystem*	
Control Sub-system	That subsystem which regulates the behaviour of a system it is monitoring. Also known as a control process or mechanism.	12, 69, 73, 74, 75, 76, 77, 78, 81, 114
Cookie	A data file placed on a user's machine by a web browser. Used by an organisation's ICT system to monitor interaction.	202
Copyright	Copyright law enables authors of an intellectual property to prevent unauthorised copying of such material. The law applies to physical transactions of written material regardless of its country of origin.	207, 209–210, 213, 267
Cost Advantage	An organisation strategy. This essentially aims to establish the organisation as a low-cost leader in the market.	284–286
Cost per acquisition	Cost per acquisition is a type of eMarketing revenue in which the advertiser pays for new acquisitions such as new customers, prospects or leads achieved through online adverts.	266

Term	Definition	Pages
D		
Data	Sets of symbols. See also *Forma*.	9, 52
Data Administration	Data administration is that function concerned with the management, planning and documentation of the data resource of some organisation.	289
Data element	A constituent part of a data structure.	20, 55–56, 85, 87, 146, 177, 181, 184
Data Flow	A data flow is a pipeline through which packets of data of known composition flow.	84–85, 114, 175
Data Format	A format for data typically consisting of data structures, data elements and data items.	191
Data item	A component of a data element.	55–56, 85, 87–88, 146, 177, 181–182
Data Management	The set of facilities needed to manage data.	16, 18, 31, 179, 181, 199, 289
Data Management Layer	See *Data Management Subsystem*	
Data Management Subsystem	That part of an *ICT system* concerned with data management.	19, 20, 172, 178–179, 186
Data Mining	The process of extracting previously unknown data from large databases and using it to make organisational decisions.	269–271
Data Model	An architecture for data.	19, 86–87, 90, 146, 180–181
Data Privacy	Ensuring the privacy of personal data.	202–203, 213, 244, 323
Data Protection	The activity of ensuring data privacy.	4, 23, 35, 185, 202–203
Data Store	A data store is a repository of data.	134–135, 138
Data structure	A structure of data that can be operated upon. A set of data elements.	11, 14, 18–20, 55–56, 85–87, 112, 146–147, 177, 180–181
Data Warehouse	A type of contemporary database system designed to fulfil decision-support needs. It utilises large amounts of data from diverse data needs to fulfil multi-dimensional query.	270
Data Warehousing	The process of building and managing data warehouses.	269
Database	An organised pool of logically related data.	18–20, 28, 86–87, 89, 174–175, 177

Term	Definition	Pages
Database Management System	A suite of computer software providing the interface between users and a *database* or databases.	179–180, 300
DBMS	See *Database Management System*	
Decision	Selecting an appropriate course of action in particular circumstances.	9, 47, 73, 79, 82, 87–88, 90
Decision Strategy	The strategy used by a comparator to arrive at a decision.	73, 75, 86
Decision-Making	The activity of deciding upon appropriate action.	3, 7, 9, 12, 14, 38, 41–45, 48, 52, 81, 87–89, 255, 261, 269–270, 310, 372
Declarative	Communicative acts that aim to change some aspect of a domain through the communication itself.	49–50, 83
Delete (formative act)	Removes the data structure from existence.	85, 146–147, 177
Dell	A US-based technology company that develops, manufactures, markets, sells, and supports personal computers, servers, data storage devices, network switches, software, televisions, computer peripherals and other technology-related products.	338–340
Demand Chain	See *Customer Chain*	107, 122
Design	A phase of the development process. Design is the process of planning a technical artefact to meet requirements established by analysis.	19, 79, 96, 117, 119, 126, 206, 247, 257, 287, 292, 294, 296, 298, 302–303, 307
Developer	See *Producer*	117, 179, 291, 294, 299
Development Information System	That information system designed to support the development process.	299, 310
Development Method	A specified approach for producing information systems.	299, 310
Development Organisation	That specialist form of organisation charged with producing some information system.	31, 297, 300
Development Process	That human activity system concerned with developing an information system.	291–292, 294–299, 304, 307, 310
Development Technique	That normally used to guide activity within one phase of the development process.	291–292, 299, 309–310

Term	Definition	Pages
eGovernment	The use of ICT to enable government processes.	24, 29, 258–263, 275, 322
EIS	See *Executive Information System*	
Electoral system (UK)	The system of voting used in the UK, particularly for parliamentary elections.	377–381
Electronic Delivery	A term used to encapsulate the delivery of services and certain products over communication networks.	13, 17, 23, 100, 106, 161, 196, 198, 199, 200–202, 226, 262, 264–265, 290, 321, 323–324
Electronic Government	See *eGovernment*	
Electronic Hierarchy	By an electronic hierarchy we mean one in which exchanges on a one-to-many basis are conducted using ICT.	27, 238, 240
Electronic Payment System	A system for the electronic transfer of monetary data.	231, 236, 274, 336
eMail	Electronic mail. The transmission and receipt of electronic text messages using communication networks.	141, 167, 169, 198, 202–203, 227–229, 232, 234, 243–244, 264–266, 303, 345
eMall	A collection of eShops.	235, 241
eMarket	An eMarket is a market in which economic exchanges are conducted using information technology and computer networks.	22
eMarketing	The process of planning and executing the conception, pricing, promotion and distribution of ideas, goods and services using electronic channels.	26, 28, 234, 263–268
Employee-Facing Information Systems	Front-end information systems used by employees.	128, 136, 143
eNabled Community	A traditional community supported by ICT.	242
Environment	Anything outside the organisation from which an organisation receives inputs and to which it passes outputs.	20, 194
eProcurement	A term used to refer to ICT-enablement of key supply chain activities.	26, 28–29, 235, 240, 262, 271, 273–274, 322
eShop	An eShop is a single firm selling their products or services online.	235, 239, 241
Executive Information System	That type of information system designed to support high-level, strategic decision-making in organisations.	137–138

Term	Definition	Pages
Expressive	Communicative acts that represent the speakers' psychological state, feelings or emotions towards some aspect of a domain.	49, 263
Extranet	Allowing access to aspects of an organisation's intranet to accredited users.	173–175, 225, 290

F

Term	Definition	Pages
Facebook	The dominant social networking site in the world.	8, 49, 243–244, 351–353, 356
Feedback	The way in which a control process adjusts the state of some system being monitored to maintain regulation or adaptation.	32, 76–78, 83, 293
Firewall	A collection of hardware and software placed between an organisation's internal network and an external network such as the internet.	174–175
Foreign key	An attribute or attributes within a table which cross-relate to data held in other tables within some database.	146, 182
Forma	Forma stands for the substance of a sign and concerns its physical representation as data.	8, 34, 41, 44–45, 53, 55–58, 60, 85–86, 146, 156, 158–159, 318
Formative act	Formative acts amount to the enactment of forma: acts of data representation and processing.	55, 60, 81, 83, 85, 90, 112, 146–148, 177, 182, 318, 319
Formative evaluation	That form of information systems evaluation concerned with monitoring the developing functionality and usability of some product.	297, 307
Formative pattern	A coherent collection of inter-related formative acts.	85
Formative system	An organised collection of formative patterns. See also *Activity System*.	
Fragmentation	A measure of the degree to which data and processing is fragmented amongst information systems.	246, 286–287
Front-End ICT Infrastructure	The organised collection of ICT systems interacting with key stakeholders.	169, 185, 198, 297, 300, 308, 383

Term	Definition	Pages
Front-End ICT System	An ICT system that supports a front-end information system.	297
Front-End Information System	An information system which interacts with internal or external stakeholders of the organisation.	128, 136–137, 145, 323
Front-End Information Systems Infrastructure	That part of the information systems infrastructure concerned with the core front-end information systems of the organisation.	238
Functionality	The functionality of an information system is what an information system does or should be able to do.	257, 291–295, 303–307, 322

G

Term	Definition	Pages
C2C eGovernment	Citizen-to-citizen eGovernment. Enablement of the community chain with eGovernment.	261
G2C eGovernment	Government-to-citizen eGovernment. The use of eGovernment in supporting relationships and activities between government and its citizens.	260–262
G2G eGovernment	Government-to–government eGovernment. The use of eGovernment in supporting relationships and activities between government agencies.	261–262
Globalisation	The process by which organisations are operating across the globe.	103, 190, 233, 285, 321
Goods	Tangible or intangible objects produced by organisations.	13–14, 21–22, 26–28, 33, 97–100, 104–108, 112–113, 325
Google	Google, as a company is now the most prominent example of an information brokerage on the web.	159, 212, 227, 266–267, 347, 354–356, 395–396
Green ICT	The use of ICT for sustainable business or the more sustainable use of ICT.	4, 24, 211

H

Term	Definition	Pages
Hierarchy	An important systems concept in which a system can be de-composed to form various levels of detail.	12, 29, 72–73, 96, 130, 146, 282
HM Revenue and Customs	The large UK government agency tasked not only with tax collection but managing customs.	262, 388, 391

Term	Definition	Pages
Impact	A pre-condition of electronic delivery. Use of remote access mechanisms must reach a critical threshold driving a virtuous cycle.	3, 20–24, 60–65, 100, 195, 199, 210, 212, 222, 244, 323
Implementation	A phase of the development process. Delivering an information system into its context of use.	5, 29, 223, 235, 291, 293–294, 298–299, 304, 306, 383
Inbound Logistics	A primary process in the internal value-chain involving the receipt and storage of raw materials and the distribution of such materials to manufacturing units.	46–47, 105, 134, 141–142, 146, 241, 288
Inconsistency	A measure of the degree to which data is treated differently in different ICT systems.	286–287
Informa	Informa relates to the meaning associated with a sign and concerns the interpretation of data as information.	8, 34, 38, 41, 44–45, 51, 56–58, 60, 65, 146, 318
Informatics Infrastructure	An informatics infrastructure consists of the sum total of information, information systems and information technology resources available to the organisation at any one time.	238, 247, 255–257, 262, 284, 286–287, 319, 321–324
Informatics Management	The management of information, information systems and ICT within organisations.	287, 289
Informatics Strategy	A definition of the structure within which information, information systems and information technology is to be applied in some organisation.	30, 268, 285–286
Information	See *Informa*.	
Information Infrastructure	This consists of definitions of information need and activities involved in the collection, storage, dissemination and use of information within the organisation	125, 144–145
Information Management	The management of the information resource of some organisation.	289–290
Information Model	An information model indicates the structure of information required by activities and processed within some information system for the purposes of business communication.	114

Term	Definition	Pages
Information Society	A term very loosely used to refer to the effect of ICT, information systems and information generally on modern society.	103, 167, 199–200, 202
Information System	A system of communication between people. Information systems are systems involved in the gathering, processing, distribution and use of information.	11, 82–83
Information System Model	A representation of an information system.	128, 144
Information Systems Infrastructure	The set of inter-related information systems used by some organisation. This consists of the information systems needed to support organisational activity in the areas of collection, storage, dissemination and use.	12, 125, 127–128, 131, 136, 138–139, 223, 238, 246–247, 381
Information Systems Strategy	That part of an informatics strategy concerned with specifying the future control of an information systems infrastructure and implementation of new elements of this infrastructure.	285
Informative act	Informative acts constitute the enactment of informa: acts of decision-making and communication involving message-making and interpretation.	41, 48–50, 60, 82–83, 318, 319
Informative pattern	A coherent collection of inter-related informative acts.	48, 50, 88
Informative system	An organised collection of informative patterns. See *Information System*.	
Input	The elements that a system takes from its environment.	18, 20, 30, 69, 73, 75, 80–81, 84, 86, 90, 99, 105, 127, 135, 138, 163, 173, 258, 291, 293
Intangible Goods	Goods that fundamentally can be represented as data and hence can be delivered to the customer electronically.	13, 99–100, 196, 198, 232, 362
Intangible Services	Services that fundamentally represent information services and hence can be delivered to the customer electronically.	100, 236
Intellectual Property Rights	A means of ensuring that creators are able to benefit from their intellectual accomplishments.	24, 206–207

Term	Definition	Pages
Intra-business eBusiness	The use of ICT to enable the internal business processes of the firm.	219, 222, 246, 336, 339
Intranet	The use of internet technology within a single organisation.	173–175, 238
IP Address	Internet Protocol Address. A unique identifier for the computers on a communications network using TCP/IP.	168–169, 208
ISDN	Integrated Service Digital Network. A broadband communication channel for the local loop.	166
Iterative Development	The style of development in which the activities of development cycle around the development of prototypes.	296

K

Term	Definition	Pages
Knowledge	Networked information. Knowledge is derived from information by integrating information with existing knowledge.	289–290
Knowledge Codification	The representation of knowledge for ease of retrieval.	290
Knowledge Creation	The acquisition of knowledge from organisational members and the creation of new organisational knowledge.	290
Knowledge Management	The management of organisational memory. Knowledge management consists of knowledge creation, knowledge codification and knowledge transfer.	289–290
Knowledge Management Systems	A group of information technologies used for managing knowledge within organisations.	305
Knowledge Transfer	The communication and sharing of knowledge amongst organisational members.	290

L

Term	Definition	Pages
LAN	See *Local Area Network*	
Linear Development	In this form of development the phases are strung out in a linear sequence with outputs from each phase triggering the start of the next phase.	295

Term	Definition	Pages
Local Area Network	A type of communication network in which the nodes of the network are situated relatively close together.	165, 168, 173
Local Loop	The communication channels between the local telephone exchange and the customer.	165–166

M

Term	Definition	Pages
Maintenance	A phase of the development process. Correcting errors in an information system and adapting an information system to changing circumstances.	172, 180, 235, 291–292
Management	A key control process for organisations.	29, 30–32, 52, 136, 138, 233, 287
Management Information System	A type of information system supporting the tactical decision-making of managers.	128, 132, 137–138, 142–143, 146, 222
Management-Facing Information Systems	Front-end information systems used by management. See also *Management Information System, Executive Information System*	136
Marketing and Sales	A primary process in the internal value-chain. Marketing is the process of planning and executing the conception, pricing, promotion and distribution of ideas, goods and services to create exchanges that satisfy individual and organisational goals. Sales is the associated activity involved in the management of purchasing activities of the customer.	105, 331, 373
Marketing Channel	A channel for the communication of marketing messages.	104, 263, 362
MIS	See *Management Information System*	
Mobile Commerce	The use of mobile access devices such as smartphones to conduct eCommerce.	29, 255
Mobile Device	A category of remote access devices including cellular telephones, laptop computers and personal digital assistants.	161, 164, 185, 257, 382–383
Modulation	A property of a communication channel. A communication signal is either modulated as digital or analogue.	155, 157

Term	Definition	Pages
Output	The elements that a system passes back to its environment.	13, 18, 20, 30, 69, 73, 75, 76, 80–81, 84, 86, 90, 96, 98, 135, 138, 140, 173, 258, 291, 296, 300
Outsourcing	The use of external organisations to produce, maintain or support the whole or a part of the informatics infrastructure.	185, 293, 298

P

Term	Definition	Pages
P2P eCommerce	The use of eCommerce in the partnership chain.	4, 26, 28, 33, 225, 246, 247, 325
Package Development	The style of development in which an organisation purchases a piece of software from a vendor organisation and frequently tailors it to organisational requirements.	294–295
Packet-Switched Network	A communications network which employs packet-switching protocols and technologies. Data are broken into individual packets which are disseminated over a communications network through the application of routers.	17, 167, 198
Partner	A key type of organisational stakeholder. Key organisations in the same industrial sector or market that participate in some partnership arrangement with an organisation.	4, 25, 28, 108, 116, 221, 301
Partner chain	The chain of relationships between an organisation and its partners.	14
Payroll Information System	That back-end information system dealing with the payment of employees of the organisation.	135–136
Performa	Performa relates to the use of the sign to facilitate coordinated activity or performance.	9, 38, 41, 44, 46, 57, 65, 78, 127, 318
Performance	The degree to which a system reaches specified levels.	9, 10, 12, 14, 16, 28, 31, 38, 40–41, 46–48, 50, 52, 73–82, 87, 90, 103, 112, 126, 128, 132, 138, 157, 194, 221–222, 259, 265, 271–272, 283, 287, 317, 321

Term	Definition	Pages
Producer	A key type of organisational stakeholder. Teams of developers that have to design, construct and maintain information systems for organisations.	27, 41, 109, 195–196, 212, 300–301
Production	That set of activities concerned with the creation of goods and services for human existence.	13, 21, 96, 106, 117, 195
Project management	The process of planning for, executing and controlling projects.	32, 297, 299, 307, 358
Prototyping	The development approach in which prototypes are produced.	296
Publish content	Publish content is one-way content. It allows the user to retrieve general information placed on the website or web page.	176

R

Term	Definition	Pages
Read (formative act)	Reads the value of some data structure.	147, 177
Record	A physical data structure composed of fields.	43, 53
Redundancy	A measure of the degree to which data are unnecessarily replicated across information systems.	212, 246, 247, 286–287
Referent	Part of the meaning triangle. That which is being signified.	41, 51, 267
Regulator	A key type of organisational stakeholder. These are groups or agencies that set environmental constraints for an information system.	301
Re-intermediation	The re-introduction of intermediaries into the supply or customer chain.	108, 109, 241
Repeat Commerce	Repeat commerce is the pattern in which regular, repeat transactions occur between trading partners.	15, 27, 196, 225, 238
Requirements Elicitation	The process of eliciting requirements for an information system from key stakeholders.	292
Requirements Specification	The process of representing the requirements for some information system.	292, 358
Rules layer	See *Rules Subsystem*	
Rules Subsystem	That part of an ICT system concerned with application logic.	18, 171–172